NOTABLE
BLACK
MEMPHIANS

NOTABLE BLACK MEMPHIANS

Miriam DeCosta-Willis

CAMBRIA PRESS

AMHERST, NEW YORK

Copyright 2008 Miriam DeCosta-Willis

All rights reserved
Printed in the United States of America

No part of this publication may be reproduced, stored in or introduced into a retrieval system, or transmitted, in any form, or by any means (electronic, mechanical, photocopying, recording, or otherwise), without the prior permission of the publisher. Requests for permission should be directed to permissions@cambriapress.com, or mailed to Permissions, Cambria Press, 20 Northpointe Parkway, Suite 188, Amherst, New York 14228.

DeCosta-Willis, Miriam.
Notable Black Memphians / Miriam DeCosta-Willis.
    p. cm.
  Includes bibliographical references and index.
  ISBN 978-1-60497-505-5 (alk. paper)
    1. African Americans—Tennessee—Memphis—Biography. 2. African Americans—Tennessee—Memphis—Biography—Pictorial works. 3. Successful people—Tennessee—Memphis—Biography. 4. Memphis (Tenn.)—Biography. I. Title.

  F444.M59N435 2008
  920'.009296076819—dc22

2007051701

For my grandchildren

*Gregory Echols
Kenneth Williamson
Angelique Williamson
Nile Sugarmon
Malik Sugarmon
Zachary McClure
Selena McClure
and their generation,
with the hope that they will be
inspired by the achievements
of these extraordinary men and women*

Table of Contents

Preface	xv
Acknowledgments	xix
Introduction: Their Lives Are a Testament	1
Notable Black Memphians	19
Albert, Laurence	19
Alston, Bettye J. Harris	21
Armstrong, Lillian Hardin "Lil"	22
Bailey, D'Army	24
Bailey, Walter Lee, Jr.	25
Bailey, William C. "Buster"	27
Bankhead, Daniel Robert "Dan"	28
Banks, Frank	29
Barry, Marion Shepilov, Jr.	31
Bisson, Wheelock Alexander	33
Blackfoot, J. "Foot"	35
Blackmon, Joyce McAnulty	36
Blackmore, Amos (a.k.a. Junior Wells)	38
Bland, Bobby "Blue"	40
Bodden, Ira Swithin	41
Booth, Benjamin Franklin	42
Boyd, Robert Richard "Bob"	44
Branch, Addison A.	45
Brandon, Otha Leon	47
Brawner, Clara Arena	48
Brewer, Harper	50
Brewster, William Herbert	51
Bridges, Josephine Valeria Johnson "Jo"	53
Broughton, Virginia E. Walker	54

Brown, Donald	56
Brown, George Henry, Jr.	57
Brown, Joe	59
Brown, Lawyer Edward	60
Bryce, Harry A.	61
Buckley, Harriet Ann	63
Bunton, Henry C.	64
Byas, Andrew D.	65
Calloway, DeVerne Lee	66
Campbell, Lucie Eddie	68
Cannon, Gus	69
Cantrell, Anderson	71
Carter, Marlin "Pee Wee"	72
Cassels, Thomas Frank	73
Champion, Charles	74
Chatman, Peter II "Memphis Slim"	76
Chisholm, Bridget	77
Church, Robert Reed	79
Church, Robert Reed, Jr.	81
Church, Sara Roberta	82
Clark, LeRoy D.	84
Clayborne, Beverly Sarah "The Pie Lady"	85
Cleaborn, Edward O.	87
Cleaves, Irene Curtis	89
Clouston, Joseph	90
Cobb, Joyce	90
Cochran, Flora Cole	92
Coleman, Veronica Freeman	93
Conley, Larry	95
Cook, Vivian Elma Johnson	96
Crawford, Alvin Howell	98
Crawford, Bennie Ross "Hank"	100
Crenshaw, Cornelia	101
Criss, William "Sonny"	103
Crossley, Callie	104
Davis, Fred	105

Table of Contents

DeBerry, Lois	106
Dickey, Eric Jerome	108
Donald, Bernice Bowen	109
Dotson, Phillip Randolph "Phil"	110
Douglas, Lizzie "Memphis Minnie"	112
Draper, O'Landa	114
Evers, O. Z.	116
Falls, Montee Theresa Norman	117
Familoni, Jumi Olajumoke	118
Finch, Larry O.	119
Flowers, Arthur R.	121
Ford, Harold Eugene	123
Ford, Harold Eugene, Jr.	124
Ford, Newton Jackson	126
Franklin, Aretha	128
Frazier, Levi, Jr.	129
Freeman, Morgan	131
Fuller, Thomas Oscar	133
Gayles, Gloria Jean Wade	134
Gilliam, Dorothy Butler	136
Gilliam, Herman Arthur, Jr. "Art"	138
Green, Leorns "Al"	140
Green, Mildred Denby	142
Griggs, Emma J. Williams	143
Griggs, Sutton Elbert	145
Guy-Sheftall, Beverly	147
Hamilton, Green Polonius	148
Hampton, Luther	149
Handy, William Christopher	151
Hardaway, Anfernee Deon "Penny"	152
Harris, Joseph "FreeJoe"	154
Harvey, Peggy Ann Prater	155
Hassell, Frances Massey	157
Hayden, Frank, Jr.	158
Hayes, Isaac	160
Hayes, Thomas Henry	161

Hedgeman, Lulah McEwen	163
Henderson, George W.	165
Henderson, Morris	166
Henry, Wiley, Jr.	167
Herenton, Willie Wilbert	169
Holloway, George L.	171
Hooks, Benjamin Lawson	172
Hooks, Julia Ann Britton	174
Horne, Onzie O.	176
Horton, Odell	177
Hoskins, Ollie Braxton "Nightingale"	179
Hulbert, Maurice "Fess"	180
Hunt, Blair Theodore, Jr.	181
Hunt, George	183
Hunter, Alberta	185
Hutchins, Fred Lew	187
Hyter, James A.	188
Jackson, Alvin O'Neal	190
Johnican, Minerva	191
Johnson, Jason Miccolo	193
Jones, Fred, Jr.	194
Jones, Thomas Oliver	195
Jones, Velma Lois	197
Jordan, Dewitt W., Jr.	199
Joysmith, Brenda	200
Kateo, Loretta Hicks	202
Kelley, Frances Burnett	203
King, Albert	204
King, Riley "B. B."	206
Kyles, Samuel Billy	207
Latting, Augustus Arvis "Doc"	209
Lawson, James Morris, Jr. "Jim"	210
Lee, George Washington	212
Lee, Tom C.	214
Lewis, Robert Stevenson	215

Table of Contents

Lewis, Walter "Furry"	216
Light, Joe Lewis	218
Lincoln, Charles Eric	219
Lipscomb, Robert	221
Little, James	222
Little, Vera	224
Lockard, Hosea T.	225
Love, John Robinson	227
Lunceford, James Melvin "Jimmie"	228
Lyke, James Patterson	229
Lynk, Miles Vandahurst	231
Maburn, Harold	233
Martin, Reginald	234
Martin, William S.	236
Mason, Charles Harrison	238
Mathis, Verdell L. "Lefty"	240
McCleave, Florence Cole Talbert	241
McCray, Shirley Yvonne	243
Miller, Mulgrew	244
Mitchell, Willie	245
Morris, Alma	247
Morris, Herman, Jr.	248
Muhammad, Talib-Karim	249
Nelson-West, Bennetta "Bennie"	251
Newborn, Phineas, Jr.	252
Olive, Benjamin Garfield, Jr.	254
Owen, Samuel Augustus	255
Pace, Harry Herbert	257
Patterson, Gilbert Earl	259
Patterson, James Oglethorpe	260
Patton, Georgia E. L.	262
Porter, David	263
Price, Hollis Freeman	265
Riley, Larry	266
Robinson, Kenneth Stanley	268

Roddy, Bert Maynard	269
Sawyer, Chew Cornelium	271
Scott, Joe Burt	272
Settle, Josiah T.	273
Shaw, Edward	275
Shaw, Lily Patricia Walker "Pat"	277
Shaw, Lucy Mae Yates	278
Smith, Maxine Atkins	280
Smith, Otis Milton	282
Smith, Vasco Albert, Jr.	283
Spillers, Hortense J.	285
Steinberg, Martha Jean	287
Stevens, Rochelle	288
Stuart, Merah Stevens	290
Stuckey, Elma Johnson	291
Stuckey, Ples Sterling	293
Sugarmon, Russell Bertram, Jr.	295
Swingler, Lewis Ossie	297
Taylor, Cora Price	298
Taylor, Lonzie Odie	299
Terrell, Mary Church	301
Thomas, Carla	303
Thomas, Rufus	304
Thomas, Sheree Renée	306
Thornton, Matthew	308
Toles, Elizabeth	309
Turner, Elaine Lee	310
Turner, Jesse Hosea	311
Urevbu, Ephraim Muvire	313
Venson, Ethyl Belle Horton	315
Wade, Theo	316
Walker, Antonio Maceo	318
Walker, Joseph Edison	320
Walter, Ronald Anderson "Ron"	322
Washington, David Whittier	323

Table of Contents xiii

Weathers, Luke J.	325
Wells, Ida Bell	326
Whalum, Kirk Wendell	328
Whalum, Wendell Phillips	329
Wharton, A C, Jr.	331
White, Augustus A. III	333
White, Maurice	334
Whittaker, John W. II	336
Wilbun, Shepperson A. "Shep"	337
Wilburn, Emma Currin Barbee	338
Williams, Eddie N.	339
Williams, James	341
Williams, Nathaniel Dowde "Nat D."	342
Williamson, Juanita V.	344
Williamson, Kenneth	345
Willis, Archie Walter, Jr.	346
Wilson, Lucious Alexander	349
Winchester, Marie Louise Amarante Loiselle "Mary"	351
Withers, Dedrick "Teddy"	352
Withers, Ernest C.	354
Woodruff, Georgia Rodgers	356
Yates, Albert Carl "Tutt"	357

Other Notables 361

Appendices
  A. Chronology by Birth Dates 385
  B. Occupations 393

Selected Bibliography 407

Photo Credits 417

Index 427

Preface

Notable Black Memphians traces the history of a Southern community through a detailed examination of the lives of the African Americans who created art forms, built landmarks, and founded institutions that strengthened the community. It includes biographical sketches of 223 men and women, as well as brief notes on 122 others, who were born in Memphis or who lived in the city for an extended period and made significant contributions to its development. Based on interviews, correspondence, and ten years of research in archives and libraries, the book documents the accomplishments of Memphians who were born between 1795 and 1972, including many who gained national prominence in the fields of business, education, law, medicine, and music. The biographical sketches are arranged alphabetically by name and there are two appendices—one by date of birth and another by occupation—that will facilitate cross-referencing for research purposes. Although there are no extant photographs of four early Memphians, the text includes 219 photographs—of varied quality due to the conditions of the original photographs—obtained from individuals and institutions such as the *Tri-State Defender*, Stax Museum, *The Commercial Appeal*, and LeMoyne-Owen College.

The introduction, "Our Lives Are a Testament," traces the evolution of the Black Memphis community, and provides a context for understanding civic and political activities and for interpreting social and cultural history.

Several autobiographies or biographies of outstanding Black Memphians have been published, including Fuller's *20 Years in Public Life, The Robert R. Churches, The Memphis Diary of Ida B. Wells*, and, recently, *Maxine Smith's Unwilling Pupils*. Between 1908 and 1989, at least fourteen books by African Americans have documented the cultural, economic, educational, and religious history of the city. Among the most significant are G. P. Hamilton's *The Bright Side of Memphis* (1908) and Roberta Church and Ronald Walter's *Nineteenth Century Families of Color* (1987). All of these biographies, autobiographies, and histories, as well as articles, programs, discography, general works, and specialized studies have been essential to this study and are listed in the Selected Bibliography. The text is designed to interest general readers and specialists, to stimulate additional research, and to serve as a reference book for schools and libraries across the country through its inclusion of national and international figures.

Although many accomplished men and women could not be included in this study because of limitations of time and space, every attempt has been made to offer a balanced and objective selection of those who represent different ages, occupations, historical periods, and social classes. Experts in art, business, music, medicine, and politics suggested the names of outstanding women and men in their fields, and the author established the following criteria for selection:

1. A pioneer in a particular field. Examples include Florence McCleave in classical music, Benjamin F. Booth in law, and Ida B. Wells in journalism.
2. A "first," such as Otha Brandon, who was Memphis's first Black accountant; Herman Morris, first Black president of Memphis Light, Gas and Water Division; and Veronica Coleman, Tennessee's first Black U.S. Attorney General.

3. A founder of a major organization or institution. Charles H. Mason, for example, founded the Church of God in Christ; Miles V. Lynk established the University of West Tennessee; and Dr. J. E. Walker founded Universal Life Insurance Company and Tri-State Bank.
4. A person with a national or international reputation, such as Aretha Franklin in music, Anfernee "Penny" Hardaway in basketball, and Augustus A. White III in orthopedic surgery.
5. Someone outstanding in more than one field. Examples include Kenneth Stanley Robinson, a physician, pastor, and state administrator; George W. Lee, an author, political leader, and insurance official; and Bettye J. Alston, a nurse, minister, and businesswoman.
6. A leader of a national organization, such as Patricia W. Shaw, former president of the National Insurance Association; Eddie N. Williams, past president of the Joint Center for Political and Economic Studies; and Benjamin L. Hooks, former executive director of the NAACP.
7. A top elected official, including Shelby County Mayor A C Wharton; Memphis Mayor W. W. Herenton; and Lois Deberry, speaker tempore of the Tennessee House of Representatives.
8. A major contributor to the Memphis community, such as activist Maxine Smith, educator Hollis Price, and businessman Fred Jones, Jr.

ACKNOWLEDGMENTS

I appreciate the generosity of Memphians who responded to my telephone calls, e-mails, letters, and requests for interviews and photographs; and, especially, the cooperation of those included in this book or their descendants, who read rough drafts, revised biographical sketches, and loaned their treasured photographs. No matter how early I called, Erma Laws provided names, answered questions, or loaned photographs; and, no matter how busy he was, Ron Walter shared with me anecdotes or details from his historical research. I borrowed liberally from the writings of David Earl Jackson, a former columnist with the *Tri-State Defender*, who knew so much about Memphis music. Jazz historian Vasco Smith made sure that I included some of the city's talented jazz players, and sports columnist Bill Little gave me a list of outstanding athletes. Phil Dotson, a close friend, former colleague, and co-editor of *Homespun Images*, supported this project from its inception, providing lists of artists and information about their work. When my computer died, Reginald Martin, a friend of many years, built a new one so that I could continue my work.

A great deal of my research was conducted in the Memphis/Shelby County Room of the Benjamin L. Hooks Central Library, where archivist Patricia La Pointe and James Johnson, head of the History Department, shared their knowledge of Memphis history and of library resources. The staff also responded graciously to every request for a book, photograph, clipping file, or item from a collection. I appreciate the help of former colleague Annette B. Hunt, LeMoyne-Owen College librarian, who searched the college archives for photographs and even permitted me to borrow reference books. A treasured friend, Herbert Rogers of Baltimore's Enoch Pratt Library responded, even on late Sunday evenings, to urgent pleas for help in documentation.

One of the most challenging tasks of this project was locating photographs of over 200 men and women, many of whom lived years ago; fortunately, several heads of cultural organizations gave me access to their collections. Journalist Wiley Henry of the *Tri-State Defender* retrieved boxes of photographs from the attic, gave me space to work, and scanned seventy-three photographs. Without his invaluable help, I would have spent countless hours searching for individual photographs. My stepson Marc Willis, head of the Stax Museum of American Soul Music, opened the archives to me and introduced me to Carol Drake, Manager of Exhibits, Archives, and Education. Carol let me select photographs from the archives, and Stax intern Terri Bokros scanned them. I am grateful for the help of Vasco "Smitty" Smith III, who loaned me photos, scanned eighty-five for the book, and prepared lunch for me in his D.C. apartment.

Frank Banks, CPA and managing partner of the Memphis African American Historical Calendar Partnership, permitted me to select photographs from his extensive collection, while Bennie Nelson-West, director of the Memphis Black Arts Alliance, sent me an electronic album of photographs that she had compiled for the organization's twentieth anniversary. Finally, Claude Jones of *The Commercial Appeal* located, scanned, and granted me permission to use photographs from the newspaper's file. Many friends, such as Alois Greer, Irvin Salky, and Sterling Stuckey, are listed in the "Photographic Credits," and I must also thank Taronda Spencer of the Spelman

College Archives and Judy Peiser of the Center for Southern Folklore for their assistance. I am particularly indebted to my friend, photographer George Hardin, for forwarding two of his photographs, and to archivist Sherman Pyatt for sending an electronic image from the Avery Research Center in Charleston.

I appreciate the support of my long-time friends, Sandra Vaughn and Patricia Bell-Scott, who kept me focused and centered throughout a long and difficult process. Most of all, I am grateful for the love of my family, including my grandchildren, to whom I dedicate this work, and my son and daughters—Tarik, Elena, Erika, and Monique. Elena clipped articles from the Memphis paper, while Erika and her husband, Eric, improved my technology skills and solved some of my computer problems. Finally, I thank the staff of Cambria Press for their assistance throughout the preparation and processing of this manuscript, especially Toni Tan.

NOTABLE BLACK MEMPHIANS

Introduction

Their Lives Are a Testament

Making a Way Out of No Way: 1820 to 1860

The early history of Memphis is inscribed in the lives of its people—Chickasaws who spread throughout Mississippi and West Tennessee, European descendants who moved from Virginia and the Carolinas to the banks of the Mississippi River, and African Americans who migrated to the city from small farms and cotton plantations in the Mid-South. Memphis was built on the labor of African Americans and on land that was taken from Native Americans. The three city founders were slave owners: John Overton had fifty slaves and a 2,300-acre cotton plantation; James Winchester's slaves worked in his cotton gin and ship-building plant, and Andrew Jackson bought and sold slaves to work on his large plantation. Jackson succeeded, through battles and bribes, in acquiring twenty million acres of land from the Chickasaws and, as president of the United States from 1829 to 1837, persuaded Congress to pass the 1830 Indian Removal

Bill and, in 1837, negotiated a forced exodus—known as the Trail of Tears—of Natives from the Mid-South. Earlier, Jackson, Overton, and Winchester divided a part of their ill-gotten land into the 362 lots that comprised the town of Memphis. Characterized by one historian as a "primitive and pestilential little mudhole" when it was founded in 1819, the settlement consisted of several cabins, a store, a tavern, and other frame buildings, as well as fifty inhabitants, including, more than likely, a few slaves and one or two free persons of color.

Although the history of Memphis's founders has been well preserved, very little is known about the townsfolk—the anonymous Natives, working-class Whites, and African-descended people who lived in and around the settlement on the Lower Chickasaw Bluff. Most of what is known about early Blacks was passed down through oral history or was obtained from official documents such as wills, church records, property deeds, census reports, and baptism records, as well as birth, marriage, and death certificates, but these documents are sketchy at best. Among the early inhabitants of Memphis and Shelby County are four notable African Americans—Joseph Harris, Marie Loiselle Winchester, Morris Henderson, and Joseph Clouston—whose life stories reveal some of the rigors of the Black experience in Memphis in the early nineteenth century. Many African Americans were born in other states and came to Memphis with the White settlers who moved from Virginia and the Carolinas after North Carolina's western territory became the state of Tennessee. Harris and Henderson, for example, were born in Virginia, while Loiselle was probably born in Louisiana. These early Memphians included free men and women such as Marie Loiselle Winchester; slaves such as Limus, a ferryboat operator who belonged to Marcus Winchester; and freedmen such as Harris, Clouston, and Henderson, who had worked as builders, barbers, and carriage drivers to purchase their freedom. Their lives reveal that, before 1830, Black Memphians had some rights and privileges: they could purchase their freedom and that of other Blacks; free men could vote, buy property, obtain mortgages, worship freely, found churches, migrate to the state, legally marry, and maintain interracial marriages in spite of Tennessee's antimiscegenation laws. For example, Harris, a former slave who had learned to read and write, purchased his wife's freedom, obtained a marriage license, founded a church, and bought and mortgaged property. The highly educated Marie Loiselle married Marcus Winchester, Memphis's first mayor and son of a founder, and she bought property in downtown Memphis, where she lived with her husband and their eight biracial children.

Free and freed Blacks had more rights in the 1820s because (1) Memphis was still a small town, with a population that increased from 50 in 1820 to only 663 by 1830; (2) most Memphians—laborers, traders, and small farmers—were not slaveholders; and (3) antislavery sentiment was evident in 1826, when Frances Wright established Nashoba, a utopian community near Memphis that promoted emancipation and interracial communal living. Those rights were taken away, however, in the 1830s, when a racial backlash ushered in a period of Negrophobia and oppression of Blacks, a reaction, in part, to Nathaniel Turner's 1831 rebellion, David Walker's 1829 *Appeal*, and the fear of slave revolts in the South. Consequently, the city and state took measures to curtail the civil rights of African Americans: in 1831, the state legislature barred the migration of free Blacks into the state; in 1834, the state constitution took away Blacks' voting rights and made manumission almost impossible; and, in 1837, the Memphis City Council passed an ordinance against "citizens keeping colored wives." Such repression forced the Winchesters to move outside of Memphis, and, after Marie's death in 1839, her children crossed the color line to become "White" in the 1840 census.

By the mid-nineteenth century, Memphis had become a major urban center. Located on the Mississippi River, at the hub of a tri-state region that includes Arkansas, Mississippi, and Tennessee, it had the resources—a railroad, steamboat landing, businesses, and retail establishments—to make it one of the Mid-South's most important trade centers. The city became famous for cotton trading and infamous for slave trading, mainly because of the efforts of Nathan Bedford Forrest, who operated one of the largest slave markets in the South. Indeed, the labor of Blacks, most of whom were enslaved, contributed substantially to the economic growth of the city. It is estimated that by 1850, there were 2,362 slaves and only 109 free Blacks in Memphis, at a ratio of 24 to 1. Larger numbers of slaves were to be found in the rural areas surrounding Memphis; according to one source, 60% of West Tennessee's population was enslaved. Although the Memphis townspeople included such accomplished freedmen as grocer Joseph Clouston and clergyman Morris Henderson, these men held a precarious position in an increasingly racialized society, where they also had to compete, economically, with European immigrants, primarily Irish and German, who moved to the city in the 1840s and '50s.

Rising Phoenix-Like from the Ashes: 1860 to 1900

By the beginning of the Civil War, in 1861, the population of Memphis had risen to 22,623, and the Black population of the city increased exponentially during the war, because of the flight to the urban center of escaped slaves from outlying plantations. As many as 6,000 fugitives lived in three contraband camps—Shiloh, New Africa, and Camp Dixie—located in South Memphis, where a cohesive Black community was emerging. When Union gunboats forced the surrender of Memphis on June 6, 1862, the soldiers built a military camp, Fort Pickering, on the outskirts of Memphis, which housed many Black Union troops. By 1865, when the Civil War ended, the number of Blacks in Memphis had increased from 4,000 in 1860, to 17,000—almost half of the total population—and that strong African American presence was threatening to some, who reacted with violence. In 1864, slave trader Nathan Bedford Forrest led Confederate troops in a massacre of Black soldiers at Fort Pillow, a Union camp located about forty miles north of Memphis. The slaughter was a prelude to the violence that erupted in Memphis two years later. In 1866, a White mob swept through the streets of Memphis in a three-day rampage that resulted in the murder of 46 Blacks, wounding of 75 others, rape of 5 women, and burning of many homes, schools, and churches. Ironically, the violence occurred during Reconstruction, at a time when the federal government guaranteed the right of citizenship to former slaves. The U.S. Civil Rights Bill was passed in 1866, and, in 1868, the Tennessee General Assembly ratified the Fourteenth Amendment, which granted citizenship, equal protection under the law, and due process to colored citizens.

During this period, two militant figures emerged in Memphis to lead the struggle for civil rights and to protest the erosion of those rights in the post-Reconstruction era. Edward Shaw and Ida B. Wells epitomize, through their efforts, the economic, political, and social struggle that Black leaders undertook to elevate their community after the devastating experience of slavery. Shaw was born free in Kentucky and, in 1867, moved to Memphis, where he became a fearless and outspoken editor, businessman, and city official who defied segregation on the railroad and returned the fire of the Ku Klux Klan. After running for the Shelby County Commission and the U.S. Congress, he was finally elected to the Memphis City Council in 1872. Wells was born a slave in Mississippi and, in 1884, moved to Memphis, where she became a public school teacher and fiery journalist. After the lynching of three Black Memphis grocers in 1892, she launched an international antilynching campaign, and she urged African Americans to leave Memphis, which they did by the droves. This exodus of Blacks from the city initiated the Great Migration of Memphians to the West and North, a movement that would continue well into the 1930s.

The lives of Wells and Shaw, as well as of other nineteenth-century notables, are a testament to the emergence of a Black consciousness movement in Memphis. Between 1860 and 1900, these Memphians built schools and churches, founded newspapers and welfare organizations, opened stores and boarding houses, and became doctors and lawyers, creating a Black working/middle class that would forge a distinctive community. In-migration increased: for example, businessman Robert R. Church and Attorney Benjamin Franklin Booth moved to Memphis from Mississippi; missionary educator Virginia Broughton from Virginia; Attorney Thomas Frank

Cassels from Ohio; and music teacher Julia Ann Britton Hooks from Kentucky. Better educated than their forbears, they achieved many "firsts": Dr. Georgia E. L. Patton finished Meharry Medical College and became the first Black woman licensed to practice medicine in Tennessee; Virginia Broughton, a graduate of Fisk University, is believed to be the first African American woman in the South to earn a college degree; and Thomas F. Cassels, an Oberlin graduate, was the first African American lawyer to practice in Memphis. Education was a high priority for these professionals, who enrolled their children in the Hooks Cottage School, founded by Julia Hooks, or in LeMoyne Normal School, founded in the 1860s by the American Missionary Association to educate former slaves. Others, such as property owner Robert R. Church, who was born a slave but became one the South's wealthiest Blacks, sent his children to schools in Ohio. The community had to rebuild after the destruction of twelve colored schools in the riot of 1866, but by 1885, when Ida B. Wells joined the Clay Street School faculty, the city had five Black schools and twenty-three Black teachers but no public high school until the end of the century.

Men and women moved to Memphis not only to acquire an education but also to gain greater economic advantages. Although most of the migrants found jobs as laborers (porters, coopers, hackers, draymen, bricklayers, boatmen, and blacksmiths), the more fortunate established grocery stores, saloons, restaurants, barbershops, shoe shops, livery stables, and print shops. Joseph Clouston, who owned a farm, grocery store, barbershop, and downtown property; and Edward Shaw, a lawyer who also had a farm, saloon, and newspaper, were among the incorporators of the Tennessee Colored Banking and Real Estate Association of Memphis. An index of the Black community's assets is the fact that the Memphis Branch of the Freedmen's Savings Bank had deposits of $56,755 by the time it closed in 1874. Most Black women worked as domestics, but some owned small businesses, such as hair salons, restaurants, and boarding houses; Mrs. Williams L. Spillman, for example, rented rooms at 15 Wright Avenue, and Louisa Ayers owned a hairdressing establishment at the time of her marriage to Robert R. Church. The citizens worked to strengthen their community. They built churches: Collins Chapel Methodist Episcopal Church was organized in 1859; Avery Chapel African Methodist Episcopal Church was founded by Black Union soldiers during the Civil War; and Morris Henderson's First Church (Beale Street Baptist Church) was erected around 1866. They formed fraternal organizations, such as the Masons, Odd Fellows, Daughters of Zion, and Independent Pole Bearers. They organized welfare societies, including the Colored Benevolent Society and the Old Folks and Orphans Home, founded by Julia Hooks in 1891. When the yellow fever epidemic decimated the city in the 1870s and the city had to relinquish its charter, colored regiments, such as the Zouaves and the McClellen Guards, secured property and buried the dead.

They also found it necessary to protect themselves from the racist backlash against their Reconstruction-era rights, and from the political reverses that heralded the end of Reconstruction. To secure their civil rights, community activists organized the Negro Mutual Protection Association and the Committee for Civil Rights. To raise social and political consciousness, Edward Shaw started the *Memphis Weekly Planet* and Ida B. Wells became part owner of the *Memphis Free Speech and Headlight*, a newspaper founded by Taylor Nightingale. When the Fifteenth Amendment gave Black men the right to vote in 1869, city leaders such as Shaw and Frederick Savage became active in Republican politics and ran for public office, gaining seats on the school board, city council, and state legislature. In the 1880s, Memphians Thomas F. Cassels and Isham F. Norris, both Republicans, served in the Tennessee General Assembly, where they lobbied against repressive legislation. In 1881, Isham introduced a bill to outlaw discrimination on the railroads, fought against racial discrimination in public facilities, worked to improve education for Blacks, and tried to revoke the ban on interracial marriage. Ironically, 1881 was the year in which Tennessee passed its first Jim Crow law mandating segregation on the railroads. Two years later, Ida B. Wells filed suit against the railroad after being forcibly dragged from the first-class car. By 1883, when the two-year legislative terms of Cassels and

Norris ended, Black political power was stifled through the erosion of voting rights, threats of violence, and economic intimidation.

By the end of the nineteenth century, the diminution of Black political power and civil rights in Memphis was buttressed by legal segregation. In its infamous 1896 case, *Plessy v. Ferguson*, the United States Supreme Court upheld the policy of "separate but equal" facilities on railroad cars and, thus, paved the way for legal segregation throughout the South.

BUILDING A COMMUNITY AND SHAPING A HISTORY: 1900 TO 1950

By the early 1900s, Beale Street had become the cultural, religious, and business center of Memphis's Black community. The street is perhaps best known as a cultural mecca, the place where W. C. Handy, Gus Cannon, and Memphis Minnie got their start. Handy, who moved to Memphis in 1908, is credited with using his formal training to transcribe rural folk music—gut-bucket blues and field hollers—into blues compositions such as "Beale Street Blues," which he wrote at Pee Wee's Club on Beale. The rural folk tradition is represented by banjo player Gus Cannon, who organized jug bands, such as Gus Cannon and the Jug Stompers. The self-taught composer of "Walk Right In" and "Come on Down to My House," blew on a jug top to make blues music with a country sound. Lizzie Douglas, known as Memphis Minnie, began playing on Beale by age fourteen and became the reigning blues queen of the 1920s, with compositions such as "Bumble Bee Blues" and "Dirty Mother For You." These artists, as well as Furry Lewis and Memphis Slim, played in Beale Street's saloons, nightclubs, and gambling joints—places like the Monarch Club, Ashford's Saloon, and the Lincoln Theater, the first Black-owned club. In the 1930s, Ethyl Venson and her husband founded the Cotton Makers' Jubilee and, in the 1940s, Nat D. Williams organized Amateur Nights and Midnight Rambles at the Palace Theater; these events became venues for Black music and other cultural forms. Memphis has also had a long tradition of sacred music, as exemplified in the gospel compositions of Lucie Campbell, a teacher and choir director, and William Brewster, a minister and educator. Campbell wrote over 100 songs, including "Hold My Hand, Precious Lord" and "He Understands, He'll Say Well Done"; Rev. Brewster, called one of the most influential gospel songwriters of the twentieth century, composed "Pay Day Someday" and "Move on Up a Little Higher."

The Beale Street Church embodies these two traditions—sacred and secular—because it was not only a religious center but also a burial society, music school, social center, and post office. And it was in the church basement that journalist Ida B. Wells published her *Memphis Free Speech and Headlight*. Founded in 1866, Beale Street Baptist produced many other churches, including Tabernacle Baptist, First Baptist on St. Paul, and Metropolitan Baptist Church. There were historic churches of other denominations in the area, such as Collins Chapel Colored Methodist Episcopal Church, to the north of Beale, and Avery Chapel African Methodist Episcopal Church on the corner of Hernando and Desoto Streets. Located in the middle of the Bible Belt, Memphis is also the headquarters of the Church of God in Christ, which was founded in 1897 by Charles H. Mason and which has become the country's largest Pentecostal church, with more than seven million members. In 1945, Bishop Mason dedicated Mason's Temple as COGIC's world headquarters, and it was in its 7,500-seat auditorium that Dr. King spoke the night before his assassination.

Significantly, the "Mother Church" (Beale Street Baptist) was located next to Church's Park and Auditorium and across the street from the Solvent Savings Bank and Trust Company. In 1900, Robert R. Church bought land to build a park, which contained a zoo, bandstand, and playground; and to construct a 2,000-seat auditorium, where operas, plays, musical shows, and political meetings were held. A banquet hall, soda fountain, Hall of Fame, and Julia Hooks's School of Music were also located in the auditorium. In 1906, Church and three other businessmen—J. T. Settle, M. L. Clay, and T. H. Hayes—founded the Solvent Bank and Trust Company, located at 392 Beale Street, which anchored the business community. Three years later, two undertakers established the Fraternal

Bank and Trust Company, which merged with Solvent in 1926 to form Solvent-Fraternal Bank, but it failed just before the Depression. Another important financial institution was founded in the Beale Street area. In 1920, Dr. J. E. Walker, a physician and insurance executive, moved Mississippi Life Insurance Company from Indianola, Mississippi to Memphis, with headquarters on Hernando Street, near Beale. When the company closed, he founded Universal Life Insurance Company at the same location, in 1923. Two years later, he relocated the company to a two-story brick building on Hernando, and, in 1940, moved Universal to a new $500,000 building at 408 Linden. In 1946, Dr. Walker and his son, A. Maceo Walker, founded Tri-State Bank of Memphis, located at 392 Beale Street on the site of the failed Solvent-Fraternal Bank.

Many Black-owned businesses, including Jackson's Drug Store, the Gillis Brothers' Hotel, Hooks Brothers Photographers, and Tri-State Casket & Coffin Company, were located in the Beale Street area. The barbershops, florists, print shops, and restaurants, such as the Iroquois Café and Johnny Mill's Barbecue Shack, drew customers to Beale. One of the most astute businesswomen of the period was Emma Currin Barbee Wilburn, who opened the Emma Wilburn Funeral Home in 1914, and bought the 75-acre New Park Cemetery in 1933. In 1919, businessman Bert M. Roddy founded the first chain of Black-owned grocery stores in Memphis—Roddy's Citizens' Co-operative Stores—with headquarters on Beale, and, within a year, he had fifteen stores, a fleet of trucks, and 9,000 investors. Although Roddy's stores failed in 1922, another business venture emerged in that decade: Negro baseball. In the early 1920s, mortician Robert S. Lewis built Lewis Park, the first baseball park in the country owned and operated by Blacks, and he organized the Memphis Red Sox, the first Black professional baseball team in the city. In 1927, the four Martin brothers—physician W. S., pharmacist J. B., physician A. T., and dentist B. B.—bought the team and the park, which they renamed Martin Stadium. Three of the brothers also built Martin Medical Building on South Third near Beale, where they had offices, a restaurant, and barbershop.

Many professional men and women, including at least sixteen lawyers, dentists, and doctors, had offices on the famous thoroughfare; among them were Dr. Fannie Kneeland, a pioneering woman physician; Dr. C. A. Terrell, founder of Terrell-Patterson Infirmary; and Dr. J. C. Hairston, who established Hairston Hospital. In 1910, Dr. William S. Martin and Dr. John T. Wilson leased land to build a 35-bed hospital, Collins Chapel Hospital and Old Folks Home at 418 Ashland, which was expanded to 53 beds in 1928. Most of Memphis's early physicians graduated from Meharry Medical College, but, in 1907, Dr. Miles V. Lynk relocated to Memphis the University of West Tennessee, which he had founded in Jackson, Tennessee in 1900. The university trained legal and medical professionals from several states and six countries; it also educated many Black Memphis physicians, including Benjamin F. McCleave, William O. Speight, and Ransom Q. Venson. Dr. Lynk also published the first medical journal in the country, co-founded the National Medical Association, published a magazine, founded a publishing house, and wrote three books, including an autobiography, *Sixty Years of Medicine or the Life and Times of Dr. Miles V. Lynk* (1930).

Through their autobiographies, biographies, and histories, Black Memphians began to tell their own stories in the first quarter of the twentieth century. One of the most important of these early writers was G. P. Hamilton, principal of Memphis's first public high school, whose books—*The Bright Side of Memphis* (1908) and *Beacon Lights of the Race* (1911)—record local and national history through biographies and photographs. He also wrote a short history of Booker T. Washington High School. T. O. Fuller published four books, including an autobiography and two church histories, but his most important work is the *Pictorial History of the American Negro* (1933), a monumental study of African American history, illuminated with more than 400 photographs. The most prolific writer was Sutton E. Griggs, pastor of Tabernacle Baptist Church, who published eighteen books between 1899 and 1929, and who is regarded as one of the most important writers to predate the New Negro movement of the 1920s. Shifting from racial militancy to accomodationism, the controversial

Griggs wrote didactic novels, such as *Imperium in Imperio* and *The Hindered Hand*. The most acclaimed creative writer was George W. Lee, known as the "Boswell of Beale Street," whose first novel, *Beale Street, Where the Blues Began* (1934) became a Book-of-the-Month Club alternate selection. He published another novel, *River George* (1937) and a collection of short stories, *Beale Street Sundown* (1942).

George W. Lee was also a political leader, insurance executive, and one of the most important men on Beale Street in the second quarter of the twentieth century. Manager of the local branch of Atlanta Life Insurance Company, he was a leader in Memphis's Black Republican organization, the Lincoln League, and he was a major player in national politics for over twenty years. Through the buck and the ballot, Lee followed in the footsteps of such Race Men and Women as Ed Shaw, Ida B. Wells, B. F. Booth, Julia Hooks, Bert Roddy, and Bob Church, who created political and civil rights organizations to attack segregation and to uplift their people.

In 1905, nine years after the U.S. Supreme Court paved the way for legal segregation in *Plessy v. Ferguson*, the Memphis streetcars were segregated. Attorneys J. T. Settle and B. F. Booth challenged the Jim Crow law, in 1905, by arguing—unsuccessfully—before the Tennessee Supreme Court that segregated streetcars were illegal. In spite of segregation, the colored citizens of Memphis—who now made up 49% of the population—reacted by creating their own institutions: banks, parks, schools, hospitals, colleges, and insurance companies. They also exerted pressure on the city through their dollars, their votes, and their organizations. Although most African Americans of the period supported the Republican Party, from 1909 to 1954 the city was controlled by Democrat E. H. "Boss" Crump, who patronized Blacks to obtain their votes. (Allegedly, he distributed watermelons on election day, and he also persuaded Handy to write his campaign song, "Mr. Crump.") In 1911, Roddy, H. H. Pace, and Bob Church founded the Colored Citizens Association, which led a registration drive and lobbied to obtain park facilities, paved streets, and sprinkling service from city government. In 1916, Roddy and

Church joined with other Memphians to organize the Lincoln League, which held voter registration drives, chose slates of candidates, and encouraged Blacks to vote. After violence broke out in the city in 1917, Roddy and Church held a meeting to organize a local branch of the NAACP, with fifty-three members; Roddy was elected the first president of the branch and Church was elected to the national board of directors. After the Depression and the resurgence of the Democratic Party under Roosevelt, Crump drove progressive leaders such as Bob Church and J. B. Martin out of town, while organizations such as the NAACP were taken over by conservative leaders. Fortuitously, a group of young, Northern-educated militants would emerge in the 1950s to hasten the demise of the Crump Machine and to initiate a political and civil rights movement.

GAINING CIVIL RIGHTS, POLITICAL POWER, AND ECONOMIC LEVERAGE: 1950 TO 2000

The second half of the twentieth century was characterized by tremendous social, political, and economic changes, as Black Memphians desegregated public facilities; created businesses; obtained corporate positions; and won election to local, state, and national offices. Three important events in the national civil rights movement fueled the desegregation movement in Memphis: the 1954 Supreme Court decision in *Brown v. Board of Education of Topeka*, the Montgomery Bus Boycott of 1955, and the 1960 student sit-ins in Greensboro, North Carolina. In the 1950s, a group of activist Memphis lawyers—H. T. Lockard, A. W. Willis, B. L. Hooks, R. B. Sugarmon, and S. A. Wilbun—with tactical support from the Legal Defense Fund of the NAACP, waged a relentless legal battle to desegregate public schools, libraries, parks, and buses.

As the cases moved slowly through the courts, impatient college and high school students initiated a sit-in at the Memphis Public Library, in 1960, that led to a city-wide direct action campaign of rallies, marches, boycotts, and demonstrations. Churches, civic clubs, and political organizations united in support of the direct action campaign, which was led by the Memphis Branch of the NAACP under the direction of Maxine A. Smith, who was named executive secretary of the branch in 1962. She helped desegregate Memphis schools in 1961, organized an eighteen-month boycott of downtown stores, and led demonstrations against the Board of Education in 1969. One of the pivotal events in the struggle was the 1967 strike by sanitation workers, led by labor leader T. O. Jones, which ended with the assassination of Martin Luther King, Jr., in Memphis on April 4, 1968. One of the other key figures in the local movement was Jesse H. Turner, an accountant and CEO of Tri-State Bank, who served as president of the Memphis Branch of the NAACP for eleven years, initiated a suit against the public library, and filed the first lawsuit to end segregation in Shelby County in 1957.

In Memphis, the struggle for civil rights and the quest for political power were concurrent in the 1960s, when civil rights leaders such as Smith, Turner, Willis, Lockard, Hooks, Sugarmon, and others were elected to public office. For example, when Turner was elected to the Shelby County Democratic Executive Committee in 1960, he became the first Black elected to such an office since Reconstruction. In 1964, Lockard won election to the Shelby County Quarterly Court, Hooks was appointed to the Shelby County Criminal Court, and Willis became the first African American elected to the Tennessee General Assembly since Reconstruction. The foundation for these political victories was laid in the 1950s, when organizations such as the Lincoln League, Council of Civic Clubs, Shelby County Democratic Club, and local branch of the NAACP launched vigorous voter registration campaigns and the political clubs supported Black candidates for public office.

Although they had little chance of winning election in a city where political banners read "Keep Memphis Down in Dixie," Black Memphians began to campaign for public office in the early 1950s. In 1951, Dr. J. E. Walker was defeated in his race for the Memphis Board of Education, but he helped organized the Nonpartisan Voters' Registration Club, which increased the number of Black registered voters to 35,000. The most significant political campaign of that decade was the 1959 election, when Hooks, Sugarmon, Roy Love, and Henry C. Bunton ran for local office on the Volunteer Ticket. That race was important because the Black community was solidly united behind a single slate of candidates, and, for the first time, there was the possibility that an African American could win elective office through single shot voting. Although none of the candidates was elected, that race increased voter registration and voter turn-out, and it led to the appointment and election of Blacks to positions in local, state, and federal government. As a result, the number of Black voters in Shelby County increased from approximately 20,000 in 1951 to 50,000 in 1959, and, by fall 1961, African Americans had been appointed to forty-three political jobs in Memphis.

The political victories of the 1960s culminated, in 1974, with the election to the U. S. Congress of Harold Ford, who built up a powerful, family centered political base during the twenty-two years that he served in the legislature. Ford's siblings—Emmitt, James, John, and, later, Ophelia—were elected city councilmen, state representatives, state senator, and general sessions clerk; while Harold Ford, Jr., succeeded his father, in 1996, in the Congress, where he served for five terms. Another major political figure to emerge during the last quarter of the century was W. W. Herenton, who was appointed the first Black superintendent of Memphis City Schools in 1979 and was elected the first Black mayor of the city in 1991, a position that he has held for four terms. One of Herenton's early supporters was A C Wharton, who, in 2002, was elected the first African American mayor of Shelby County, with 62% of the vote and substantial support across party and racial lines. Unfortunately, the emergence of strong individuals has created some disunity and divisiveness in the Black community, as political organizations have competed for influence and financial support.

One of the primary sources of support for political and civil rights activities has been the churches and Black businesses; ironically, however, the desegregation movement of the 1960s has led to the demise of many small businesses, such as florists, nightclubs, restaurants, and barbershops. Although Tri-State Bank has opened three branches in the past twenty years, other financial institutions—Mutual Federal Savings and Loan Association, Supreme Mortgage Company, and Union Protective Life Insurance Company—closed for lack of leadership, insufficient capital, or an inability to compete in a changed market. For example, the untimely death of president and CEO Patricia Walker Shaw, who was developing new market initiatives for Universal Life Insurance Company, led to the collapse of the company, which had 36 branch offices, $62 million in assets, and $610 million in policies. A new breed of business leaders has created opportunities in the fields of technology, entertainment, and communications. In 1975, Art Gilliam founded Gilliam Communications, Inc., which purchased WLOK radio station, one of the most successful gospel music stations in the country. In 1984, Fred Jones, Jr., founded Summitt Management Corporation and, six years later, created the Southern Heritage Classic, a sports and entertainment institution that pours millions into the city. One of the most successful entrepreneurs is Frank Banks, who co-founded Banks, Finley, White & Company, one of the largest accounting firms in the South; created Banks and Holeyfield Management Company; and raised millions to open MemphisFirst Community Bank, renamed Landmark Community Bank. More recently, Bridget Chisholm has used her knowledge of finance and marketing to form BBC Consulting, LLC, a professional services firm, and to found Delta Bluff, LLC and Mosaic, LLC, which have bought several Memphis restaurants.

In the past three decades, opportunities have opened up for African Americans in Memphis corporations. Ronald Walter became president and station manager of WREG-TV, and Herman Morris rose from general council to president of Memphis Light, Gas and Water Division in 1989. Black women have also gained leadership positions in corporations: Peggy Harvey became vice president of Human Resources at MLGW in 1987, and Joyce Blackmon became one of only two senior vice presidents at the Division in 1991. Before she was appointed Tennessee's first woman and first Black U.S. attorney general, Veronica Coleman served as senior litigator for

Federal Express Corporation. In 1990, Lucy Yates Shaw was the first woman and first Black to become president and CEO of The Med, a nonprofit hospital with 2,800 employees and an annual budget of $200 million. In the past decade, several entrepreneurs have created innovative businesses; Olympic Gold Medalist Rochelle Stevens opened Rochelle's Health and Wellness Center in 1999; Brenda Joysmith and her husband created Joysmith Gallery and Studio in the Main Street Historic District; and Bettye Alston founded the Inside and Out Wellness Center.

Opportunities in business, education, and medicine have attracted or produced a cadre of Black Memphis professionals, including Northern-educated and board-certified specialists in such fields as urology and cardiology. The pastor of a church and a national authority on community health, Kenneth S. Robinson, was an administrator at the University of Tennessee College of Medicine before being named commissioner of the Tennessee Department of Health. Although they no longer live in Memphis, Alvin H. Crawford is a world-renowned orthopedic surgeon and professor of pediatrics, who has authored six books; and Augustus A. White III co-founded Beth Israel Hospital's Orthopedic Biomechanics Laboratory and was professor of orthopedic surgery at Harvard Medical School. With a doctorate in theoretical chemical physics, Albert C. Yates became vice president and provost of Washington State University and, later, president of Colorado State University and chancellor of the Colorado State System. These Memphians have achieved a great deal through their individual efforts—their training, discipline, commitment, and work ethic—but they are also indebted to their families and to those in the community who have created opportunities for them. Their lives bear witness to the support they have received and to the struggles made on their behalf: the labor of grandparents and single mothers, the encouragement of teachers and ministers, the cautionary tales of village elders, and the sacrifices of those who preceded them.

NOTABLE BLACK MEMPHIANS

Albert, Laurence (1953–), opera singer. A renowned baritone with an international reputation, he has performed operatic roles in twenty-five countries. The son of Laurence and Elizabeth Kilpatrick Albert, he was born in Memphis on April 9, 1953. The singer has deep roots in the Memphis community; his great-grandfather, Isaac Gooden, was a major figure at Avery Chapel A.M.E. Church, and his grandfather, Frank Kilpatrick, was prominent in the political and civil rights struggles of the 1950s and '60s. Albert's interest in music began in church and public school, where he took clarinet lessons with Thomas Doggett and sang in glee clubs directed by John Clayborne, Hattie Swearengen, and Lulah Hedgeman. After graduating from Hamilton High School in 1971, he entered Morehouse College, where he sang with the celebrated Morehouse Glee Club, under the direction of Memphian Wendell Whalum. After completing a bachelor's degree in music, he enrolled in the opera program at the University of Michigan, where he studied voice with Willis Patterson and Czechoslovakian soprano Eva Likova. Just before completing a master's degree, he auditioned for and won a role in the Houston Grand Opera production of *Porgy and Bess*, which toured Europe in 1978. When the tour ended, he returned to Memphis, studied voice with Ethel Taylor Maxwell, and served for two years as artist-in-residence with the Southern Opera Theater, before moving to St. Louis. For the next four and a half years, he studied voice with Edward Zambara at the St. Louis Conservatory.

In 1984, Albert went to Paris to study and perform, after winning a major prize in the Concours de Chant de Paris. He toured Germany with the Kaiserslautern Platztheater, and, in 1987, returned to Paris to assume a demanding schedule of concerts, recitals, and operatic performances. Later, he worked to elevate the range of his voice, moving from bass to baritone, because, as he pointed out, "baritone roles better suit my personality than those of stoic bass roles." The vocal transition took three years to accomplish, and it is significant that his first attempt at the Italian baritone repertoire took place in Memphis. In October 1995, Albert played the title role in the Opera Memphis production of *Rigoletto*, performing at the Orpheum and Germantown Performing Arts Center. A 1992 convert to Buddhism, he has added Negro spirituals to his repertoire, because of "the incredible strength of emotional and spiritual values Black people have exhibited in overcoming many negative forces." In a career that spans three decades, he has won acclaim in Europe and the United States. He has sung with the Paris Opera Company and with the Strasbourg, Nancy, and Kaisersalutem Opera Companies in Germany. In this country, he has performed with the Santa Fe Opera, Opera Theatre of St. Louis, Nashville Opera, and Opera Memphis. In September 2005, he appeared with the Memphis Symphony Opera in a free concert to raise money for musicians victimized by Hurricane Katrina, and he made his Memphis Symphony Orchestra debut in January 2006.

Alston, Bettye J. Harris (1938–), entrepreneur, religious leader. One of Memphis's most prominent women clerics, she became an A.M.E. minister before organizing an independent church. Born in Memphis on December 17, 1938, to Thomas L. and Bettie Marie Golden Harris, she grew up in Orange Mound, where she attended Melrose Elementary and High School before dropping out in the tenth grade. She graduated from the Memphis Area Vocational School in 1961 and Memphis State University School of Nursing eight years later. A recruiter and chief nurse with the United States Army Reserve Nurse Corps, she attained the rank of captain before resigning in 1975. After graduating cum laude from Memphis Theological Seminary in 1984, she acquired two other advanced degrees: a Doctorate of Ministry degree from St. Paul School of Theology in Missouri and a Ph.D. in counseling psychology from Emanuel Baptist University in North Carolina.

As a licensed practical nurse, Bettye Alston worked at the City of Memphis Hospital, Tennessee Psychiatric Hospital, and University of West Tennessee Tuberculosis Hospital; as a registered nurse, she worked at the Regional Medical Center, from which she retired as director of nursing in 1987. She opened BeNea Travel, Entertainment and Fashions in the 1980s and later founded BeNea's House of Fashion, but her work is her ministry. She and three other women ministers resigned from the A.M.E. denomination in October 1988, because, although Dr. Alston was a college and seminary graduate who had pastored for a decade, less educated and less experienced male colleagues were promoted to larger churches. It is ironic and painful, she noted, that Black women who participated in the freedom movement are rejected by male colleagues who worked with them to achieve civil rights for Blacks.

Dr. Alston's response to rejection by the all-male church hierarchy was to found an independent church, the New Beginning Ministries Church of Our Lord and Savior Jesus Christ, in 1988. She also founded the Interdenominational Women's Ministerial Alliance, a coalition of forty Black Memphis women pastors, evangelists, and missionaries. Active in community and service organizations, she is an alumna of Leadership Memphis Class of 1991, a recipient of the "She Knows Where She's Going" award from Girls, Inc., and she was selected as one of the 1998 "Fifty Women Who Make a Difference." She has received many other awards, including the M. L. King, Jr., Service Award for Religion; Outstanding Student Nurse at MSU; Outstanding Pastor of the A.M.E. Church; and Academic Excellence in Christian Education. Vice president and executive director of the Alston Family Evangelistic Association, Reverend Alston was the founder of the Ecumenical Christian Leadership School and is the former president of the Henry Logan Starks Alumni at the Memphis Theological Seminary. She made history on May 6, 2007, when she was consecrated as the first female African American bishop in New Day Church International.

On November 28, 1980, she married Reverend Neasbie Alston, presently the pastor of Gospel Temple Missionary Baptist Church; they are the parents of eight adult children and they host the Alston Family Prayer Time on cable television. She helped plan the Women's Holy Convocation Mid-Year Service and, two years later, published *Building Bricks Without Straw: The Impossible Mission*, an inspirational book that describes the skills for leading a balanced life. In recent years, Dr. Alston joined First Fitness International and rose to the position of crown presidential director in the company. With natural products from First Fitness, she opened the Inside and Out Wellness Center, thus extending her ministry to include health and wellness.

Armstrong, Lillian Hardin "Lil" (1898–1971), singer, pianist, and composer. One of Memphis's pioneering jazz artists, she reached her height as a performer in the 1930s, when she led several all-star bands in a series of recording sessions for Decca. Lillian Hardin was born in Memphis on February 3, 1898, and nineteen years later, moved with her family to Chicago, where she worked as a song demonstrator at Jones's Music Store. After studying classical music at Fisk University for three years, she joined Freddie Keppard and then formed her own band in 1920 at Chicago's Dreamland Ballroom. Her February 5, 1924, marriage to Louis Armstrong ended with a separation in 1931 and a divorce in 1938. In the 1920s, she performed with such band leaders as King Oliver and Hugh Swift, and she was featured on Louis Armstrong's *Hot Five* and *Hot Seven* recordings. She is depicted in a 1923 photograph of King Oliver's seven-member Creole Jazz Band as a petite and curvaceous young woman in a stylish, flapper dress. Leaning against the piano with her fingers on the keyboard, she looks like the serious and consummate artist that she was.

Her training as a concert pianist was evident in her unique keyboard styling. Lil Armstrong continued the study of classical music, earning a teachers' diploma, in 1928, from the Chicago College of Music, where she studied with Louis Victor Saar. A year later, she was awarded a postgraduate diploma by the New York College of Music, after completing studies with August Fraemoke. She spent most of her professional career in Chicago, leading her all-female or all-male bands on tours of the country or doing solo performances at clubs such as the Garrick Stage Bar, Nob Hill Club, or Mark Twain Lounge. She lived for a while in New York, appearing with Ralph Cooper's Orchestra at the Harlem Opera House in 1931, broadcasting on local radio stations, and performing in *Hot Chocolate* and *Shuffle Along* revues. After a European tour in early 1952, she returned to the Chicago area, where she continued to perform throughout the 1950s and '60s. Lillian Armstrong died in Chicago on August 27, 1971, while participating in a memorial concert for Louis Armstrong.

Bailey, D'Army (1941–), attorney, judge, civil rights activist. Characterized as a "radical activist" while serving on the Berkeley City Council, Bailey became a prominent figure in the cultural and political life of Memphis. The son of Will Ella and Walter L. Bailey, Sr., he was born in Memphis on November 29, 1941, and grew up in a South Memphis neighborhood near Mississippi and Walker Avenue. His early experiences in the segregated city—sitting in movie theater balconies, riding in the backs of buses, and going to the zoo on Thursdays—helped to shape his militance and interest in law. After graduating from Booker T. Washington High School in 1959, he entered Southern University in Baton Rouge but was suspended in 1962 for taking part in a demonstration near the state capitol. Fortuitously, he received a scholarship to Clark University in Worchester, Massachusetts, where he organized the Worchester Student movement. During his summers in Memphis, he cut his political teeth working in the legislative campaigns of Russell Sugarmon and A. W. Willis. Bailey received a bachelor's degree in 1964 and a law degree from Yale University in 1967. While at Yale, he helped organize a chapter of the Law Students Civil Rights Research Council and, upon graduation, became national director of the LSCRRC in New York. A year later, he joined the staff of San Francisco Legal Services. When he was elected to the Berkeley City Council in 1971, he worked for changes in city government, moderate-income housing, a graduated income tax, and an end to police brutality. In spite of his progressive politics, he lost his council seat in a 1973 recall election.

When he returned to Memphis in 1974, Bailey became an assistant Shelby County public defender and opened a law office with his older brother, Walter L. Bailey, Jr. In 1983, he was unsuccessful in his candidacy for mayor of Memphis but was elected a Circuit Court Judge in Tennessee's 30th Judicial District. Active in civic and cultural affairs, he was one of the founders of the Lorraine Civil Rights Museum and served for several years as chairman of the museum board. He has also served on the boards of the Vollintine Boys Club, Tennessee Historical Commission, and Tennessee Commission on the Humanities. A member of the Grand Krewe of the Nile, he has appeared in several movies and has published editorial columns for *The Commercial Appeal*, law review articles, and a book on Martin Luther King. In *Mine Eyes Have Seen: Dr. Martin Luther King Jr.'s Final Journey*, Bailey reflects on his involvement in the civil rights movement and chronicles, through photographs and archival materials, King's participation in the Sanitation Workers' Strike during his final days in Memphis. D'Army Bailey is married to Adrienne Marie Leslie Bailey, and they have two children, Justin and Merritt.

Bailey, Walter Lee, Jr. (1940–), attorney, county commissioner. One of the longest-serving members of the Shelby County Commission, Bailey has been in the forefront of the legal profession in Memphis. The older of two sons, he was born in Memphis on August 21, 1940, to Will Ella Bailey, a practical nurse, and Walter L. Bailey, a Pullman porter. After attending Rosebud and LaRose Elementary Schools, he entered Booker T. Washington High School, where he played football and from which he graduated with honors. While at Southern University in Baton Rouge, he and his brother, D'Army, became involved in civil rights activities: marching on the state capitol and sitting-in at lunch counters. Bailey was among the expelled students who were readmitted conditionally, probably because of his value to the football team. He was assigned to the faculty dormitory and then to the law school dormitory, where he would have less influence over other students. After graduating from college, he entered Southern Law School. In 1962, he married Elsie Lewis, an educator, and they have three sons and a daughter: Javier, Steve, Taurus, and Pamela. The couple have since divorced. Walter and D'Army Bailey organized a law partnership but dissolved the firm when D'Army was appointed to the Circuit Court. Since then, two of his sons, Javier and Taurus, have joined him in the practice of law.

A civil and criminal trial lawyer, Walter Bailey filed the first housing discrimination lawsuit in the area, and he also sued Memphis State University over a policy that kept Vietnam veterans from distributing antiwar material on campus. One of his major achievements is the successful prosecution of a 1984 lawsuit that limits police use of deadly force in apprehending suspects. This suit went to the United States Supreme Court, which ruled that it is unconstitutional to shoot unarmed suspects who pose no threat. Bailey contends that his most important case is his defense of Dr. Martin Luther King during the Sanitation Strike. After city officials enjoined King from organizing additional marches, Bailey and other lawyers filed an injunction against the city that they argued before the Supreme Court. Bailey has become increasingly involved in politics: he served as president of the Shelby County Democratic Club, and he campaigned for Senator Albert Gore, Sr. and for gubernatorial candidate John Jay Hooker. In 1971, he was elected to the Shelby County Commission in a narrow victory, and he has been returned to office in every election since then without any serious opposition. As a commissioner, he has worked to eliminate poverty, to encourage county vendors to hire more Blacks, and to consolidate city and county services, especially the police department and public schools. In 1989, he was named chairman of the Shelby County Commission, but he left the Commission in 2006 because of the new term limit law. For three years,

Bailey served on the American Civil Liberties Union Board, and he was active with the NAACP Legal Defense Fund.

Bailey, William C. "Buster" (1902–1967), jazz musician. Noted for his fluent and highly personal style, Buster Bailey was the first academically trained clarinetist to gain fame as a jazz musician. He was born in Memphis on July 19, 1902, and began playing the clarinet at the Clay Street School when he was thirteen years old. Two years later, he joined W. C. Handy's orchestra and toured with him until 1919, when he moved to Chicago to play with Erskine Tate and to study under Franz Schoepp of the Chicago Symphony. In the 1920s, he performed with the top band leaders of the period, including King Oliver, Fletcher Henderson, and Oscar "Bernie" Young. In May 1929, he accompanied Noble Sissle on a European tour and, on his return, joined several bandleaders—Edgar Hayes, Dave Nelson, Louis Armstrong, Stuff Smith, and John Kirby—for various periods during the 1930s. In 1940, he was depicted in a photograph playing the clarinet with the John Kirby sextette, known as the "biggest little band in America." A tall, handsome, light-brown-skinned man, he is elegantly attired, as are the other band members, in a white tuxedo. A member of the sextet said: "Buster Bailey was a genius. Buster could play anywhere, whether it be the Philharmonic, a pit band, a radio program or a blues session. He was brilliant." During that period, Bailey also formed his own bands, including a quartet and a small combo at New York's Spotlite Club. He performed occasionally with symphony orchestras in New York and worked in the pit orchestra for the 1953 production of *Porgy and Bess*. Featured at several jazz festivals in the 1950s and 1960s, he also appeared in the 1962 film *Splendor in the Grass*. In July 1965, Buster Bailey joined Louis Armstrong's All Stars and remained with the group until his death in Brooklyn on April 12, 1967.

Bankhead, Daniel Robert "Dan" (1920–1976), baseball player. Called the "next Satchel Paige" and the "colored Bob Feller," Bankhead became the first Black pitcher in the major leagues. He was born in Empire, Alabama, on May 30, 1920, and grew up in a family of baseball players who came up through the Negro Leagues. His father was a first baseman in the Cotton Belt League; his oldest brother, Sam, became the first Black manager in organized baseball, after playing in the Negro League for twenty years; his brother, Fred, was his teammate with the Memphis Red Sox; and his brothers, Garnett and Joe, also played in the Negro Leagues. The six-foot-one ballplayer joined the Birmingham Black Barons as a shortstop in 1940, but, after two years with the team, joined the Marines; while in the service, he organized a Black baseball team. On his return to the Memphis Red Sox in 1946, he was voted to the All-Star team twice and was the winning pitcher in both All-Star games; his outstanding performances as a pitcher soon made him the highest-paid player on the team. In 1947, Branch Rickey flew to Memphis to watch Bankhead pitch and, a few days later, the ballplayer joined the Dodgers, becoming the first Black pitcher in the major league. The reported $15,000 that Rickey paid for Bankhead's contract was the highest paid in 1947 for the contract of a Black player.

In his first season with the Dodgers, Bankhead played in only four games. After his first game, the 184-pound athlete commented, "I was scared as hell. When I stepped on the mound, I was perspiring all over and tight as a drum." In spite of his nervousness, he brought in a homer during his first game, a feat that no other National League pitcher had accomplished. In 1948, he was sent to Class B Nashua, where he won twenty games, tossed a no-hitter, and struck out 240 in 202 innings. Called the "wild man of the International League," he had a spectacular season: he won ten games, hit seven home runs, and secured the Puerto Rican League pennant with a five-hit shutout. In 1950, on his return to the majors, he shut out the Cardinals and earned the number three spot in the Dodger rotation, behind Don Newcombe and Preacher Roe. Later that summer, Bankhead dislocated his shoulder and had financial problems; he and his family had to live in an expensive hotel because he could not find a Brooklyn apartment that would accept children. In 1951, following a poor start, he was farmed out to Montreal and then sold to a team in the Dominican Republic. After a provocation, Bankhead attacked another player, landed in jail, and was fired by the Escogido Lions. In 1954, he began a 12-season stint with various Mexican teams as a pitcher-outfielder-first baseman, compiling decent statistics, with a lifetime pitching record of 32–19. He died on May 2, 1976, in Houston, Texas.

Banks, Frank (1941–), accountant, entrepreneur, banker. Known as one of the "movers and shakers" in the Memphis business community, he has organized several important Black-owned and-operated businesses and financial institutions. The youngest of George and Maggie Malone Banks's eleven children, he was born in Memphis on September 22, 1941, three months after the death of his 47-year-old father, who had a heart attack while working for the Illinois Central Railroad. His mother did housework, sold Avon products, and taught kindergarten to support her children. He and his family lived across the street from Jesse Turner, president of Tri-State Bank, in whose footsteps he followed to become a business major and an accountant. After graduating from Hamilton High School in 1960 and from Xavier University in 1964, with a degree in accounting, he became federal auditor of Chicago's Department of Housing and Urban Development and, later, an accountant with a social agency in Milwaukee. On the advice of Turner, he returned to Memphis, where he obtained important positions: head of accounting for the local War on Poverty Committee, financial officer for the Community Action Agency, accountant with the national firm of Ernst & Ernst, and accountant for the firm of CPA Otha L. Brandon, who also became a role model. In 1973, Banks served as treasurer of Harold Ford's congressional campaign and, five years later, Ford nominated him for a seat on the three-member board of directors of the Tennessee Valley Authority, but he did not get the appointment.

In May 1973, he co-founded Banks, Finley, White & Company, a regional accounting firm, which was the first CPA firm in Mississippi and Alabama. He and his partners, Mack Finley, Jr., and James C. White, obtained a loan from a Birmingham bank after Memphis banks turned down their application, and they opened offices in three states. It became one of the largest CPA firms in the country: it employed sixty people, including ten CPAs; handled the accounts of Tri-State Bank and LeMoyne-Owen College; and had $2 million in annual billings by 1987. Banks left the firm in 1985 and sold his interest to the present owner, Stan Sawyer, in 1987. That year, with partner Mabra Holeyfield, he founded Banks and Holeyfield Management Company, which managed the Tennessee Valley Center for Minority Economic Development, Southern Cooperative Development Fund (Memphis office), American History Calendar Partnership, West Tennessee Venture Capital Corporation, Days Inn Hotel, and Banks Investment Building. Banks also became president and CEO of the Tennessee Valley Center, a regional, nonprofit economic development firm that he created in 1979 to generate jobs and business opportunities for minorities. During his affiliation with the Center, from 1979 to 1988, 2,778 jobs were created or saved and over $23 million was leveraged for economic development. Among the Center's projects was the Benchmark Hotel, which reopened as the Days Inn on Union and Third Streets, across from the Peabody Hotel.

In 1999, Banks helped raise $4.75 million to found MemphisFirst Community Bank, which he serves as chairman. The first bank in the country with almost equal holdings by Black and White shareholders, it is located in Whitehaven and had earnings of $178,000 in the first nine months of 2005. With an injection of $10 million, a group of investors bought a majority interest in MemphisFirst in 2006, renamed it Landmark Community Bank, and made plans to open a branch in Collierville and new headquarters in Germantown.

Married to the former Brenda Tervalon of New Orleans, Frank Banks and his wife have two daughters, Tracey and Danese.

Barnett, Ida B. Wells. See Ida B. Wells.

Barry, Marion Shepilov, Jr. (1936–), school board member, city councilman, mayor. The first civil rights activist to become mayor of a large city, Barry won election to the D.C. City Council and an unprecedented fourth term as mayor of Washington, D.C., after serving a six-month prison sentence. The son of Marion S. Barry, a sharecropper, and Mattie Barry, a domestic, he was born in Itta Bena, Mississippi, on March 6, 1936. After the death of his father when he was four years old, he moved with his family to Memphis, where his mother married David Cummings, a butcher. Young Barry excelled in school, became an Eagle Scout, and worked at menial jobs to help raise his seven younger sisters. After graduating from

Booker T. Washington High School, he entered LeMoyne College, where, as president of the NAACP college chapter, he led a movement to oust a White member of the trustee board who had used a racial slur in a bus desegregation trial. After graduating with a bachelor's degree in chemistry in 1958, Barry entered Fisk University, where he established an NAACP chapter and organized the first lunch counter sit-ins in Nashville. He met with other student leaders at Shaw University to organize the Student Nonviolent Coordinating Committee and was named its first national chairman. After receiving a master's degree from Fisk in 1960, he began doctoral studies at the University of Kansas and later transferred to the University of Tennessee, but he left UT in 1964 to work full time for SNCC.

Barry moved to New York but then settled in Washington, D.C., where he became active in civil rights and politics: in January 1966, he led a one-day bus boycott; the following month, he organized the "Free D.C. movement" to wrest control of the city from Congress; and then he led a boycott of merchants who refused to back the movement. Described by supporters as a "man with a mission" and by detractors as an "extortionist and caged panther," Marion Barry created Youth Pride, a federally funded project that led to the founding of Pride Economic Enterprises, a for-profit body that operated several small businesses and a 55-unit housing development. Barry also began to climb the city's political ladder: in 1970 he was elected to the citizen's board of the Pilot Police District Project; in 1971, he won a seat on the school board and served as its president from 1972 to 1974; in 1974, he was elected to an at-large seat on the city council; and in 1976, he won reelection with 78% of the vote. His career almost came to an end, however, in 1977, when the Hanafi Muslims took over the District Building and, in the confusion, accidentally shot Barry in the chest, barely missing his heart.

In 1978, Barry married Effi Slaughter with whom he had a son, Marion Christopher Barry. That same year, he was elected mayor of Washington, D.C. He created housing projects, job programs, and employment opportunities, particularly for youth, but he also had to contend with a teachers' strike, cuts in jobs and services, and a $409 million budget deficit. In 1979, his former wife, Mary Treadwell, was convicted of taking federal money from a Pride housing project. Nevertheless, Barry won a second term in 1982 and a third term by a landslide in 1986. He was credited with the renewal of downtown and the decline in crime and unemployment; he was also blamed for prison disturbances, the loss of federal grants, increased taxes, and a fiscal crisis. After surviving several scandals, he was arrested at the Vista Hotel on a charge of drug possession, convicted on a charge of cocaine usage, and began serving a six-month prison term in September 1991. After his release, he won a two-year term on the city council, representing Ward 8, and married Cora Lavonne Master, whom he has since divorced. In 1994, Marion S. Barry won a fourth term as mayor of the nation's capital and, after a brief hiatus from politics, won reelection to the D.C. City Council, representing Ward 8.

Bisson, Wheelock Alexander (1898–1985), physician. Dr. Bisson, who practiced medicine in Tennessee for many years, had a distinguished career as a private physician, medical examiner, and director of health clinics. He was born on January 5, 1898, in Key West, Florida, to George Henry Bisson, a carpenter who had worked on the Panama Canal, and Sarah Jane Bisson, a dressmaker who operated a sewing school for thirty years. A talented and precocious child, he decided at age five that he wanted to be a doctor, but he also took piano and violin lessons, and, as a member of the Jolly Boys Orchestra, played for dances and concerts. When he was nine years old, Bisson learned tailoring and worked for eight years at a tailor shop while attending school. He graduated from Douglass Junior High School as president of the student body and valedictorian of the class of 1917, and that fall entered Florida A&M

College, completing the last two years of high school during his freshman year.

After graduating from college as valedictorian, he taught physics and mathematics for two years at the State Teachers College at Winston-Salem, North Carolina, and he pursued graduate studies in science and mathematics at Harvard University. In 1925, he entered Meharry Medical College, receiving the M.D. degree in 1929. On June 1, 1930, he married Maude Lee Voorhies, a teacher, who later served as X-ray technician and physical therapist in her husband's office. After practicing medicine for a year in Bolivar, Tennessee, Dr. Bisson moved to Memphis and spent the first two years (1930–1932) interning at Royal Circle Hospital. In 1932, he founded and directed the Park Avenue Clinic in the Orange Mound neighborhood, where he lived and practiced medicine for fifty-five years until his retirement in 1978. Through the efforts of Dr. Bisson and five other Black doctors, the Memphis Health Department established well-baby clinics at Dunbar, Melrose, and Park Avenue Schools; in 1982, one of the clinics was named the W. A. Bisson Primary Health Clinic in recognition of his thirty-seven years of volunteer work in that program. Beginning in 1933, he spent ten years working with the Chest Clinic sponsored by the Memphis and Shelby County Tuberculosis Society.

During the 1937 Mississippi River flood, Dr. Bisson supervised the 200-bed refugee hospital established at Carnes School by the Red Cross. After completing a course on venereal diseases at Eve Hall Clinic in 1938, he was appointed clinician and, later, director of the Wellington Health Clinic, the largest facility for the treatment of venereal diseases in the United States. In the 1940s, he received a number of significant appointments: Shelby County Tennessee Examiner of the National Youth Administration, examiner for the Tennessee Department of Vocational Rehabilitation, and medical advisor to Local Draft Board #83. Dr. Bisson continued his professional development: in 1944, he studied at the U.S. Public Health Research Hospital in Hot Springs, Arkansas, and, nine years later, he studied at Chicago's Providence Hospital. Highly regarded by business leaders, he served as medical examiner for the Tri-State Boxing Commission and for Universal, Union Protective, and North Carolina Mutual Insurance Companies. He was also active in professional organizations, serving as vice president of the National Medical Association, secretary of the Bluff County Medical Society, and member of the Tennessee Academy of Science, Tennessee State Medical Association, and Memphis and Shelby County Medical Society. In 1978, he received the Governor's Outstanding Tennessean Award in recognition of his many years of professional service. Reflecting on his life, Dr. Bisson said, "I tried to be an old-style doctor where interest in the condition of the patient exceeded interest in the condition of the pocketbook." At the time of his death on October 23, 1985, he was writing his autobiography.

Blackfoot, J. "Foot" (1946–), singer. This Stax legend is noted for his rousing, foot-stomping performance of blues and R&B. Born John Colbert on November 20, 1946, in Greenville, Mississippi, he grew up in the South Memphis neighborhood of Suzette Bottom, near LeMoyne Gardens Housing Project. The first part of his life was hard: he got the nickname "Foot" because he walked barefoot on the tarred streets of Memphis in the hot summers and, as a teenager, he spent time in jail for stealing a car. At Porter School, in the "doo-wop" days, he was exposed to the music and teaching of Harry Winfield. "You know how it was back then," he said. "We didn't have much money, so we'd get a little bottle of wine, stand under the corner and do some singing." He was discovered when music maestro David Porter came to hear him at Payne's, a little juke joint on McLemore Street, where "Foot" was belting out a spirited rendition of "Shout-Bama-Lama" and Wilson Pickett's "I'm in Love." He began his musical career in 1967 at age twenty-one, traveling with the Bar-Kays after the original members and Otis Redding died in a plane crash. When Porter and Isaac Hayes formed the Soul Children, they asked him to be the lead vocalist, along with Anita Louis, Shelbra Bennett, and Norman West. He recalled: "Our first gig was at the Apollo in Harlem...I went from singing behind a liquor store to performing at the Apollo almost overnight." The group recorded their first hit, "Give 'Em Love," a Hayes-Porter composition, on the 1968 album *The Soul Children*. Between 1968 and 1978, they also recorded three albums—*The Best of Two Worlds*, *Genesis*, and *Friction*—for Stax, as well as two LPs for Epic—*Finders Keepers* and *Where Is Your Woman Tonite*. After the collapse of Stax, he began singing in local clubs.

Blackfoot went solo in 1978, and scored a mega-hit with the single, "Taxi," which made Billboard's Top Five and climbed to the R&B Top Ten in 1984. During his comeback, he made seven guest appearances on *Soul Train* and *Hollywood Live*. His performance style, described as "energy, energy and flat-out soul singing," is characterized by enthusiasm, red hot heat, and a lot of jumping around. He explained, "I love to entertain people. My thing is, if it's just three people out there I'm going to give those three people their money's worth." Blackfoot collaborated with former Staxmen, composer Homer Banks and composer/musician Lester Snell, to reissue "Taxi," which was the last major record created by a Memphis artist and released by a local production team. Several years after the demise of Stax, Blackfoot released his *LoveAholic* album, which placed him solidly in the R&B genre. In 1986, he recorded *U-Turn* with the popular track "Tearjerker" on the Edge label, and he continued to record through the 1990s on the Basic label, which released *Same Time, Same Place* in 2001.

Blackmon, Joyce McAnulty (1937–), educator, businesswoman, public utilities administrator. The former public school teacher, counselor, and administrator became the first African American executive at Memphis Light, Gas and Water Division. The oldest of the two daughters of Evelyn and Samuel G. McAnulty, a playground and community center director, she was born on November 25, 1937, and grew up in the Klondyke neighborhood. In 1955, she entered Tennessee State University but left in 1957 to join her husband, Lawrence Blackmon, who was attending LeMoyne College, and they became the parents of two sons, Lawrence, Jr., and David Gardner. She began teaching in the Memphis City Schools in 1959, while continuing work toward a bachelor's degree in education, which she received from Memphis State University in 1966. For ten years, from 1959 to 1969, she taught elementary, junior, and senior high school but, after obtaining a master's degree in education from MSU in 1970, she became a guidance counselor at several schools. Eventually, she became director of Memphis Volunteer Placement Program, which helped students obtain financial aid for college and jobs after graduation. After almost twenty years with the school system, Blackmon, who describes herself as a risk-taker, accepted a new challenge.

She became vice president for personnel and training at MLGW in 1979, after Black employees filed a class-action lawsuit against the division, alleging discrimination in hiring and promotions. As a part of the consent decree, Blackmon was hired to set up training programs, a basic education program, and a center with hands-on technical training. The highest ranking female employee, she became vice president for Economic Development and External Affairs in 1991, and one of only two senior vice presidents. The division's Joyce McAnulty Blackmon Training Center on Raleigh-LaGrange, which was dedicated in 2002, is a testament to her seventeen and a half years of service to MLGW. Her life, however, has not been without challenges: she had brain surgery in 1982, and her husband, who was principal of Westwood Elementary School, died in 1985. An active member of Mississippi Boulevard Christian Church, she says that her faith sustained her during those trying times. "I am blessed to be alive. God spared me to do some other things." When she retired from her position with MLGW, in 1996, she became more active in the event management firm, J. Blackmon and Associates, which she founded in 1994.

A former trustee board member of Tougaloo College and a member of the Memphis and Shelby County Film and Television Commission, she was president of the Memphis Chapter of Links, as well as national director of The Arts for The Links, Inc. As a board member and then president of the Memphis in May International Festival, she had an opportunity to travel to Kenya, New Zealand, Russia, Thailand, and Côte d'Ivoire. She has received many awards from organizations such as March of Dimes, Big Brothers/Big Sisters, Black Business Association, *Grace* magazine, United Way, and the Memphis Branch of the NAACP. Under the headline "Great Catches for the Over-40 Crowd," Joyce M. Blackmon was featured with other singles in the September 1990 issue of *Ebony* magazine.

Blackmore, Amos (a.k.a. Junior Wells) (1934–1998), blues vocalist, harmonica player. Known professionally as Junior Wells, the legendary musician helped shape the Chicago blues sound and influenced generations of blues harmonica players. He was born in Memphis on December 9, 1934, but was raised in Arkansas. Although his parents wanted him to become a gospel singer, he started playing harmonica on city streets after picking up lessons from local bluesmen Junior Parker and Howlin' Wolf. He recalled that, as a boy, he didn't have $2.00 for a harmonica, so he left $1.50 on the counter, grabbed a harp, and ran. The police picked him up but, when the judge heard him play, he gave the store owner fifty cents and let the boy go.

In 1946, Blackmore moved to Chicago, formed a trio—known as the Little Chicago Devils, then the Three Deuces, and, finally, the Three Aces—and reinvented himself as Junior Wells, probably in honor of his mentor, Junior Parker. By age eighteen, he had joined the band of blues great Muddy Waters, with whom he recorded his first solo hit, the classic "Hoodoo Man Blues," the title song from his 1965 Delmark album. His unique harmonica style and musical sense of adventure are evident on such hits as "Messin' With the Kid," "Early in the Morning," and "Good Morning Little Schoolgirl."

After a brief stint in the Army, Junior Wells returned to the stage and the studio in 1957, when he released *Little by Little* and *Messin' With the Kid*. In the 1960s, he began an on and off, thirty-year association with guitarist Buddy Guy. During the 1970s, the pair opened several tour dates for the Rolling Stones, and they released a half-dozen albums, including *Buddy Guy and Junior Walker Play the Blues*, with guest artist Eric Clapton; *South Side Blues Jam*; *It's My Life Baby*; and the phenomenal *Hoodoo Man Blues*, called one of the finest Chicago blues albums, which features Wells's impressive styling and Guy's supportive playing. He became known for his song writing, unique style of blues, spirited performances, tireless touring schedule, and flamboyant style of dress. His music even influenced non-blues musicians such as Carlos Santana and Van Morrison. Harmonica player Sugar Blue said: "He had such a power in him, such emotive presence, that even listening to him on a record you could almost see him."

In 1997, Wells's *Come on in This House* won the W. C. Handy Blues Award for traditional blues album, and it was also nominated for a Grammy Award in the category of Best Traditional Blues Album. Before he became ill in September 1997, he completed work on the film *Blues Brothers 2000* in which he had a cameo part, and he recorded a sizzling number, "(I Can't Get No) Satisfaction," for a Rolling Stones tribute album called *Paint It Blue: Songs of the Rolling Stones*. After a four-month battle with lymphoma, Junior Wells died on January 15, 1998, at age sixty-three.

Bland, Bobby "Blue" (1930–), singer. Called one of the greatest blues vocalists of all times, he has recorded over thirty Top 20 R&B singles in a career spanning more than fifty years. Born Robert Calvin Bland in Rosemark, Tennessee (outside of Memphis) on January 27, 1930, he grew up singing spirituals in a rural church and listening to Nat King Cole and the Grand Ole Opry on the radio. He dropped out of school in the third grade and, at seventeen, moved with his mother to Memphis. Later, his mother opened the Sterling Grill on Third Street, and her son got a job at Bender's making $27 a week and singing spirituals on weekends with the Pilgrim Travelers. For several years, he worked for Little Junior Parker as a combination chauffeur, valet, and opening act, but he eventually came into his own. Rufus Thomas invited him to appear on WDIA Radio; he and Johnny Ace formed a band called The Beale Streeters; he won prizes at the Palace Theater's Amateur Night; and he performed in clubs like the Domino Lounge, Club Handy on Beale, and Sunshine Mitchell's. Bland made his first recording at the home of band leader Richard "Tuff" Green, but his recording career was interrupted, in 1952, by a two and a half year stint in the U.S. Army. Recording with Duke-Peacock Records in the 1950s and '60s, Bland developed his unique singing style, described as slow and deliberate, with an "unrelenting intensity and a down-on-your-knees fervor." He produced great albums like *Two Steps From the Blues* and memorable singles such as "I Pity the Fool" (1961), "Cry, Cry, Cry," and "Turn on Your Love Light," a favorite of the Grateful Dead. As one critic noted, "his evocative vocal style has taken the blues out of the barroom and into the bedroom" with lyrics such as "Without a warning you broke my heart / You took it darlin' and you tore it apart."

Fame and fortune did not come easily to Bland. He led a hard life and, although he battled booze, drugs, and depression for two decades, he never missed a gig, performing 300 shows a year and spending forty-nine weeks on the road. In the 1970s, he divorced his wife Marty and began traveling with Willie Mae, his wife of over twenty years. For the past two decades, he has reached a wider audience and been headlined at blues festivals. In 1979, he performed with B. B. King in the Dixon-Myers Auditorium and, in 1980, he headlined the International Blues Festival at the Mid-South Coliseum. Described as a "blues ballad stylist without peer," he created the soul-blues hybrid in such albums as *Two Steps From the Blues* and, more recently, *Members Only* and *After All*. In 1992, Bland was inducted into the Rock and Roll Hall of Fame and was honored by the Memphis Chapter of NARAS when a brass note in his honor was etched on Beale Street in April 1996. In 1997, he received a Grammy for Lifetime Achievement and his CD *Sad Street* was nominated for best contemporary blues album. Among his many other awards are Billboard's Special Achievement Award and the Rhythm and Blues Foundation's Pioneer Award; he was also inducted into the Blues Foundation's Hall of Fame. Although triple bypass surgery, in 1995, slowed him down a bit, Bobby "Blue" Bland has continued to perform up to a hundred shows a year, sometimes collaborating with his friend, blues legend B. B. King. In 1998, he released a CD/cassette/video *Live on Beale Street*, received a Lifetime Achievement Award from the Blues Foundation, and his Beale Street concert was filmed in *The Night, the Street, and Man*.

Bodden, Ira Swithin (1902–1985), tailor, businessman. A skilled craftsman and enterprising business owner, Bodden was acknowledged as one of Memphis's most meticulous tailors. One of the seven children of Sarah and Ethelbert Bodden, he was born on September 10, 1902, in Roatan Republic, Honduras, where his father worked as a tailor. After completing high school in Central America, Ira Bodden followed one of his brothers to Tuskegee

Institute, from which he graduated with a degree in tailoring. He then moved to Memphis to become designer, cutter, and manager for Buffington Tailoring Company. Although he planned to remain in Memphis for just one summer and then pursue studies at Meharry Medical College, his dream of becoming a physician ended with the onset of the Depression. In the ten years that he worked at Buffington's, he earned a reputation as an expert craftsman who took pride in his work and gave attention to detail. Over the years, he continued to study at prestigious schools throughout the country, including the American Gentlemen's School of Designing in New York, Stone Tailoring College, and Master Designing College in Chicago.

In 1939, he accepted a position as head of the Tailoring Division at Tuskegee but returned to Memphis in 1947 to establish the Bodden Tailoring Company on Beale Street in the old Urban League Building. Several years later, he founded the Bodden Tailoring School, after receiving approval by the State Department of Education and the Veterans Administration for a school of designing and tailoring technology. Many of the students whom he trained have attested to the impact that Bodden's school and business have had on Memphis and the Tri-State area. In 1962, he married Frankie Holliday, a nurse, and the couple traveled to many countries, including Egypt, Greece, Canada, Mexico, Hawaii, and the Holy Land. A communicant of Emmanuel Episcopal Church and a member of Phi Beta Sigma, he received special recognition for fifty years of devoted service to the fraternity. Although he retired in the 1970s, he continued to teach individuals at his home. Ira S. Bodden, a gentleman noted for his honesty and integrity, died on April 18, 1995, at age ninety-two, and he is buried in Elmwood Cemetery.

Booth, Benjamin Franklin (1858–1941), attorney. Acknowledged as the most prominent African American attorney in Memphis and Shelby County during the early twentieth century, Booth gained a reputation as a brilliant criminal attorney and as an early defender of civil rights. Born to slave parents on October 17, 1858, he grew up on a farm in Prentiss County, Mississippi. The Booth family soon moved to Tippah County, Mississippi, where young Ben attended rural schools until age sixteen. The early death of his father meant that he had to work to support himself and his widowed mother, so he began teaching, as well as working on the farm. In 1880, he entered the State Normal School for Colored in Holly Springs, Mississippi, and he graduated with honors four years later. That same year, he began reading law books on his own and, later, under the supervision of Colonel William Inge, a criminal lawyer and Speaker of the Mississippi House of Representatives, and under Judge Francis Fentress. Booth taught in Mississippi and Tennessee before accepting the principalship of a school in Bolivar, Tennessee. On September 8, 1885, he opened a law practice in Bolivar, while working in the public schools.

A resourceful attorney with a remarkable memory, Booth moved to Memphis in January 1889, in search of greater professional opportunities. In one of his first cases, *Eaton v. Phelan*, he represented Republican Lucian Bonaparte Eaton in a contested election for the United States Congress, the first time that an African American was hired in a contested election in the South. In preparing for the case, Booth took 1,400 depositions and canvassed four counties in the Tenth Congressional District. This case brought him fame and fortune, for he soon became one of the most prominent and prosperous Black attorneys in the South. Acclaimed as a great criminal lawyer, he won the acquittal of Mrs. Willie Anderson for the murder of her husband by arguing that her indictment should be thrown out because Blacks were excluded from the jury. He also handled civil cases, such as a divorce suit between the Scurlocks that had been in the courts for twelve years. Booth had a judgment against the husband set aside, got a new trial, obtained a judgment in favor of his client, and then won two appeals to the Tennessee State Supreme Court.

In 1905, he and Josiah T. Settle unsuccessfully challenged the state Jim Crow law mandating segregated streetcars, when they argued the case before the Tennessee State Supreme Court. By the early 1900s, Booth had become one of the most successful Black men in the city; he owned a large home, downtown property, and a forty-acre farm near Millington. One of the founders of the Fraternal Savings Bank & Trust Company of Memphis, he served as a lawyer for the bank, as well as an attorney for the Knights of Pythias. On March 16, 1923, he signed the charter of Universal Life Insurance Company along with four other prominent businessmen. The B. F. Booth Park in South Memphis is named after the legendary attorney. After his death on May 31, 1941, the Chancery, Circuit, and Probate Courts recessed for his funeral, and the Memphis and Shelby County Bar Association paid tribute to him at a special meeting. In 2001, Mary E. Booth, published a biography of her grandfather: *B. F. Booth: The Legacy*.

Boyd, Robert Richard "Bob" (1919–2004), baseball player. A first baseman for the Memphis Red Sox for four years, Boyd was one of the first Blacks to be drafted into the major leagues, playing first for the Chicago White Sox and then for the Baltimore Orioles. He was born in Potts Camp, Mississippi on October 1, 1919, but spent most of his youth in New Albany, Mississippi. While he was in high school, his mother died, so he moved to Memphis to live with his father, who had also played baseball. After three years in military service, he returned to Memphis and began working in a warehouse. When he and his brother Jimmy tried out for the Red Sox in 1946, Bob—now 5' 10' and 170 pounds—was signed on the spot after hitting line drives to all fields. Over the next four years, he broke Negro American League hitting records and, in 1950, became the first Black player signed by the Chicago White Sox.

In spite of the fact that he hit .373 in the Western League and led the Pacific Coast League with forty-one stolen bases, he was sent to the minors three times in as many years, allegedly because of racial prejudice. In retrospect, the soft-spoken Boyd admitted that he was probably treated unfairly: "Looking back, I really feel that the early black ballplayers had to do a little better than the white players to make it to the majors." At age thirty, when he finally made it to the majors to stay, his frozen line drives earned him the nickname of "Rope." In 1957, he finished fourth in the American League batting competition after Ted Williams, Mickey Mantle, and Gene Woodling, and the following year he had seven hits in a doubleheader and led the AL in night-game hitting. In the 1950s, he had several successful seasons with Caribbean teams: the Ponce in Puerto Rico (1951–1952) and the Cienfuegos in Cuba (1954–1955), where he had a batting average of .300. Boyd played nine years in the majors, completing his career with them in 1961, and then he played three additional seasons in the minors as a pinch hitter with Oklahoma City, before calling it quits in 1964. He then worked for several years as a scout for the Orioles and, later, organized autograph shows for major league baseball players in Wichita and Kansas City. He died on September 7, 2004.

Branch, Addison A. (1898–1997), educator. A noted science professor at LeMoyne College for twenty-one years and interim president of Tougaloo College, he served the Memphis community during a period of social and political turmoil. One of five children born to the Albert Branches, he grew up in Lynchburg, Virginia, and attended the Weyland Academy in Richmond. He served in the Armed Forces during World

War I and received an honorable discharge on December 20, 1918. In 1923, after completing the bachelor's degree in chemistry with highest honors from Virginia Union University, he acquired two master's degrees—one in 1925 and the other in 1930. Additional graduate study included two years toward a Ph.D. in science at Teachers College, Columbia University, as well as courses in college administration at Harvard University. In 1930, he married Rose H., and they had a son, Addison A. Branch, Jr. The American Missionary Association sent him to Memphis in 1931 to develop the Chemistry Department at LeMoyne College, where his chemistry class became a rite of passage for pre-medical students. There, he served as professor of chemistry, chair of the Natural Sciences Department, and director of the summer in-service program for public school teachers.

Dr. Branch left Memphis in 1952 to become academic dean of Tougaloo College, where he served as interim president in 1955 and vice-president in 1964. While at the college, he harbored several leaders of the civil rights movement and kept a book with the signatures of Martin L. King, Ralph Bunche, Medgar Evers, Jesse Jackson, and others. His son explained that their home "was like a safe haven because Tougaloo was a private institution that the police couldn't enter without some kind of cause." Branch established the Tougaloo College Summer Science Program (SSP), designed to introduce high school juniors and seniors to the health professions. Widely traveled, he served on a panel, in 1972, to study educational programs in Egypt, Kenya, Ethiopia, Tanzania, and Kenya. Through a program sponsored by the Comparative Education Society, he also studied educational systems in Austria, England, Denmark, Germany, Scotland, and the Soviet Union. On his return to Memphis following his 1975 retirement from Tougaloo, he received many awards, including the Doctor of Law Degree from Tougaloo College in 1975 and the Doctor of Science Degree from LeMoyne-Owen College in 1992.

A committed civic worker and community activist, Branch was a founder and president of the Bluff City Council of Civic Clubs. A board member of the Memphis Branch of the NAACP, he participated in the 1963 March on Washington and the 1966 march in

Jackson, Mississippi, when Martin Luther King and other civil rights leaders met at his home. He was a member of the Second Congregational Church, Omega Psi Phi fraternity, and Sigma Pi Phi fraternity. The Chi Psi Chapter of Omega Psi Phi Fraternity at LeMoyne College established the A. A. Branch Loan Fund in his honor, because he was a prominent member of the fraternity. A devoted husband, he cared for his wife during the protracted illness that claimed her life, and he died of heart disease at Graceland Nursing Home in 1997.

Brandon, Otha Leon (1921–1980), educator, accountant, businessman. Called the "Accounting Dean" because of his contributions to the profession, Brandon opened the first Black-owned, full-service, full-time Certified Public Accounting practice in Tennessee in 1969. He was born on December 29, 1921, in Shelby, Mississippi, to Calvin and Delia Washington Brandon. After graduating from the public schools of Mound Bayou, Mississippi, he applied for the position of surveyor for the Federal Soil Conservation Project but was given, instead, the job of pulling the measuring chain. He worked long enough to earn money to enter LeMoyne College in Memphis. He received a bachelor's degree in accounting and did postgraduate work at the University of Illinois in Urbana. He also studied at the University of Omaha, University of Texas, and University of Tennessee-Memphis Branch. After serving in the United States Armed Forces for four years, he was honorably discharged with the rank of master sergeant. He married Deta Dozier, and they had six children: Carolyn, LaVerne, Otha Leon, Louietta, Carmen, and Norma.

Brandon had a distinguished career in higher education, serving as chief accounting officer of Rust College, LeMoyne College, and Tuskegee Institute. Under the auspices of the U.S. Agency for International Development, he spent two years in Liberia, where he updated the government's business and financial policies. In appreciation of his work, the Liberians appointed him an Honorary Paramount Chief. On his return to the United States, he founded and served as senior partner in Brandon, Smith and Jones, Certified Public Accountants. He began his practice in a small frame house on Mississippi Boulevard with three employees and two clients. Later, the firm moved to the Exchange Building in downtown Memphis with 243 clients in twenty-three states; offices in three states; associated facilities in Nigeria; and a joint venture with the largest CPA firm in the world. Brandon mentored numerous young people and tutored many of the CPAs in the Memphis Chapter of the National Association of Black Accountants. He was president of the National Business League-Memphis Chapter, a founder of the Memphis Business Resource Center, and a member of the advisory committee for Community Development Block Grants. He served on the Riverfront Harbor Commission, Revenue Finance Corporation, Center City Commission, and Governor's Advisory Board for Economic Development. He was active in the American Institute of Certified Public Accountants and the Tennessee Society of Certified Public Accountants, and he was a licensed Chartered Accountant in the United Kingdom of Africa. He died in Memphis on July 27, 1980.

Brawner, Clara Arena (1929–1991), physician. One of Memphis's pioneering African American women physicians, she was the daughter of Rena Darden Brawner, a registered nurse, and Jeff Brawner, a medical doctor who was instrumental in getting Blacks admitted to John Gaston Hospital. She was born in Georgia but moved to Memphis at an early age. Determined to excel even as a little girl, she accompanied her father on his house calls. Brawner graduated from Manassas High School and Spelman College, before entering Meharry Medical College, from which she received a degree twenty-eight years after her father had graduated from that institution. A specialist in family medicine, she was the only Black woman physician in Memphis when she began practicing with her father in 1955. Later, she continued study at such universities as Vanderbilt, Kentucky, Tennessee, and Southern California. When Memphis hospitals were desegregated, she joined the staffs of Baptist Memorial and St. Joseph Hospitals.

Throughout her life, Clara Brawner was active in her profession. In 1963, she became the first woman president of the Volunteer State Medical Association during its 63rd convention at Meharry. She also served as national chair of the Family Practice Section of the National Medical Association, diplomat of the American Board of Family Practice, Fellow of the American Academy of Family Physicians, and president for an unprecedented fifteen years of the Bluff City Medical Society. She was a member of the Mid-South Medical Center Council, Mayor's Medical Society, and Tennessee Medicaid Reimbursement Commission; and she was on the boards of the Mid-South Medical Center, Meharry Medical College, and chair of the board of governors of the Memphis Health Center. In recognition of her outstanding service to the community, she received many awards, including the Dr. Martin Luther King Service Award, Mayor's Staff Aide-de-Camp from the City of Memphis, Physician's Achievement Award, and Family Practice Service Award. She also received awards from Memphians Inc., the National Medical Association, Memphis Health Center, and North Memphis Civic Club.

A very spiritual person, Dr. Brawner was active in Gospel Temple Baptist Church, where she served as a Sunday School and Bible class teacher, member of the Trustee Board, chair of the Ministerial Council, and superintendent of Junior Ushers. In 1979, Gospel Temple dedicated its September Festival of Hymns to Clara Brawner and her sister, soprano Alpha Brawner Floyd. In 1989, the physician received a call to the ministry, entered Memphis Theological Seminary, studied under Rev. W. A. Suggs of Friendship Baptist Church, and preached her first sermon at Gospel Temple on March 4, 1990. A year and a half later, on October 4, 1991, the prominent physician died at age sixty-two. She is survived by a daughter, Jewell Campbell.

Brewer, Harper (1937–1990), state representative, school administrator, real estate broker. A member of the Tennessee House of Representatives from 1972 to 1986, Brewer became the first Black to serve as Speaker pro tempore. The son of Daisy and Harper Brewer, he was born in Memphis on December 22, 1937. After graduating from Melrose High School, he attended Fisk University, from which he received a B.A. degree in chemistry in 1958, and an M.A. degree in science education in 1964. Several years later, he acquired a law degree from the UMCA Night Law School in Nashville. He taught at Lester High School and was an instructor at Southwestern at Memphis in the High School Scholars Program, before becoming a resource specialist for the Memphis City Schools. During his fourteen-year tenure as a representative from District 98 in North Memphis, he served as assistant majority leader and whip of the Democratic Caucus, and he also organized the first Legislative Retreat of the Tennessee Black Caucus of State Legislators in 1974. He was noted for his contemplative manner and knowledge of the legislative system. With the support of Speaker Ned McWherter, he was elected House Speaker pro tempore of the Tennessee General Assembly, a position that he held from 1978 to 1984. An even-tempered and low-key leader who worked well with others, he supported bills to help the elderly, fund the Civil Rights Museum, support Brooks Museum of Art, and increase teachers' salaries. After his defeat by Ulysses Jones, Jr., in 1986, he founded Brewer's Delivery Service and taught mathematics and science at Snowden School. A member of the National Association of Real

Estate Brokers, he also worked as a real estate broker at Comfort Realty Company.

Active in civic affairs, he was a member of Goals for Memphis, the Klondyke Civic Club, National Business League, and Vollentine-Evergreen Community Association. A Shriner and 32nd Degree Mason, he also served on the NAACP Freedom Fund Dinner Committee and was a board member of the Memphis Jobs Conference. In 1980, he was appointed to the National Highway Safety Advisory Committee by former President Jimmy Carter. He and his wife, Peggy Cox Brewer, were the parents of two daughters, Kimberly Michelle and Kaia Mignon. On April 11, 1990, Harper Brewer died at age fifty-two.

Brewster, William Herbert (1897–1987), minister, educator, religious leader, composer. A Baptist minister who was called "a giant among gospel composers," he gained national acclaim as a poet, religious dramatist, and theologian. Born at the turn of the century in a one-room shanty on a plantation near Somerville, Tennessee, he was the grandson of slaves and the son of sharecroppers—William Herbert Brewster and his wife. Since his birth was not recorded, he chose 1897, a time of gnat infestation, as the year of his birth because, like the gnat, he had no pretensions to greatness. According to his family, he was a strange child who walked early, had a photographic memory, and recalled events that had happened when he was a baby. Like many plantation children, he attended school only a few months a year, but he excelled at Jones High School and graduated from Howe Institute in Memphis. In 1922, he graduated from Roger Williams College, but he credits his achievements to the inspiration of teachers and family members such as his grandmother, a devout Christian with a gift for singing and praying, who nurtured his spiritual and creative gifts.

On September 31, 1914, when he was only seventeen years old, Reverend Brewster preached his first sermon, "Witnesses for Christ," at Smith Chapel Baptist Church. While leading a church outside of Somerville, he met Julianna Nelson, whom he married on November 28, 1918, and they had a daughter, Juanita. Between 1918 and 1930, he pastored churches in Forrest City, Arkansas; and in Somerville, Mason, and Russell Grove, Tennessee. He accepted the pastorate of Pilgrim Baptist Church in 1925 and of the East Trigg Baptist Church in 1930, dividing his time between the two Memphis churches for over fifty years. Noted for his profound messages and stirring oratory, he was a college-educated minister, fluent in Greek and Hebrew and inspired by the works of Plato, Aquinas, Buber, and Tillich. He served as dean of the Baptist Education Center in Chicago, dean of religious education of three organizations, and founder of the Brewster Theological Seminary, which educated many Memphis ministers and had branches in twenty-five cities.

One of the most influential gospel songwriters of the twentieth century, Herbert Brewster composed at least 200 gospel songs, including, "Lord I Tried," "Move Upstairs," "Pay Day Someday," and "Move on Up a Little Higher," which was recorded by Mahalia Jackson and became one of the first gospel recordings by an African American to sell over a million copies. During the 1940s and 1950s, he hosted a gospel radio show on WDIA. His "sermons in song," such as "I'm Leaning and Depending on the Lord," composed in 1939, are based on Bible stories. An eloquent poet, storyteller, and scholar with an extraordinary knowledge of the Bible, Dr. Brewster pioneered in a dramatic genre that is unique to Black Americans: pageants inspired by allegory and dramatized into choreographed scenes. His religious dramas include *Old Ship of Zion*, *The Birth of Christ*, *Children of Freedom*, *Sowing the Wind*, and *Reaping the Whirlwind*. His most famous pageant, *From the Auction Block*, was composed in 1941 and staged in 1958 with a chorus of one thousand and a cast of hundreds as part of a massive campaign to register Black voters. As a minister and composer, he influenced the careers of B. B. King, Elvis Presley, and Clara Ward and the Ward Singers, among others. Although he was honored by many organizations, including the Smithsonian Institution, Dr. Brewster was an humble man who wanted to be known merely as "God's sharecropper." He said, "I've never been able to feel the deep-down desire for lots of credits and honors." He was dynamic and vigorous almost until the day of his death at age ninety.

Bridges, Josephine Valeria Johnson "Jo" (1932–), educator, event planner, entrepreneur. One of the city's most creative and enterprising women, she used her talent and professional training to carve out careers in business and public relations. The daughter of Zenobia and Cleopas Johnson, she was born on March 7, 1932, in North Memphis, where she attended Manassas Elementary and High School. There, she was a drum majorette and founder of the Double Ten Society, a girls' club that still exists. She attended Tennessee State University, where she met her future husband, and was a health and physical education graduate of Mississippi Industrial College in Holly Springs. For thirteen years, Bridges taught in the Memphis Public Schools, primarily at Porter Junior High School, and then she worked at the government-funded Memphis Community Learning Lab. After opening her own public relations firm, Positive Public Relations, she joined Stax Records, Incorporated, where she became vice president of "We Produce Records." While at Stax, she and Deanie Parker handled all of the press parties for musicians such as David Porter and the Staple Singers, and, with a budget of $90,000, she planned Isaac Hayes's Academy Award party at the Rivermont and also organized trips to Los Angeles by Stax artists for benefit concerts in Watts.

"Josie knows everybody in the country, especially in the music and entertainment industry," said Reverend Billy Kyles. "That connection started with Stax, and she has used those contacts quite effectively." Her political connections were effective in raising money for Memphis mayoral candidates A. W. Willis and Otis Higgs, as well as for the presidential campaign of her friend Jesse Jackson, and, in 1991, she worked with Reverend Alvin Jackson as co-chair of the inaugural committee of W. W. Herenton, Memphis's first elected Black mayor. Her experience in event planning led to several other opportunities: she was the first African American to plan the inaugural dinner for a Wonder Series exhibition (the Napoleon exhibition); she worked with the NAACP in planning its annual banquet; and she organized dinners and fashion shows for Women in the NAACP. For fifteen years, the businesswoman operated Jo Bridges Boutique in Whitehaven, where women could buy designer fashions at reasonable prices. In 1953, she and Sarah Chandler founded the J.U.G.S. (Justice, Unity, Generosity, and Service), a service organization with fourteen chapters nation-wide, which raises money for charities such as the Goodwill Homes for Children. She is also active in Operation PUSH, the Rainbow Coalition, NAACP, Delta Sigma Theta Sorority, and the Coalition of 100 Black Women.

Josephine and Anderson Bridges, a junior high school principal who died in 1990, had four daughters: Veta, Kimberly, Keath, and Kyle.

Broughton, Virginia E. Walker (1856–1934), educator, missionary, journalist. Believed to be the first African American woman in the South to earn a college degree, she served as a principal, became a Baptist missionary, edited a newspaper, and wrote two books. Virginia E. Walker was born free in Virginia, grew up in Nashville, Tennessee, and graduated from Fisk University in 1875 at age nineteen. After her marriage to Memphian Julius A. Broughton, a postal clerk, she worked for twelve years in the Memphis public schools, first as a teacher and later as assistant principal of Kortrecht School. In 1886, when she was demoted to a teaching position following an illness, she resigned from the school system and became a Baptist evangelical missionary, traveling extensively, raising money for the church, and founding a training school for girls. Her gender consciousness came from her feminist interpretation of the Bible. Believing that Black women should have a more significant role in the church, she gave public lectures, made house calls, and organized Bible bands—groups of women who met weekly to study the Bible, do charitable work, and share their religious experiences.

Broughton became one of the foremost women in the Baptist Church, traveling throughout Tennessee to help organize a state-wide association of Black Baptist women. Active in the Woman's Christian Temperance Union, she was a strong advocate of higher education and religious training for women. She served as chair of the Educational Committee of the Negro Department of the Tennessee Centennial Exposition in 1897 and was secretary of the Women's Auxiliary to the National Baptist Convention. In his *History of the Negro Baptists of Tennessee*, T. O. Fuller wrote that she "was an important factor in all religious work in Tennessee...She knew the Scriptures and was an effective speaker yet she never claimed the pulpit as a place for her services..." She was the publisher and editor of *Woman's Messenger*, a Memphis newspaper for Black women, and she served as chair of the Educational Committee in the Negro Department of the Tennessee Centennial. Her two books include *Women's Work, as Gleaned from the Women of the Bible* (1904), which examines biblical precedents for gender equality, and *Twenty Years' Experience of a Missionary* (1907), which describes her religious work in Tennessee.

Brown, Donald (1954–), jazz pianist, composer, arranger, band leader, and educator. An accomplished musician and prolific composer, Brown has been called one of the most original and versatile piano players of his generation. He was born on March 28, 1954, in Hernando, Mississippi, but moved with his family to Memphis when he was two years old. Although his five sisters played the piano, Brown studied the trumpet, drums, and baritone horn. He began his career as a drummer and received a scholarship to Memphis State University in 1972 as a trumpet player, but he soon began studying piano. Another music student, James Williams, encouraged him to concentrate on jazz, and he became one of the Memphis Three—Donald Brown, James Williams, and Mulgrew Miller—a trio of outstanding keyboardists who studied at Memphis State in the 1970s. For five years, he played R&B (which is still recognizable in his playing) in Memphis clubs, before replacing Williams with Art Blakey's Jazz Messengers, from 1981 to 1982. After developing rheumatoid arthritis in his hands, he taught at Berklee from 1983 to 1985, and, since 1988, has been on the music faculty of the University of Tennessee, where he teaches jazz piano, improvisation, and jazz history. He recently commented: "I'm at the point in my career where I am starting to get a lot of recognition and praise for my compositions, but I definitely am a teacher more than anything. I know that is where I am spending more of my time and getting the most satisfaction."

Donald Brown has recorded over a dozen albums for Sunnyside, Muse, and Space Time Records, including *Cause And Effect* (1991); *Piano Short Stories* (1996), a solo album that has received rave reviews; *Wurd on the Skreet*, an urban album of the late 1990s; *French Kiss* (2000), called "the most funky he has ever recorded"; and *Enchanté* (2002), a tribute to France. The *New York Times* named his

Autumn in New York (Space Time, 2002) one of the best recordings outside of the mainstream music industry. Brown's original compositions have been recorded by many internationally known jazz artists, such as Javon Jackson, RS Monk, and Charlie Sepulveda; and two of his compositions—"Insane Asylum," recorded by Wynton Marsalis, and "Theme for Malcolm," recorded by Donald Byrd—were nominated for Grammy awards. According to one critic: "In his highly inspired solos one can discover the entire history of jazz from Stride to New Thing, from Bud Powell to Herbie Hancock, through Thelonious Monk and Ahmad Jamal."

Brown, George Henry, Jr. (1939–), attorney, judge, entrepreneur. The first African American president of the Memphis Board of Education and the first Black to sit on the state's highest court, he has earned a reputation as a conscientious, thoughtful, and no-nonsense member of the judiciary. The son of George H. Brown, an employee of the Illinois Central Railroad, and Sara Pinkston Brown, an elementary school teacher, he was born in Memphis on July 16, 1939. After attending LaRose Elementary School and Booker T. Washington High School, he entered Florida A&M University on a music scholarship, graduating in 1960 with a B.S. in political science and a commission in the ROTC. He was assigned to duty with the Army Signal Corps and, after three years of service, received an honorable discharge. In the years that followed, he taught at Carver High School, attained a law degree from Howard University, worked for the Housing and Home Finance Agency and the Department of Housing and Urban Development in Washington, and joined the law offices of Attorney A. A. Latting. He resigned a position as acting deputy director of the Equal Employment Opportunity Commission (EEOC) in Memphis to serve as director of the Memphis and

Shelby County Legal Services Association between 1970 and 1973. Eventually, he and Walter Evans organized the firm of Brown & Evans.

In 1980, Governor Lamar Alexander appointed Brown to the Tennessee Supreme Court, making him the first Black to sit on the state's highest court. Although he lost in the November election, he was appointed, in 1983, to fill an unexpired term in Division VI of the 30th Circuit Court Division and, in 1984, he won election to that court. After being elected to two eight-year terms as a Circuit Court Judge, he left the bench on February 18, 2005, explaining, "I'm not retiring. I'm transforming." Judge Brown has provided outstanding service to his profession, as well as to the community, particularly in the fields of education and the arts. After the successful boycott of the city schools in 1969, he and Hollis F. Price were named advisory members of the Memphis Board of Education. In 1971, Brown was elected to the board from his district, serving as vice chairman in 1973 and 1978, and becoming its first Black chairman on January 1, 1974. While on the board, he was elected chairman of the Council of Urban Boards of Education, a major branch of the National School Boards Association.

In 1979, he became the second Black attorney to receive the prestigious San A. Myar, Jr., Memorial Award from the Memphis State University Law school for outstanding service to the legal profession. A former trustee of Lane College and a board member of the Memphis Academy of Arts, he served on the executive council of the Memphis NAACP and executive committee of the National Legal Aid and Defense Association. He was coordinator of the Governor's Job Conference, chairman of the board of Jobs for Tennessee Graduates, and a board member of the Memphis in May Festival. In November 2000, he and Charles Barnes bought Memphis Chemical & Janitorial Supply Company. Under Brown's leadership as CEO, the company has grown five-fold in five years to become one of the more successful minority-owned businesses in Memphis.

George Brown married Margaret Solomon, who was a teacher and supervisor at the MLGW, and they were the parents of two children, Laurita and George Henry "Hank" Brown III. After Margaret's death, he married Lillian Fisher Hammond, a retired higher education administrator who also was widowed, on March 2, 2002. Believing that "life is to be lived and enjoyed and the time savored," he travels often and is a piano-playing jazz aficionado. Brown is perhaps best known to movie fans for his cameo role as a basketball-playing judge in the Tom Cruise film *The Firm*, which was filmed in Memphis in 1992–1993.

Brown, Joe (1947–), attorney, judge, television personality. Known for his unconventional sentencing as a Shelby County Criminal Court judge, he gained national prominence as star of the television show, *Judge Joe Brown*. The only son of hardworking teachers, he was born on July 5, 1947, in Washington, D.C., but grew up in a tough neighborhood in South Central Los Angeles. A street-savvy kid who valued education, he graduated from Dorsey High School at the top of his class and paid his way to UCLA by digging ditches and loading trucks. At UCLA, he obtained a bachelor's degree in political science and a law degree in 1973, while working as a substitute teacher. In 1974, he moved to Memphis to assume a position at Legal Services and then at the Equal Employment Opportunity Commission. Memphis's first Black prosecutor, Attorney Brown was later named director of the city's Public Defender's Office. He went into private practice in 1978, but gave up his practice after being elected judge of Division 9 of the State Criminal Courts for Shelby County in 1990. As a judge, he was noted for his alternative sentencing; for example, he permitted victims to take items from burglars' homes and he required forgers to copy "I will not write bad paper" 100,000 times.

Charismatic and dynamic, Brown gained national attention in 1998, when he presided over the appeal of James Earl Ray, convicted assassin of Martin Luther King, Jr., but he was removed from the bench by the Criminal Court of Appeals after being charged with bias in the high-profile case. The publicity led to an appearance on *Nightline*, where he impressed the producer of *Judge Judy*, who offered him a television show, commenting that Brown's "from-the-streets upbringing gives him a tough-love approach to justice that will endear him to viewers nationwide." The *Judge Joe Brown* show, which aired nationwide in September 1998, has become one of the most highly rated courtroom reality shows. For a year and a half, Brown commuted between Los Angeles and Memphis, where he continued to serve as judge, but he retired from the judgeship in April 2000. He still lives in Memphis, where he often spends weekends working with at-risk adolescents, sharing his experiences and imparting his tough-love philosophy. A former scoutmaster, he was inducted into Phi Alpha Delta, a noted law fraternity, in 1999, and, a year later, he was given the Advocate for Justice Award by The Olender Foundation at the Kennedy Center in recognition of his work with inner-city youth. The father of two young sons from his first marriage to Wanda Jones, he married Deborah Herron on December 29, 2001.

Brown, Lawyer Edward (1871–1947), educator. One of Memphis's most respected early educators, L. E. Brown served as principal of Porter School during a career of fifty-two years in the city's public schools. He was born in Whitehaven, Mississippi, where his parents were farmers, and he came to Memphis at age sixteen to attend LeMoyne Normal Institute at the urging of his life-long friend, W. S. Ellington of Nashville. He received a B.A. degree from Fisk University and spent two years at Meharry Medical College, but he gave up the study of medicine to care for his ailing mother. He began teaching at Kortretch High School, where he developed an extraordinary group of children. Later, he became assistant principal of Kortrecht and principal of LaRose Elementary School. Regarded as one of the finest principals in the city, he was responsible in large measure for the construction, in 1920, of Porter School, the first modern school for African American children built in Memphis. When Universal Life Insurance Company was founded in 1923, he was one of the first investors.

For thirty-six years, he was married to Sarah Brown for whom a YWCA branch—located on the site of the Browns' home at 1044 Mississippi Boulevard—was named. According to his wife, "he was a cultured, high-class, Christian gentleman at home and in life." In 1950, the L. E. Brown Park and Playground on Orleans Street behind Porter School was named for the former principal, and St. Patrick Catholic Church established the L. E. Brown Neighborhood Association to help inner-city residents. Called a "jolly good fellow," he liked to play croquet and was a member of the Republican Party, Memphis Grand Lodge, Knights of Pythias, Order of the Eastern Star, and Delta Boulé of Sigma Psi Phi Fraternity. He and Mrs. Brown were long-time members of Second Congregational Church, where he served as chairman of the Trustee Board. Professor L. E. Brown retired in 1946, and a year later, on January 22, 1947, he died of a heart attack at his home.

Bryce, Harry A. (1951–), choreographer, theater director, arts educator. Bryce became a significant cultural figure in Memphis with the founding of the Harry Bryce Dance Theatre and the Memphis Black Repertory Theatre Company. A native of Richmond, Virginia, he was born on August 16, 1951, and came to Memphis as a protégé of poet Margaret

Danner, who was teaching at LeMoyne-Owen College. He has studied dance under such noted choreographers as Alvin Ailey, Katherine Dunham, Martha Graham, Michael Olatunji, Bella Lewitzsky, and Arthur Mitchell. Between 1968 and 1983, he choreographed fourteen major musicals, including *The Wiz, Emperor Jones, West Side Story, El Grande de Coca Cola,* and *Don't Bother Me, I Can't Cope.* In the 1980s, he was founding artistic staff member for Vinnette Carroll Repertory Theatre in Ft. Lauderdale, Florida, and in 1989, he received the Carbonell Award nomination for Choreography. Since 1974, he has also choreographed fourteen major dance productions, including *The Path, Missa Luba, Still I Rise, Tubular Bells, Tryin' Times,* and *The Sound of Thunder Didn't It Rain.* Bryce has led professional dance companies in Richmond and Atlanta, where his original concert ballet *Beyond the Canebrake: Moments in the Life of Harriet Tubman* received critical acclaim at the National Black Arts Festival. He has performed in schools, colleges, and universities, appearing on television programs such as the Dinah Shore and Merv Griffin Shows, and performing at Carnegie Hall in a one-man program of dance and poetry. He has received the Mid-South Talent Award, Isaac Hayes Talent Award, and Blues City Cultural Center's "Bess Award."

In the 1980s, he returned to Richmond, where he served as arts consultant for the Amber Gallery, and assistant coordinator of the 1984 June Jubilee Fine Arts Festival. While living in Atlanta and teaching at Spelman College, he came to Memphis to guest direct plays such as *Five Guys Named Moe.* He moved back to the city in 1997 to found and direct the Memphis Black Repertory Theatre Company, which began under the auspices of Playhouse on the Square. As artistic director of the company, he produced twenty-one plays, including *Having Our Say, Blues for an Alabama Sky, Shakin' the Mess Outta Misery, The Old Settler, Dreamgirls, Ain't Misbehavin,' Spunk,* and *Master Harold and the Boys.* In 2000, he received the Carter G. Woodson Award of Merit for Lifetime Achievement in the Performing Arts. By the beginning of the third season (1999–2000), the company had an operating budget of $169,000, but it closed in the fall of 2002 because of a budget deficit and inadequate fund raising, as well as a dispute between Bryce and the board of directors. Harry Bryce presently lives in Daytona Beach, Florida, where he has directed such works as *Five Guys Named Moe* and *Once On This Island* for the Seaside Music Theater.

Buckley, Harriet Ann (1948–) artist. One of the city's most versatile artists, she has had individual and group shows throughout the region. She was born in Memphis on July 28, 1948, to John Ella Griffin Buckley, a teacher, and Urias Buckley, an employee of the Veterans Administration Hospital. Young Harriet began creating art in kindergarten, and her mother, who was her first grade teacher, encouraged her to make pictures out of construction paper. At Lester Elementary and High School, she designed bulletin boards and excelled in Percy Washington's art classes. An oboe player, she won a band scholarship to Arkansas AM&N College but transferred, after a year, to the Memphis Academy of Art, from which she was graduated in 1971, with a concentration in painting. Buckley works in various media, including watercolor, block printing, sculpture, wood carving, leather craft, papier-maché, storytelling, quilts, and black and white photography. Her paintings were exhibited in group shows at the Memphis Brooks Museum of Art in 1970, University of Georgia in 1994, and Joysmith Gallery in 2001; and her fabrics and quilts were featured in shows at Scarett College and the University of Memphis Gallery. In 1993, she had a one-woman exhibition at LeMoyne-Owen College, a retrospective at Sidewalk University Gallery in 1998, and a one-woman show in Union City, Tennessee, in 2006. One of her paintings was selected for the cover of Patricia Bell-Scott's *Flat-Footed Truths: Telling Black Women's Lives*, published in 1998. Harriet Buckley completed a piece of public art for the Memphis Area Transit Authority in

2004; created out of concrete and mosaic blocks, the work, entitled "We Ride On," is located at Madison and Pauline.

Bunton, Henry C. (1903–1999), clergyman. The long-time pastor of Memphis's Mount Olive Cathedral C.M.E. Church, he was a distinguished bishop of the Christian Methodist Episcopal Church. The sixth of eleven children, he was born to sharecropping parents in Coker, Arkansas, on October 19, 1903. After graduating from a one-teacher elementary school, located in a church in rural Tuscaloosa County, he entered Miles High School and then completed two years at Miles College. He received a bachelor's degree from Florida A&M College and later attended the Perkins School of Theology on the campus of Southern Methodist University in Dallas, Texas; Garrett Seminary; and the Iliff School of Theology in Denver, Colorado, from which he received the Alumni Award of the Year for Parish Ministry in 1988. In 1923, he married Estelle McKinney, and they were the parents of three children: Mattye Lou, Marjorie, and Henry C., Jr. After the death of his wife, he married Alfreda Gibbs Carpenter, with whom he had a fourth child, Joseph.

Henry C. Bunton began his ministry in 1925, was ordained an elder of the C.M.E. Church in 1930, and pastored churches in Alabama, Arkansas, Texas, Colorado, and Tennessee. He was a chaplain in Europe during world War II, earning three battle stars and achieving the rank of major. He served as national director of youth work for the C.M.E. Church office in Chicago and as president of the Interdenominational Ministers' Alliance, an organization of C.M.E. pastors. He was elected the 33rd bishop of the C.M.E. Church in 1962, serving the Seventh Episcopal District, which included churches in New England, North and South Carolina. In May 1962, following his election to the episcopacy, a testimonial banquet in his honor was held at Universal Life Insurance Company. Before his retirement in 1978, he organized more than thirty churches and initiated the C.M.E. Conference in Haiti. Active in civic and educational affairs, he served on the boards of the Southern Christian Leadership Conference in Atlanta and of Miles College in Birmingham, which established The Bishop Henry C. Bunton Scholarship in his honor. Bishop Bunton wrote an autobiography, *A Dreamer of Dreams*, which was published by the C.M.E. Publishing House, and he donated the Henry C. Bunton Papers, 1871–1989, to the Schomburg Center for Research in Black Culture in New York. He died in October 1999.

Byas, Andrew D. (1871–?), physician, businessman. One of Memphis's most prominent doctors in the early part of the twentieth century, he owned property in Shelby County and was part owner of a pharmacy. The son of James and Laura C. Byas, former slaves who acquired a 500-acre farm near Kosciusko, Mississippi, he was born on May 9, 1871. His parents sent their nine children to Rust College, M. I. College, Central Mississippi College, LeMoyne Normal Institute, and Meharry Medical College. Four of the sons became physicians, a daughter became a truant officer with the Memphis City Schools, while the others became teachers and homemakers. The second of the Byas offspring, Andrew attended local schools and, in 1888, entered Rust University, but it took him seven years to complete college because he taught school to pay his expenses. From 1890 until 1899, he taught in Attala County, Mississippi, as well as in the Hardeman and Shelby County schools in Tennessee. Although, as a boy, he had never seen a Black physician, he was inspired to enter the medical profession by watching the old neighborhood doctor, who carried a leather saddlebag and rode a decrepit horse. So, in the fall of 1895, he headed to Nashville, Tennessee, to enroll at Meharry Medical College, and by teaching during summer vacations, he was able to graduate with honors in 1899.

Right after graduation, Dr. Byas opened his first office near Benjestown, Tennessee, where he built up the largest medical practice in that part of the county. In 1901, he married Lula McPherson of Shelby County, an alumna of and teacher at LeMoyne Normal Institute. Four years later, the Byases moved to Memphis, where he became one of the leading physicians in the city. Within twelve years, he had acquired two or three farms in Shelby County and several pieces of real estate in Memphis; he was also president and co-owner of the North Memphis Drug Company. At a cost of $7,000—a considerable amount for the period—he built an eight-room, two-story house of brick and slate, which G. P. Hamilton called "one of the most substantial residences in the city of Memphis, Tenn." During that period, four of his brothers graduated from LeMoyne and went on to Meharry Medical College, and his brother, Dr. John V. Byas, opened a practice in Millington, Tennessee before he, too, moved to Memphis.

Calloway, DeVerne Lee (1916–1993), civic leader, state representative. The first Black woman elected to the General Assembly of the State of Missouri, she advocated for welfare reform, women's rights, and public education. The daughter of Sadie White-Lee and Charles Howard Lee, she was born in Memphis on June 17, 1916. She graduated with honors from Booker T. Washington High School and then entered LeMoyne College, from which she received a B.A. degree. She pursued graduate studies at Atlanta and Northwestern Universities, Pendle-Hill in Pennsylvania, and the University of Missouri at

St. Louis. In the 1940s, she worked for the United Service Organizations (U.S.O.), as well as with the American Red Cross in India, where she protested the Red Cross policy of segregated facilities for U.S. servicemen. On her return to Chicago, she met journalist Earnest Calloway and they married in 1947; three years later, the Calloways moved to St. Louis, where they published a newspaper, *The New Citizen*. Mrs. Calloway also became active in the YWCA, Americans for Democratic Action, Delta Sigma Theta Sorority, People's Art Center, and National Council of Negro Women. Committed to the struggle for civil rights, she was a life member of the NAACP, a founder of the Congress of Racial Equality (CORE), and a frequent demonstrator and protester for racial justice.

DeVerne Lee Calloway's activism and community service eventually led her into politics. In 1962, she was elected state representative from District 13 (the St. Louis area) and became the first African American woman to serve in the Missouri General Assembly. During her two decades in office, she advocated social welfare reform, support of urban areas, and state aid for public education, and passed legislation that changed Harris-Stowe Teachers College into a state college. A crusader for women's rights and, especially, for reproductive rights, she co-sponsored an unsuccessful bill to reform Missouri's abortion law, as well as a bill to provide equal pay for equal work. She also spearheaded legislation for prison reform after chairing a committee that uncovered the inhumane conditions at the Missouri State Penitentiary, and her efforts resulted in a lawsuit that led to the construction of a medium-security prison at Pacific, Missouri. Her work gained national attention: President John F. Kennedy invited her to the White House for a conference to consider women's roles in solving civil rights problems, and President Jimmy Carter appointed her to the U.S. Circuit Judge Nominating Panel for the 8th Circuit Court. She was also listed in *Ebony* magazine's "Success Library—1000 Successful Blacks."

Representative Calloway retired in 1982, after serving nine terms in the Missouri House of Representatives. The governor then appointed her to the Board of Regents of Harris-Stowe State College.

After her retirement as chair in 1989, the college awarded her an honorary degree and the Golden Palm Laureate. Since her death in 1993, the Women Legislators of Missouri have presented the "DeVerne Lee Calloway Award" annually to "a Missouri woman... who has made major contributions to equality and justice."

Campbell, Lucie Eddie (1885–1963), teacher, composer, music director. One of the foremost composers of gospel music in the United States, she was also one of Memphis's most outstanding public school teachers. The youngest of nine children, Campbell was born on April 3, 1885, in Duck Hill (Carroll County), Mississippi to Isabella Wilkerson Campbell, a cook, and Burrell Campbell, a railroad worker. When her father died in a train accident soon after her birth, her mother moved the family, in 1889, to Memphis, where her children attended the public schools. Lucie graduated, in 1899, from Kortrecht High School as class valedictorian, and she began teaching at Carnes Avenue Grammar School. In 1911, she returned to her alma mater (later, Booker T. Washington High School), where she taught English and American history for forty-two years. During those years, she also acquired a B.A. degree from Rust College and an M.A. degree from Tennessee A&I State College. A gifted teacher, she achieved national acclaim for her service to the profession: she was president of the Tennessee Negro Teachers Association from 1941 to 1946; she was named to the National Policy Planning Commission of the National Education Association in 1946; and she was elected vice president of the American Teachers Association. In 1934, President Franklin D. Roosevelt invited her to attend a conference on Negro Child Welfare in Washington, D.C. During her five-year tenure as president of the TNTA, she struggled with officials to equalize the salaries and increase the benefits of Afro-American teachers. A decade before Rosa Parks refused to move to the back of the bus, Miss Campbell defied the Jim Crow laws by refusing to give up her seat in the "White section" of the streetcar.

When she was only nineteen, Lucie Campbell organized the Music Club, which increased from a small group of Beale Street musicians to a thousand-voice choir that performed at the National Baptist Convention. She was one of the founders of the National Sunday and Baptist Training Union Congress of the National Baptist Convention, U.S.A., and, when it held its organizational meeting in Memphis in 1915, she was elected director of music. As director, she invited several singers, including Marian Anderson, Thomas A. Dorsey, and Mahalia Jackson, to perform at Baptist conventions. "Miss Lucie" was a devout Christian and an outstanding music teacher and composer, who published her first gospel song, "Something Within," in 1919. Among her more than 100 compositions are "Touch Me, Lord Jesus," "Hold My Hand, Precious Lord," "Something Within," and "He Understands, He'll Say Well Done." During the 1940s and '50s, she gave recitals, directed choirs, and taught music to future singers such as J. Robert Bradley, a baritone with the Hall-Johnson Choir; Dorothy Clark, a member of the Wings Over Jordan Choir; and Georgia Woodruff, a church organist, actress, and singer.

On January 14, 1960, she married Reverend C. R. Williams, her long-time companion, and dedicated her song, "They That Wait Upon the Lord," to him. While preparing to attend the banquet and celebration of "Lucie E. Campbell Appreciation Day," sponsored by the National Baptist Convention on June 20, 1962, she had to be rushed to the hospital. She died in Nashville on January 3, 1963, and her funeral was held at Memphis's Mount Nebo Baptist Church, with burial at Mount Carmel Cemetery.

Cannon, Gus (1883–1979), banjo player. Although fame eluded him for most of his life, this banjo-playing, self-taught composer of "Walk Right In" and "Come on Down to My House" had a major influence on future generations of blues and rock and roll musicians. He was born on September 12, 1883, on Henderson Newell's plantation in Red Banks, Mississippi, the youngest of the ten sons of Ellen and John Cannon, a former slave. As a boy, he worked in the cotton fields but, at twelve, he traveled to Clarksdale, where W. C. Handy's band was playing. He made his first banjo from a guitar neck and a bread pan and, at fifteen, acquired a guitar, which his brother had won in a crap game. Bud Jackson taught the boy to finger-pick the strings so that, by nineteen, he was making $2.50 playing at Saturday night balls. Although he worked on a railroad in Mississippi and a plantation in Tennessee, music was his passion. As "Banjo Joe," he joined the medicine show circuit and, by 1914, was playing in Memphis clubs such as The Monarch, The Red Light, and The Hole in the Wall. In 1916, he finally moved from Clarksdale to Memphis, where jug bands—playing music that was a mixture of jazz and country/pop, with its roots in ragtime—were all the rage. They were called jug bands because a band member would blow on the top of a jug to make a blues style of music with a country sound. Cannon, who was proficient on the banjo, guitar, and fiddle, went one step further: he played the banjo while blowing on a jug strapped around his neck.

In 1928, he organized Gus Cannon and the Jug Stompers, with Noah Lewis on harmonica and vocals, and three guitarists: Ashley Thompson, Hosea Woods, and Elijah Avery. Between January 30, 1928, and November 28, 1930, the Stompers recorded twenty-six sides for the Victor label, but the Depression effectively ended Cannon's career as a performer and recording artist. For the next twenty-five years, he resumed playing on the streets for money and was practically destitute when he made a comeback with the blues revival of the Sixties. He recorded with Folkways and Stax Records, played at folk festivals, hit the top of the charts with the album *Walk Right In*, appeared in videos like *The Blues* and *The Devils's Music: A History of the Blues*, and gained the acclaim of artists such as Bob Dylan, the Rooftop Singers, and the Grateful Dead. When Gus Cannon died in 1979, the Lovin' Spoonful and other musicians gave a benefit concert in Memphis to raise money for his tombstone.

Cantrell, Anderson (1939–1997), photographer, businessman. Widely recognized as one of Memphis's outstanding photojournalists, he captured the images of many local and national figures. Born in Louisville, Kentucky on April 24, 1939, he was the son of Anderson and Emma Orr Cantrell. In 1971, he moved to Memphis, where he worked as a painting contractor specializing in large contracts. "Cantrell," as he was known, served as the personal photographer for B. B. King, James Cleveland, and many other celebrities. A quiet, soft-spoken gentleman, he was noted for the way that he captured the dignity and strength of ordinary people, as well as of the rich and famous. He was honored for his work by former congressman Harold Ford and by both city and county mayors. A long-time member of Temple of Love C.M.E. Church, he published *The Pictorial History of the Christian Methodist Episcopal Church* and also created a pictorial collage entitled *Some African Americans*, which features the faces of over one thousand Black historical figures. In the course of his career, he served as staff photographer for LeMoyne-Owen College, the *Tri-State Defender* newspaper, *B. Visible* magazine, and he was a contributor to *Jet*, *Ebony*, and *Life* magazines. According to one account, "his work is recognized nationally for its gripping depiction of historical, religious, political, and cultural events." At one time, he was an associate of photojournalist Ernest Withers. He and his wife, Christine Cantrell, had four children: Martha Ann, Karen Denise, Winona Jean, and Anderson III. He died of cancer on April 4, 1997.

Carter, Marlin "Pee Wee" (1912–1993), athlete. Called one of Negro baseball's finest and most durable infielders, he played for the Memphis Red Sox and other Negro American League teams from 1922 to 1950. The youngest child of Albert and Missouri Carter, he was born in Hasslin, Texas on December 27, 1912. He was educated in the public schools of Hasslin and Houston and began playing sports in high school, with the encouragement of his coaches and his brother Talmadge. In the late 1920s, he began playing with the Texas Negro Leagues and eventually moved on to the Cincinnati Tigers and the Chicago American Giants. In 1932, he joined the Monroe Monarchs, and was short stop, second and third baseman for the San Antonio Black Indians. According to sports writer Bill Little, Carter was a "smooth fielding third baseman who swung one of the heaviest bats on the Red Sox team." The team, owned by the Martin brothers, had its greatest success in 1938, when it won the Negro American League first half with a 21–4 record. At various times, Carter also played for the Baltimore Elite Giants, Harrisburg Stars, and Rochester Royals. In 1942, during the golden era of Negro baseball, he appeared in the East-West All Star Game. Six years later, he married Mollie Jackson, and they had a daughter, Marilyn.

His baseball career was interrupted during World War II, when Coast Guardsman Carter served aboard a ship with Russian sailors in international waters. In 1983, he was inducted into the Baseball Hall of Fame in Ashland, Kentucky, and, in 1989, Carter, along with other Negro League players, was honored as a "Living Legend" by the Atlanta Braves and Southwestern Bell Company. The baseball pioneers, who did not have an opportunity to participate in organized baseball, were honored at a banquet in Atlanta, presented watches at the Atlanta Stadium Club, and introduced to the crowd at a doubleheader between the Braves and Dodgers. A member of Metropolitan Baptist Church, Carter died on December 21, 1993, and was buried in Elmwood Cemetery on what would have been his birthday. Former Negro League players Verdell Mathis, Sam Brown, Casey Jones, and Frank Pearson attended his funeral. Marilyn Carter Williams, a counselor in the Memphis City Schools, paid tribute to her father and his baseball friends: "They had a right to be bitter, hostile, volatile, but they didn't exercise it. They remained gentlemen."

Cassels, Thomas Frank (1847–1903), attorney, state legislator. Said to be the first African American lawyer to practice in Memphis, he was elected to the 42nd Tennessee General Assembly in 1881. Cassels was born around 1847 in Jackson, Ohio, to Thomas James Cassels (1814–1876) and his wife, who were free persons of color. After graduating from Oberlin College, he moved to Memphis, where he opened a law practice, and on February 1, 1868, he was admitted to the bar, becoming the first African American to achieve this distinction. He was also the first Black lawyer to present a case to the Supreme Court of West Tennessee. In 1978, he was appointed assistant attorney general of Memphis, and he was elected to represent Shelby County in the 42nd General Assembly. A Republican, he served one term in the legislature, from 1881 to 1883. He introduced House Bill No. 478 to compensate families of victims of mob violence, and he signed House Bill No. 289 to admit colored students to a school for the blind in Nashville and to a school for the deaf and dumb in Knoxville.

He also introduced a bill prohibiting "the unlawful carnal intercourse of white persons with negroes, mulatoes and persons of mixed blood descended from the negro race," the first attempt to pass a law designed to prevent the rape of Black women by White men, but the bill did not pass. Activist Ida B. Wells hired Cassels, in 1884, to represent her in a law suit against the Chesapeake & Ohio Railroad for discrimination on public transportation, but the railroad company persuaded him to drop the suit. Another attorney subsequently won the case, which was reversed by the State Supreme Court. He served as a Republican presidential elector in 1888. A member of the Second Congregational Church, Thomas F. Cassels was married twice (to Emma and Sallie) and had three children: Francis DeWitt, Hattie, and Ella. After a year-long battle with tuberculosis, he died in Memphis on April 2, 1903, at the family home at 861 Lauderdale. In 1991, the Ben F. Jones Chapter of the National Bar Association and its affiliate unveiled an historic marker honoring the attorney, whose first office was located at 350 Second Street (under the old numbering system). The marker is located on Second Street, between Union and Gayoso, near where Cassels established his office.

Champion, Charles (1930–), pharmacist, herbalist. An award-winning pharmacist with a national reputation as an herbalist, Dr. Champion, known as "The Herb Doctor," combines traditional folk medicines with modern pharmaceuticals. He was born in Memphis on August 20, 1930, the son of Minnie Lee Allen and James A. Champion, but he was raised by his grandparents in Greenfield, Tennessee. It was there among the old people that he learned about folk medicine. He explained: "I can remember my great-grandmother using remedies like mutton tallow, which was rubbed on the chest for colds, and a mixture of goose grease and honey for coughs." After completing high school, he entered Xavier University, where, in 1953, he took a course in pharmacognosy, which deals with drugs made from plants and animals. This course increased his interest in herbalism and folk medicine. After receiving the B.S. degree from Xavier University College of Pharmacy in 1955 and interning in New Orleans, he worked as a pharmacist in the Army between 1955 and 1957. When he left the service, he worked as a pharmacist at John Gaston Hospital for twelve years and then in a chain drugstore.

In 1981, he opened Champion's Pharmacy at 2220 South Third Street in a low-income neighborhood, and his business increased rapidly after he set out a small display of herbs. One of the few herbal druggists in Tennessee, he carries a collection of home remedies, including roots, leaves, tonics, teas, oils, and herbs, as well as a line of patent medicines—swamp root, horehound candy, Pluto water, snake oil, and Grandpa's pine tar soap—which were once sold by traveling medicine men. In January 1991, Champion's Pharmacy and Herb Store opened a 2,700-square-foot store at 2369 Elvis Presley Boulevard, where Dr. Champion set aside a room at the front for herbal products. His staff includes his business-manager wife, two pharmacy technician daughters, and a pharmacist daughter. He does a mail-order business in herbs, as well as "pre-selected companion selling," packaged medicines such as cough syrup, vitamin C, and Echinacea in a zip lock bag for cold sufferers. A holistic practitioner interested in the health, fitness, and well-being of his customers, Champion is much more than a pharmacist, particularly to older people in the neighborhood.

A life-long student of folk medicine, Champion has talked with old-time practitioners, and his research has led to several publications: *Common Herbs*; a book of recipes, which is a record of folk medicine; a booklet of grandma's home remedies; and a treatise on medicinal plants found in the Bible. He notes that, in the Bible, Balm of Gilead is recommended as a sedative, mandrake is considered a love plant, and salt peter is suggested as a sedative. In 1987, Champion was presented the "Pharmacist of the Year Award" at the annual meeting of the National Pharmaceutical Association, and he was featured in the fall 1997 issue of *Xavier Gold* in an article, "Herbal Medicines Make the Difference." In the October 1997 issue of *American Druggist*, he was listed as one of the fifty most influential pharmacists in the United States, and his work in the field has earned him an honorary Doctor of Pharmacy Degree from the state of Tennessee. Dr. Champion and his wife, Carolyn Frances Bailey Champion, have three daughters: Chandra, Charita, and Carol.

Chatman, Peter II "Memphis Slim" (1915–1988), blues singer, pianist, and composer. Named "America's Ambassador at Large for Goodwill" by the United States Senate, Memphis Slim was a talented musician, who became one of the first blues artists to tour Europe. Born on September 3, 1915, in Memphis, he was the only son of Ella Kennedy and Peter Chatman, Sr. His mother died when he was two years old, so he was raised by his father and stepmother, Lillie Chatman. His father, who played the guitar and piano, owned nightclubs in Earle and Crawfordsville, Arkansas. Young Peter grew up in the Binghamton community and graduated from Lester School. By age sixteen, he was singing and playing the piano professionally in such Beale Street venues as the old Mid-Way Café.

In 1937, he left for Chicago, where he was dubbed "Memphis Slim" because of his slender build and place of origin. His prowess at the keyboard and versatile singing style brought him to the attention of recording companies, and his first recording, "Beer-Drinking Woman," for Bluebird Records became a hit. As he noted in an interview, "To be successful in the blues field you've got to play all type of blues, all styles, all beats." At first, he adopted the heavy, electric sound that characterized the Chicago blues, but then he changed to the more sophisticated sound of the small combos. With Muddy Waters, Blind Lemon Jefferson, and Willie Dixon, he recorded a classic album, *Just Blues*, in 1938. In 1940, he joined William "Big Bill" Broonzy's band as a pianist but eventually formed his own bands and began recording on several labels, first as "Memphis Slim and His Solid Band," and later as "Memphis Slim and His House Rockers." In the late 1950s, he changed his musical style again to folk blues and began recording for Folkways Records, accompanied solely by his own piano. Soon after his first tour of Europe in 1960, he moved to Paris, where he found more work and greater acclaim as an artist. He appeared in two films—*The Sergeant* in 1968 and *Carry It On* in 1970—and he scored a 1970 French film, *A Nous Deux La France*.

Memphis Slim wrote more than 300 songs but is best remembered for "Every Day I Have the Blues," which became a signature piece for musicians such as B. B. King and Count Basie. His other well-known compositions include "Born with the Blues," "Double Crossing Blues," "Slim's Life Blues," and the autobiographical "Born in Memphis Tennessee," which details his journey from Memphis to Chicago. Described in his later years as a tall, imposing man with a gray streak in his hair, Memphis Slim had an integrity, dignity, and serenity that set him apart from many musicians. In 1978, he performed in a Memphis Symphony pops concert, and, eight years later, he was named Commander in the Order of the Arts and Letters by the French Ministry of Culture. He married Doris Owen of Chicago in 1946, and later wed Christini Freys, daughter of a Paris nightclub owner. His six children include Helen, John L., Natalie, Peter III, Vivian, and Tyrone. He died on February 24, 1988, at Necker Hospital in Paris and was buried in Memphis after a ceremonial funeral strut down Beale Street.

Chisholm, Bridget (1964–), businesswoman, county commissioner. A prime example of the new breed of dynamic young city leaders and entrepreneurs, Chisholm has leveraged her strength in finance, marketing, and management to found companies and acquire property. She was born on December 12, 1964, in Fayetteville, North Carolina, to Winston and Mary Deyampert Chisholm, and she has a younger brother. She attended Ferguson Elementary School and graduated from Reid Ross High School, where she was salutatorian and senior class president, and received the Challenge Cup Award for leadership, character, and academic achievement. In 1986, she was awarded a bachelor's degree, cum laude, in economics and computer science by Wake Forest University. After three years with RJR Nabisco, she acquired a master's degree in marketing and finance from the famed Wharton School of Business in 1991. Chisholm then became branch manager for General Mills and, from 1994 to 1996, general manager of Maybelline's "Shades of You" brand of cosmetics in Memphis. She was hired, in 1996, to be director of marketing for the Applebee's Division of Apple South, where her experience in putting together mergers and acquisitions gave her an opportunity to buy franchises. Characterized as "bright, savvy, and somewhat bold," she and a former colleague founded Delta Bluff, LLC on her return to Memphis in 1998. With three other investors, she bought thirteen Applebee Restaurants at a cost of about $1.3 million each.

In 1999, Chisholm and two women partners founded Mosaic, LLC; they bought a Church's Restaurant, with plans to acquire three more. Then, she obtained tax freezes, in 2000, for two restaurants in which she was a partner: Applebee's on Union and Church's Chicken Restaurant on Poplar. Wanting to help people in the neighborhood, the owners of the Poplar Avenue restaurant hired ten workers from Dixie Homes because, as Chisholm explains: "In Memphis, you have a responsibility to give back. It can be gut-wrenching how have-and-have-not oriented this town can be." In 2004, she founded BBC Consulting, LLC, a professional services firm, which targets firms and communities that can empower women and African Americans.

Two years later, she secured Shelby County's first investment inside Memphis for one of her clients, the LeMoyne College Community Development Corporation, when the County allocated $700,000 for the Towne Center at Soulsville U.S.A.

Businesswoman Bridget Chisholm surprised the politicians when she was appointed, by an 8 to 3 margin, to fill a vacancy on the County Commission from 2001 to 2002. Her business experience was invaluable in shaping the budget and helping secure the largest bond issue for a capital project—the $250-million FedEx Forum. She also serves the community through her work on the Shelby County LINKS, Inc., Memphis Brooks Museum of Art Trustee Board, University of Memphis Board of Visitors, and the University Neighborhood Development Corporation, where she is president of the board. As chair of LeMoyne-Owen College's UNCF fund drive, she launched the Celebrity Sunset 5K race, which has raised over $100,000 in scholarships. Although her 100-hour work week leaves little time for leisure, she manages to run, work out, and play the piano.

Church, Robert Reed (1839–1912), businessman, philanthropist. After accumulating substantial wealth through his real estate holdings, Church became one of Memphis's most astute businessmen and respected philanthropists. The son of a slave seamstress, Emmeline, and Charles B. Church, a White steamboat captain who became a director of Union & Planters Bank, he was born a slave in Holly Springs, Mississippi, on June 18, 1839. After his mother's death in 1851, he came to Memphis to work on his father's boat, first as a dishwasher and then as a steward. At the height of the Civil War, he witnessed the capture of Captain Church's boat by the Federal Fleet. When young Church was freed at the end of the Civil War, he invested his small savings in the purchase of a saloon located at Main and Gayoso Streets, which he renamed the Bob Church Saloon. During the violence that erupted in the city in 1866, when a White mob burned down houses, churches, and schools in Black neighborhoods, Church was shot and later testified before a congressional committee investigating the riot.

The young entrepreneur continued to buy real estate, including a restaurant and downtown hotel on the corner of South Second and Gayoso, which was advertised as the "only first-class Colored hotel in the city," with dining facilities and large rooms furnished with the best equipment of the day. When Memphis was reduced to a taxing district after the yellow fever epidemic of 1878, he was the first citizen to purchase a $1,000 bond to restore the city charter. In 1899, concerned that there were no public parks for Negroes, he bought six acres of land on Beale Street to establish Church's Park and Auditorium at a cost of $50,000. The park had gardens, playgrounds, picnic areas, and a bandstand, while the 2,000-seat auditorium, where President Theodore Roosevelt and Booker T. Washington spoke, was used for political rallies, graduation exercises, vaudeville shows, and a Thanksgiving dinner for the underprivileged.

His interest in public service led Church to make two ventures into politics: in 1882, he ran unsuccessfully for the Board of Public Works on both the People's Ticket and the Independent Ticket, and in 1900, he served as a delegate to the Republican National Convention as a McKinley supporter. Economic development, however, continued to be his forte and his major interest. In 1906, he founded and served as the first president of the Solvent Savings Bank and Trust Company, the first Black-owned-and-operated bank in Memphis and the third largest Black bank in the country, with deposits by 1912 in excess of $100,000. In 1908, when the Beale Street Baptist Church faced foreclosure, Church, through his personal and business resources, paid off the creditors with liberal repayment terms. Robert R. Church was devoted to his family. He first married Louisa Ayers, a milliner and shop owner, with whom he had two children, Mary and Thomas. That marriage ended in divorce and, in 1885, he married school principal Anna Wright, and they became the parents of Robert, Jr., and Annette. After a brief illness, he died on August 2, 1912, leaving an estate in excess of a million dollars, and is buried in a mausoleum at Elmwood Cemetery. In 1984, the Memphis Chamber of Commerce named him one of Memphis's pioneer businessmen.

Church, Robert Reed, Jr. (1885–1952), businessman, political leader. One of the most powerful Blacks in the Republican Party for two decades, he founded the Lincoln League and the Memphis Branch of the NAACP. Born in Memphis on October 26, 1885, to Robert R. and Anna Wright Church, he received his early education at Hooks's kindergarten and Memphis parochial schools, and he obtained further education at Morgan Park Military Academy in Illinois, Oberlin College in Ohio, and the Packard School of Business in New York. Following a two-year apprenticeship at a New York bank, Church returned to Memphis to manage Church's Park and Auditorium on Beale Street. In 1907, he became cashier of the Solvent Savings Bank and Trust Company, which had been founded by his father, who also served as bank president. The elder Church stepped aside in 1909, so that his son could assume the presidency. Two years later, on July 26, 1911, Church married Sara P. Johnson of Washington, D.C., and they became the parents of a daughter, Sara Roberta. On the death of his father in 1912, Church resigned the presidency of the bank to become executor and manager of the Church properties, which included over 300 pieces of real estate.

Although he was a prominent businessman, young Church's real passion was politics. In 1916, he founded and financed the Lincoln League, an organization of Black Republicans, which eventually expanded into a state and national organization. The Lincoln League sponsored voter registration drives, paid voters' poll taxes, and fielded a slate of candidates, including a Black candidate for Congress in the 1916 campaign. Although the "Black and Tan" ticket lost, the campaign established Church as a formidable political player: he was a strategist whose advice was sought by national leaders; he controlled the Black Republican vote in Memphis and Shelby County; he was consulted on federal patronage; and he was a Memphis delegate to eight successive Republican conventions between 1912 and 1940. Aware of the connection between politics and civil rights, he organized the Memphis Branch of the National Association for the Advancement of Colored People (the first branch in Tennessee), and, in 1919, he represented fourteen Southern states as a member of the NAACP's national board of directors.

Church's political nemesis was E. H. "Boss" Crump, the patronizing Democratic leader who ruled Memphis with an iron fist. In the 1930s, with the Depression, Democratic resurgence under President Franklin D. Roosevelt, and Crump's control of local politics, Church sustained financial setbacks and a loss of political influence. In 1940, the Crump administration seized his property, allegedly for back taxes, in a move to destroy his political base. As a result, he relocated to Washington, D.C., where he served on the board of directors of the National Council for a Permanent Fair Employment Practices Committee (now the EEOC). In 1944, he organized and served as chairman of the Republican American Committee, a group of Black Republicans who lobbied for equal employment and civil rights legislation. On April 17, 1952, after campaigning for Dwight D. Eisenhower, he died of a heart attack and was buried in Elmwood Cemetery.

Church, Sara Roberta (1914–1995), author, civic worker, government administrator. A third-generation Memphian, Church dedicated her life to public service, locally and nationally. The only daughter of Robert R. and Sara Johnson Church, Jr., and the granddaughter of pioneer Memphians Robert R. and Anna Wright Church, she was born in Memphis on June 5, 1914. She was raised by her paternal aunt and grandmother after the death of her mother, when Roberta was only eight years old. After graduating from LeMoyne High School, she attended Oberlin College for two years and graduated from Northwestern University in 1935. After receiving a master's degree in social work from Northwestern in 1937, she was a social worker in Chicago for thirteen years at the Family and Child Welfare Division of the Chicago Welfare Administration and then with the adoption division of the Illinois Children's Home and Aid Society. Following the death of her father in 1952, she took his place as a candidate for the Republican State Executive Committee of Tennessee, becoming the first Black woman in Memphis and Shelby County to be elected to public office. In 1953, she was appointed to the Department of Labor as Minority Groups Consultant, becoming the highest ranking Black woman in the federal government.

Roberta Church resigned from that position to accept a career civil service appointment with the Department of Health, Education, and Welfare as a consultant with the Rehabilitation Services Administration. In 1977, she published "Migrants: The Last Human Frontier" in the journal *American Rehabilitation*. In 1970, President Nixon appointed her to the National Council on Adult Education; in her second term, she served as chair of the Research Committee. Returning to Memphis frequently to speak, she addressed the Memphis Pan-Hellenic Council in 1955 and gave the Black History Week lecture for the Memphis-Shelby County Public Library in 1975.

After retiring from government service in 1982, she returned to Memphis, where she became active in community work and historical research. A May 1959 *Ebony* magazine article, "In the Steps of Her Father," underscored one of her main objectives: to preserve the memory of her family. With her aunt, Annette E. Church, she coauthored *The Robert R. Churches of Memphis*, a biography of her father and grandfather, published in 1974, and she co-authored with Ronald Walter, *Nineteenth Century Memphis Families of Color* in 1987, which featured biographical sketches of thirty-two pioneers. She also played a major role in the effort to gain local and state government support for the historical recognition of Church's Park, located on Beale Street. Miss Church received numerous awards: Delta Sigma Theta Sorority held a tribute for her in 1984; Leadership Memphis gave her the Kate Gooch Award in 1988; and, in 1987, the Kiwanis Club selected her as Senior Citizen of the Year. After a brief illness, she died in Memphis on July 15, 1995.

Clark, LeRoy D. (1918–1988), trade unionist, civil rights leader. The first executive director of Local 1733 of the American Federation of State, County and Municipal Employees, Clark was active in civic affairs, political activities, and civil rights in Memphis for over twenty years. One of three children, he was born on November 19, 1918, in the Panama Canal Zone but grew up in New York City, where he attended the public schools. His father was David Clark, a Jamaican carpenter who worked on the Panama Canal, and his mother, a Cuban by birth, was Alexandrina Clark. After completing a tour of duty with the U.S. Army in World War II, he worked as an upholsterer and joined the United Furniture Workers Union in 1949. During his forty years with the UFWU, he held many responsible positions, from labor negotiator to international representative. In fact, it was his investigative work for the union in the early 1950s that first brought him to Memphis, where he and Alzeda Clark, who was also a representative of the furniture workers' union, were married on Thanksgiving Day 1952. The couple lived in High Point, North Carolina, and New York City, before moving to Memphis in 1961, at a time when the civil rights struggle was in full swing and Blacks were campaigning vigorously for political office. County Commissioner Jesse Turner recalled that LeRoy Clark "would register people to vote and make sure that people got out to vote. He was always available with ideas and his own personal effort."

Clark was the first president of the Shelby County Democratic Voters Council and, later, chairman of the Shelby County Democratic Executive Committee. A neat dresser and a smooth speaker, he was noted for his calm and efficient management style. In an interview, he described himself as the type of person who makes decisions "based on logical deduction instead of emotional reaction." Active in the NAACP, he was elected president of the Memphis branch, and he also served as NAACP field director in Tennessee and Arkansas. Clark provided service to the community in other ways: he was on the board of directors of Shelby United Neighbors and was a Shelby County housing commissioner. He died on December 22, 1988, leaving, besides his wife, a son, LeRoy Clark Jr., who was an attorney for the NAACP Legal Defense Fund and professor of law at New York City University.

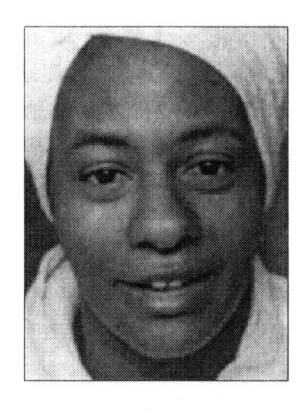

Clayborne, Beverly Sarah "The Pie Lady" (1949–), chef, restauranteur. One of Memphis's most creative and celebrated cooks, she started out as a chef but opened her own restaurant. She was born on May 1, 1949. In 1982, after a failed marriage, she moved from Chicago to Memphis, where she worked as a chef at Sherrod's, Mood Indigo, and La Montagne Restaurants. Five years later, her pregnant daughter, Eugenia Binkins, was shot in the head during a robbery in Glenview Park and, when Eugenia slipped into a coma, her mother needed money to pay the medical bills. Clayborne had no insurance, no job, and a burned-out house, but she knew how to cook because she had grown up "around lots of wonderful African American women who were very fine cooks." In fact, she had been cooking since age five, had owned a Chicago seafood restaurant, and had just graduated from the Memphis Culinary Academy. So she started selling pies out of her house: exotic pies like "Glory Hallelujah," made of pears topped by a lemon-glazed crust; "Amen Pie," concocted out of walnuts and chocolate; and "Hosanna Hosanna," a sinfully delicious mixture of coconut and almonds. Soon, word got around that The Pie Lady could "burn," so there was a market for her wares at eateries such as Houston's, Sleep Out Louies, and King's Palace Café; and Memphis notables—State Senator Steve Cohen, fashion designer Pat Kerr Tigrett, and opera star Kallen Esperian—had a taste for her pastries. In 1990, with a $250 used stove, she rented—in good faith and against all odds—a small, plain house at 1482 Florida Street and opened The Pie Lady, a restaurant where she served lunch Monday through Friday and dinner on Friday nights.

In 1993, when the Shelby County Health Department prohibited her from baking pies at her restaurant, her friends raised $7,500 at Zinnie's East to help her with her pie business. Later that year, under the headline "Pie High," she and her baked goods were featured in *People* magazine because celebrities had a penchant for her pies. In spite of the restaurant's ups and downs, she was proud of her South Memphis location, pointing out: "I think we African Americans need to rebuild our neighborhoods and not run away. We need to build up what we have and make it nice and make it grow." The restaurant's typically Southern menu of turnip greens, fried corn and smothered chicken and dressing reflected her healthy lifestyle: soul food with no pork, seasoning without fats, and cakes without milk or eggs. She has cooked for celebrities such as film star Tom Cruise, actor Ben Vereen, and director Sydney Pollack, who paid $100 for one of her "Glory Hallelujahs."

In spite of all the hard work, Mrs. Clayborne was never too busy to help others. She worked with the Center for Independent Living, helped the disabled, and baked pies for charities such as Youth Villages' Soup Sunday, where she was awarded the Best Dessert ribbon in competition with fifty local restaurants. Her restaurant's Jazz

Tuesdays, featuring Calvin Newborn on guitar, began as a fund-raiser for the Phineas Newborn Family Foundation. In 2004, she created the "Saveahoe Foundation" to offer prostitutes job training and financial counseling. "Women need to learn how to use their mind and not their behind," she insisted. Clayborne had plans for the future: franchising recipes, teaching cooking classes, doing motivational speaking, and opening a rehabilitation center for indigents. In 1994, she opened a new restaurant at 144 Madison, but continued to sell at her Florida Street restaurant. After those closed, she began selling pies at the Farmer's Market on Saturday.

Cleaborn, Edward O. (1933–1951), soldier. A hero of the Korean War at age eighteen, Cleaborn was posthumously awarded the Distinguished Service Cross, the second highest military award of the United States. Born in Merigold, Mississippi to Florence C. and Everett Cleaborn, he moved with his family to Memphis in 1936. He and his eight brothers and sisters grew up in the slums of southwest Memphis in an unpainted, two-room, shotgun house at 196 Bailey's Alley. A personable and conscientious young man, intent on making something of himself, he was active in the Shiloh Baptist Church and joined Boy Scout Troop 161, Seminole Division. He attended Florida Street School and then entered Booker T. Washington High School but dropped out after less than a year to help support his large family. For a while, he worked with his father at the South Memphis stockyards and then became a busboy at Hotel Claridge. According to his mother, he worked hard but was often laid off of low-paying, menial jobs when the work ran out. Like other young men growing up

Black, impoverished, and poorly educated in the post-World War II South, he believed that military service offered the only opportunity for economic advancement. So, on February 13, 1950, at age seventeen, Cleaborn joined the Army "because he couldn't find a job," said his mother.

On August 15, 1951, Marine Private Edward O. Cleaborn stood alone on a ridge near Kuri, Korea. While his comrades in Company A of the all-Black 24th Regiment of the 25th Division withdrew from battle, he protected his platoon from enemy fire. Although his gun burned his hands from continual firing, he managed to wipe out the enemy machine gunners before being killed. In death Pvt. Cleaborn found the acclaim that had eluded him in life. After a funeral with full military honors, he was buried in National Cemetery. Several days later, a parade that included bands from all of the Black public and private schools proceeded from the Beale Street Auditorium to Booker T. Washington High School, where more than 4,000 Memphians—Black and White, dignitaries and ordinary folk, military officials and fellow soldiers—crowded into the gymnasium to pay tribute to a man who had given his life for his comrades. Before a standing-room-only crowd, the young soldier was posthumously awarded the Distinguished Service Cross for "extraordinary heroism in action in Korea." His mother was interviewed by Edward R. Murrow on CBS's "Hear It Now." City officials considered naming a 15-acre park and a 69-unit housing development after the young hero; eventually, the Edward O. Cleaborn Homes, a public housing project located on South Lauderdale, was named in his honor.

Three days after his death, Florence Cleaborn received a letter from her son that ended, "Tell Dad don't work too hard and be sure you write and tell me when you move to your new house..." Ironically, the $350 that his parents had put down on a new house—money that had probably been sent to them by their son—was lost to an unscrupulous real estate dealer. Touched by Cleaborn's heroism and his family's plight, friends and neighbors established a fund to help the family buy a new house.

Cleaves, Irene Curtis (1908–1998), restauranteur, businesswoman. Operator of the legendary Four Way Grill for more than fifty years, she was nationally acclaimed for her soul food cooking and warm Southern hospitality. She was one of eight children born to a C.M.E. minister and his wife in Sardis, Mississippi, on July 12, 1908. She explained in an interview, "See, my husband loved to eat, and my mama told me, 'the way to a man's heart is through his stomach,' so I'd whip him some short ribs, turnip greens and candy yams for love sake." She and her husband, Clint Cleaves, borrowed $1,500 and put up their house for collateral to start the business. Located at 998 Mississippi Boulevard and Walker Avenue in South Memphis, the Four Way Grill was a small restaurant with only 100 seats, where you could get fried fish, chitterlings, meatloaf, and peach cobbler "to die for." Notables such as Jesse Jackson, Isaac Hayes, Bishop Charles Mason, Harry Belafonte, and Dr. J. E. Walker have dined at the humble restaurant and, in gratitude, left autographed photographs to embellish the grease-stained walls. Martin Luther King, Jr., for example, wrote "Thanks for the good home cooking. Tastes just like mama cooked it."

Cleaves was not only a culinary wizard, she was also a student of African American history and of soul food, which originated on large plantations in Delta cotton country, along the Yazoo and Mississippi Railroads from Jackson to Memphis. "Soul cooking," she explained, "is a strong element of our country's Black heritage. Recipes are passed down from mother to daughter to preserve the dignity, love, and pride of Black culture." After she became ill, the restaurant was co-managed by her sister and nephew, but closed from November 1996 through April 1997 because of failure to pay about $20,000 in taxes owed to the Tennessee Department of Revenue. After Mayor

Herenton created an advisory committee to find ways to save the landmark, the Four Way Grill reopened in April 1997. Irene Cleaves died on March 17, 1998.

Clouston, Joseph (1814–1894), businessman. One of the first African Americans to own property on Beale Street and in downtown Memphis, he served on the Memphis City Council in the 1870s. Born a slave in Fayette County, Tennessee, in 1814, he worked as a barber to buy his freedom and that of his mother. In 1860, he is reported to have owned a grocery store on Brown Avenue and, according to the *Memphis City Directory* of 1867–1869, he had a barbershop and grocery store at 145 Beale Avenue. As a city councilman, he moved at an 1874 meeting of the Council that the city add ten colored men to the fire department and twenty-five to the police force. Although he ran unsuccessfully for reelection as a Fifth Ward councilman in 1876, he had a great deal of political influence. He and his wife Dora had three children: Arthur, born in 1866; a son, Alma; and a daughter, Teresa, who died tragically in a home fire. The Cloustons, who amassed considerable wealth in farm land and city property, lived in a large house across from Zion Cemetery on a road that later became South Parkway East.

Cobb, Joyce (1945–), singer, performer, songwriter. The first woman on Beale Street to have her name on a nightclub marquee, the jazz diva is one of Memphis's most talented and celebrated vocalists. Born on June 2, 1945, in Okmulgee, Oklahoma and raised in Nashville, she is the daughter of Florence Cobb, a teacher and dance director, and Robert S. Cobb, a former professor at Tennessee State University, who had an extensive collection of jazz records. She began singing in her Catholic school glee club and in her grandmother's church choir before earning a bachelor's degree at Central State University in Dayton, Ohio. While pursuing a master's in social work and playing in coffee houses, she was offered a job singing for the Ramada Hotel chain. After two and a half years on the road working for Ramada, she returned to Nashville and took up country music, singing in clubs and on radio, appearing on television, and performing with a Dixieland band at Opryland. In 1976, she signed with Stax Records—just before it folded—but she was intrigued by Memphis. "Everything was black—black music, black bands. I said, 'Oh, I want to stay here.'" She began writing songs, including such hits as "Dig the Gold" and "Another Lonely Night"; recording albums like *Good to Me* and *Jazzin' on Beale*; and touring with Taj Mahal, Muddy Waters, Al Jareau, and the Temptations.

Singing everything from jazz and blues to country and reggae, the multitalented Joyce Cobb, who also plays the piano, guitar, and harmonica, has done it all: she wrote songs for record producer Willie Mitchell, toured Europe in 1992 with blues singer Otis Clay, hosted shows such as "Voices" and "Songs for My Father" on WEVL FM90, sang the National Anthem at a 1993 all-star baseball game at Tim McCarver Stadium, taught jazz vocals at the University of Memphis, and performed with the Memphis Symphony. In April 2005, she starred as the legendary Billie Holiday in Theatre Memphis's one-woman show, *Lady Day at Emerson's Bar & Grill*, a performance that was characterized as "as gracefully natural and as easy to swallow as a smooth gin and tonic," and, in 2006, she captured the soul-stirring magic of blues singer Bessie Smith in the musical *The Devil's Music* at Theatre Memphis. A reviewer wrote that "she is so natural, you close your eyes and you see Bessie herself."

One of the highlights of her career came on April 1, 1992, when Joyce Cobb's, a club owned by John Robertson, opened on Beale Street and she became not only the star attraction but also part manager, promoter, and PR person. Cobb has received many honors and awards: she was voted "Best Female Singer" by the Memphis chapter of NARAS and "Best Female Entertainer in 1995" by the Beale

Street Merchant's Association; she was honored at the 18th annual Women of Achievement dinner when she received the "Initiative Award"; she received her own brass music note on the "Beale Street Walk of Fame"; and she was awarded an honorary doctorate of music by Grand Valley State College in 1995. The lead singer on "We Shall Overcome," one of the songs on an album to raise funds for the National Civil Rights Museum, Joyce Cobb has given generously of her time and talent to raise money for local and national organizations such as the Exchange Club of Memphis, an organization that helps abused women and children; Memphis and Shelby County Coalition for the Homeless; and the Make-A-Wish Foundation.

Cochran, Flora Cole (1906–1989), florist. Founder of Memphis's first Black-owned floral shop, she operated her own business for forty-five years, until her retirement in 1981. She was born to Essie and Robert Cole on January 29, 1906, in Earle, Arkansas. After completing high school in the early 1920s, she moved to Memphis, where she worked her way up from a maid to an arranger at Tri-State Floral Company. At Tri-State she learned to grow, arrange, and sell unique floral arrangements. In 1936, she opened Flora's Flower Shop in the livingroom of her home at 1044 Neptune Street, where she introduced Memphians to the significance of fresh flowers for their wedding celebrations and funeral observances. Her husband, Socrates C. Cochran, whom she married in the 1940s, worked with his wife in the business. When the flower shop grew too large for that location, she bought a house at 964 Mississippi Boulevard, where she used the front room for designing arrangements and an enclosed porch for a showroom. In 1952, she bought a house and an adjacent lot at 729 and 733 Vance Avenue, where she built a modern, 2,500-square-foot building for her large retail flower business. Among its many rooms, the building contained a wedding chapel, where many couples were married.

Although she learned the flower trade at the Tri-State Floral Company, Mrs. Cochran developed her business acumen from her association with members of the Negro Business League such as B. G. Olive, J. E. Walker, and H. D. Whalum, who advocated Black pride, independence, and ownership. Through her business contacts, she gained the support of Black clubs, schools, colleges, and churches, whose members were impressed by her creative floral designs, competitive prices, and professional service. By the same token, she offered service to her community through membership in and leadership of many civic, church, and educational organizations. Mrs. Cochrane, who truly lived up to the name Flora ("Goddess of flowers"), died on August 31, 1989, and is buried in National Cemetery.

Colbert, John. See J. Blackfoot.

Coleman, Veronica Freeman (1945–), lawyer, judge, United States attorney. Since her 1975 graduation from law school, Coleman has moved rapidly through the legal system to become the first woman and first Black United States Attorney in Tennessee. She was born in Washington, D.C. on January 1, 1945, to Mary and Robert T. Freeman, but the family moved to Brooklyn when she was nine months old. Ten years later, the Freemans moved to Ghana, where her father co-founded the Gold Coast Life Insurance Company. In 1958, Veronica Freeman returned to the States to enter Solebury, a private boarding school from which she was graduated in 1962. After receiving a bachelor's degree in sociology from Howard University in 1966, she married

Wisdom F. Coleman, a dental student, on August 13, 1966. While living in Washington, St. Louis, and Atlanta, Veronica Coleman worked for the Redevelopment Land Agency, International Business Machines, and the Model Cities Agency.

In 1971, the Colemans moved to Memphis, where she began taking night classes at Memphis State University Law School. After receiving a law degree in 1975, she served briefly as assistant public defender for Memphis and then became the first full-time female assistant in the Shelby County Public Defender's Office. In 1977, she was a founding partner in the first all-female law firm in Tennessee: Coleman, Sorak and Williams. Three years later, she became the first Black woman hired as assistant district attorney general for the 30th Judicial District of Tennessee. For eighteen months, she served as in-house counsel to the president of Memphis State University; after leaving that office, she volunteered as a member of Greater Memphis State's Board of Directors, MSU Law School's Board of Visitors, MSU Foundation's Board of Trustees, and the Academic Fund's Century Club. She became a litigation attorney for Federal Express Corporation and rose to the rank of senior attorney, before accepting a position as a Juvenile Court referee, the first Black woman in the state to hold that position.

Veronica Freeman Coleman was sworn in as United States attorney for the Western District of Tennessee on October 18, 1993. Well prepared and articulate, Coleman advocates the vigorous enforcement of the law and has gained a reputation for being tough but fair. She supports, for example, alternative sentencing programs, such as Parents Fair Share, a holistic approach to child support. At the request of the Bush Administration, she tendered her resignation as United States attorney on March 29, 2000, and, in 2006, she finished second in the election for Shelby County Juvenile Court judge. Through her legal work, Coleman became interested in social issues that affect women and young people. She is founder and president of the National Institute for Law and Equity, a member of the Volunteer Women's Roundtable, and founding president of the Coalition of 100 Black Women. She has served on the boards of Leadership Memphis,

Goals for Memphis, Free the Children, Blues City Cultural Center, and the Black-on-Black Crime Task force. The recipient of awards from the University of Memphis, Girls Club Incorporated of Memphis, and the YWCA, she was a member of the Memphis Shelby County Crime Commission, and her office adopted a junior high school in 1995 through the Adopt-A-School program. She and her former husband, Dr. Wisdom Coleman, are the parents of three sons: Wisdom, Jr., David, and Anthony.

Conley, Larry (1953–), journalist, editor, college professor. The only Black city magazine editor in the country in 1986, he became the first native Memphian and the first African American to edit *Memphis* magazine. Born on June 30, 1953, the oldest of eight children, he was the surrogate parent of his younger siblings while his mother, Bessie Conley, was working. He grew up in North Memphis, attended Chicago Park Elementary School and, in 1971, graduated from Manassas High School, where he was president of the student council, vice president of the honor society, and a member of the basketball team. Although he applied to several colleges, he was so impressed by the Black student recruiter—"who was so smooth and self-assured, I said 'Wow, I could be like that!'" Conley exclaimed—that he decided to attend Dartmouth College on a four-year National Merit Scholarship from McGraw-Hill. He earned a B.A. degree in English from Dartmouth College in 1975, and, a year later, received an M.S. in journalism from Columbia University. Along the way, he married (but is now divorced from) Memphis native Clarice Gordon, who is also a journalist, and they have a son, Alan.

Larry Conley's first job, writing for the Metro Section of *The Commercial Appeal*, was a "real baptism," he chuckled, because at the time there were only four Blacks on the staff. He went on to edit the Memphis Light Gas and Water Division's newsletter and did freelance writing in his spare time. Later, he edited *Racquetball* magazine, published by Towery Press (which also published *Memphis*), and for two years (1980–1982), he had a dual position at the University of Mississippi as professor of journalism and staff writer for the Center for the Study of Southern Culture. From 1982 to 1986, he taught writing and journalism at Memphis State University, where he had a tenured position on the faculty. Although he began writing for *Memphis* in 1976, and his article on disco trends became the cover story of the June 1977 issue, he did not join the staff until the 1980s. He is most proud of the October 1983 issue on race relations, which contains two of his articles and which won the Sigma Delta Chi Award for Distinguished Public Service in Magazine Journalism. On June 1, 1986, when he was only thirty-two years old, Conley was appointed executive editor of *Memphis*, an appointment about which he observed: "I think it means something that *Memphis* magazine will have a black editor—it's a sign of change in the city." When he left the magazine in 1990, he explained, "I reached the end of my stream." Looking back on the experience in a 1993 editorial, he wrote: "I had to overcome all the normal obstacles of life that my white colleagues faced—*plus* the obstacles of race that they didn't face. And I resent it, deeply." Larry Conley's articles have appeared in *Essence*, *Stars & Stripes*, the Los Angeles *Daily News*, Tampa *Tribune*, Kansas City *Star*, and *Maui* (Hawaii) *News*, and he is presently the Dekalb County Bureau Chief of the *Atlanta Journal-Constitution*.

Cook, Vivian Elma Johnson (1889–1977), teacher, administrator, civic worker. She was the first female guidance counselor in the Baltimore schools and the first woman principal of the largest coeducational high school in Maryland. Born on October 6, 1889, to Caroline and Spencer Johnson in Collierville, Tennessee, she was the youngest of eight children. Her mother was the first Black teacher in Fayette County, Tennessee, and her father became principal of Manassas High School in Memphis, where Vivian Johnson received her elementary and secondary school education. After graduating from Howard University in 1912, she taught at Tuskegee Institute for a year, until Booker T. Washington offered her the principalship of The Children's House. She also taught at McCall School in Cincinnati and Sumner High School in St. Louis until her 1918 marriage to Ralph Victor Cook, an engineer who graduated from Cornell in the 1890s. The couple moved to Baltimore but, because married women could not teach in public schools, Mrs. Cook put her career on hold until the ban was lifted during World War II.

After the loss of their baby, she began teaching in the Baltimore City Public Schools and acquired a number of "firsts": she was the first woman guidance counselor, first Black female administrator in the secondary schools, and first woman principal of Dunbar High School, which had an enrollment of 3,800 students. After her retirement from the Baltimore City Schools in 1956, she taught at Morgan State College, where she trained practice teachers until 1963. Throughout her career, she took a leadership role in community affairs, serving on the board of the Metropolitan YWCA and as vice chairperson of its Committee on Administration of the International Center. She was also president of the Cooperative Women's Civic League and a member of the Baltimore Commission on Problems of the Aging for ten years. A patron of the arts, Vivian Cook was chairperson of the CWCL's Art Committee, which sponsored contests for art students and exhibits at the Baltimore Museum of Art. Her work on the Art Committee led to the desegregation of the Baltimore Museum of Art, when Howard University artist and professor Elton Fox was invited to exhibit his works at the museum. As chair of the public school's Negro History Week Committee, she and Milton Dugger presented an oil painting, Hayward Rivers's "Baptism," to the museum on behalf of Black teachers and administrators. She was also instrumental in acquiring artifacts from the Harmon Foundation for exhibit at the Peale Museum. Mrs. Cook was devoted to the younger members of her family and was quick to reward deserving youngsters with financial aid for school. Known as "Aunt Sweet," she kept in touch with family throughout the country and initiated reunions of the Johnson clan. Her grandnephew, historian Sterling Stuckey, recalled: "Aunt Vivian was a formidable, very demanding person, who inspired a certain admiring distance. She had an aristocratic, regal bearing that gained her the respect and admiration of Whites and Blacks alike."

Crawford, Alvin Howell (1939–), physician, professor. The author of six books, sixty chapters, and 200 scientific articles and abstracts, Dr. Crawford is presently director of Pediatric Orthopaedics at Cincinnati Children's Hospital Medical Center and professor of pediatrics at the University of Cincinnati College of Medicine. He was born in Memphis on August 28, 1939, and was a 1957 graduate of Melrose High School. In 1960, he received a B.S. degree in chemistry and biochemistry with a minor in music from Tennessee A&I University, from which he graduated with highest distinction. After completing a quarter at Meharry Medical College, he entered the University of Tennessee College of Medicine in Memphis. With National Defense loans and a scholarship from the National Medical Foundation, he was the first African American to attend the medical college, from which he graduated, in 1964. When asked about his experiences in medical school, he replied, "My years at UT? They were hard, not so much from the academic side as from the social." The young physician interned at Boston Naval Hospital, taught at Harvard and the University of California at San Diego, and, in 1977, was appointed to the Children's Hospital

Medical Center in Cincinnati and to the faculty of the University of Cincinnati College of Medicine. He has presented papers at international conferences throughout the world; served as visiting professor at universities such as Columbia, Michigan, and Washington; trained forty fellows in pediatric orthopaedic surgery; and presented orthopaedic techniques at several hospitals, where he lectured and performed video-assisted thorascopic surgeries.

Dr. Crawford is editor of the *Journal of the National Medical Association*, is on the editorial board of the *Journal of Pediatric Orthopaedics*, and is consulting editor of *Clinical Orthopaedics and Related Research*. He belongs to some thirty medical associations, including the American College of Surgeons, National Medical Association, and the American Academy of Orthopaedic Surgeons. In 1991–1992, he was a member of the board of directors of the Scoliosis Research Society, and he served as a member of the Orthopaedic Research and Education Foundation's Board of Trustees in 1995–1996. In 1998, he was named to the board of directors of the American Academy of Orthopaedic Surgeons as a member-at-large. Over the span of his illustrious career, he has received more than fifty honors, awards, and traveling fellowships, including the American Orthopaedic Association's Alfred Shands Lectureship Award in 1991, Pediatric Orthopaedic Society of North America's Pioneer Award in 1993, National Medical Association's Orthopaedic Scholar Award in 1995, and *Applause* magazine's Image Maker Award in the Field of Medicine. In 2000, he was elected the Neurofibromatosis, Inc. Scholar for the Year and was named one of the Best Doctors in America for 2000 and 2001. In 2003, he was inducted into the Memphis City Schools' Alumni Hall of Fame, and, in 2006, he was presented the Daniel Drake Medal, the highest honor the University of Cincinnati College of Medicine can bestow on a graduate or faculty member. Alvin H. Crawford served in the military during Operation Desert Storm and is presently retired as senior captain in the U.S. Naval Reserves. He and his wife, the former Alva Jean Jamison of Memphis, have two children: Carol and Alvin, Jr.

Crawford, Bennie Ross "Hank" (1934–), jazz musician. Saxophonist Crawford draws heavily on the Memphis rhythm-and-blues sound to create a distinctive soul-jazz and blues style. One critic characterized his alto style as "an intense wail filled with blues-drenched grace notes, slow grinding slurred phrases, and goose bump-inducing, vibrato-rich sustains." Born on December 21, 1934, Crawford grew up in North Memphis and began studying the piano at age nine and playing for his church choir. When he entered Manassas High School, his father bought him an alto saxophone so that he could play in the school band. While in high school, he hung out with Phineas Newborn, Jr., Frank Strozier, and Harold Mabern, who became acclaimed jazz figures. Dubbed "Hank" after legendary Memphis saxophonist Hank O'Day, he joined groups led by Tuff Green and Ben Branch, and he also played the piano and saxophone at the Palace Theater and Club Paradise with B. B. King and Bobby "Blue" Bland, before going to Nashville to study music at Tennessee A&I State College. At Tennessee State he led the college's dance band and organized a quartet called Little Hank and the Rhythm Kings, which performed in area clubs. His early work reveals the influences of Louis Jordan, Charlie Parker, Earl Bostic, and Johnny Hodges.

One night while working at the Subway Lounge, Roy Hall, a country music producer, heard him play and paved the way for him to cut his first records, "The House of Pink Lights" and "Christine." After a 1958 performance at Tennessee State, Ray Charles asked him to join his band, and, two years later, Crawford became music director of the Ray Charles Band. He recorded "Sherry," his first composition and arrangement for the Charles Septet, on the album *Ray Charles At Newport*. During the five years that he was with Charles, Crawford perfected his style, "blending bebop, R&B, and blues—dishing out tasty offerings of funky cuts and mellow ballads" (David Earl Jackson). After going solo in 1963, he began recording some of his most important albums—*Soul of the Ballad*, *True Blue*, and *After Hours*—for Atlantic Records. In the 1970s, his reputation increased when he produced a series of crossover records for Creed Taylor's CTI label, but in the 1980s he returned to his R&B background, producing records for Milestone. In the 1990s release, *After Dark*, he pays homage to his hometown with the soulful "Beale Street After Dark," while his haunting rendition of "Amazing Grace" evokes Sunday mornings at Memphis's Missionary Baptist Church, where he first performed.

Crenshaw, Cornelia (1916–1994), community activist. Called a "gadfly in the ointment of elected officialdom," Crenshaw worked to make public institutions and government agencies accountable to ordinary citizens. She was born to Beatrice Crenshaw on March 25, 1916, in Millington, Tennessee, and moved to Memphis with her mother when she was five years old. After graduating from Booker T. Washington High School, she attended LeMoyne College for a year. She worked as a receptionist for a physician, became a project manager for the Memphis Housing Authority, and served as a public relations representative for a trading stamp firm. Cornelia Crenshaw waged a long battle against the Memphis Light, Gas & Water Division, which began in 1969, when she refused to pay the city service fee for garbage collection. As a result, MLGW cut off her utilities, and she went without electricity, gas, or running water for years. Finally, the Health Department took her to court on a charge of breaking the city ordinance against unsanitary conditions, but she won the case and then held an open-house to prove that there were no unsanitary conditions in her house. She lost the income from a Vance Avenue duplex because she was unable to rent the property without utilities, and she mortgaged her car and furniture to pay her legal fees.

Calling herself an advocate for the underdog, she attended meetings of the utility company and the City Council but was barred from council executive meetings, arrested for disorderly conduct, and spent two nights in jail after staging a sleep-in at MLGW. With the "righteous wrath of an Old Testament prophet," she filed a suit, in 1974, against twelve public figures charging that they "conspired to defame" her character. Although she campaigned for Harold Ford in his first bid for Congress, she ran against his brother, John Ford, in the 1974 race for the Tennessee State Senate. She lost the campaign and then charged in court that the election was illegal because the senator lived outside of the district. She also supported William B. Ingram in his race for mayor, but campaigned against him when he withdrew as her attorney. An outspoken and often angry critic, she attacked Black political leaders such as Councilman J. O. Patterson and candidate for mayor, A. W. Willis, Jr.

Crenshaw filed a complaint with the Equal Employment Opportunities Commission in 1975, accusing the city and the Memphis Housing Authority of discrimination for refusing to appoint her executive director of MHA. A year later, she filed a bankruptcy petition, stating that she had been unemployed since 1974 and lived solely on Social Security income. Finally, in 1979, after ten years without utilities, she was forced to abandon her house at 603 Vance Avenue. Far from defeated, however, she filed another suit against MLGW in 1980, charging that rate increases by the utility company were excessive. Although she lost the suit, one result of her campaign was that MLGW began accepting partial payments from low-income citizens to prevent a service cutoff and a high reconnection fee. She was also arrested in 1980 for refusing to leave the City Council chambers. In 1992, she appealed to citizens on her own behalf. Dressed in a safari hat and a tan overcoat, she stood outside of her house amidst helium-filled balloons, soliciting financial help. A year later, she entered Court Manor Nursing Home and died on February 19, 1994, after suffering a stroke. In her honor, the Vance Avenue Library was renamed the Cornelia Crenshaw Library in October 1997.

Criss, William "Sonny" (1927–1977), jazz musician. One of the first generation of alto saxophonists influenced by Charlie Parker, Criss achieved an intense and distinctive style of his own that made him a major figure in the jazz world. Born in Memphis' John Gaston Hospital on October 23, 1927, he grew up listening to music. "I used to sit in a theater and listen to the great artists who changed my life," he recalled. "My parents would give me enough money to sit there Saturday and Sunday and listen to everybody in the world who was important in music. They all came through Beale Street." When he was fourteen, Criss moved to California. During the 1940s, he joined the bands of Howard McGhee, Johnny Otis, and Gerald Wilson, and, in the 1950s, he played with jazz greats, such as Billy Eckstine, Charlie Parker, Dizzy Gillespie, and Stan Kenton, while periodically organizing his own groups. He performed in Memphis, in 1962, pointing out that local musicians are better known around the world than at home. That same year, Criss moved to Europe, where he lived for three years, appearing on radio and television programs and performing in films and at nightclubs.

In Europe, in the 1960s, Sonny Criss found the acclaim that had eluded him in the States. He said, "When I go to foreign lands, I'm treated like a king. They know who my mother was and who my father was and when I first recorded." After returning to Los Angeles, he began working with children, as well as with alcoholics and drug addicts, and he also offered a series of jazz programs for children at the Hollywood Bowl. After a second tour of Europe in 1974, he appeared with Dizzy Gillespie at Monterey. The saxophonist was at the height of his career in 1977: in May, he released *The Joy of Sax* and played at the Beale Street Music Festival, along with B. B. King and Rufus Thomas; in the fall, he scheduled a concert tour of Japan and planned to record a new album on his return. The year, however, ended tragically. Sonny Criss died in his Los Angeles apartment on November 19,

1977, at age fifty, of a self-inflicted gunshot wound. He is survived by a son, Steven Criss, who was twenty-eight years old at the time of his father's death.

Crossley, Callie (1952?–), producer, commentator, broadcast journalist. Formerly a reporter for WREG-TV in Memphis, she co-produced the award-winning PBS documentary *Eyes on the Prize: America's Civil Rights Years, 1954–1965*. A native Memphian, she is the daughter of the late Mattie R. Crossley, an instructional consultant for the Memphis City Schools, and Samuel Crossley, a cost analyst for the U.S. Postal Service. In 1966, she and eighteen other students desegregated Central High School, where she was one of only two Blacks on the newspaper staff. Twenty years later, she spoke about the experience to a group of Central honors students: "It was just day after day of this psychological assault, [but] I lived through it and benefitted from it." After graduation from Wellesley College in 1973, she worked as a reporter for WREG-TV and for an Indianapolis station before moving, in 1977, to Boston, where she produced the "10 O'Clock News" at WGHB-TV and then became a producer of health and medical features at ABC News 20/20 for thirteen years. A social and cultural commentator, she contributes regularly to such radio programs as "On the Media" and "NPR News and Notes," and she appears frequently on CNN and WGBH-TV's "Beat the Press."

For two and a half years, Crossley worked on *Eyes on the Prize*, produced by Blackside, Inc., a small, minority-owned Boston film company with a $2.5 million budget. The series, which premiered on January 21, 1987, chronicles the civil rights movement from the Montgomery Bus Boycott to the 1965 Voting Rights Act. With James A. Divveney, she produced the fourth and sixth episodes in the series. Episode six, "Bridge to Freedom, 1965" was nominated for an Academy Award and won an Emmy for Best Documentary Feature in 1988.

She also served as senior producer on the 2003 PBS documentary series *This Far by Faith: African-American Spiritual Journeys*. Her work has garnered major journalism awards, including the Edward R. Murrow and Alfred I. Dupont-Columbia Awards, and she has received a Nieman Fellowship from Harvard University, Woodrow Wilson Visiting Fellowship, and an Institute of Politics Fellowship at the John F. Kennedy School of Government. Crediting much of her success to committed mentors—her mother, who exposed her to people from different cultures, and Blackside's Henry Hampton, who gave her support and encouragement—she, in turn, has become a mentor to aspiring journalists and filmmakers.

Davis, Fred (1934–) businessman, city councilman. When he was named chairman of the Memphis City Council in 1972, he attained the highest city office ever held by a Black. Davis was born in Memphis on May 8, 1934, at 1385 Horace Street. He grew up in a split family, spending time with his mother and then his father, who was a barber. While a student at Florida and Hyde Park Elementary Schools, he picked cotton to pay for his education and for piano lessons at twenty-five cents a session. Although he worked as a busboy to get through Manassas High School, he excelled academically and served as president of the student council and editor of the school paper. He received a B.S. degree in business administration from Tennessee A&I University and later obtained an M.A. degree in public administration from Memphis State University. After a tour of duty in the United States Army, he worked in the Shelby County Register's Office and sold insurance policies at night. In 1967, he opened the Fred L. Davis Agency at 1374 Airways, the first general agency owned and operated by a Black; he represented the Hartford Insurance Group and other agencies, as well as earned membership in the President's Club in his first year of operation.

Davis also became active in politics. In 1962, he became the youngest person elected to the Democratic Executive Committee, with a total of 46,580 votes. Five years later, he was elected, as a dark horse, to District 4 of the Memphis City Council, but in the next election he was the only candidate to win without a runoff, receiving more than 60% of the vote. After being elected chairman of the Council by a vote of 8 to 3, he took office on January 1, 1972. Ironically, the "Kansas Street Boy," who chaired the city's Housing, Building and Public Works Department, voted for the demolition of his former home in one of the poorest sections of Memphis, when the Council approved the Kansas Street Urban Renewal Project. In the late 1960s, Davis, a quiet and unassuming man, was criticized by some Blacks for not aggressively supporting the sanitation strike and the boycott of public schools. A member of the NAACP and president of the Orange Mound Civic Club, he received the Silver Quill Award as "Communicator of the Year" from the Memphis Chapter of the Public Relations Society of America. Fred L. Davis married Ella Josephine Singleton of Wartrace, Tennessee, an accountant, and they have three children: Michael, Sheila, and Marvin.

DeBerry, Lois (1945–), educator, state legislator. One of the most influential Black elected officials in Memphis and one of the two most powerful Black officials in state government, DeBerry has served over thirty years in the Tennessee State Legislature. The second of five children, she was born on May 5, 1945, and was raised by her mother, Mary DeBerry, in a one-bedroom duplex in the Bunker Hill neighborhood. After graduation from Hamilton High School, she received a bachelor's degree in education from LeMoyne College; although teachers were her role models growing up, she soon realized that teaching was not for her. DeBerry became the first Black woman elected to the Tennessee House of Representatives from Memphis and is presently the top-ranking woman and Black in the legislature, as well as the first woman chair of the Shelby County Democratic Caucus. During her long tenure in office, she has supported family issues such as teen pregnancy and school absenteeism; she has advocated counseling for teens, family life curricula in schools, crime prevention, and better prison facilities. Her legislative concerns include improving the state's juvenile justice system and mandating a family life curriculum in school districts with high teen pregnancy rates; she successfully steered bills on both subjects to passage in 1989.

As a founding member and president of the Tennessee Legislative Black Caucus, DeBerry has helped organize annual retreats beginning in 1974, which have attracted over 3,000 representatives of business, education, and government every year. In 1986, after a tough fight, she was elected Speaker pro tempore of the Tennessee House of Representatives and fought off a conservative challenge, in 1988, to win a second term. The first woman elected to this top legislative post in Tennessee, she presides over the chamber in the absence of the speaker and automatically votes on all standing committees. In 1994, she was elected to a two-year term as president of the 540-member National Black Caucus of State Legislators, of which she is a founding member and, in 1997, she was offered a presidential appointment to a one-year diplomatic post as assistant to the United Nations Ambassador. Lois DeBerry has earned the title "Madame Speaker" for her political dexterity, negotiating skills, and lengthy experience. In spite of her success as an elected official, her life has not been easy. She recalls that, within a span of thirty days, her father was fatally shot, her nineteen-year-old sister died from taking the wrong medication, and her brother, a Vietnam veteran, died after being hit by a softball bat. She is married to Charles M. Traughber, a member of the Board of Paroles, and she has an adult son, Michael Boyer. Although The DeBerry Correctional Facility bears her name, she became the object of controversy in 2004 for taking $200 from an undercover FBI agent at a gambling casino in

Tunica, Mississippi. In response, she resigned from a legislative ethics committee that she co-chaired.

Dickey, Eric Jerome (1961–), novelist. Author of twelve novels, seven of which have been *New York Times* bestsellers, he has been called "one of the original male voices in contemporary African American fiction." Born on July 7, 1961, he grew up in South Memphis, where he attended Riverdale Elementary and Junior High, Carver High School, and the University of Memphis, from which he received a B.S. degree in 1983. After working for Federal Express and as a bill collector for Lowenstein's downtown, he accepted a job in California as a software engineer for Rockwell (now Boeing). In his spare time, he moonlighted as an actor and did stand-up comedy from Seattle to San Antonio. He also began writing short stories and realized that he had a book underway when one of the stories developed into 300 pages. While attending graduate school, he studied information systems, took writing courses at a community college, and was accepted into UCLA's writing program.

After several rejections and a couple of years spent looking for an agent, Dickey finally published his first novel, *Sister Sister*, in 1996, and quit his day job. Since then, he has been on a roll, often publishing two novels in a single year, including *Milk in My Coffee* (1998), *Cheaters* (1999), *Liar's Game* (2002), *Between Lovers* (2001), *Thieves' Paradise* (2002), *Black Silk* (2002), *Naughty or Nice* (2003), *The Other Woman* (2003), *Drive Me Crazy* (2004), *Genevieve* (2005), and *Chasing Destiny* (2006). His contemporary romance novels, which focus on young professional Black men and women trying to establish long-lasting relationships, have been called "provocative and complex" by *Ebony* magazine and "smart, gritty, and gripping" by *Publisher's Weekly*. Several of his novels have been made into films, and his short stories have appeared in two anthologies: *Got to Be Real* and *Gumbo: A Celebration of African American Writing*. Recently, he cut a deal with Marvel Comics to produce six issues in the Storm series, a series that focuses on two super heroes—Ororo (Storm of the X-men) and Tchalla (The Black Panther) in comics that blend romance and adventure. Dickey was nominated four times for an NAACP Image Award, and he received the University of Memphis Alumni Award in 2002.

Donald, Bernice Bowen (1951–), attorney, judge, law professor. One of the country's most respected and learned judges, she was the first Black women elected to a judgeship in Tennessee, the first appointed to the U.S. Bankruptcy Court, and the first appointed to the federal court in the Western District of Tennessee. The sixth of Perry and Willie Bowen's ten children, she was born on September 17, 1951, on a plantation in Desoto County, Mississippi. She grew up in a four-room house in the Pleasant Hill community near Olive Branch, where her father was a sharecropper and her mother was a domestic. She attended all-Black public schools until her junior year in high school, when she transferred from East Side High School to the desegregated Olive Branch High School. One of only four African Americans in the school at the time of her admission, she was the first member of her family to graduate from high school. In 1969, she entered Memphis State University as a commuting student, but moved to the city in 1971, when she became a mail clerk at South Central Bell Telephone Company. She continued to work and attend college after her 1973 marriage to salesman W. L. "Don" Donald, with whom she has raised a stepson. A year after receiving her bachelor's degree in sociology from

Memphis State University in 1974, she was promoted to dispatch supervisor at South Central Bell. That same year, she began night classes at Memphis State University Law School, from which she received a degree in 1979.

A quiet and thoughtful attorney, Bernice B. Donald worked for several months at Memphis Area Legal Services before becoming an Assistant Shelby County Public Defender in 1980. In 1982, she entered the race for Shelby County General Sessions Judge and became the first Black woman elected to a judgeship in Tennessee. She served in that position until 1988, when she was appointed U.S. Bankruptcy Court Judge for the Western District of Tennessee—another first. Not content to rest on her laurels, Judge Donald became a law professor, serving on the faculties of Shelby State Community College, University of Memphis, Federal Judicial Center in Washington, and the National Judicial College in Reno. In 1995, Bernice B. Donald was appointed U.S. District Judge for the Western District of Tennessee. Active in many professional organizations, she was president of the National Association of Women Judges, chair of the American Bar Association's Judicial Administration Division, and chair of the National Conference of Special Court Judges. She has been profiled in *Essence*, *Ebony*, and *Black Enterprise* magazines, and has received many honors and awards, including the Arabella Mansfield Award from the National Association of Women Lawyers. In 1988, *Dollars and Sense* magazine named her one of "America's Best and Brightest." This soft-spoken woman is known as a defender of the underdog and a passionate advocate of equal rights.

Dotson, Phillip Randolph "Phil" (1948–), artist, educator, entrepreneur. An award-winning artist whose works have been widely exhibited, he has shaped the cultural ambience of the city through his teaching and promotion of other painters, sculptors, and photographers. He was born on October 10, 1948, on a farm near the town of Carthage in Leake County, Mississippi, to Velma Earnest Dotson and Jim O. R. Singleton Dotson. After completing the sixth grade at Harmony High School, he was bused fifteen miles to O. E. Jordan High School in Carthage, Mississippi, where teachers encouraged him. Growing up during the civil rights movement, he remembers the freedom riders, Medgar and Charles Evers's visits to his church, and his father-son photograph in the Smithsonian exhibition *We Shall Never Turn Back*. After graduating from high school in 1966, he won a scholarship to Jackson State College, where he studied under painter Lawrence A. Jones. He received a bachelor's degree in art education in 1970, as well as a master of fine arts in painting from the University of Mississippi in 1972.

Dotson joined the faculty of LeMoyne-Owen College in 1972, serving as director of art, curator of collections, and chairman of the Division of Fine Arts & Humanities. As an educator, he has organized exhibitions and cultural programs, served on the boards of the Memphis Arts Festival and Memphis Arts Council's Arts in the Schools, been artistic consultant for businesses and cultural organizations, illustrated three medical books, and co-edited *Homespun Images: An Anthology of Black Memphis Writers and Artists*. As an artist who works in various media, he has moved from surrealism to an expressionism that has been heavily influenced by his travels to African countries. His large, vibrant canvases have been exhibited at museums, galleries, and universities such as the Studio Museum in Harlem, Stax Museum, and Beach Institute in Savannah. His first one-man show opened at Gestine's Gallery on Beale Street in 1989, when 24 of his paintings were exhibited. With motifs such as cotton bolls and magnolia flowers, these dreamlike, surrealistic paintings evoke the artist's Southern roots. More recent paintings, including "If I Had Some Strings On It, It Would Really Sound Good," from the 2003 *Vision From Within: New Images from Historically Black Colleges and Universities* exhibition in Dallas, depict the rich colors and tribal images of West Africa's Ashanti tribe. Dotson's spiritual growth has led to the creation of another group of paintings called "works of praise," which reveal how he found strength in God after the breakup of his twenty-five-year marriage to Judith Kerr Dotson, a teacher and mother of their three children: Phillip, Tiffany, and Brian. In 2006, the Memphis Theological Seminary presented an exhibition of Dotson's work, entitled *Is It Life or Is It Art?*, at Lindenwood Christian Church. The opening reception included dance, as well as vocal and instrumental interpretations of his paintings, which included "She Loves Gospel Music and African Art" and "Transformation Experience." Chosen an Outstanding Young Man of America in 1979, he has received awards from Memphis in May, Memphis City Council, Black Academy of Arts and Letters, and West Virginia State College. His papers and paintings are in the permanent collection of the Amistad Research Center; he is listed in *Who's Who in Black America*; and he received the People's Choice Award from the Memphis Arts Festival.

Douglas, Lizzie "Memphis Minnie" (1897–1973), blues singer, guitarist, and composer. Called one of the greatest blues singers of all time, she began performing on Beale Street, where she became the reigning blues queen in the 1920s. Lizzie Douglas was born on June 3, 1897, in Algiers, Louisiana, the oldest of thirteen children born to Abe and Gertrude Wells Douglas, but the family moved to Walls, Mississippi, in 1904. A year later, she was given a guitar as a Christmas present, and began her love affair with music. By age fourteen, she was singing and strumming her guitar in Memphis streets under the tutelage of guitarists Frank Stokes and Furry Lewis. A dynamic performer, Douglas joined a Ringling Brothers show and toured the South during World War I. Something of a hellcat, she could keep fresh spectators at bay with a pistol or knife, both of which she knew how to use. While in her teens, she supposedly married Will Weldon, known as "Casey Bill, the Hawaiian Guitar Wizard," a former member of Will Shade's Memphis Jug Band. Douglas and her new partner, guitarist Kansas Joe McCoy, were discovered playing in a Beale Street barber shop by a Columbia scout, who arranged a New York recording session for them in 1929. The couple married later that year. After "Bumble Bee Blues" made her famous, Memphis Minnie moved with Kansas Joe to Chicago, where they played with such blues greats as Big Bill Broozy, Memphis Slim, and Blind John Davis. In 1933, she faced Big Bill in a legendary blues contest; the judges were Tampa Red and Sleepy John Estes, and the prize was two bottles of liquor. Minnie won the contest, but Bill made off with the whiskey. Although Chicago was her home base, Minnie returned often to Memphis and the Mississippi Delta. She played at the Palace and Royal Theatre on Beale Street, but she also sang at friends' houses, Saturday night fish fries, and her celebrated Blue Monday parties.

Douglas and McCoy stopped recording and performing together in 1934, and their marriage soon broke up, primarily because he could not deal with his wife's fame and allure. Memphis Minnie was an independent woman who lived life on her own terms, and she also had a rough edge: she shot craps, chewed tobacco, dipped snuff, drank moonshine, and cussed like a sailor. Noted for her silver dollar bracelet and sparkling gold teeth, she was attractive to men and knew it; a friend reports that "they had to fight the mens away from her." Looks notwithstanding, Douglas was a consummate artist. In the 1930s, she began to experiment with new sounds and produced a more modern, urban guitar style, characterized by single string picking. Later, she began working with Ernest Lawlars, a talented Memphis guitarist known as "Little Son Joe," whom she married in 1939. Minnie and Son Joe began recording in 1940, and her style was constantly evolving, from country to urban blues and from Chicago to postwar blues. In three decades, she recorded over 200 sides on the race labels of Columbia, Vocalion, Okeh, Decca, and Bluebird, and her records were available continuously from 1930 to 1960. One of the first blues artists to use a steel-bodied National guitar, she was an exceptional musician with remarkable guitar skills and tremendous verbal agility and creativity. She was also an outstanding composer of songs with exceptional lyrics, including "I'm a Gambling Woman," "If You See My Rooster," and "Dirty Mother For You." Douglas influenced artists in the blues, jazz, and country idioms, and her songs have been performed by vocalists such as Muddy Waters, Big Mama Thornton, Joyce Cobb, and Bonnie Raitt.

In 1958, Minnie and Son moved back to Memphis because of his heart condition, but Son's health worsened and they had serious money problems. On Saturday nights, they played in a small band at the Red Light in Millington; Minnie even appeared on WDIA and made her last recording session in Memphis in 1959. Subsisting on welfare, they first lived with her brother at 1701 Kansas Street and finally rented a duplex on Linden Avenue. When Minnie suffered a stroke, they moved in with her younger sister at 1355 Adelaide, but—after Son's death, in 1961, and a second stroke—Minnie was taken to Jell Nursing Home. She died in Memphis on August 6, 1973, and was buried without a marker in New Hope Cemetery. She was among the first twenty performers elected to the Hall of Fame at the W. C. Handy Awards presentation in 1980, and she won the top female vocalist award in the first *Blues Unlimited* readers' poll in 1973.

Draper, O'Landa (1963–1998) minister, composer, choir director. A five-time Grammy nominee known for his flamboyant style, Draper was one of the hottest gospel directors in the country. He was born in Chattanooga, Tennessee, on September 29, 1963, to Marie Draper but did not know his natural father until years later. After living in Huntsville, Alabama and Washington, D.C., he and his mother moved to

Memphis when he was eleven years old. At Graceland Junior High School, he joined the glee club, and at Overton High School, where he was a student of the legendary Lulah Hedgeman, he directed his first gospel choir. He also directed the gospel choir at Memphis State University, before dropping out of college. In 1986, while working part-time at FedEx, he formed The Associates, a gospel choir that grew from twelve to sixty members. His mother, a former promoter and recording artist, served as publicist and business manager of the group.

Three years later, Draper, who composed most of the songs for The Associates, wrote a song for Shirley Caesar that landed him a four-year contract with Word Records. Since then, the group has produced six albums and received many awards: a Grammy nomination for *Above and Beyond*; a Grammy and three Stellar nominations for *All the Bases*; and Dove and Stellar awards for the gospel video *Live in Memphis*. In 1998, The Associates won the best choir category at the Premier Player Awards and sang "Oh Happy Day" with the Staple Singers at the ceremony. The choir has cut albums with Shirley Caesar, Yolanda Adams, and Jennifer Holliday, and it has performed with the San Francisco and Memphis Symphony Orchestras. In 1994, Draper and The Associates performed with Billy Joel at the 36th Annual Grammy Awards ceremony and, in 1996, the choir produced its first album for Warner Alliance: *O'Landa Draper and The Associates: Gotta Feelin.'* The group's last release, *Reflection*, became a Top Ten record on Billboard's gospel charts. Called a pioneer in contemporary gospel, Draper got in on the beginning of the boom in gospel music and made a name for Memphis in the process. A former board member of NARAS, he also participated in its Grammy in the Schools program. Known for his charisma, "drop-dead good looks," and energetic directing style, he was constantly on the go, traveling, training choirs, conducting workshops, composing songs, and performing on television. A member of the Greater Community Temple Church of God in Christ, Draper was also an ordained COGIC minister, who directed his own ministry program, counseling inner-city youth, organizing youth retreats, and holding gospel workshops. He recruited choir members, including troubled youth and unwed mothers, from churches throughout the city, and they ministered to others: the homeless, drug addicts, and AIDS patients. His many fans were stunned by O'Landa Draper's untimely death from liver failure, at age thirty-four, on July 21, 1998.

Evers, O. Z. (1925–2001), businessman, politician, civil rights activist. In the vanguard of Memphis's civil rights movement, he was a political leader and successful entrepreneur in the city for more than twenty-five years. Born in Holly Grove, Arkansas, on May 8, 1925, he joined the Navy, in 1943, and earned a Purple Heart after being wounded in the South Pacific. After studying entomology at UCLA, O. Z. Evers (whose initials are his name) spent six months with the California forestry service and then moved to Chicago, where he worked as a policeman for two and a half years. In 1955, he moved to Memphis with money for only one night's lodging at the old Queen Ann Hotel, but a hotel maid opened her home to the Evers family. He soon got a job as a railway mail clerk for the postal service and obtained a license as a public accountant after studying accounting for five years at the segregated University of Tennessee. In April 1956, he boarded a city bus at Bellevue and Lamar and sat on the front seat, but the bus driver ordered him to move to the rear. Evers did not realize that the buses were segregated. He explained: "Over in Arkansas, where I was from, we didn't have no damned buses. So I just didn't know the difference." He was arrested and filed a federal law suit that led to the desegregation of Memphis buses in 1958, when the Supreme Court ruled in his favor. As a result, he was subjected to threats, vandalism, and cross burnings; he was also fired from his post office job. Eventually, he regained his position and received four years' back pay, but he quit after nine days and told Postmaster Moreland, "Get yourself another boy."

After this incident, O. Z. became actively involved in politics and civil rights. He served as president of the Binghamton Civic League and of the local chapter of CORE, and he founded the Unity League Democratic Council, which turned out voters in large numbers. His supporters credited him with making advances in hiring and obtaining city services for Blacks, while his detractors accused him of being a "troublemaker, seller of votes, buyer of politicians, and violator of the Hatch act." Undaunted, the pipe-smoking Evers led marches and a protest against the Greyhound bus station; he was instrumental in desegregating the Memphis Zoo and the Memphis Fairgrounds; he was the first to try to unionize the city's sanitation workers; and he also made several unsuccessful bids for public office. He was more successful in developing his own business. Using the two-year pest control course that he had taken in California under the G. I. Bill, he started the Evers Termite and Pest Control Company and became the first Black to win a Tennessee pest control license from a board that was stacked against African Americans. Ironically, he was later appointed to the Pest Control Board of Tennessee and served as president of the West Tennessee Pest Control Association. He married Dorothy Lee Hatchett on September 8, 1948, and they had six children—Gwendolyn, Portia, Sherri, Kimberly, Kenneth, and Ovell—all of whom went to college. O. Z. Evers died at age seventy-six from complications of diabetes at the Memphis Veterans Medical Center.

Falls, Montee Therese Norman (1897–1980), teacher, pastor, community worker. The daughter of John and Lou Augusta Harris Norman, she was born in Osceola, Arkansas, on July 6, 1897. After a storm, the family moved to Memphis, where young Montee graduated from Kortrecht High School. She received bachelor's and master's degrees from Tennessee A&I State University, and she was awarded two honorary degrees: the Doctor of Divinity from the Association of Unity Churches and the Doctor of Humanities from Monrovia College in Liberia, West Africa. She married Joseph W. Falls, principal of Geeter High School, and they had three children: Mildred, Joseph, Jr., and Phyllis. A committed educator, Montee Falls taught at Geeter and Mitchell High Schools in Shelby County, and she directed the Memphis Division of Tennessee State University. She was also active in community affairs, especially with the Shelby County Tuberculosis Association.

On October 20, 1952, Dr. Falls founded and became the first presiding minister of Unity Center of Memphis (UCOM), conducting services at the Abe Scharff Branch of the YMCA with only twelve members. Two years later, the church, which had grown to a large congregation, moved to a house on the corner of Wellington and LaClede Streets. In 1961, she became the first woman to be licensed and ordained as a Unity minister, serving as minister of UCOM until 1976, during which time she organized three tours to Europe and the Holy Land. In 1971, she received the Outstanding Women's Award in Religion in Memphis. Because of her vision, leadership, and personal achievements, the Unity Center of Memphis dedicated its first annual Dr. Montee Falls Founder's Award at its anniversary celebration in 2002.

Familoni, Jumi Olajumoke (1958–), banker, marketing analyst, dress designer. She was born in March 1958, and grew up in Lagos, Nigeria, with a lifelong interest in clothing design because her mother runs a sewing shop in her homeland. After obtaining a degree in economics, Familoni became a banker in Nigeria, where she served as vice president of the letters of credit division of NAL Merchant Bank in Lagos. She married Babadije Familoni in July 1981, and a month later, they moved to Canada, where her husband completed his doctorate and she worked as a market researcher for radio stations. They are the parents of a son, Eniadewole—meaning "a child of the crown has come"—who is called "Enny" by his classmates. After the family moved to Memphis in 1987, Dr. Familoni became chair of the electrical engineering department at the University of Memphis, and Jumi Familoni received a master's degree, cum laude, in public administration. For a while, she worked as a marketing representative for Mortgage Market Financial Company of Germantown and as an adjunct faculty member at Shelby State Community College, where she taught management and small-business courses.

In 1991, after completing a two-year marketing study, Familoni opened Jumi's International, a dress design store that features African patterns and fabrics, such as Guinea brocade, Kente cotton print, and African royal cloth. Until 1993, she sent her sketches to Lagos, where they were sewn into finished garments. At first, she contracted with a New York garment manufacturer to fill orders from J. C. Penney and other stores. In one of its 1995 specialty catalogs, J. C. Penney featured two of her outfits, including a skirt and top of African Guinea brocade in purple or orange that sold for $179. Her designs sold in Memphis, New York, London, and Nigeria. In 1996, with a loan from Tri-State Bank of Memphis for equipment to set up production, she started a small garment-making operation in Ashland, Mississippi, fifty-five miles southeast of Memphis, where she had a staff of four. She also had a small workshop on Summer Avenue. Locally, her clothes were sold at Dee's Hats and Fashions, a Whitehaven boutique, and at Lowe-Down Sportswear in the Mall of Memphis.

Finch, Larry O. (1951–), athlete, basketball coach. Called the "most important figure in Memphis sports history," he became the first Black to serve as men's basketball coach at Memphis State University. The oldest of seven children, he was born in Memphis on February 16, 1951, and grew up on Select Street in the Orange Mound neighborhood. His father died of a war wound when Larry was only ten years old, so his mother, Mable Finch, worked in private homes to support her children. As a youngster, he played pick-up games in neighborhood parks and playgrounds, and began his illustrious career at Melrose High School, where he perfected his game under William Collins and Verties Sails. A 6' 2" star guard at Melrose, he was an all-state performer. Finch played three seasons, from 1970 to 1973, for Memphis State University, where he compiled an outstanding record. He was named Missouri Valley Conference Athlete of the Year two years in a row, received the Hall of Fame trophy, and All-American Honors from the Associated Press and United Press International. As Tiger captain in his senior year, he led the team to the Final Four championship game against the UCLA Bruins. Finch scored 29 points in the game, racked up 13 MSU scoring records in college, and graduated as the all-time leading scorer in Memphis history with a career total of 1,869 points. His coach declared that Finch was "a great player, a great person, and a great team leader."

After graduating from Memphis State with a B.S. in secondary education in 1973, he had a disappointing two-year stint with the American Basketball Association's Memphis Tams, coached basketball teams at Richland and Messick High Schools for two years, and became assistant coach at the University of Alabama at Birmingham. In 1979, he returned to Memphis State as assistant coach, and, in 1986, was named head coach of the men's basketball team. The legendary coach became "the most recognized name in Memphis basketball history," leading the Tigers to three 20-win seasons, one Metro Tournament championship, and back-to-back appearances in the NCAA Tournament. Twice named Metro Conference Coach of the Year, he took his 1991–1992 team, led by Anfernee Hardaway and David Vaughn, to the Elite Eight of the NCAA tournament. His teams were also impressive in the classroom; his 1988–1989 squad had a cumulative grade point average of 2.79, the highest GPA in men's athletics at MSU.

The charismatic and much-loved hometown hero resigned under pressure in January 1997, ostensibly because of poor recruiting and decreased attendance at The Pyramid. Many fans believed that he was poorly compensated for four decades of service to the University as a Tiger player and coach. His record as the University's winningest men's basketball coach still stands, and he has continued to receive honors and awards: the 1982 Dr. Martin Luther King Humanitarian Award and 2005 Arthur S. Holman Lifetime Achievement Award; and the new basketball wing of the student recreation building was named the Larry O. Finch Recreation Complex. In 1998, he campaigned for Shelby County Registrar but lost by 127 votes to the incumbent. Finch is married to his high school sweetheart, Vickie Stephens Finch, and they have three children: Shanae, Larry, Jr., and James Allawrence. In recent years, he has developed health problems, so his friends have organized Larry Finch Benefit Golf Tournaments to help defray his medical expenses.

Flowers, Arthur R. (1950–), essayist, novelist, cultural activist. One of Memphis's most accomplished creative writers, Flowers has incorporated Black Southern culture into his novels and nonfiction. Born in Nashville on July 30, 1950, he is the son of Memphis physician A. R. Flowers and his wife Eloise. He attended Riverview Elementary School and Carver Junior High School before entering Hamilton High School, where he was named "Mr. Brains" of the 1968 graduating class. After a year at Memphis State University, he served in the U.S. Army for two years. When he completed a tour of duty in Vietnam, he moved to New York to pursue a career in writing. There, for thirteen years, he attended the writing workshop of John Oliver Killens, founder of the Harlem Writers' Guild in the 1950s. Strongly influenced in his philosophy and craftsmanship by Killens, Flowers co-founded and served as executive director of the New Renaissance Writers' Guild in New York and, in the 1990s, he founded the Griot Shop, a literary workshop in Memphis.

A talented singer and harmonica player, Flowers describes himself as a literary blues and hoodoo man who has a social and political responsibility to shape values and to reconceptualize African American identity. His first novel, *De Mojo Blues* (1986), traces the lives of three Vietnam veterans who choose different lifestyles and methods of redefining Black masculinity in the 1970s; one of the characters, Tucept Highjohn, returns to Memphis, where he becomes an apprentice of hoodoo on Beale Street. His second novel, *Another Good Loving Blues* (1993), describes the love affair of a conjure woman and a bluesman during the Great Migration, a period of increased racial tension and violence, when Blacks struggled to survive. His third book, *Mojo Rising: Confessions of a 21st-Century Hoodoo Man*, which he calls an intellectual memoir, was published in 2003 by Wanagegresse Press, the publishing arm of Sheree Thomas, another Memphis writer/editor/publisher.

Flowers is presently working on *Rest for the Weary*, based on the myth of Highjohn the Conqueror, which "attempts to define memphis and the delta as african american holyground," he writes. In all of his creative writing, Flowers, who calls himself a contemporary griot, draws heavily upon Black folk culture, particularly blues music, hoodoo spirituality, Delta dialect, folk tales, toasts, and other elements of the oral tradition. He writes that he is "also working on a hoodoo sacred text, the hoodoo book of flowers, and trying to modernize and reconcept the hoodoo tradition into one of the world's great spiritual/magical traditions." The recipient of a National Endowment for the Arts Fellowship for fiction, A. R. Flowers taught writing workshops at the City University of New York (CUNY), and, presently, teaches creative writing in the M.F.A. program at Syracuse University.

Ford, Harold Eugene (1945–), funeral director, state legislator, congressman, lobbyist. The patriarch of a powerful Black political family, he served for four years in the Tennessee State Legislature and for twenty-two years in the United States Congress. One of the twelve surviving children of Vera Davis Ford and Newton Jackson Ford, he was born in Memphis on May 20, 1945. In 1963, he graduated from Geeter High School, which was named for his paternal great grandfather. While a student at Tennessee State University, he worked as a waiter at the Jackson Hotel and was chosen "Mr. Esquire" in his senior year. In summer 1966, he planned and managed his father's unsuccessful campaign for the state legislature. After earning a bachelor's degree in business administration from Tennessee State in 1967, he entered John A. Gupton College, from which he received an associate degree in mortuary science in 1969. A year later, he defeated incumbent James I. Taylor to gain a seat in the Tennessee General Assembly from District Five, while continuing to work in the family business, N. J. Ford & Sons Funeral Parlor. He married the former Dorothy Bowles of Memphis, from whom he is now divorced, and they are the parents of three sons: Harold, Jr., Jake, and Isaac. A savvy South Memphis street politician and Kennedy-style Democrat, Ford served two terms as a state legislator. In 1974, he narrowly defeated four-term Republican incumbent Dan Kuykendall to win the Eighth Congressional District (presently the Ninth District) seat by only 600 votes, becoming the youngest member of the U.S. Congress at age twenty-nine, as well as the first African American to represent Tennessee in the twentieth century. He easily won reelection in 1976 and 1978, ran unopposed in 1980, and had little opposition thereafter.

During his eleven terms in the House, Harold Ford supported a liberal agenda: he favored national health insurance, extension of the Voting Rights Act, and welfare for two-parent families; he worked to eliminate Black unemployment and to prevent teen pregnancy; and he picketed the big oil companies and protested apartheid in South Africa. In the Congress, he was a member of the powerful Ways and Means Committee, chaired the Subcommittee on Human Resources, and served on the House Select Committee on Assassinations, which investigated the assassination of Martin Luther King, Jr. After helping to craft the Welfare Reform Bill, he was named 1987 Child Advocate of the Year by the Child Welfare League of America. As Democratic Zone Whip, he served on the Democratic Steering and Policy Committee, which defines party policy and chooses committee leaders. Charismatic and personable, the congressman, who made the best-dressed lists of both *Ebony* and the weekly *Roll Call*, was a dashing figure on Capitol Hill. For three and a half years, he attended night classes twice a week to earn an MBA with honors from Howard University in 1982.

Known to his siblings as "The Rock." Ford built up a strong, family-centered political base and established himself as the dominant political force in Memphis through "hard work, constituent service, a great family name, and service to the Black community," according to supporters. His detractors suggest, however, that he has built up a machine to back his friends and family. In one election, for example, seven members of the Ford family were candidates for public office. He was also criticized for grooming his son as his successor, as well as for supporting his brother, John, in the divisive mayoral race that led to the victory of Dick Hackett in 1983. In the 1980s, he struggled with personal and business debts, and he fought federal bank fraud, mail fraud, and conspiracy charges for six years. Many observers felt that the charges were politically motivated and, after his acquittal in 1993, he blamed the ordeal on White racists. When he completed his last congressional term in 1996, Harold Ford retired from public office and moved to Miami, where he works as a lobbyist.

Ford, Harold Eugene, Jr. (1970–), congressman. The first son to succeed his father in the U.S. House of Representatives, he represents a new generation of political leaders with a pragmatic, centrist approach to social and economic issues. He was born in Memphis on May 11, 1970, the eldest of the three sons of Harold E. Ford and Dorothy Bowles Ford. He recalls, "There were three things we had no choice about doing when we were growing up: our homework, going to church, and working in political campaigns." At age four, he cut a radio spot for his father supporting better schools, better housing, and "lower cookie prices," and, later, he stood up and raised his right hand as Harold, Sr., was sworn into office. When he was in the fourth grade, the family moved to Washington, where he attended the prestigious St. Albans School for Boys. In 1992, he received a bachelor's degree in American history from the University of Pennsylvania and a law degree from the University of Michigan School of Law in 1996. During breaks, he held government internships, worked on the Clinton/Gore Transition Team, and campaigned for his father's reelection in 1992 and 1994.

In 1996, at age twenty-six, Harold Ford, Jr., was elected, with 62% of the vote, to the U.S. House of Representatives from Tennessee's heavily Democratic, Black-majority Ninth Congressional District. During the second session of the 106th Congress, he was chosen freshman class president. In his second election, he won 80% of the vote, including 42% in predominantly White districts and, two years later, he ran uncontested. He was cast into the national limelight when he delivered the keynote address at the 2000 Democratic National Convention. A centrist New Democrat, described as "smart, articulate, politically tough and wise beyond his years," he has focused on education, health care, and campaign reform as a member of the House Education and Workforce Committee, Government Reform Committee, and Subcommittee on the Census. As a member of the Congressional Black Caucus, he supports affirmative action and is against tax cuts, but as the youngest member of the moderate-to-conservative Blue Dog Coalition, he supports trade agreements and national education testing.

In spite of his moderate voting record, he opposes the president's energy proposals, wants to reform the illegal drug policy, and introduced legislation in 2006 to require the president to budget for wars in Iraq and Afghanistan. Many consider his good looks a political plus. At 6' 1" and about 180 pounds, the trim, young Democrat, who wears Gucci loafers and tailored suits, was cited as a "fresh face" in *People* magazine's "50 Most Beautiful People" issue in 2001. After the 2002 elections, Ford upset some members of Congress by announcing his candidacy for House Democratic Leader, challenging then-House Minority Whip Nancy Pelosi. He lost by a margin of 29 to 177, but, after five terms in Congress, he announced his candidacy for the Senate seat vacated by Bill Frist. In the 2006 Senate race, he won the Democratic primary but lost the November general election to Republican Bob Corker by a statewide margin of less than 3 percentage points or about 50,000 votes.

Ford, Newton Jackson (1914–1986), businessman, mortician. Described by his son as "a champion, who knew how to live with pain and move right ahead," he founded one of Memphis's largest Black funeral homes. He was born in Memphis on June 12, 1914, to Ophelia Edna Geeter Ford, a teacher, and Lewie C. Ford, owner of a funeral home. His family had deep roots in Shelby County: his maternal grandfather, Jackson Geeter, for whom Geeter School is named, served in the Civil War; and his paternal grandfather, Newton F. Ford, for whom Ford Road School is named, served as a county squire. He attended elementary school in Shelby County and, after graduating from Manassas High School, became a busboy and keeper of the ducks at the Peabody Hotel, where he met his future wife, Vera Davis.

Although he was unable to attend college, he used his pay to help finance his sister's education. In 1932, he followed in his father's footsteps and opened the N. J. Ford Funeral Home, later renamed the N. J. Ford & Sons Funeral Parlor, now located at 12 S. Parkway West. A mortician and licensed funeral director, he was active in his profession, serving as president of the Bluff City Funeral Directors, chairman of the Tennessee State Funeral Directors and Morticians Association, and assistant executive secretary of the National Funeral Directors and Morticians Association, which named him "Man of the Year" in 1978.

N. J. Ford was perhaps best known as a devoted family man and patriarch of the Ford family. He and his wife had fifteen children, twelve of whom survived. Although their children grew up in a small house on Horn Lake Road, near Boxtown, they all graduated from Tennessee State University, and four of the sons entered politics. In 1974, Harold was elected to the United States Congress and Emmit became a member of the Tennessee State Legislature; John served as a city councilman, state senator, and clerk of the General Sessions Office; and James was elected to the City Council and served as chair. Throughout his life, Ford was active in civic and community affairs. In 1966, he made an unsuccessful bid for the state legislature and, in 1977, he became a delegate to the State Constitutional Convention. Active in scouting for many years, he served as chairman of the Southwest District Chickasaw Council of Boy Scouts and received the Boy Scouts' Silver Beaver Award in 1979. He was a lifelong member of Ford's Chapel A.M.E. Zion Church, which was founded by his grandfather, Squire Newton F. Ford. In 1977, he and his family were cited for their "significant contributions on the local, state, and national levels" at a banquet at the Holiday Inn-Rivermont. A life member of the NAACP, he participated in the civil rights movement and often provided cars for Martin Luther King and other leaders. N. J. Ford died unexpectedly of a heart attack on September 13, 1986, and is buried in the cemetery at Ford's Chapel A.M.E. Zion Church.

Franklin, Aretha (1942–). singer, composer. For forty-five years, the "Queen of Soul" has performed before kings and presidents, produced award-winning singles and albums, and thrilled audiences with her jazz, R&B, and gospel compositions. One of the five children of Clarence L. Franklin and Barbara Siggers Franklin, Aretha was born in Memphis on March 25, 1942. Her father was pastor of New Salem Baptist Church, and the family lived at 406 Lucy, but, when she was two years old, the family moved to Buffalo, New York, and then to Detroit, Michigan, where her father pastored New Bethel Baptist Church. After teaching herself to sing and play the piano when she about nine years old, Aretha cut her first single for Chess Records at age twelve. She also began touring with her father's evangelist group and singing in local churches with a group that included her sister and two other girls. At age fifteen, she gave birth to her first son, Clarence, Jr., and, a year later, she dropped out of Northern High School after her second son, Edward (Eddie), was born. In 1960, Franklin went to New York, hired a manager, took singing and dancing lessons, and signed a contract with Columbia Records. During her five years with Columbia, she made nine albums, including *Electrifying Aretha Franklin*, *Runnin' Out of Fools*, and *Unforgettable*, but her recordings of ballads and jazz songs achieved only moderate success. Having triumphed on the gospel circuit as a teenager, she toured the "chitlin'" circuit in the early 1960s, making one-night stands in southern towns, where hotels and restaurants were closed to Blacks. She married Ted White in 1962, and they had a son, Theodore "Teddy" White, but the marriage ended in 1969. After performing at the Newport and Lower Ohio Jazz festivals and touring Bermuda, the Bahamas, and Puerto Rico, she gained a wider audience, but it was not until the mid-1960s that her career took off.

In 1967, Franklin signed with Atlantic Records, a small company specializing in R&B, whose producers encouraged her to sing her own compositions, do her own arrangements, and accompany herself on the piano. That year, she recorded five golden singles, including "Respect" and "Baby, I Love you," made two albums—*I Never Loved a Man* and *Aretha Arrives*—that passed the one million mark, and was named top female vocalist of 1967 by *Billboard*, *Cashbox*, and *Record World* magazines. A year later, her soul version of "The Star Spangled Banner" opened the National Democratic Convention in Chicago. She married actor Glynn Turman in 1978, but they were divorced in 1984. Although her career suffered a down-turn during the disco craze of the 1970s, she made a strong comeback in the 1980s, when she appeared in *The Blues Brothers* film. Since then, "Lady Soul," who sings jazz, rock, blues, pop, gospel, and even opera, has won 41 Grammy nominations and 19 Grammys, including 11 for Best Female R&B Vocal Performer. Reported to have a vocal range of four octaves, the diva sang "Nessun Dorma" at the 1999 Grammy telecast, after Luciano Pavarotti became ill.

Aretha Franklin has received numerous awards. In 1987, she became the first woman named to the Rock and Roll Hall of Fame and she received the National Medal of Arts from President Bill Clinton in 1999. In 2005, she received the Presidential Medal of Freedom from President George W. Bush as well as an honorary Doctor of Music from Berklee College of Music in 2006. She was also cited by the Southern Christian Leadership Conference for her work on behalf of civil rights causes.

Frazier, Levi, Jr. (1951–), actor, director, poet, screen- and scriptwriter. The son of Sallie Mae Keith Frazier and Levi Frazier, he was born in Memphis on July 3, 1951. He graduated from Catholic High School for Boys in 1969, received a bachelor's degree in psychology and communication arts from Southwestern at Memphis in 1973, and a master's in speech and communications from Memphis State University in 1975. While a high school student, he developed an interest in theater and began acting in the Memphis Youth Theater and, later, performing at Southwestern. His work in communications led to positions at WREC radio, Southwest Tennessee Community College, Memphis State University, and State Technical Institute, where he was a scriptwriter and audio-visual coordinator. In 1974, he helped found the Beale Street Repertory Company and, in 1979, he and his wife, Deborah Glass Frazier, co-founded the Blues City Cultural Center, Memphis's only Black professional theater company. With Levi as artistic director and Deborah as general manager, the performing and visual arts organization presented plays about the Southern Black experience, such as Tom Dent's *Ritual Murder*; offered Saturday classes in dance, theater, and music; performed in churches and community centers; put on workshops and conferences; and created the Trolley Stop Creative Arts Camp for children.

Levi Frazier has written poetry, nonfiction—*151 Things That Happen or Don't Happen When You Turn Fifty*—and short stories such as "The Witch Doctor," published in *Homeworks '96: A Book of Tennessee Writers*. He is best known, however, as a playwright whose works include *Sis' Moses*; *The Way We Was or The Wrong Place at the Right Time*; *Lies, Legends and Tales of Tennessee*; and *Paul Robeson All-American*, which he wrote and staged at Southwestern in 1974 and at Mud Island's Mississippi River Museum in 1986. His musical, *Down on Beale*, was first performed at LeMoyne-Owen College in 1972, as part of the W. C. Handy Festival, and was later performed at numerous venues both in and outside Memphis, including off-off Broadway at The Richard Allen Center for Culture & Art in New York in 1979 and at the New Daisy Theater in 1985. His *Beale Street Back Again*, presented at the Tennessee Performing Arts Center, was part of the state's bicentennial celebration in 1996. Frazier was invited to produce his *Tribute to Richard Wright* in Paris as part of an international festival on African American writers in

France. In 1992, he was one of three writers chosen nationally to be a Fellow at the Alabama Shakespeare Festival as part of the Southern Writers Project. *When It Rains...*, which premiered in New Orleans at the Contemporary Art Center as part of the 1994 Playwright's Festival, won first place in the Chattanooga Theater Center's 2002 Play Writing Contest and received a featured reading in 1993 at the National Black Theater Festival in North Carolina.

Freeman, Morgan (1937–), actor. An Academy Award-winning movie star, he has appeared in Shakespearean dramas, Broadway plays, musical theater, television programs, and more than forty films. He was born in Memphis on June 1, 1937, the son of Morgan Porterfield Freeman and Mayme Edna Revere. When he was two years old, he was sent to live with his paternal grandmother, Evie Freeman, in Charleston, Mississippi, and, after her death, he and his sister joined their mother in Chicago. Later, he and his sister moved to Gary to live with their father and, finally, his maternal grandmother, Lenore Greenlee Revere, took the children, their pregnant mother, and two older brothers to live with her in Greenwood, Mississippi. Morgan began acting in junior high school and won the Best Actor Award in the 1950 state tournament, while his school won the district and state championships. After graduating from high school, he joined the Air Force and then went to Hollywood to become an actor, working as a clerk to pay for acting and tap dancing lessons at Los Angeles City College. In the early 1960s, he moved to New York, where he landed his first significant role in an off-Broadway play, *The Nigger-Lovers*, in 1967, which led to roles in the all-Black production of *Hello, Dolly*; the children's television program, *The Electric Company*; and the NBC soap opera, *Another World*.

In the 1970s and early '80s, Morgan Freeman won awards for his performances in *Coriolanus, Julius Caesar,* and *Mother Courage* in the New York Shakespeare Festival, and he won an Obie as best actor in the 1983 production of *The Gospel at Colonus,* as well as for his starring role in the stage play *Driving Miss Daisy.* He also appeared in films, such as *Street Smart,* in which he gave a powerful performance as a half-psychotic pimp; and *Glory,* which depicted the heroism of an all-Black regiment during the Civil War. He received three Oscar nominations: Best Supporting Actor for *Street Smart* (1987) and Best Actor for *Driving Miss Daisy* (1989) and *The Shawshank Redemption* (1994). Critical of the negative representations of Blacks in films and on stage, he chooses his roles carefully, selecting those in which the character is portrayed as a person of depth and substance. An intuitive actor, he brings sensitivity, subtlety of expression, and a profound understanding of character to his craft. In the past two decades, he has directed *Bopha!,* narrated documentaries, won a 2004 NAACP Image Award; and received an Oscar in 2005 for Best Supporting Actor in *Million Dollar Baby.*

Freeman often relaxes by plying the waters of the Caribbean and North America in his 38-foot sailboat, accompanied by his wife and one of his seven grandchildren. The actor, who has four children—Alphonse, Saifoulaye, Deena, and Morgana—was married to Jeanette Adair Bradshaw between 1967 and 1979, and wed costume designer Myrna Colley-Lee on June 16, 1984. The Freemans now live on a 12-acre estate, "Sonedna," in Charleston, Mississippi, where they are active in the cultural, economic, and educational life of the Mid-South. Committed to the education of young people, he funded scholarships at Mississippi State and The University of Mississippi, created the Myrna Colley-Lee and Edena Hines Creative Dramatics Chair at The Hutchinson School, and established the Morgan Freeman Foundation to improve education in Mississippi. He also owns an upscale restaurant (Madidi) and blues club (Ground Zero) in Clarksdale, and, in 2003, he introduced his film, *Levity,* at the fourth annual Memphis International Film Festival. In 2004, he received the inaugural "Cast in Memphis" award from Theatre Memphis and, two years later, was awarded an honorary Doctor of Arts and Letters by Delta State University. Journalist Kathleen Trace has traced the actor's life in *Morgan Freeman: A Biography*, which was published in 2006.

Fuller, Thomas Oscar (1867–1942), author, educator, state senator, religious leader. As a proponent of racial accommodationism, Fuller became an influential community spokesman during the first quarter of the twentieth century. The son of Mary Eliza Kearney and J. Henderson Fuller, he was born in Franklin County, North Carolina, on October 25, 1867, the youngest of fourteen children. His father, a carpenter and wheelwright, bought his family's freedom from slavery before the Civil War. After graduating from the State Normal School in Franklin, Fuller attended Shaw University, from which he received a bachelor's degree in 1890 and a master's in 1893. After teaching in the public schools, he became principal of Shiloh Institute and founded the Girl's Training School in Franklin. The sole Black elected to the North Carolina State Senate in 1898, Fuller took office two days after a mob of Whites burned a newspaper office and shot innocent Blacks in Wilmington, North Carolina. In response, the senator urged nonviolence and nonresistance rather than militant protest. In 1899, he lobbied unsuccessfully against an amendment that would disenfranchise Blacks. In 1900, he accepted the pastorate of Memphis's First Baptist Church, where he continued to preach his philosophy of racial accommodationism, based on the precepts of Booker T. Washington. After the death of his first wife, Laura Faulkner Fuller in 1902, he married Memphian Rosa B. Baker in 1904, and the Fullers had two children, Thomas Oscar, Jr., and Erskine.

Called the "Apostle of Peace," he urged compliance with the law mandating segregation on Memphis streetcars. Subsequently, he was appointed chairman of the Negro Advisory Board to the Memphis Housing Authority, and E. H. "Boss" Crump paid tribute to him on his death. Fuller was frequently criticized by militant Black leaders, particularly members of the NAACP, who did not share his views or approve of his actions, particularly his efforts to rename the Negro Industrial School the Booker T. Washington High School. He believed in appeal rather than protest, proclaiming, "I shall DEMAND nothing, but shall gently and earnestly PLEAD..." He founded the Inter-Racial League to lobby for better schools and recreational facilities for Blacks; the League also organized a parade against crime and requested less brutal treatment of Blacks by policemen and streetcar conductors.

A strong supporter of education, T. O. Fuller taught at Howe Institute, a private elementary and secondary institution in Memphis. A well-educated man, he distributed weekly sermon outlines to the Black ministers who attended his classes in theology, homiletics, and church history. When he became principal of Howe in 1902, Fuller expanded the curriculum and increased enrollment to 300 students. After Howe merged with Nashville's Roger Williams College in 1927, Fuller became the first president of the combined institution. An author and lay historian, he wrote and published several pamphlets and books to underscore the achievements of Blacks. Two of his earliest works were *Banks and Banking* (1920), designed as a textbook, and *Flashes and Gems of Thought and Eloquence* (1920), which includes statements that he heard at National Baptist conventions. In 1933, he published *Pictorial History of the American Negro...A Story of Progress and Development Along Social, Economic and Spiritual Lines*, a monumental work of research and scholarship. He also wrote an autobiography, *Twenty Years in Public Life* (1910), and *History of the Negro Baptists of Tennessee* (1936). Nine days before his death in 1942, Shelby Bluffs State Park, a 1,000-acre facility on Mitchell Road, was renamed the T. O. Fuller State Park.

Gayles, Gloria Jean Wade (1937–), activist, poet, scholar, college professor. Described as a master teacher, she was born on July 1 as the third child of Bertha Reese Wade and Robert Wade. Although she was born in Memphis, she and her sister Faye spent summers in Chicago with their father who took them on visits to the University of Chicago. In her memoir, *Pushed Back to Strength: A Black Woman's Journey Home*, she describes her growing-up years in Foote Homes Housing Project, where her mother and grandmother stimulated her intellectual growth. As class salutatorian at Booker T. Washington High School, she followed in the footsteps of her mother, who had been valedictorian of her class. Wade graduated from LeMoyne College "with distinction" and, as a Woodrow Wilson Fellow, continued her education at Boston University. After receiving a master's degree in 1963, she joined the faculty at Spelman College. Because of her participation in the civil rights movement, which resulted in her spending four and a half days in solitary confinement, the College did not renew her contract. The following summer, she worked in Mississippi, registering voters and teaching in a Freedom School. These and other experiences fueled her early writing, including her first published poems and an essay for *The Atlantic Monthly*. That fall, she moved to Washington, D.C., where she joined the faculty at Howard University. In 1967, she married Joseph Gayles and two children—Jonathan and Monica—were born to the union. After two years in San José, California, the couple moved to Atlanta, where Wade-Gayles rejoined the faculty at Spelman and completed a doctorate in American Studies from Emory University in 1981. She has taught at Talladega, Morehouse, Howard, and Bennett, and, for three years, served as Eminent Scholar's Chair in the Humanities at Dillard University, but her most sustained work has been at Spelman, where she began her teaching career.

In 1991, Dr. Gayles was named recipient of the President's Award for Outstanding Scholarship; in 1997, inducted into Phi Beta

Kappa; and in 2000, named Eminent Scholar's Chair in Independent Scholarship and Service Learning. In that same year, she began mentoring students in Spelman's Independent Scholars (SIS) and founded the SIS Oral History Project, which collects the life stories of older African American women in the South and preserves the stories in published volumes entitled *Their Memories, Our Treasure: Conversations with African American Women of Wisdom*. A prolific writer, she has authored *Push Back to Strength*; *No Crystal Stair: Visions of Race and Sex in Black Women's Novels*; *Anointed to Fly* (poetry); and *Rooted Against the Wind: Personal Essays*. She has edited *"My Soul Is a Witness": African American Women's Spirituality*; *Father Songs: Testimonies by African-American Sons and Daughters*; *In Praise of Our Teachers*; and *Conversations with Gwendolyn Brooks*. A former DuBois Fellow at Harvard University, she has received many awards for her teaching and scholarship, including an honorary degree from Meadville-Lombard Theological School, Emory Medal for outstanding scholarship and service, LeMoyne-Owen Dubois Scholar's Award, and CASE Professor of Teaching Excellence for the State of Georgia.

Gilliam, Dorothy Butler (1936–), journalist. One of the first Black women to break into the predominantly White, male-controlled media, she has served as a newspaper reporter, editor, and columnist, as well as a television newswoman. She was born on November 24, 1936, in Memphis, the eighth of Jessie Mae Norment Butler and Adee Conklin Butler's ten children. When Dorothy was five years old, the family moved to Louisville, Kentucky, where her father pastored Young's Chapel A.M.E. Church. She was only fourteen when her father died and her mother had to work as a domestic to support her children. As a sixteen-year-old freshman at Ursuline

College, she worked after classes as a secretary for the *Louisville Defender*, a Black weekly newspaper. One day, the editor asked her to substitute for a sick reporter, and she was forever hooked on journalism. After graduation from historically Black Lincoln University, she was hired by Alex Wilson, editor of the *Tri-State Defender* in Memphis. At the time, he was covering the integration of schools in Little Rock but would not let her accompany him because he said that it was too dangerous. She went anyway and, as a result, came to the attention of reporters from *Jet*, and she was hired to work for that periodical.

After serving an apprenticeship in the Black press and graduating from Columbia University Graduate School of Journalism, she was hired by *The Washington Post* in 1961. One of the few African American journalists at *The Post*, she had to overcome many personal and professional obstacles, but she had some challenging assignments, including covering James Meredith's entry into The University of Mississippi. In the meantime, she married Sam Gilliam, an acclaimed artist, and they had three children. Wanting to spend more time with their children, she took a part-time job with Channel 5 and became one of the first Blacks hired in television. Seven years later, she was rehired as an assistant editor in *The Post*'s Style section. After writing several articles on Paul Robeson, she published *Paul Robeson: All American* in 1976. In 1979, she became a *Post* columnist, a position that, she says, gave her an opportunity to find her voice, "to grow and develop as a writer and thinker." In the eighteen years that Gilliam served as a columnist, she wrote more than 1,500 columns dealing with issues and problems that affect the country, from the perspective of an African American woman. In 1998, she took on a new position at *The Post* as director of a program to train young, prospective journalists in the Washington area. Under the supervision of forty *Post* editors and reporters, local high school and college students published newspapers, attended classes and workshops, and received journalism scholarships

Dorothy Gilliam, as a career professional and a volunteer, has worked to increase racial diversity in the news industry. In 1977, she and several colleagues incorporated the Institute for Journalism Education, a nonprofit organization based in California, to help train minorities for careers in journalism. She was one of the founding directors and served as board chair from 1985 to 1993. She also served as head of the 3,000-member National Association of Black Journalists from 1993 to 1995. Under her leadership, the NABJ held an historic unity convention in 1994, which brought together 7,000 journalists of color to advance racial diversity in the media. Working continuously to master her craft, Gilliam spent a 1991 sabbatical at the Freedom Forum in New York and a 1996 sabbatical at Harvard University's Institute of Politics. In the summer of 1998, she trained journalists at newspapers in Johannesburg and Cape Town, South Africa, as part of the Knight International Press Fellowship Program. She is presently director of Prime Movers at the George Washington University School of Media and Public Affairs. The program, which began in 2004, is designed to initiate or revitalize print and broadcast programs at four senior high schools in the Washington, D.C. area.

Gilliam, Herman Arthur, Jr. "Art" (1943–), businessman. One of the city's most successful broadcasters, he has been a leader in community and professional organizations. The son of Leola and H. A. Gilliam, an officer of Universal Life Insurance Company, he was born on May 1, 1943. He grew up in Memphis, where he attended Hamilton Elementary and High School from the fourth through tenth grades, after which he transferred to Westminster Preparatory School in Simsbury, Connecticut. At age sixteen, he was among the top three or four graduates of Westminister. After receiving a bachelor's degree in economics from Yale University, he completed a master's in business administration from the University of Michigan. On his return to Memphis in 1967, he began full-time work as a claims manager and assistant actuary at Universal Life Insurance Company and was promoted to vice president in charge of claims and underwriting in 1970. During this period, he also became involved in communications, serving as an editorial columnist for *The Commercial Appeal* and as a weekend news anchor for Channel 5, WMC-TV. In 1974, he was named one of the Ten Outstanding Young Men in America by the U.S. Jaycees. When he became an administrative assistant to Congressman Harold Ford in 1974, he relocated to Washington, D.C. but returned to Memphis a year later to found Gilliam Communications, Inc. "I enjoyed media and I formed the company in 1975," he said, "because I saw it as the direction that I wanted to go in. That allowed me to return to what I had been doing but in an ownership capacity." As president and chairman of the board, he spent a year pursuing financing for the purchase of WLOK, a twenty-six-year-old radio station, which Gilliam Communications bought from Starr Broadcasting for $725,000.

As station manager, Art Gilliam has reached out to the African American community through such crowd-pleasing initiatives as the annual Stone Soul Picnic, more than doubling the size of the listening audience and making WLOK among the top five Memphis radio stations. Convinced that the station ought "to be uplifting to the community," he changed the format of the station from soul/pop to gospel in 1983, and, four years later, it received the 1987 Black Business of the Year Award from the Memphis Black Business Association. Designated as a Tennessee historic landmark, the station gives away food baskets, sponsors voter registration drives, holds live concerts for local churches, and offers scholarships to LeMoyne-Owen College and the University of Memphis. "WLOK has one of the most loyal audiences in Memphis," he said. "We are successful because of our listeners; they are the core of the station's success." Art Gilliam has also been active in the educational and professional fields. He has served on the Memphis State University Board of Visitors and he succeeded his father on the board of trustees of LeMoyne-Owen College in 1973. He also served on the board of the Memphis Zoo, Inc., as well as as treasurer of the Memphis Black Business Association. A member of the Tennessee Association of Broadcasting, National Association of Broadcasters, and National Association of Black Owned Broadcasters, he was treasurer and a member of the board of governors of the National Academy of Recording Arts and Science.

Green, Leorns "Al" (1946–), singer, composer, clergyman. One of the most critically acclaimed soul singers of the 1970s, Green became a minister and gospel singer. He was born on April 13, 1946, to sharecroppers in Forrest City, Arkansas, forty miles outside of Memphis. Influenced by the gospel style of Claude Jeter of the Swan Silvertones, he started performing at age nine in a family gospel group called The Green Brothers. When he was thirteen, his family moved to Grand Rapids, Michigan, where he continued to sing gospel music, but several years later, he was dropped from the act for listening to the secular music of Jackie Wilson. Green then formed an R&B group called the Creations, cut his first record, "Back Up Train," in 1967, and produced a national hit in 1970 with "I Can't Get Next to You." Often compared to Sam Cooke and Otis Redding, Al Green opened the show for Memphis bandleader Willie Mitchell in Midland, Texas, in 1968. That meeting was fortuitous for both men. Green moved to Memphis in 1971 to record for Mitchell, who became his mentor and producer at Hi Recording Studios. Under Mitchell's guidance, he racked up seven Top Ten hits in one three-year stretch. Known for his "sweet, soulful falsetto," he sang sophisticated arrangements in hits such as "Tired of Being Alone," "Let's Stay Together," and "L-O-V-E." He often performs in Memphis; in 1973, "Al Green Day" was held in Memphis's Mid-South Coliseum to benefit the Police Service Centers, and he performed at the Beale Street Music Festival in Tom Lee Park in 1992.

Although he enjoyed critical and commercial success in the early 1970s, fame and fortune led him into the fast life of sex, booze, and drugs. In 1974, Mary Woodson, a married lover, threw hot Cream of Wheat (not grits, as was reported) on him while he was bathing and then shot herself to death with his gun. His June 15, 1977, marriage to Shirley Anne Watts Kyles, a member of his backup singing group, ended in divorce and three children. In 1979, the singer fell off of a stage during a performance in Cincinnati. Green realized that he had to change his way of living after having a religious epiphany in a motel room in Orange County, California. At the time, he had a fourteen-piece band, was at the top of the soul music charts, and had twenty-four gold and platinum records. He gave that all up to become a Baptist minister and bought a church in Whitehaven for $355,000. Reverend Green held his first worship service at the Full Gospel Tabernacle Church on December 17, 1976. His new vocation had a dramatic impact on his music—he moved from soul music back to gospel. But the singer did not miss a beat. He won a Grammy in 1980 for his first gospel album, *The Lord Will Make a Way*, and he won seven more gospel Grammys between 1981 and 1990. In 1995, he returned to the music that made him famous—soul and R&B. That year, he recorded *Your Heart Is in Good Hands*, his first secular album in twenty years.

One thing led to another. In 1982, Green co-starred with Patti LaBelle as a minister in *Your Arm's Too Short to Box with God* at the Alvin Theater on Broadway. A musical portrait of Green appeared in the 1984 film *The Gospel According to Al Green*. Many honors and awards were presented to him in the 1990s. He received Memphis State University's 19th Annual Distinguished Achievement Award for the Creative and Performing Arts in 1990. That same year, he won a Grammy for Best Soul Gospel Vocal Performance for the single "As Long as We're Together," and he also won the first pop music Grammy for a duet, "Funny How Time Slips Away," with Lyle Lovett. In 1994, he was inducted into the Rock and Roll Hall of Fame, in recognition of the million-selling hits that he had recorded for Hi Records, and he gave the final performance in the closing ceremony at the 1996 Olympics in Atlanta. Calling himself a "down-home country boy," Green has lived since 1972 on a farm in Shelby Forest, eight miles west of Millington. He lives there with his second wife and son, Al, Jr., who was born in 1995.

Green, Mildred Denby (1938–), college professor, choir director, composer, music scholar. One of Memphis's foremost historians of Black music, she has taught at two of the city's historically Black colleges for forty years. The daughter of Howard C. Denby, a painting contractor, and his wife, Wanetah Benn Denby, she was born on August 25, 1938, in Portsmouth, Virginia, where she attended Truxton Elementary School and graduated from I. C. Norcom High School. She attributes her interest in music to early experiences and to studies with noted musicians such as Noah F. Ryder, Undine Moore and Altona Johns. After two years at Oberlin, she transferred to Ohio State University, from which she received a bachelor's degree in music education in 1959. A few months after graduation, on August 15, 1959, she married Reuben Green, an ordained minister who later became a college professor, and they have two sons, Reuben II and Howard. In 1962, she received a master's in music education, and thirteen years later, she completed a doctorate in music education from the University of Oklahoma.

Dr. Mildred Green has made significant contributions to the Memphis community through her work as a college professor and music historian. She and her husband moved to Memphis in 1963, when they joined the faculty of Owen College, a private Baptist college, where she directed the choir and taught music appreciation and humanities. When Owen merged with LeMoyne College in 1968 to form LeMoyne-Owen College, Dr. Green became a professor of music and director of the choir. In addition to traditional music courses, she introduced a seminar on Black women composers and one on Black Memphis musicians. The seminar was based on research for her doctoral dissertation, which led to publication of a book, *Black Women Composers: A Genesis* (1983), that traces the lives and works of composers Julia Perry, Florence Price, Margaret Bonds, Evelyn Pittman, and Lena McLin. The course on Black Memphis musicians developed from a grant that she received from the United Negro College Fund to document the accomplishments of more than 300 musicians, including singer Carla Thomas, saxophonist Herman Green, classical pianist Thomas Flagg, and music educator Wendell P. Whalum. She explains, "I teach about these musicians in class because I believe it helps students research and learn their heritage."

Dr. Green's articles on African American musicians have appeared in the *Historical Anthology of Music by Women* (1987); her essay, "A Matter of Fact: Selected Black Memphis Musicians, 1950–1980," was published in *Homespun Images: An Anthology of Black Memphis Writers and Artists* (1989); and her articles on Marian Anderson, women composers, and women in concert music were published in the revised edition of *Black Women in America* (2005), edited by Darlene Clark-Hine. She has also arranged spirituals and composed songs—"O Clap Your Hands," based on Psalm 47, for example—which have been performed by the LeMoyne-Owen Choir, but her best known composition is "I Have a Dream," based on the 1963 speech of Dr. Martin Luther King, Jr. "I wrote it the night King was killed," she explained. "There was something pressing that night. I don't know why it took the shape of a song. I was obsessed with it." In recognition of her scholarship and service in the field of music education, Dr. Mildred D. Green was honored on February 8, 1987, when she received the Florence Cole Talbert McCleave Award from the Delta Sigma Theta Sorority at Memphis Brooks Museum of Art.

Griggs, Emma J. Williams (1875?–1948), educator. The founder of Griggs Business College, Emma Williams was born in Portsmouth,

Virginia, where she received her primary education. She then attended the Norfolk Mission College, a Portsmouth high school, and Richmond's Hartshorn Memorial College. She began teaching at age seventeen, but her marriage to Sutton E. Griggs on May 10, 1897, led her into the field of religious education. After moving to Nashville, Tennessee with her husband in 1902, she began studying at Roger Williams Baptist College and, later, completed a course in commercial science at the old Walden University. Mrs. Griggs also pursued advanced study in domestic science at Chicago University, the American School of Home Economics, and Dennison School. In 1906, Emma Griggs established her first school in Nashville, with an enrollment of fifty students. In 1912, she moved to Memphis with Reverend Griggs, who became pastor of Tabernacle Baptist Church, and four years later, she founded a practical arts school. When her husband became pastor of Hopewell church in 1930, the couple moved to Deniston, Texas, and then to Houston, where Sutton Griggs died in 1933.

After her husband's death, Mrs. Griggs returned to Memphis and resumed her career in education. She founded and served as president of a business college on Walker Avenue, which she later moved to 302 South Lauderdale. The institution developed rapidly; it was chartered in 1944 as the Griggs Business and Practical Arts College (in memory of her late husband), and in 1947, the college was certified by the Veterans Administration to educate veterans. The chairman of the board of directors was S. A. Owen, pastor of Metropolitan Baptist Church and head of the State Baptist Convention. Mrs. Griggs was a member of Metropolitan and an active worker in women's circles of the Baptist Church. A few days before her death, she was honored on her birthday by Griggs students and faculty; at the time, she would not disclose her age, but was said to be in her seventies. Emma Williams Griggs died at Collins Chapel Hospital in early 1948. An adopted daughter, Eunice Griggs Jones, preceded her in death.

Griggs, Sutton Elbert (1872–1933), author, minister, religious leader. A renowned clergyman and one of the most prolific Black writers of the first quarter of the twentieth century, the controversial Griggs moved from racial militancy to a conservative accommodationism. Born on June 19, 1872, in Chatfield, Texas, he was the son of the Reverend Allen R. Griggs, Sr., a former slave from Georgia, and his wife. After attending the Dallas public schools, he entered Bishop College, from which he graduated in 1890, and Richmond Theological Seminary, from which he received a degree in 1893. On May 10, 1897, he married Emma J. Williams of Portsmouth, Virginia, and then accepted a two-year pastorate at the First Baptist Church in Berkley, Virginia. In 1902, the couple moved to Nashville, where he became pastor of the First Baptist Church. In the early years of his ministry, he published the novel *Imperium in Imperio*, the first of eighteen books that he wrote between 1899 and 1929. A complex thinker, Griggs is acknowledged as one of the most important writers and intellectuals to emerge in the years predating the New Negro movement of the 1920s. His didactic novels, such as *Overshadowed*, *Unfettered*, and *The Hindered Hand*, are innovative works of protest that advocate civil rights for African Americans and reject the white supremacist views of Southern writers.

Less well known than his novels are Griggs' theological, sociological, and philosophical works, which at first challenged and then supported the racial nostrums of that period. The cost of his self-published works, which sold poorly, placed a severe financial strain on Griggs, who underwrote the publication and distribution of his books through the National Public Welfare League, which he founded. He was particularly disenchanted over the failure of his fourth novel, *The Hindered Hand* (1905), because it was written at the request of the National Baptist Convention; after setting up a stock corporation to finance the work, Griggs failed to get support from members of the NBC. On the other hand, a 1911 publication, *Wisdom's Call*, was more successful, primarily because it was endorsed by southern Whites. In that polemical text, Griggs suggested that a philosophy of social efficiency (i.e., separatism) would create more harmony between the races. By 1911, Griggs began to embrace the doctrine of racial accommodationism, a move that signaled a philosophic change, as well as a response to financial exigencies, as he intimates in his autobiography, *The Story of My Struggles* (1914). His philosophy of interracial cooperation garnered the support of Whites: he was invited to address the Southern Baptist Convention in 1913, and the Convention gave financial support to the American Baptist Theological Seminary in Nashville. Griggs was one of the co-founders of the seminary, and he served as its president from 1925 to 1926.

One of Sutton Griggs' major accomplishments was his work with the Tabernacle Baptist Church. He was called to the Memphis church, located on Turley Street, in 1913, but by 1916 he had begun construction of an imposing structure on Lauderdale. He envisioned an institutional church that would serve the religious, educational, and social needs of his congregation and of the wider community. The church provided a gymnasium, swimming pool, employment bureau, educational facilities, and classes in domestic service for women. Griggs used the church as the base for the National Public Welfare League. With the support of both races, he also began publication, in 1919, of a free weekly newspaper, *The Neighbor*, to demonstrate the progress of Black Memphians. By 1925, however, Griggs and his church faced severe financial problems, which were exacerbated by the stock market crash of 1929. On October 30, 1930, the church was sold at public auction to satisfy the delinquent mortgage held by Universal Life Insurance Company. After the loss of Tabernacle, Griggs moved to Denison, Texas, to head the Hopewell Baptist Church, which his father had pastored. In 1932, after two years at Hopewell, he resigned to found a religious institute in Houston. On January 2, 1933, after less than a month in Houston, Sutton E. Griggs died.

After his death, Emma W. Griggs established the Griggs Institute of Memphis in memory of her husband.

Guy-Sheftall, Beverly (1946–), scholar, college professor. Considered one of the country's foremost Black feminist scholars, she has played a major role in the national women's studies movement. The daughter of Ernestine Varnado Guy and Walter P. Guy, a high school art teacher, she was born in Memphis on June 1, 1946, and grew up in the home of her grandfather, an accomplished Baptist minister. Her mother—a college accountant and independent woman who stressed education—helped shape the intellectual development of her three daughters. Beverly attended Lutheran Cooperative, graduated from Manassas High School, and, at age sixteen, entered Spelman College, where she majored in English and minored in secondary education. After receiving a bachelor's degree with honors, she completed a fifth year of study at Wellesley College. In 1968–1969, while pursuing a master's in English at Atlanta University, her thesis, "Faulkner's Treatment of Women in His Major Novels," stimulated what would be a life-long interest in women's issues. After her May 1969 marriage to Willis B. Sheftall, Jr., she moved to Montgomery to teach at Alabama State University but returned to Atlanta, in 1971, to join Spelman's faculty. The recipient of a Woodrow Wilson Fellowship for her dissertation, she completed a doctorate in American Studies at Emory University, where she now teaches graduate courses as an adjunct professor in the Institute for Women's Studies.

Dr. Guy-Sheftall was named the Anna Julia Cooper Professor of Women's Studies at Spelman College and was awarded Spelman's Presidential Faculty Award for Outstanding Scholarship. The founding director, in 1981, of the Women's Research And Resource Center, she obtained funding from the Charles Stewart Mott Foundation and other agencies to plan exhibitions, organize conferences, and develop curricula and internship programs. In 1983, she was founding co-editor of *Sage: A Scholarly Journal of Black Women*, the first journal to examine the experiences of African-descended women. A prolific scholar who became interested in research and writing while teaching English and working on the first anthology of Black women's literature, she has published her dissertation, *Daughters of Sorrow: Attitudes Toward Black Women, 1880–1920* (1991) and *Gender Talk: The Struggle for Women's Equality in African American Communities*, co-authored with Johnnetta Betsch Cole (2003); edited *Words of Fire: An Anthology of African American Feminist Thought* (1995); and co-edited two anthologies, *Sturdy Black Bridges: Visions of Black Women in Literature* (1979) and *Traps: African American Men on Gender and Sexuality* (2001). She has received many awards and fellowships, including a National Kellogg Fellowship and the 2006 Kathleen Carlin Justice Seeker's Award.

Hamilton, Green Polonius (1867–1932), writer, educator. Principal of the first public high school for Blacks in Memphis, he published two books that are important historical documents. He was born in Memphis and raised by his mother, Laura Hamilton. After graduating with honors from LeMoyne Normal Institute in 1882, he began teaching in the Memphis public schools but eventually continued his education at Rust College and Columbia University. In 1884, he became a sixth grade teacher at Kortrecht School and, in 1892, he was appointed principal of Kortrecht High School, the first public high school for Blacks in Memphis. Around 1900, Hamilton organized the first high school band at Kortrecht. The school moved into a new building in 1904 and again in 1910, as graduates from LeMoyne, Roger Williams, and Tougaloo College joined the faculty. In 1926, Kortrecht was renamed Booker T. Washington High School, and Hamilton later wrote a history of the school.

One of the first writers to record the history of Memphis's Black community, G. P. Hamilton published two books, including *The Bright Side of Memphis* (1908), which chronicles the social, political, and economic growth of the community and which includes photographs of churches and biographical sketches of leading citizens. In 1911, he published *Beacon Lights of the Race*, with biographies and photographs of outstanding African Americans. One of the photographs is of his wife, Alice Richmond Hamilton, an Arkansan who taught in Memphis. Hamilton High School is named in honor of this pioneering educator.

Hampton, Luther (1942–), sculptor. A gifted artist who works in various media, he has created sculptures that are displayed in galleries and universities around the country. The fourth of the eleven children of Alberta Hampton, a beautician, and Louis Hampton, an upholsterer, he was born on November 15, 1942, and grew up on McDowell Street, behind LeMoyne-Owen College. By the time he entered kindergarten, he realized that he had artistic talent, because he was always painting and sketching in the classroom. After graduating from Booker T. Washington High School, Hampton served for three years in the Navy, painting murals on ships' walls and whittling away with his military knife. After the assassination of Martin Luther King, Jr., he carved "Wounded America," a three-foot, abstract sculpture of oak, which underscores his unique style and approach to art. In 1973, he graduated from the Memphis Academy of Art. Noted for his sculptures of African American female nudes, he works in clay, wood, bronze, marble, sandstone, and bone; once, he even carved a tooth of his that had fallen out. Describing himself as a "struggling artist," he often transforms discarded stones and trees into statues; after a dream one night, he carved an angel with a head of walnut and wings of fish jawbones. In his fifty years as an artist, Hampton has experienced tough times: in 1982, five wood and two stone sculptures were stolen but were recovered by the police, and, in 1993, while living on Alabama Avenue, someone stole several of his large paintings, as well as his chisels—these were never found. The artist has had to be resourceful, working in small spaces and even on the landing outside his second-story apartment.

Luther Hampton's world now consists of a two-room apartment near downtown Memphis that serves as his home and studio, with photographs on the walls and sculptures everywhere. Over the course of his lifetime, a variety of jobs have paid the rent; he once taught in Arkansas and West Tennessee, and now he works as a Beale Street sketch artist. Hampton has had many successes: in 2000 and 2006, he won the first place award in the VA's Creative Arts Festival, and he received the 2003 Governor's Distinguished Award, which was presented to him at the Memphis Brooks Museum of Art. His stone sculptures were displayed at the museum, and he was credited with "fostering the community of African American artists in Memphis" through his work with young people and other artists. On November 29–30, 2002, a two-day exhibit of his art, "'As Real as It Gets,' Luther Hampton: One Artist, Two-Day Retrospective," was held in a vacant building at 387 South Main Street. The opening reception featured music, a slide show of his work, and interpretive dances by his goddaughter, who organized the event. The twelve sculptures on display included "Praise Phase I," a near life-size black walnut carving of a woman; "Head of a God," a log carving; "Alligator Woman," which depicts a female with the head of a reptile; and "Spirit of the Dance," made from a small forked stick. According to an art critic, Luther Hampton's "works document the history of his life experiences as an African American growing up during the 1950s."

Handy, William Christopher (1873–1958), musician, composer, band leader. Known as the "Father of the Blues," he is credited with documenting and popularizing the Black musical tradition of the South. The son of a Methodist minister, he was born in Florence, Alabama, on November 18, 1873. His parents, Charles Bernard and Elizabeth Brewer Handy, were former slaves who did not want their son to play blues or ragtime, which they considered "low down." After studying music at the Florence District School, Handy joined a minstrel band and became bandmaster at A&M College in Huntsville, Alabama. Later, he organized a quartet that performed at the Chicago Columbian Exposition in 1893, and, in 1896, he toured with his own band throughout the United States, Cuba, and Mexico, before returning to the minstrel circuit as director of brass bands for Mahara's Minstrel Troop. About 1903, Handy began a five-year stint in the Mississippi Delta, working as a bandmaster and director of dance orchestras. In the Delta, he began to appreciate the rich musical tradition of Black, guitar-picking bluesmen, and he started collecting the blues, using his formal training in music to transcribe rural folk music.

About 1908, Handy moved to Memphis and, four years later, published his first blues composition, "The Memphis Blues," which had been written three years before as a campaign song entitled "Mr. Crump," for mayoral candidate Edward H. "Boss" Crump. Two years later, he published the "St. Louis Blues," which brought him national fame. With Harry Pace, a lyricist and businessman, Handy founded a successful music publishing company that they moved to New York in 1918. The company published pamphlets, small books, and popular music that was sung by entertainers such as Sophie Tucker. During the 1920s, when blues music was at its height, many of Handy's compositions, such as "Careless Love," "Aunt Hagar's Blues," and "A Good Man Is Hard to Find," became best-sellers and popular hits. Handy almost lost his sight after World War I and became totally blind after a fall from a subway station in 1943, but he continued to perform; he toured with his band, played trumpet, made recordings, and wrote blues, hymns, marches, and spirituals. Besides those mentioned above, his best known compositions are "Joe Turner Blues," "Beale Street Blues," and "Make Me a Pallet on the Floor." His publications include *Blues: An Anthology* (1926), *Negro Authors and Composers of the United States* (1935), and *Father of the Blues* (1941), an autobiography.

In 1898, Handy married Elizabeth V. Price, his childhood sweetheart, and they were the parents of six children. She died in 1937, and he married Louise Logan in 1954, when he was eighty years old. That same year, he suffered a stroke, which left him confined to a wheelchair. He died of bronchial pneumonia on November 17, 1957, and is buried in Woodlawn Cemetery in the Bronx. The Handy Heights Housing Development and Museum, which includes a restored cabin containing his piano, trumpet, and other memorabilia, was established in Florence, Alabama. A bronze statue of the musician was erected in W. C. Handy Park, located at the corner of Beale and Second Streets in downtown Memphis, and his home has been moved to Beale Street and converted into a museum.

Hardaway, Anfernee Deon "Penny" (1971–), basketball player, Olympic medalist. Named the best all-around player in the

National Basketball Association, he was an outstanding athlete and an inspiration to young people. On July 18, 1971, nineteen-year-old Fae Hardaway gave birth to Anfernee, who was nicknamed "Penny" because his grandmother, who raised him, thought that he was "pretty as a penny." He did not meet his father until he was six years old, and Eddie Golden never became actively involved in his son's life. When not in school or church, Lil Penny could be found playing for hours on the neighborhood basketball courts. He became Treadwell High School's star player, scoring as many as 70 points in a single game, and was considered one of the top ten college picks in the country, but a low score on the ACT exam made him ineligible to play college basketball. At his own expense, Hardaway entered Memphis State University and earned a 3.0 GPA in his freshman year. In April 1991, he and a friend were robbed and shot, and doctors thought that he would never play basketball again, but he returned to the court in his sophomore year, made the dean's list, and earned the highest grade point average of any player on the team.

In his first game as an MSU Tiger, in December 1991, Hardaway scored 18 points and sent the game into overtime. His team made it to the Final Eight of the NCAA tournament, and Penny was voted the Great Midwest Player of the Year. The following summer, his team won the gold medal at the Olympic Festival, and he was invited to scrimmage against the U.S. Olympic "Dream Team." The next year, he led the Great Midwest Conference in scoring, rebounding, and minutes played; was named *Sports Illustrated*'s Player of the Week; was voted the Great Midwest Player of the Year; and was named a first-team all-American. In 1993, prior to his senior year, Hardaway turned pro, ending up—after a trade—with the Orlando Magic, who agreed to pay him $68 million over thirteen years. He became one of the Magic's most outstanding players, winning the Most Valuable Player award during the 1994 Rookie All-Star Game, after scoring 22 points. The 6' 7" point guard/shooting guard won a gold medal for men's basketball at the 1996 Summer Olympics, and he made the NBA All-Star team from 1995 to 1998. After an injury to his left knee early in the 1997–1998 season and four later surgeries, he was traded to the Phoenix Suns, whom he led to the semifinals in the 2000 NBA playoffs. Knee problems, however, forced him to miss most of the 2001 season and, after a stint with the New York Knicks, he was traded back to Orlando on February 22, 2006. He was recently waived by the Orlando Magic and is currently a free agent.

Throughout his career, Penny Hardaway did not forget his family or his hometown. He bought a $150,000 house for his mother and grandmother, and, in 1995, he held his first annual summer basketball camp for Memphis youngsters, which provided 200 scholarships for those who could not afford to participate. The camp is followed each year by the Penny Charity Classic basketball game, featuring stars of the NBA. In its first two years, the classic earned $300,000 for area charities. Hardaway has proved to be one of Memphis's brightest stars.

Hardin, Lil. See Lillian Hardin Armstrong.

Harris, Joseph "FreeJoe" (1796–1875), builder, minister, inn owner. A freed slave, he and his wife, who operated a stagecoach inn east of Bartlett in the mid-1800s, are believed to be the first Blacks to be issued a marriage license in Shelby County. Born into slavery on the Goochland, Virginia, plantation of Elizabeth and John Harris, who appears to have been his father, young Joseph learned to read and write, possibly at the neighboring plantation of Samuel Leake, who also might have taught him the building trade. Soon after his emancipation on September 5, 1832, he followed Leake to Shelby

County, Tennessee, because his wife and four of their children belonged to Leake. After arriving in Tennessee, Harris bought Fannie and their daughter Virginia for $300–$150 in cash and the balance in a mortgage. Eventually, he bought the other three children, and he and his wife had six additional children, who were born free in Shelby County. On April 18, 1835, FreeJoe and Fannie were issued a marriage license to formalize their undocumented union. In the mid-1800s, the Harrises operated a stagecoach inn east of Bartlett, which is believed to be the oldest brick structure in West Tennessee. After he died, their daughter Martha and her husband, George Branch, operated the inn.

A Baptist minister, Joseph Harris became the first pastor of Gray's Creek Church, located on U.S. 64 at Airline Road, and his oldest son, Peter, became the first pastor of Morning Grove Church near Arlington and possibly a co-founder of the all-Black town of Mound Bayou, Mississippi. FreeJoe died in 1875, leaving an estate valued at about $3,500, including 700 acres of property in the Eads community. He left 100 acres each to five of his children, and the property remained in the family until around 1967, when a part of the land was sold and the remainder was donated to a home for troubled youth—Dogwood Village, operated by Youth Villages, Inc. According to his great-great-great grandson Earnest Edward Lacey, whose research culminated in the biographical novel *FreeJoe: A Story of Faith, Love and Perseverance*, Joseph Harris "had the strength of character to overcome incredible odds and become a powerful and influential businessman in Shelby County." FreeJoe died in 1875, and he is buried in the cemetery of Gray's Creek Church.

Harvey, Peggy Ann Prater (1949–1997), psychologist, businesswoman, commissioner. Trained as an educational psychologist, she dedicated her life to public service and had a distinguished career as an administrator with the Memphis Light, Gas and Water Division. Born in Memphis on October 9, 1949, she was the only child of Edwin and Helen Prater. After graduating from Father Bertrand

High School, she received the B.S. and M.S. degrees from the University of Tennessee at Knoxville and completed additional postgraduate work at The Johns Hopkins University. On August 18, 1973, she married her high school sweetheart, Percy H. Harvey, a Memphis attorney, and they adopted Nicole Elizabeth on February 17, 1989. Noted for her grace, beauty, and petite figure, she was always elegantly attired in the latest fashion. In her personal life, she was devoted to her family, including her in-laws; in her public life, she was committed to education, the arts, social welfare, and human rights.

Harvey served as an educational psychologist and certified psychological examiner in Maryland, Massachusetts, and Tennessee. She became a training coordinator for the Memphis Light, Gas and Water Division in 1980 and, later, served as supervisor of Management Development and as manager of training and development. In March 1987, she was appointed vice president of human resources. As an MLGW executive on loan to the Memphis City Schools, she assisted the superintendent in developing the district's strategic plan and the site-based management structure. Elected to the Memphis Board of Education in 1995, she took office in January 1996, and became vice president of the board in December 1996. Chairperson of Leadership Memphis, she was actively involved in many service clubs and organizations, including the Memphis Arts Council, Memphis Branch NAACP, National Civil Rights Museum, and Memphis and Shelby County Sports Authority. She is, perhaps, best remembered for her volunteer work with Girls Incorporated of Memphis, where she had a significant impact on the lives of young people in the community. As president of the board of directors, she outlined the agency's mission in providing services to girls and in developing methods for tracking their success rate. She moderated the "She Knows Where She's Going" Forum in which girls interact with women role models.

A financial contributor to the agency, she also served as solicitor of the G.I.F.T.S. Campaign and was second chairperson of the Celebration Luncheon. Peggy Prater Harvey died on July 2, 1997, while vacationing with her family in Kailua, Hawaii.

Hassell, Frances Massey (1925–1996), writer, artist, insurance executive. The only female senior vice president at Universal Life Insurance Company, she was the first Black to prepare and distribute a Black History calendar, free of charge, in the United States. The seventh of the nine children of Dilcie and Conley Massey, a sharecropper, she was born on March 26, 1925, in Lucy, Tennessee. A member of the girls' basketball team, she graduated first in the Class of 1943 at the Shelby County Training School, where the principal, R. J. Roddy, encouraged her skills in spelling, writing, and mathematics. Her father said, "That girl can't chop cotton, she can't pick cotton, and her food is either too salty or burnt. She needs to go to school so she can learn how to take of herself." Frances entered Lane College, attended the Memphis Branch of Tennessee State University and Memphis State University, and received a bachelor's degree from Louisiana Baptist College at age sixty-five. A year before her death, she completed all the requirements for a Master of Arts degree in religious education and counseling from Louisiana Baptist University.

Frances Hassell joined the staff of Universal Life Insurance Company on June 1, 1947, as a cashier/clerk at the Memphis district office. During her forty-eight years with the company, she also served as personal secretary and administrative assistant to B. G. Olive, Jr., as well as assistant vice president and director of public relations and customer service. She was the second woman to hold a senior administrative position in the company. Responsible for the company's corporate communications, she researched and edited Universal's Black

Legacy Calendars; a resource booklet entitled "From the Pages of Black History"; and two cookbooks, including a booklet of bread recipes, and the 175-page *Reflections of an African American Kitchen*. Profits from book sales went to promote community projects, such as the company's Adopt-A-School program. On occasion, Mrs. Hassell taught typing and shorthand at S. A. Owen Junior College. She also wrote poetry and created fiber art, making designs out of paper or silk fabrics, or combining macrame knots with knitting and crochet stitches.

An active member of her profession, she received the 1990 Outstanding Woman in Business Award from *Dollars and Sense* and two Awards of Excellence from the Life Communicators Association. Secretary and vice president of the Home Office Section of the National Insurance Association, she held the highest degree, FLMI, in the insurance business and was the first African American woman to attain this degree. She also taught courses at Universal that enabled others to advance in the insurance business. She served on many boards, including the Memphis Volunteer Placement Program, Shelby State Community College, Memphis Chamber of Commerce, Afro-American Arts and Crafts Council, and Jobs for Tennessee Graduates. Frances M. Hassell died on March 12, 1996, and is survived by a daughter, Dr. Marian H. Whitson, professor of criminology and criminal justice at East Tennessee State University.

Hayden, Frank, Jr. (1934–1988), sculptor, professor of art. A world-renowned artist, he was selected to create a sculpture for Pope John Paul II during the pontiff's visit to New Orleans. Born on June 10, 1934, he and his sister Hazel were raised by their mother, Myrtle Hayden, in LeMoyne Gardens Housing Project. After completing kindergarten at Bethlehem Center on Walker Avenue, he graduated from St. Augustine High School, where he played basketball and football. In spite of his interest in sports, he was committed to art, so he accepted a scholarship to Xavier University, which awarded him a bachelor's degree in fine arts with a minor in German. Because of his academic achievements, ten universities offered him graduate fellowships, but he went to the University of Notre Dame to study under Ivan Mestrovec and to earn a Master of Fine Arts in sculpture. A gifted artist and an accomplished student, Hayden did postgraduate work at Iowa State University and, in 1959, received a Fulbright Fellowship to study at the Munich Art Academy in West Germany. In 1987, he was awarded an honorary doctorate by Madonna College in Michigan. A board member of the National Faculty of Humanities, Arts and Sciences, he was also an American-Scandinavian Artist at the Royal Academy in Copenhagen and a Southern Foundation Fellow at the Academy of Fine Arts in Stockholm. In spite of such honors, friends remember him as an humble, unpretentious, and unassuming man. A colleague recalls that, when Hayden's bust of coaching legend A. W. Mumford was unveiled, the artist "stayed inconspicuous in the background."

Between 1961 and 1988, Frank Hayden taught drawing, sculpture, aesthetics, and art appreciation at Southern University in Baton Rouge and, in recognition of his outstanding teaching, the faculty named him Southern University's first distinguished professor in 1985. Hayden gained international attention for his sculpture, and his works in clay, wood, plaster, and stone have been exhibited in Illinois, New York, Texas, and throughout Louisiana. His creations have been displayed in churches, synagogues, banks, and college campuses, as well as in museums; for example, "A Sequence of Life," a Honduran mahogany relief sculpture, was purchased by a bank but was on loan to the Louisiana Arts and Science Museum. His strong religious and philosophical beliefs are reflected in many of his sculptures, including one of his last works, "The Prodigal Son," which is carved out of white alabaster. He often used his artistic ability and religious faith to interpret the lives and deeds of historical figures, such as St. Martin de Porres, the sixteenth-century Peruvian saint of African descent. When Pope John Paul II visited New Orleans in 1987, Hayden presented him with a small bronze, "St. Martin de Porres," on behalf of African American Catholics. Frank Hayden and his wife, Joyce, lived in Scotlandville, Louisiana, with their four children: Frank III, David, Anna Marie, and Claudia. In January 1988, their son, Frank—a disturbed young man—shot his father to death with a 32-caliber pistol as he lay sleeping on a couch. A Memphis friend reported that thousands packed Baton Rouge's St. Joseph's Cathedral for the funeral of the acclaimed sculptor.

Hayes, Isaac (1941–), actor, pianist, vocalist, arranger, saxophonist, songwriter. A soul icon and music superstar, he was the first African American to win an Oscar for best song. The son of Eula and Isaac Hayes, Sr., he was born in Covington, Tennessee on August 20, 1941, but moved to Memphis with his grandparents after his mother's death when he was two years old. Although he eventually graduated from Manassas High School in 1962, he dropped out in his teens to make recordings and form a band, Sir Isaac and the Doo-Dads. After an apprenticeship with the Teen Tones and the Morning Stars, he joined Stax in 1964, and co-wrote, with lyricist David Porter, over 200 songs, including such hits as "Soul Man," "B-A-B-Y," "Hold On, I'm Comin," and "When Something Is Wrong with My Baby." Working as backup musicians for such stars as Carla Thomas and Otis Redding, the dynamic duo helped to create the Memphis Sound and to make Stax into Soulsville U.S.A. Hayes went solo with *Hot Buttered Soul*, which climbed to the top of the charts in 1969, and he became a superstar when "The Theme from Shaft" won an Academy Award in 1971, reached number one on the pop chart, and went platinum, earning Hayes—dubbed Black Moses—a Grammy, Golden Globe, Edison Award, and NAACP Image Award. When bad management forced him into bankruptcy in 1976, he soon rebounded, releasing over twenty albums and recording such hits as "Walk On By," "Say a Little Prayer," and "By the Time I Get to Phoenix."

Noted for his bald head and deep basso profundo voice, the legendary Hayes is a man of many talents, who has carved out separate careers as an actor, disk jockey, restauranteur, and cookbook author. He created a radio program, "Isaac Hayes and Friends in the Morning" for a New York station; he has appeared in films, such as the 2006 Oscar-winning *Hustle and Flow*; and he has performed in television hits like *Miami Vice* and *The Rockford Files*. His grandmother's cooking inspired his first cookbook, *Cooking with Heart & Soul: Making Music in the Kitchen with Family and Friends*, and his second cookbook, *Kidney Friendly Comfort Foods: A Collection of Recipes for Eating Well with Chronic Kidney Disease*, pays tribute to his father and others who died of kidney failure. His cooking skills led to his role as the voice of a school cafeteria cook on the *South Park* cartoon show, which revived his career, and the album, "*Chef Aid: The South Park Album*," which went platinum, gave him his first hit in many years. In the 1990s, he opened a restaurant and store in Memphis's Peabody Place: Isaac Hayes Food-Passion and Isaac Hayes Studio Kitchen and Wares. He has received many honors and awards: he was crowned a king in Ghana and a chief in Nigeria; he received the Governor's Award from the Memphis Chapter of NARAS in 1994; he and Porter earned the Pyramid Award for lifetime achievement in 1999; and, in 2005, they were inducted into the Songwriters Hall of Fame. A divorcé who has been married three times, he has eleven children. Since 1993, he has been a member of the Church of Scientology.

Hayes, Thomas Henry (1868–1949), businessman, funeral director. With a limited education and very little capital, one of Memphis's most successful entrepreneurs was founder of the oldest Black business still in operation. Born on August 15, 1868, in Richmond, Virginia, he moved with his parents to LaGrange, Tennessee, when he was three years old. Seeking financial opportunities, he came to Memphis at age sixteen and found employment at the Millburn Iron Works Company. After working for ten years as a porter on Front Street, he saved enough money to realize his dream of becoming a grocer. His first grocery store on Gholson Street failed, as did the next two that he opened on Beale Street and South Second. Realizing the importance of education to an aspiring businessman, Hayes entered Howe Institute, where he made rapid progress, advancing to the eighth grade in only two years. To finance his education, he opened a barbershop on Poplar Street, which he sold to become a traveling salesman for the Red Star Supply Company. His success at selling clocks and Bibles motivated him to become an independent salesman for a year, during which time he raised the capital to open his fourth store, Central Grocery Company on Front Street. When that business failed, he worked to repay his debts and then, with $35 in savings, he opened a fifth store on Ross Avenue. Through that successful venture, he acquired a horse, buggy, and $1,400.

When the undertaking firm of Carroway and Randle went bankrupt, friends persuaded him to buy the company. With no experience in the undertaking business, he opened T. H. Hayes Company at 245 Poplar on May 20, 1902, and immediately began studying embalming and anatomy. His funeral establishment was well equipped and elegantly appointed: it included a morgue, chapel, and storage rooms; and it provided an ambulance, five hearses, coaches, and horse-drawn buggies. The success of his company led T. H. Hayes into other ventures. He bought stock in Mississippi Beneficial Life Insurance

Company, Standard Life Insurance Company of Georgia, and Blocker Coal Company of Oklahoma. A life member of the National Negro Business League, he served as first vice president of the Solvent Savings Bank & Trust Company and was co-founder of Union Protective Life Insurance Company. He was also president of Tri-State Casket Company, advertised as the "Largest in the South." His business successes led him into politics and public service. In 1916, he ran for state senator on the ticket of the Lincoln League, a Black Republican organization, and, in 1917, he became a charter member of the Memphis Branch of the NAACP. A humanitarian and philanthropist noted for his honesty and integrity, he served as treasurer of the Reform School Association and of the Old Folks and Orphans Home.

Hayes acquired property in several neighborhoods throughout the city—Mid-Town, Orange Mound, Klondike, New Chicago, and East Memphis—and he bought a luxurious Victorian house at 680 S. Lauderdale, which he remodeled in 1918; the funeral business was located on the first floor, while the family's quarters were on the second floor. A large, handsome man with a commanding presence, Hayes married Florence Taylor of Covington, Tennessee, on March 31, 1898, and they had two sons, Thomas, Jr., and Taylor. When his sons joined the firm, he changed the name of the business to T. H. Hayes and Sons, which became known as the "refuge of the rich and the poor."

Hedgeman, Lulah McEwen (1938–1997), educator, musician. An award-winning choir director and music educator, she was called the "Pied Piper for kids" because she influenced the lives of hundreds of young people. The youngest child of Johanna Wells McEwen, a teacher, and A. B. McEwen, Bishop of the Church of God in Christ, she was born on January 30, 1938. After completing the tenth grade at

Hamilton High School, she entered Fisk University, from which she received a B.A. degree in music. Later, she was awarded a master's degree in music from Memphis State University. As a youngster, Lulah McEwen dreamed of becoming a performer, but it was difficult then for a Black women to have a professional career as an instrumentalist. She explained, "I'm a performer. I wanted to be a concert pianist, and I even have two degrees in piano performance. But my mother sat me down and told me what to do if I wanted to make some money."

During the 1960s, she taught in Chicago, where she married Herbert L. Hedgeman and had a daughter, Denita Jo. After her divorce, she returned to Memphis and began teaching at Melrose, Treadwell, and Hamilton High Schools before joining the faculty of Overton High School of the Creative and Performing Arts in 1976. As a teacher, she shaped the work of many music professionals, including R&B singer Wendy Moten, gospel choir director O'Landa Draper, and bass baritone Charles Billings. After eight years at Overton, she built a twenty-six-member concert choir into an ensemble of 104 voices, called the Overton CAPA Swingers. A tough and demanding teacher with high standards, she served as director of the Overton High School Choirs, including a concert choir; chamber group that performed Renaissance, Medieval, and contemporary chamber music; a gospel group; and jazz show choir that put on a sixty-six-minute program of music from shows such as *A Chorus Line*, *Chicago*, and *All That Jazz*. In 1983, she raised $40,000 to take her choir to France for an international competition. She held workshops, judged music festivals, and conducted college choirs throughout the country. In 1994, she was chosen as the assistant conductor of the Grammy Awards All-American High School Jazz Choir.

A strict disciplinarian who is described as a caring and concerned teacher, Lulah Hedgeman won numerous awards for her work. In 1984, she was named "Teacher of the Year" for the Memphis Public Schools, and in 1991, she won the Governor's Award from NARAS. She gained nationwide acclaim in 1990, after winning Disney's Outstanding Performing Arts Teacher in America Award.

The Maybelline Corporation selected her as one of several Black women who have made outstanding contributions to Memphis, and the Association of Black Business and Professional Women honored her for her contributions to music. In 1994, she was named Teacher of the Year by the Memphis Alliance of Black School Educators and was awarded the Honorary Doctor of Fine Arts Degree by Rhodes College. Three themes—religion, education, and the arts—shaped her life. A member of Mississippi Boulevard Christian Church, she served as coordinator of the music committee. On December 8, 1997, Lulah McEwen Hedgeman died suddenly of a heart attack.

Henderson, George W. (1888–1944), writer, educator, businessman. Professor Henderson's life exemplifies the motto of the business college that he founded: "He Profits Most Who Serves Best." Born in Knoxville, Tennessee on August 5, 1888, he was the son of poor parents. He began working as a shoeshine boy, newspaper carrier, and janitor when he was very young to help support his family. After graduating from Austin High School in Knoxville, he acquired degrees and certificates from such institutions as Cuyahoga Teachers College, Roger Williams University, Dyer's College of Commercial Law, and Spencer's School of Commerce. Early in his career, he demonstrated an aptitude for business administration, and, while attending college in Nashville, he gained a reputation as a typing and shorthand "wizard." In 1914, he developed a system of shorthand about which he wrote a book, and he created a correspondence school in Nashville to sell the book. A prolific writer, he published short stories and articles in magazines and wrote *Miracle System of Mind Training*.

On January 1, 1912, with $2.20 in cash and two used typewriters, he founded Henderson Business College in Knoxville, and, two years later, he opened a branch of the college in Memphis. According to

Henderson, he was invited to move to Memphis by W. C. Handy, the noted musician and composer, and M. W. Thornton, the "Mayor of Beale Street." After opening Henderson Business College in a house located at 528 St. Paul Avenue, the enterprising businessman visited ministers and professionals to get support for the college. He moved the school to a larger facility at 590 St. Paul but, when the Memphis Housing Authority bought the property in 1939, he relocated to 530 Linden Avenue. Under Henderson's presidency, the institution acquired modern equipment for student training and three spacious buildings—an administration building where classes in typing and accounting were held, a graphic arts building for courses in printing and allied trades, and a dormitory for young women from out of town. The college was recognized by the State Department of Education, and it was commissioned by the National Bureau of Office Proficiency Standards to prepare applicants for administrative tests. In 1956, twelve years after the death of its founder, Henderson Business College had property and equipment valued at $100,000, and it had graduated 1,800 students, many of whom held positions in local and federal government.

A member of the Baha'i faith, Professor Henderson was highly esteemed by members of the Memphis community. In 1936, he was endorsed for the position of Minister to Liberia during the Roosevelt administration, and, although he did not get the appointment, he became well known in diplomatic circles. In 1940, he was selected to be King of the Cotton Makers' Jubilee. After a long illness, George W. Henderson died on December 24, 1944, and was survived by a son, Hale Henderson.

Henderson, Morris (1802–1877), religious leader. Called "the most influential man of his race in Memphis" at the time of his death, Henderson was the founding pastor of the Beale Street Baptist Church. Born in Virginia in 1802, he came to Memphis in 1849 to work as a carriage driver. When he became disenchanted with the beliefs and practices of the African Church, he formed a small congregation to which he ministered for more than ten years, but he was not ordained until 1864. When the Civil War ended in 1865, his church members held a fair and raised $406.50 with which Reverend Henderson made a down payment on a Beale Street lot. By October 1866, the congregation had raised $5,000 to complete the purchase of the site, and by 1869, the first floor of the large and impressive brick church was completed. Between 1865 and 1877, the congregation, under Henderson's leadership, raised $44,408.72 to erect one of the largest churches in Memphis.

Henderson was a dedicated clergyman who underscored the importance of religious institutions in the intellectual and spiritual development of the community. A man of high character and exacting principles, he attempted to raise the moral standards and educational training of the clergy. He was a member of the Tennessee Missionary Baptist Association, which reviewed candidates for the ministry and published a semimonthly journal, the *Missionary Baptist*, to promote the professional development of Baptist ministers. First published in 1871, the journal was edited by the clerk of Henderson's church. He was highly respected by his colleagues, who invited him to deliver the first sermon at the annual conference of the Tennessee Colored Missionary Baptist Association in 1867. Although he was unlettered, he was a strong advocate of education; with his encouragement, his congregation organized a day school and two Sunday schools, operated by two teachers and a supervisor. He died on October 26, 1877, before the completion of his church. It is reported that 5,000 Memphians attended his funeral service, when he was eulogized by the Reverend Landrum, pastor of Central Baptist Church, and that his funeral cortege extended for almost a mile.

Henry, Wiley, Jr. (1957–), artist, journalist. One of the eight children of Dessie and Wiley Henry, he was born in Memphis on September 12, 1957, and grew up at 1029 Breedlove. He began drawing as a preschooler and received his first commission in the ninth grade. After graduating from Northside High School in 1975, he was awarded a merit scholarship to the Memphis Academy of Art, from which he received a bachelor's degree in advertising design and fine arts in 1980. While a sophomore at the Academy, he had a small exhibition of oil and charcoal portraits in the library of Christian Brothers College; one of the larger canvases was a double self-portrait of the artist as a toddler and teenager. His artwork has been exhibited at several venues, including the First Tennessee Bank, Parthenon Gallery in Nashville, and National Civil Rights Museum; and he has completed commissioned portraits of musician Stevie Wonder, Mayor W. W. Herenton, actor Clifton Davis, and civil rights leader Benjamin Hooks, among others. One of his paintings—of King and Ghandi superimposed over the American flag—hangs at the Martin Luther King Jr. Labor Center. The artist has also created posters for the Memphis Urban League and for WLOK's Stone Soul Picnic; a 4' × 10' mural of the Memphis Chicks baseball team; and several portrait series: one, in charcoal, of twenty-one Black religious pioneers, and another, of ten historical Blacks, drawn in pen and ink for Leader Federal Bank's "African-American Check Series."

A columnist for the *Tri-State Defender* newspaper for over twenty years, Wiley Henry is an award-winning journalist who has won or been a finalist in competitions sponsored by the National Newspaper Publishers Association and the Memphis Chapter of the Society of Professional Journalists. He has written and produced public service commercials on Black art for television station WREG, developed promotional material for expositions and trade shows, written op-ed pieces for *The Commercial Appeal*, and served as editor-in-chief of the *Golden Gate Gazette* newspaper. Noted for his service to the Memphis community, he received the Satterfield Award in 2000 for his volunteer work at the North Branch Library, where he led workshops in cartooning and art appreciation. For eight years, he served as vice president of the nonprofit Memphis Black Arts Alliance, utilizing his skills as an artist, writer, and designer of promotional material. On January 19, 2002, the artist and journalist married Debra Royston.

Herenton, Willie Wilbert (1940–). The first Black superintendent of the Memphis Public Schools and the first Black elected mayor of Memphis, he is one of the most significant political figures in the city. The son of Ruby Herenton and Willie Witherspoon, he was born in Memphis on April 23, 1940, and was raised in a public housing project, where he lived with his mother, grandmother, sister, and stepfather, Joe Harris. At age eleven, he began delivering groceries and working on coal trucks; at age twelve, he started boxing and became a Golden Gloves champion, winning five straight city championships. After graduating from Booker T. Washington High School in 1958, he entered LeMoyne College, from which he received a bachelor's degree in 1963. Herenton first made his mark as a teacher in the Memphis Public Schools and then as principal of Bethel Grove and La Rose Elementary Schools. In 1966, he received a master's degree in educational administration from Memphis State University and, two years later, became the only principal to participate in Black Monday protests to gain Black representation on the School Board. In 1971, he earned a doctorate in education from Southern Illinois University, with a dissertation entitled "A Historical Study of Desegregation in the Memphis City Schools, 1954–1970." One of ten minority school administrators, Dr. Herenton was chosen, in 1973, to participate in a training program for future superintendents, sponsored by the Rockefeller Foundation.

After serving from 1975 to 1978 as deputy superintendent for instruction in Memphis, he was one of forty-two applicants for the superintendent's job. The majority-White Memphis Board of Education first offered the position to Dr. William Coats, who declined the job because of the Black backlash. Subsequently, Herenton was appointed the first African American superintendent of Memphis City Schools in 1979, becoming chief executive of the 18th largest school system in the country and head of a $200-million operation. He developed the Optional School Program, which offered special academic courses at twenty-two schools, and instituted the Adopt-A-School Program, which garnered support from businesses; he reduced busing, improved student test scores, mandated tougher promotion standards, and initiated programs for at-risk students. He was selected three times as one of the top 100 school executives in the United States and Canada by *Executive Educator*, and he was one of ten winners of the Horatio Alger Award for Distinguished Americans in 1988. A year later, however, he was beset with problems: a difficult divorce, a breach-of-promise lawsuit by a teacher with whom he had been romantically involved, and a consultants' report that criticized city school management. Memphians assumed that he had been given a knock-out punch, but he rebounded and ran for mayor.

On October 3, 1991, Dr. W. W. Herenton was elected the first Black mayor in a race against incumbent Dick Hackett that he won by only 142 votes—the closest race in Memphis history. Sixteen years later, on October 4, 2007, he was elected to an unprecedented fifth term as mayor of the city with 42% of the vote over his two closest challengers, City Councilwoman Carol Chumney and former Memphis Light, Gas and Water Division CEO Herman Morris. As mayor, he has focused on economic, educational, and cultural development of the city through the infusion of private investments; revitalization of downtown; construction of FedExForum, AutoZone Park, and Stax Museum and Music Academy; riverfront development; revitalization of neighborhoods such as LeMoyne Gardens and New Chicago; creation of jobs, including summer jobs for teens; support for public schools; increase in police officers and firefighters; and construction of community centers. Mayor Herenton has received two honorary Doctor of Humanities degrees from Rhodes College and Christian

Brothers College, was named to the Memphis City Schools Alumni Hall of Fame, received the Arthur S. Holman Lifetime Achievement Award from the University of Memphis in 2002, and was selected as the 2003 Municipal Leader of the Year by *American City and County Magazine*. He and his former wife, Ida Jones Herenton, have three children—Duke, Rodney, and Andrea—and he has a fourth child, born in 2004.

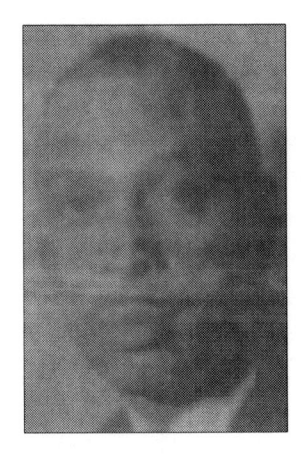

Holloway, George L. (1915–1990), labor leader, civil rights activist. One of Memphis's most powerful union leaders, he viewed the labor movement as a civil rights struggle. Born in Memphis on June 8, 1915, he attended Porter, Klondyke, and Grant Elementary Schools. After graduating from Manassas High School, he attended Tuskegee Institute for three years and became an All-American prep at the college in 1934. Two years later, he began work at Firestone Tire & Rubber Company, where he tried without success to organize his co-workers. Early on, Holloway developed a strong belief in unionization as a vital element in the Black freedom struggle. After leaving Firestone in 1942, he went to work for Pullman Company and was successful in getting 500 Black men to join the Pullman Porters Union. He believed that unionization would bring higher salaries and increased benefits, as well as eliminate segregated bathrooms and water fountains. In 1947, he joined International Harvester, helped workers join the United Auto Workers Union, and served as a union committeeman in the International Harvester plant for twenty years. As a result of his efforts, Holloway was not only the first Black to negotiate a contract for workers at a UAW plant, but he was also the first Black man to operate a machine at International Harvester. He was thus able to open up skilled jobs to African Americans, but he did so at a price, because his machine was sabotaged by jealous Whites who nearly maimed him.

Because of his work ethic and leadership ability, George Holloway moved up quickly in union ranks: on August 3, 1963, he was appointed to the international staff of the UAW, and he was the first servicing staff member of the UAW in the South, with responsibility for local unions in Delaware, Maryland, and Virginia. According to T. O. Jones, leader of the 1968 Sanitation Strike and founder of AFSCME Local Union 1733, Holloway had a major influence on him. Holloway told Jones, who was trying to unionize sanitation workers, "to organize six men at a time, so as not to raise suspicion." After his retirement on June 30, 1980, Holloway continued his service to the labor movement: he was vice chairman of Local 344 Retired Workers Chapter and served four terms on the UAW Retired Workers Advisory Council. Active in the Baltimore community, he was a board member of the Maryland State Council of Senior Citizens. Although he lived in Baltimore for the last two decades of his life, he had been active in Memphis's civil rights movement, participating in protests and demonstrations sponsored by the NAACP, SCLC, and UAW. He claims to have been the first Black man to be elected to the Democratic Party in Tennessee at a time when most Blacks were Republicans. He was also the first African American to receive a Goldsmith Department Store credit card, when "they were not giving them to Blacks," he said. He also claimed responsibility for getting nine of the thirteen Black children who desegregated Memphis city schools, while the NAACP got the other four. A member of Collins Chapel C.M.E. Church in Memphis and of Howard Park United Methodist Church in Baltimore, he died on December 8, 1990, and was buried in Baltimore.

Hooks, Benjamin Lawson (1925–), attorney, judge, clergyman, civil rights activist. The first Black criminal court judge in Tennessee and the first appointed to the Federal Communications Commission, he became an FCC commissioner and executive director of the NAACP.

The fifth of the seven children of Robert B. Hooks, Sr., and Bessie White Hooks, he was born in Memphis on January 31, 1925. He attended Porter Elementary School and Booker T. Washington High School, from which he graduated in 1941. After two years at LeMoyne College, he was drafted into the United States Army and, on his discharge in 1946, entered De Paul University, which awarded him the J.D. degree in 1948. On his return to Memphis the following year, Hooks began practicing law and became active in business, politics, and civil rights. On March 21, 1952, he married Frances Dancy, a teacher and guidance counselor, and they adopted Patricia Hooks. In 1954, he made an unsuccessful bid for the state legislature and, in 1959, ran for Juvenile Court Judge on the Volunteer Ticket with three other Blacks. In the 1950s, he and other Black Memphis lawyers filed suits in city, state, and federal courts to desegregate public facilities in the city. In 1956, he co-founded and served as vice president of Mutual Federal Savings and Loan Association, the first Black-owned institution of its kind in Memphis and the Mid-South. After serving as assistant public defender of Shelby County from 1961 to 1964, he was appointed to fill a vacancy on the Shelby County Criminal Court. Hooks thus became the first Black judge of a court of record in Tennessee and the South. He resigned from the court, in 1968, to devote more time to the pastorate of two churches: Greater Middle Baptist Church in Memphis and Greater New Mount Moriah Baptist Church in Detroit. He also produced and hosted television programs such as "Conversations in Black and White," "Forty Percent Speaks," and "What Is Your Faith?"

In 1972, President Nixon appointed Hooks, a Republican, to the seven-member Federal Communications Commission and, in 1976, he became executive director of the NAACP, which he led for fifteen years. On his retirement from the NAACP in 1993, he became senior vice president of the Chapman Company, professor of social justice at Fisk University, and adjunct professor of political science at the University of Memphis, which established the Benjamin L. Hooks Institute for Social Change in 1996. He has served on the boards of the National Civil Rights Museum, LeMoyne-Owen College, Universal Life Insurance Company, and Tri-State Bank of Memphis. Hooks has won many awards, including honorary degrees from several universities, NAACP's Spingarn Award, and Man of the Year Award from the Masons. He was inducted into the National Bar Association's Hall of Fame in 1998, and Memphis City Schools' Alumni Hall of Fame in 2002. The Memphis/Shelby County Library named its main library the Benjamin L. Hooks Central Library in 2005. On November 5, 2007, in a ceremony at the White House, Hooks was awarded the Presidential Medal of Freedom, the nation's highest civilian honor, by President Bush. The highlights of his life are recounted in an autobiography, *The March of Civil Rights: The Benjamin Hooks Story*, published in 2003.

Hooks, Julia Ann Britton (1852–1942), musician, teacher, social worker. Called the "Angel of Beale Street" because of her compassion for others, Hooks founded a private school, a home for the elderly and orphaned, and a music school on Beale Street. Born in Frankfort, Kentucy in 1852, she was reared in Lexington by her mother, a musician, who had been freed from slavery at age sixteen. Known as "Kentucky's little musical prodigy," Julia was taught to sing and play the piano by an English woman. Later, she and her mother played Beethoven and Mozart for their White friends, while Julia performed in parlor concerts in Lexington. One of the first women to attend college and the first Black woman to teach integrated classes in Kentucky, Julia Britton entered Berea College in 1869. As an advanced student, she taught music at the college from 1870 to 1872. After moving to Greenville, Mississippi, in 1872, to teach in the public schools, she became active in Blanche K. Bruce's campaign for the U.S. Senate. In 1876, she moved to Memphis, where she became one of the city's first Black public school teachers. On November 9, 1879, she was appointed to teach at the Monroe Street School and then at the Clay Street School; eventually, she became principal of the Virginia Avenue School. A voice teacher and concert pianist, Julia Hooks belonged to the Liszt-Mullard Club, which gave recitals and musical concerts, and she also directed choirs for various churches. On July 4, 1886, Memphis diarist Ida B. Wells described a social affair at her home: "Went to Mrs. H[ooks]'s concert & recited 'The Letter Reading' & Sleep-walking scenes from 'Lady McBeth'."

After teaching in the public schools of Mississippi and Tennessee for twenty-eight years, she founded the Hooks Cottage School, a private kindergarten and elementary school for grades one to three in her home at 578 South Lauderdale Street. Later, she founded the Hooks School of Music, located in Church's Auditorium, where her pupils included W. C. Handy, who studied harmony; Sidney Woodard, a concert artist; and mezzo-soprano Nell Hunter. The young matron, described as a "beautiful woman with long black hair," was actively involved in the community. She founded and was a charter member of a club that purchased twenty-five acres on Hernando Street to build the Old Folks and Orphans Home in 1891. Julia Hooks paid off the mortgage on the home within three years by giving concerts to raise money. In 1902, she persuaded E. H. "Boss" Crump to open a detention home for Negroes at 576 South Lauderdale, next to her house, and she was selected to supervise the facility. Although her husband was killed by one of the inmates, she continued to assist the young people. Her lengthy essay, "Duty of the Hour," was featured in the 1895 *Afro-American Encyclopedia*, and in 1917, she became a charter member of the Memphis branch of the NAACP. She and her husband, Charles F. Hooks, had two sons, Henry and Robert, who opened the Hooks Brothers Photographers at 162 Beale Street in

1907. Julia Britton Hooks died in 1942, at the Old Folks and Orphans Home. She was eulogized by Reverend T. O. Fuller and buried in Mt. Zion Cemetery.

Horne, Onzie O. (1923–1973), educator, businessman, conductor, composer, arranger. The first African American to conduct the Chicago Symphony Orchestra, he composed and arranged music for Count Basie, Lionel Hampton, and Duke Ellington. Born in Memphis on September 5, 1923, he and his brother, Eugene, Jr., as well as three sisters—Mary, Martha, and Almeta—were the children of the Eugene G. Hornes. A graduate of the Memphis public schools, he received a bachelor's degree from LeMoyne College and also attended the Chicago Music Conservatory and University of Tennessee. With additional degrees from Charter Life Underwriters, Life Office Management Association, and Life Underwriters Training, he prepared for careers in business and education. Horne had a successful career in insurance, working up from a salesman to secretary, treasurer, and, eventually, executive vice president of Union Protective Life Insurance Company, one of the nation's largest Black-owned insurance companies. He had a parallel career as a music teacher and band director at Woodstock, Geeter, and Manassas High Schools, where he trained many outstanding jazz musicians, including Hank Crawford, Phineas Newborn, and Charles Lloyd, to whom he offered classes in the evening and on weekends. As owner and manager of The Living Room, he combined his business acumen and musical skills in a restaurant and nightclub that offered fine cuisine and entertainment by his jazz band, The Maestros.

As a performer, Onzie Horne started out on Beale Street, conducting live interviews for his talk show, "Man On the Street," on radio station WDIA. He was also director of music at such Beale

Street landmarks as the Palace Theater, Old Daisy, and New Daisy Theaters, where bands from across the country were featured, and he directed music for the Royal American Shows. Horne is perhaps best known as a consummate musician, who played strings, horns, reeds, keyboards, and vibraphone, his favorite; studied with Billy Strayhorn and Quincy Jones; played for band leader Lionel Hampton; arranged for B. B. King and Al Jackson; and worked with Isaac Hayes, assisting with his signature piece, "Theme from Shaft." His arrangements were featured on American, Satellite, and Stax Records, and his music clients ranged from Glen Campbell to Rufus and Carla Thomas, and from Willie Mitchell to Sammy Davis, Jr. According to Mitchell, he learned a lot about production and music chart writing from Horne, and Isaac Hayes credited him with inspiring "many musicians who have gone abroad and become successful."

Dedicated to community progress, he spearheaded the restoration of the W. C. Handy Performance Arts Park and accompanied Mrs. Handy in the rededication of the park and installation of W. C. Handy's statue. Posthumously, he was given a musical note on Beale Street, near the entrance to the park, and he received the W. C. Handy Heritage Award that honors authentic Beale Street musicians. President and "Man of the Year" of the Memphis Junior Chamber of Commerce, Horne was on the board of directors of the Boys Club of America, Memphians Civic and Social Club, Memphis and Shelby County Insurance Committee, American Federation of Musicians, National Urban League, Masons, and Elks, as well as a life member of the NAACP and Alpha Phi Alpha Fraternity. Married to the former Mildred Peace of Memphis, he and his wife had two sons—Onzie, Jr., and Merrick—who grew up in the family home at 1602 South Parkway East. Onzie O. Horne died on February 9, 1973, at age forty-nine.

Horton, Odell (1929–2006), attorney, college president, judge. The first Black federal judge in Tennessee since Reconstruction, he had a reputation as a man of unfailing courtesy and fairness. The eldest of the five children of Odell and Rosa Lee Horton, he was born in Bolivar,

Tennessee, on May 13, 1929. When his father, a laborer at Western State Hospital, died, he helped his mother support the family by delivering laundry and working as a shoeshine boy. After graduating from Allen White High School in Whiteville, Tennessee, he entered Morehouse College, from which he received a bachelor's degree in 1951. Between college and law school, he served in the United States Marine Corps and attended the United States Navy School of Journalism. In 1953, he married his childhood sweetheart, Evie Randolph, and they had two sons, Odell, Jr., and Christopher. Horton graduated from Howard University Law School in 1956, and, a year later, opened a one-room law office on Beale Street. In 1962, he became an assistant United States attorney, a position that he held for five years. At the height of the civil rights struggle, Mayor Henry Loeb appointed him director of Hospitals and Health Services for Memphis, making him the only Black division director in city hall at the time. When he had to deal with a strike by hospital workers, he said, "I'm as much interested in social change as any other Negro, but I'm interested in orderly social change." He confronted officials at the University of Tennessee Medical School over the way that physicians treated patients, and he also required that indigent patients be accepted at city hospitals.

In 1969, he was appointed to the Shelby County Criminal Court and, a year later, he became president of LeMoyne-Owen College, serving for four years. He was an unsuccessful candidate for Shelby County District Attorney General in 1974, but served as a federal bankruptcy judge from 1976 to 1980. Nominated by President Jimmy Carter to be United States judge in the Western District of Tennessee, Judge Horton took office in 1980. The first Black Tennessean to serve as a federal judge, he handled a number of high-profile cases, including the toxic waste case against Velsicol Chemical Company and the criminal proceedings against former Memphis State basketball coach Dana

Kirk. He also presided over the controversial 1990 bank fraud trial of Congressman Harold Ford, who was critical of Horton's handling of his case. A trustee of Mt. Pisgah C.M.E. Church, Odell Horton was active in professional organizations and received numerous awards for community service. A Fellow of the American Bar Association, he was chair of the National Conference of Federal Trial Judges and president of the Sixth Circuit District Judges Association; he served on the United States Judicial Conference Committee on Defender Services and on the Circuit Council for the Sixth Circuit. With honorary degrees from Howard University and Mississippi Industrial College, he received awards from the C.M.E. Church, LeMoyne-Owen College, and the National Conference of Christians and Jews. After a lengthy illness, Judge Horton died of respiratory failure on February 22, 2006.

Hoskins, Ollie Braxton "Nightingale" (1936–1997), singer. A soul singer noted for his powerful voice and dynamic stage presence, Nightingale had a tremendous talent but struggled for over thirty years to gain national recognition. Born in Batesville, Mississippi, on September 6, 1936, he was the son of Glenda Jones. His early training in music was acquired from his grandmother and from his church choir. An Army veteran, he began his career as a gospel singer in the early 1950s, when he helped organize and became the lead singer of the Memphis-based gospel group, the Dixie Nightingales. The group took its name from the Dixie Homes Housing Project, where Hoskins and his wife, Rosie, lived and raised their four children: Diane, LaChelle, Veronica, and Xavier. The Nightingales began recording for Pepper and Nashboro Records, as well as for Stax's Chalice gospel label. In 1968, Al Bell, head of Stax, persuaded the group to switch from gospel to soul music. Singing in the style that made the Temptations famous, Ollie and the Nightingales recorded a number of hits for Stax, including

"I've Got a Sure Thing," "I've Got a Feeling," and "Bracing Myself for the Fall." Between 1968 and 1970, the group toured the country, playing in such places as New York's Apollo Theater.

Hoskins went solo in 1970, and became noted for expressive renditions of songs like "I'll Take a Big Fat Woman," and "I'll Drink Your Bathwater, Baby," recorded for the Memphis-based Ecko Records. Known for his dynamic live performances, he recently made a comeback on the soul circuit, playing at festivals such as the annual Sweet Soul Music Festival in Poretta Terme, Italy. Just weeks before his death, he released *Make It Sweet*, his third album for Ecko Records, considered one of his best works. One of his hit singles appears on *The Best of Ecko Records, Volume I*, along with two other Nightingale songs, "I'm Ready to Party" and "If You're Lucky Enough to Have a Good Woman." According to one critic, Nightingale was "a downhome urbane Soul Man who knew that the strength of soul music has always been the knowledge of how to survive tragedy." He did a cameo gig in *The Firm*, filmed in Memphis, while he was working for Metropolitan Inter-Faith Association. His last performance was with Bobby Rush and Marvin Sease at Club Paradise on October 4, 1997. Ollie Nightingale died unexpectedly of heart failure on October 26, 1997, four days after burying his 84-year-old mother.

Hulburt, Maurice "Fess" (1896–1984), dancer, businessman, civic leader. One of Beale Street's most beloved and enterprising promoters, Hulburt devoted sixty years of his life to helping others. A native of Coffeeville, Mississippi, he graduated from high school in Helena, Arkansas, and then attended Arkansas Baptist College in Little Rock for two years. As a young man, he traveled to St. Louis, Chicago, and Gary, where he taught dancing and entertained under the stage name "Fess" Hulburt, a name acquired from his status as a professional dance instructor. In 1921, he moved to Memphis and began working on Beale Street, where he became known as "Mr. Beale Street" because he loved the people who frequented the clubs and businesses on the Black thoroughfare. A sharp and savvy promoter, he booked Black baseball teams, brought entertainers such as Duke Ellington and Ethel Waters to Memphis, organized a musical combo called Hulburt's Low Down Hounds, founded the first Black dance school on Beale Street, and opened several restaurants, including the Ritz Café, Blue Zephyr, Manhattan, Flamingo, and Harlem House. During his final years on Beale, he operated a printing shop, but urban renewal in the 1960s forced him to move the shop to Lauderdale Street.

"He did a lot to promote the positive side of Black life here in Memphis. So many people who made it here were touched in some way by Maurice Hulburt," noted one observer. For six decades, this kind and gentle man worked to strengthen the cultural and economic fiber of the community. He founded the Artists and Models Club, as well as the Robert R. Church Elks Lodge No. 1477; he sponsored Blues Bowl Games in the 1950s and '60s to provide scholarships for students; and he raised money for numerous projects. When he died at age eighty-eight on October 29, 1984, his friends organized a funeral service that included a New Orleans-style jazz procession from the Orpheum Theater to Handy Park on Beale, where Rufus Thomas, Roberta Church, and other notables paid homage to a man who lived a life of service to others. A charming and dapper man, known for his sporty clothes, Maurice Hulburt went out as he had lived: dressed to kill in a white, pin-striped suit and a black tie with blue swirls. He left three children: Maurice, Jr. (Hot Rod), Donjulian, and Faye. Speaking about death, he once said, "When the big man takes me, I'm gone and that's the end of my blues. But then you can't be sure about that because you can't ever be sure what the good Lord's got in store for you on the other side."

Hunt, Blair Theodore, Jr. (1888–1978), educator, clergyman, civic leader. As principal of Memphis's largest Black high school and pastor of one of the city's most prestigious African American churches, he became an influential power broker during the Crump era. The son of former slaves, Emma Shoust Hunt and Blair T. Hunt, he was born in Memphis on October 1, 1888. He received his elementary and high school education at LeMoyne Institute and, during the summer, worked as a busboy at the Peabody Hotel and bartender at the Jockey Club to pay his way through college. After receiving a bachelor's degree from Morehouse College and an associate of arts degree from Harvard University, he earned a master's degree from Tennessee State A&I College. When he obtained his first teaching position at Porter School in 1913, he was one of only three college-educated Black teachers in the public schools. During World War I, Hunt served in France as a first lieutenant in the Chaplain's Corps with the 340th Service Battalion. After his discharge, he advanced rapidly in the Memphis school system, teaching at Kortrecht High School and serving as principal of La Rose and Kortrecht before his appointment as principal of Booker T. Washington High School in 1932. Professor Hunt was principal of Washington for twenty-seven years, until his retirement in 1959. Known as a strict disciplinarian "who could pull a strap faster than Wild Bill Hickock could pull a pistol," according to a former student, he carried a brass bell that he rang in the halls. He became a powerful figure during the Jim Crow era, serving as a political "go-between" in the segregated city. When he was criticized for his racial accommodationism by Black civil rights leaders, he replied, "I'm a desegregationalist but with it a gradualist. I'm not a revolutionist, but an evolutionist."

After receiving a bachelor's degree in theology from Roger Williams College in Nashville, Hunt was ordained a Baptist minister and became assistant pastor of First Baptist Lauderdale. In March 1922, he became the first pastor of Mississippi Boulevard Church and, after fifty-one years of service, was named pastor emeritus, following his retirement in 1973. A skilled orator with a deep voice and keen sense of humor, he said that his most popular sermon was "Goodbye, God—I'm Gone to College." Also active in the community, he became a deputy probation officer for Juvenile Court in 1960, and was the first Black to serve on the Tennessee Draft Board, as well as the first appointed to the Shelby County School Board in 1961. He was president of the Bluff City Education Association, trustee of Tougaloo College and Owen Junior College, and chairman of the board of the Abe Scharff YMCA. A board member of the Memphis Urban League, he was president of the Tri-State Fair, National Convention of Christian Churches, and West Tennessee Educational Congress. On July 12, 1918, Professor Hunt married a former student, eighteen-year-old Ernestine Jacobs, who bore him three sons in three years: Blair III, Wilson, and Ernest. Raised by their maternal grandmother, the sons made infrequent visits to Memphis and, later, two of them committed suicide. In *Repossessing Ernestine: A Granddaughter Uncovers the Secret History of Her American Family*, Hunt's granddaughter, Marsha Hunt, criticized the fifty-year confinement of Ernestine Jacobs Hunt to the Western State Mental Hospital, beginning in 1929. She also questioned the propriety of her grandfather's appointment of his longtime companion as his wife's guardian and executrix of his estate. Blair T. Hunt, Jr., died on June 29, 1978, at age ninety.

Hunt, George (1940–), artist, educator. One of Memphis's most prolific artists, he has acquired a national reputation for his visual interpretations of blues music and culture. The son of Hettie Griffin and Nolan Hunt, he was born on July 6, 1940, on a sugarcane plantation in rural Louisiana. He was raised by his grandmother, Addie Alexander, and great grandmother, Cilla Amos, an herb doctor who delivered him and discovered his ability to "see thangs." The young artist began drawing at age four and sold his first piece of art in grade school for a quarter. A sickly child, he drew chickens with the crayons that his grandmother gave him and made collages out of magazines that his mother, a plantation cook, brought home. Hunt won a football scholarship to the University of Arkansas at Pine Bluff and, after graduating from college in 1960, studied with artist Hale Woodruff at New York University. In 1972, he became a football coach and art director at Carver High School, where he taught for over three decades, until his retirement in 1998. His colorful canvases are inspired by the Black Southern folk tradition, African American men and women, and the civil rights movement, which he witnessed first hand. He was living in Arkansas when nine students desegregated the Little Rock High School, and he helped put the body of Martin Luther King, Jr., on the plane after his assassination.

Known primarily as a visual translator of the blues, George Hunt's bold, dramatic, artistic style captures the musical genius of bluesmen such as John Lee Hooker, Robert Johnson, and B. B. King. He grew up in the deep South, listening to music in his mother-in-law's Dreamland Café in Helena, Arkansas, where he heard blues legends such as Sonny Boy Williamson and watched customers drink, dance, and party hardy. One of his paintings was featured in the Memphis Arts Council calendar, and he was one of five artists invited to participate in the 1991 Memphis Arts Festival Invitational Exhibition. Since 1992, he has designed posters for the Beale Street Music Festival and, in 1994, he was chosen from thirty-four artists to design the Memphis in May poster honoring the Ivory Coast. In 1996, Hunt was commissioned to paint twenty-four portraits and a large exterior mural for the Blues & Legends Hall of Fame Museum in Robinsonville, Mississippi. His painting, "America Cares," which was commissioned in 1997 as a tribute to the Little Rock Nine, won the 1998 Arkansas Advertising Federation Silver Award, hung in the White House for four years, and was chosen, along with paintings by Romare Bearden and Jacob Lawrence, for a series of 37-cent postal stamps depicting the civil rights movement.

Two of his multimedia works, "Adam" and "Eve," were exhibited at "Visions of My People: African-American Art in Tennessee" at the Tennessee State Museum in Nashville in 1997, and "Adam" was used on the front cover of the exhibition catalog, brochure, and gallery viewing guide. Hunt was the featured artist for the Rock and Roll Hall of Fame Museum's American Music Master's 1998 and 2000 conferences; the '98 conference, "Hellhound on My Trail: Robert Johnson and the Blues," used his painting for the poster and gave the artist a one-man exhibition at Cleveland's 9th Street Gallery. His exhibit, "Conjurating the Blues: The High Cotton Tour," was on view at Seattle Center's Experience Music Project in the summer of 2003. More recently, he created the 2006 Memphis in May poster, "Ridin' with the King." A founding member of the Memphis Black Arts Alliance, he is co-author of *Twenty-Five Black Artists in Memphis*. George Hunt is married to the former Marva Woods of Helena, Arkansas, and they have a son, Kylon, and a daughter, Harlyn.

Hunter, Alberta (1895–1984), blues singer, composer. Memphis-born Hunter became the toast of Black Chicago nightclubs in the 1920s and the queen of European blues cafes in the 1930s. She was born on April 1, 1895, in a clapboard house on High Street to Charles E. and Laura Peterson Hunter. When her father, a railroad porter, abandoned his wife and two children, her mother worked as a domestic in a "sporting house" on Gayoso to support the family. Alberta attended Grant School and worshiped at Collins Chapel C.M.E. Church. At age sixteen, she ran away from home and, after months of peeling potatoes in Chicago, landed a job singing at Dago Frank's, a bordello, for $10 a week. Later, she sang at small, Black-owned clubs such as Hugh Hoskins and Elite Number One, where her throaty blues numbers made her one of Chicago's most promising new talents. After singing at the prestigious Panama Club, she began a five-year stint, in 1917, at the famous Dreamland Ballroom, where she was hailed as the "South Side's Sweetheart." A private person who preferred the company of women, Hunter married Willard Saxby Townsend on January 27, 1919, but the marriage lasted only two months.

In the 1920s, Hunter moved to New York, bought a Harlem apartment, and traveled the Vaudeville circuit with a song-and-dance act called "Alberta Hunter and Company." From 1927 to 1939, she spent most of her time in Europe. There, she became fluent in French and learned to sing in several languages; performed at cabarets in Cairo, Istanbul, and Copenhagen; wore designer clothes and befriended European artists and aristocrats; and performed with Paul Robeson before Queen Mary and King George V. Unable to find singing engagements on her return to the United States in 1940, she did volunteer work, gave benefit performances for the NAACP and the Harlem Children's Fund, and worked as a USO entertainer during the Second World War and Korean War. The gifted composer, who could neither read nor write music, wrote at least seventy songs, including "The Love I Have for You," "My Castle Rockin'," and "Down Hearted Blues." She wrote bawdy lyrics and plaintive pieces, such as "When I Go Home," as well as religious songs like "You Got to Reap Just What You Sow."

When she was sixty-one and unable to find work as a singer, Alberta Hunter put her age back to forty-nine and took a nurses' training course, which led to a twenty-year career as a practical nurse at New York's Goldwater Hospital. She was furious when she was forced to retire at "age 70," although she was actually eighty-two years old. In 1977, the "little lady with the big voice" made a spectacular comeback as a singer: she debuted at Carnegie Hall, sang at the Kennedy Center, and performed for President Jimmy Carter at the White House. She returned to Memphis, in 1978, for the world premier of the film *Remember My Name* for which, at age eighty-three, she composed and performed all the songs, including the title number. Just before her death in October 1980, Hunter came home to receive the Blues Foundation's W. C. Handy Award as the Traditional

Female Blues Artist of the Year. This dynamic and spirited woman was a survivor, who overcame many obstacles—childhood poverty and sexual abuse, exploitation and unemployment—to become an acclaimed artist. She captures that spirit in one of her last songs: "I've been sloughed way down, but / I'll slow drag up again. / When that big day arrives / Remember my name."

Hutchins, Fred Lew (1888–1984), postman, historian. Noted for his prodigious memory and interest in local history, he published two books that chronicled Memphis history at the turn of the century. Born on January 14, 1888, he was the twelfth of fourteen children born to Tobias and Henrietta "Rette" Hutchins. The family lived in Michigan, Mississippi, but moved to Memphis when Fred was four years old. His father opened a shoe store near the corner of Mississippi and Walker Avenue but, after the 1892 lynching of three Blacks at the Curve, he moved his shop to St. Paul Street. Fred attended Julia Hooks's kindergarten and then entered LeMoyne Normal Institute, where he served as class leader in three grades. After nine years at the Institute, he dropped out but eventually received a high school diploma at night school. In 1904, he began delivering the *Memphis News-Scimitar* on his bicycle and became a self-appointed "side-walk superintendent" of early twentieth-century Memphis life. *What Happened in Memphis*, which he published privately in 1965, is a collection of anecdotes, folk tales, and character sketches of noted Memphians such as Bob Church, W. C. Handy, and Tom Lee. The folk historian wrote in his preface: "I have tried to draw a series of word pictures that will capture…the flavor, the atmosphere, the color and the spirit…of Memphis." Gifted with a sharp memory, he could recall, after 75 years, the snowfall of 1892, and the names of his LeMoyne classmates.

In 1912, Hutchins became a letter carrier for the U.S. Postal Service, a job that he held for forty-four years. With a twinkle in his eye, he recalled that he came in last the first time he took the postal examination but, on the third try, he made the highest score. As a result, he was given a prestigious job: traveling on trains to weigh the mail. On November 10, 1927, he married Edna Nicholson, and they built a spacious brick house at 1087 Mississippi Boulevard at a cost of $4,797. The gregarious gentleman enjoyed Christmas: on December 24, he entertained friends on the telephone by playing his violin, and he served his special, homemade eggnog at his annual Christmas parties. After his retirement from the post office, in 1956, Hutchins began writing in earnest; he published articles on local history in periodicals and journals such as the *West Tennessee Society Papers* and, in 1972, he read a paper about Beale Street at a meeting of the West Tennessee Historical Society. In the late 1960s, he published *Sketch History of Second Congregational Church Centennial, 1868–1968*. In 1923, he joined the church and served as its treasurer for fifty years. In recognition of his contributions to local history, the Memphis/Shelby County Library and LeMoyne-Owen College sponsored "A Tribute to Fred Hutchins" on February 26, 1982, and County Mayor William Morris declared it "Fred Hutchins Day" in Shelby County. Two years later, on February 11, 1984, he died at age ninety-seven.

Hyter, James A. (1922–), vocalist, businessman. Noted for his moving rendition of "Ol Man River" at the Memphis in May Sunset Symphony, he has performed at concerts, churches, and conventions throughout the country and abroad. He was born in Athens, Alabama, to a piano-playing mother and a restauranteur father. His mother died when he was just a week old, so his father and grandmother moved to Memphis, where he grew up. While in grammar school, he began singing in the Centenary United Methodist Church choir and, later, joined his high school glee club. In 1940, he graduated from Booker T. Washington High School, where he was encouraged by his music teacher, Emma Corporal, and he began studying voice under Madame Florence McCleave. After turning down a four-year scholarship to Rust College, he served three years in the Army during World War II, worked in his father's restaurants—Flakes Lunchroom and the Griddle Playhouse at Vance and Lauderdale—in the 1950s, sold insurance for Atlanta Life Insurance Company, and tended bar at Colonial Country Club. While bartending, he met the former president of Blue Cross-Blue Shield, who offered him a job with the company; Hyter accepted and worked his way up to marketing representative for BC/BS. Around 1961, he married Flora, a former school crossing guard and Memphis City Schools cashier, whom he met at church, and they have a daughter, Beverly.

Hyter gained fame—if not fortune—late in life. His big break came in 1968, when he played Joe in the Memphis State University production of *Show Boat*. He made his first Sunset Symphony appearance in 1977, singing "Ol Man River" before an audience of 100,000, and, since then, has sung the song more than 2,000 times. In 1996, he recorded his first album, *Musically Yours, James A. Hyter*, which consists primarily of spirituals such as "Swing Lo, Sweet Chariot," and "Bound for the Kingdom," but classical music is his forte. For more than thirty years, he has sung in the Memphis Symphony chorus, starred in local operas, and toured Europe as a soloist with the Greater Memphis Chorale. He has performed with the Santa Fe Opera and the Little Rock Symphony; he has appeared at the Kansas City Lyric Theater; and he participated in a Jackson (Mississippi) Symphony Orchestra Pops concert. James A. Hyter has served for many years on the boards of Opera Memphis, Memphis Orchestral Society, and Charter Lakeside Hospital. Every year during Christmas, he entertained cancer patients at Baptist and Methodist Hospitals. Such service has earned him many awards, including the 1988 Annual Host Award by the Memphis Convention and Visitors Bureau and the 1989 Citizen of the Year Award by the Memphis and Shelby County Optimist

Committee. He was featured in the May/June issue of *Tennessee Illustrated* magazine, and the James A. Hyter Music Scholarship was established to benefit vocal students in the Mid-South area.

Jackson, Alvin O'Neal (1950–), clergyman, religious leader. For almost twenty years, this dynamic spiritual leader led one of the largest and fastest growing congregations in the nation. He was born on July 10, 1950, in Laurel, Mississippi, and grew up in Indianola, Mississippi, where his parents were public school teachers. After graduating from high school in Indianola, he entered Chapman College in California, and visited Asia and Africa through the college's World Campus Afloat Program. One summer, after working at a vacation Bible school in Indianapolis, Indiana, he decided to transfer to Butler University, from which he received a bachelor's degree in sociology. He then enrolled in Andover-Newton Seminary in Boston. During a summer pastorate at a church in Roanoke, Virginia, he met and married Tina Brown, and they have a son, Cullen O'Neal. Persuaded to remain in Virginia, he entered Duke University School of Divinity from which he received a master's degree. He wrote a dissertation, "A Preaching Model for Equipping Disciples (Making Numbers Count)," and received the Doctor of Ministry Degree from United Theological Seminary in Dayton, Ohio. In 1977, the young clergyman returned to Indianapolis as associate minister of the Second Christian Church.

When a snow storm stranded him in Memphis on a flight from Houston in 1979, Jackson visited Mississippi Boulevard Christian Church, which had not had a pastor for two years. He was invited back to preach a trial sermon and, five months later, became senior pastor of the church, one of the few Black congregations affiliated with the Christian Church (Disciples of Christ) denomination. A charismatic minister noted for his scholarly treatment of contemporary topics, Jackson was hailed for his outstanding preaching ministry. Under his leadership, Mississippi Boulevard became one of the largest and fastest growing churches in the nation with two morning services on Sunday, a radio ministry, and outreach programs for children and young adults. The congregation eventually purchased a larger facility at 250 E. Raines in Whitehaven, which included a large sanctuary, 125 classrooms, day care center, library, and gymnasium. By 1988, the church had an operating budget of $1.5 million, 10% of which went toward a day care center, community clothes closet, and a meal program called "Manna from Heaven." When the congregation outgrew the Raines Road facility, it relocated to the former site of Bellevue Baptist Church, where the church established a school, ministry for children and youth, program to feed the hungry, and drugs and AIDS support groups.

Active in religious circles on the local and national levels, Reverend Jackson was elected president of the predominantly White Memphis Ministers' Association in 1982. He was also elected national vice president of the Black Fellowship within the predominantly White Christian Church, and he became a Convocation Trustee of the Christian Church in 1986. When he resigned the pastorate of Mississippi Boulevard Church in 1997, after serving for eighteen years, the church had the largest Christian Church congregation in the nation, with 8,600 members. On April 1, 1998, Jackson became senior minister of the National City Christian Church of Washington, the church to which Presidents James Garfield and Lyndon Johnson belonged. Known as the denomination's national cathedral, it has a membership of 500, which is 83% White and 15% Black and Hispanic. Reverend Alvin O. Jackson took a leave of absence from the church in 2003, and he later resigned the pastorate after admitting that he borrowed sermons from other ministers without permission.

Johnican, Minerva (1938–), educator, businesswoman, city councilwoman, county commissioner. The only woman to serve on the City Council and the Shelby County Commission, she was a powerful political figure for over two decades. The sixth of the seven children of Annie Mae Rounsoville Johnican and John Bruce Johnican, she was born on November 16, 1938, and lives in the house of her birth. After graduating from Hamilton High School in 1956, she received a B.A. degree in elementary education from Tennessee A&I State University and pursued graduate study in library science at Memphis State University. She worked for seventeen years in the Memphis City Schools, first as a teacher at Dunn Avenue, A. B. Hill, and Georgia Avenue Schools, and later, as a school librarian at Colonial Elementary School. In 1975, she defeated Walter L. Evans in a six-candidate race by only 29 votes to win the District 6 seat on the Shelby County Court, becoming the first woman in recent years to be elected to that position. While on the court, she was a Shelby County delegate to the National Democratic Convention; she co-chaired the 1979 mini-convention in Memphis; and she was elected the first Black and first female president of the Tennessee County Commission Association. In 1982, after serving two terms, Squire Johnican was defeated in a hotly contested battle by Julian Bolton, who had the support of Congressman Harold Ford.

Two years later, Minerva Johnican was elected to the Memphis City Council with strong Republican support in a run-off with David Hill, who was backed by the Fords. In the run-off, she received 84% of the Black vote and 40% of the White, which underscored, she said, the importance of coalition building. In 1987, she resigned from the Council to run for mayor against Dick Hackett, with a "Building Bridges for a Better Memphis" campaign. In 1988, she finished third in her race for reelection to the City Council. In spite of her claim ("People like me because I'm gutsy and because I deliver"), she was defeated in what was described as an under-financed, lackluster campaign. Undaunted by her two defeats, she ran successfully for criminal court clerk in 1990, and served for four years. Minerva Johnican has also gained success as a businesswoman. She founded Alpha Termite and Pest Control Company at 1565 Lamar, co-founded a public relations firm, and, later, formed Commonwealth Consultants Limited, a business and political consulting firm. In 1997, she founded OMO [On My Own] Mortgage and Financial Services, located at 4466 Elvis Presley Boulevard.

Johnson, Jason Miccolo (1956–), photographer. An award-winning photographer whose visual images have appeared in many books and periodicals, he has lectured and exhibited his work throughout the country. The youngest of five sons, he was born on November 21, 1956, in Hayti, Missouri, and, nine years later, moved to South Memphis and entered Kansas Street School. In 1974, he graduated from George Washington Carver High School, where he played baseball, was school photographer, and served on the newspaper and yearbook staffs. He attended Memphis State University but moved to Washington, D.C. to continue at Howard University, from which he received a bachelor's degree in journalism in 1994. Inspired by Gordon Parks's *The Learning Tree*, he used his extracurricular activities, educational training, and experiences as a photographer in the U.S. Navy to shape a professional career as a documentary, editorial, and fine arts photographer. In the 1980s, he was photo editor at USA Today's *Sports Weekly* and production assistant at ABC Network News's *Good Morning America*. He gained more artistic freedom in 1989, when he became a freelance photographer: he took exclusive photographs of Thurgood Marshall, Nelson Mandela, and Oprah Winfrey; covered President Clinton's inauguration and the Million Man March; lectured at universities and conferences; and became official photographer of the National Association of Black Journalists and of the A.M.E. Church's general conference.

A resident of Washington, D.C., Jason Miccolo Johnson is a board member of Beacon House, which supports education for at-risk youth; a member of the American Society of Media Photographers; and president of The Exposure Group African American Photographers Association, Inc. His photographs have appeared in *Ebony*, *Newsweek*, and *Black Enterprise*, as well as in books such as *Songs of My People*, *Standing in the Need of Prayer*, and *Q: The Autobiography of Quincy Jones*. In 2006, he published his first solo photography book, *Soul Sanctuary: Images of the African American Worship Experience*, a collection that captures the spiritual dimensions of the Black church. It contains a foreword by Gordon Parks, 170 black and white photographs, and essays by noted clergymen. Johnson's work has appeared in two major Smithsonian exhibitions—*Reflections in Black* and *Speak to My Heart*—and is included in the permanent collections of the St. Louis Art Museum and Houston's Museum of Fine Arts. In 2007, an exhibition of photographs from his book was held at the Stax Museum of American Soul Music in Memphis.

Jones, Fred, Jr. (1948–), businessman. One of Memphis's most successful entrepreneurs, he created the Southern Heritage Classic, a sports and entertainment institution that pours millions of dollars into the city's economy. The fourth of Lula and Fred Jones's five children, he was born in Memphis on January 2, 1948, and walked to school from the housing project where the family lived. He attended W. Alonzo Locke Elementary School and Porter Junior High School, where he was inducted into the honor society, and graduated from Booker T. Washington High School in 1966. While studying for a bachelor's degree in business administration at Memphis State University, he worked as an auditor and assistant branch manager at Union Planters Bank. After graduating from college in 1971, he used his background in music and business to serve as tour manager for Isaac Hayes for four years. In 1975, he became an independent producer, staging concerts for such national celebrities as Aretha Franklin, Sting, and Bobby "Blue" Bland, and he recently handled Usher's breakout tour of 2004.

In 1984, Jones founded and now serves as president of Summitt Management Corporation. Six years later, he founded and produced the Southern Heritage Classic, a three-day event that leads up to a football game between Jackson State and Tennessee State Colleges at FedEx Forum. The event, supported by corporate partner FedEx and others, includes a golf tournament, fashion show, luncheon, parade, battle of the bands, and concerts with headliners such as Usher and Kanye West. It is estimated that the Classic brings $5–11 million annually to the Memphis economy, and the Southern Heritage Foundation donates tens of thousands of dollars to nonprofits and schools. Part-owner of the Memphis Grizzles NBA sports team, Jones has won many awards: the 1996 Black Business of the Year Award, 2000 Outstanding Community Sales Award, 2002 African American Male Image Award, 2004 Kate Gooch Award for Service to the Community, and 2005 Entrepreneur of the Year Award. A life member of the NAACP and member of the Memphis Black Business Association, he was inducted into the Alumni Hall of Fame for the Memphis City Schools in 2002, and into the Society of Entrepreneurs in 2006. Carolyn and Fred Jones have six children.

Jones, Thomas Oliver (1924–1989), labor leader. Known as the father of the labor movement in Memphis, he led a strike of the city's sanitation workers that paved the way for the unionization of policemen, firefighters, and other public employees. He was born in Memphis on September 27, 1924. Jones, who was a veteran of World War II, became a sanitation worker in 1959, and soon began complaining about the intolerable working conditions. Under his leadership, a small group of men began holding monthly meetings at the old AFL-CIO labor temple at Beale and Lauderdale to discuss their problems. One of the union leaders noted that "T. O. used to run the meetings back in the days when it was really dangerous, when the mayor and them would just as soon run you out of town." In the summer of 1963, Jones led thirty-three men in a short-lived, disorganized strike, but the city refused to recognize unions for public employees. A year later, he founded and became the first president of a small, independent union that eventually became Local 1733 (number "33" in honor of the thirty-three men who walked out in 1963) of the American Federation of State, County and Municipal Employees (AFSCME). Today, the union is the largest local in the AFL-CIO, with a membership of almost 7,000.

On February 1, 1968, two sanitation workers were crushed to death in the back of a garbage truck and, several days later, Jones called a meeting of sanitation workers to protest the unsafe conditions, low salaries, inadequate benefits, lack of workers' compensation, and other problems. Approximately 500 men attended the meeting and called for a strike to demand salary increases, union recognition, a dues checkoff, and other benefits, but Mayor Henry Loeb, who considered the strike illegal, refused to negotiate with union leaders. When 1,300 sanitation workers walked off their jobs in protest, carrying signs stating "I Am a Man," the strike escalated into a mass movement, as churches, civic groups, and civil rights organizations became involved in what has been called "one of the biggest and most pervasive protests in the labor/civil rights movement." On April 4, 1968, the strike led to the assassination of Martin Luther King, Jr., who had come to Memphis in support of the sanitation workers.

The strike finally ended on April 16, twelve days after King's assassination, when city officials acceded to most of the union's demands and recognized Local 1733. T. O. Jones, described as a tough-talking man of "character, compassion, courage, and consistency," said that he and his co-workers had waited five years, from 1963 to 1968, to be treated "like men." After serving as president of the local chapter of AFSCME, he joined the union's international staff and then worked for the AFL-CIO labor council. He retired in the late 1970s, and he had a series of heart attacks. He spent the last four years of his life at Paul Borda Tower, a public housing facility, where he became "part of neglected Black history in Memphis," according to his niece. After a long illness, T. O. Jones died at the Memphis Veterans Medical Center on April 12, 1989. His funeral was held at his church, Union Grove Baptist Church, with sanitation workers serving as honorary pallbearers, and he was buried at National Cemetery. A memorial service was held on April 16, at Clayborne Temple A.M.E. Church, the site of many civil rights rallies. In his honor, members of the International Brotherhood of Electrical Workers Local Union 1288 named its hall at 4000 Clearpool Circle the T. O. Jones Union Hall. He and his wife Helen, whom he called "Precious," were the parents of six daughters—Myquitia, Tamika, Charlotte, Yolanda, Reiko, and Ruth—and four sons: Richard, Jesse, Thomas, and Tyrone.

Jones, Velma Lois (1930–), educator. The first African American classroom teacher to serve as president of the 44,000-member Tennessee Education Association, she taught mathematics in the Memphis City Schools for forty-three years. The only child of Ethel Crotie Joyner Smith and Eddie Lee Jones, she was born on September 7, 1930, and was raised by her mother after the deaths of her father and stepfather. She still lives in the house on Edward Avenue in the Vollintine-Evergreen neighborhood, five blocks from where she was born. "Living in the community was one of the things that endeared me to my students and my parents," she says. She attended Manassas Elementary and High School and received a bachelor's degree in elementary education from LeMoyne College in 1952, as well as a master's degree from Teacher's College of Columbia University in 1957. The woman who always wanted to be a teacher worked in the Memphis City Schools for almost fifty years, first at Hyde Park Elementary School and later at Cypress Junior High School. When Memphis schools were desegregated, the middle grades of Hyde Park School were combined with those of Hollywood School to form Cypress Junior High School. Her colleagues described Jones as a "visionary who works hard and cares about public school children and [their] teachers."

Active for over four decades in civic, political, and educational organizations, Jones served as president of the Memphis Education Association and of the West Tennessee Education Association, and she was the first woman president of the Memphis Branch of the NAACP, from 1972 to 1976. In 1987, she ran for District 7 of the Memphis City Council but lost to Ricky Peete in the runoff election. A delegate to the 1992, 1996, and 2000 Democratic National Conventions, she attended President Clinton's inaugurations and campaigned for Congressmen Harold Ford, Sr., and Jr., as well as other candidates for public office. After serving as vice president of the Tennessee Education Association from 1994 to 1996, she became president of the organization in September 1996, after her friend and former president of the TEA, Kathy Woodall, died of cancer. The state affiliate of the National Education Association, the TEA lobbies the state legislature, negotiates for pay raises, and serves the interests of Tennessee teachers. Under her six-year, three-term leadership, the Association had to deal with issues such as reductions in class size, programs for at-risk students, planning time for teachers, and funding for the Basic Education Program. A member of the board of trustees of LeMoyne-Owen College from 1987 to 2001, Velma Lois Jones belongs to many organizations and is a life-long member of Trinity C.M.E. Church.

Jordan, Dewitt W., Jr. (1932–1977), artist. Called one of the top ten American artists by *Time* magazine, Jordan gained critical and commercial success as a painter in the 1960s. Born on December 12, 1932, to the Dewitt W. Jordans in Nashville, Tennessee, he grew up in West Helena, Arkansas, where he graduated from high school. His father sold burial policies and his mother, who occasionally passed for White, was an embalmer. After attending college in Ohio and Tennessee, he received his training at the California School of Arts and Crafts in San Francisco and the Chouinard Art Institute in Los Angeles. When he finished art school in 1956, he spent six months with Native Americans in Arizona and then worked briefly as a sketch artist for Warner Brothers movie studio in California. In the early 1960s, he moved to Memphis, where his work came to the attention of developer Harry Bloomfield, who commissioned paintings for the Rivermont, 100 North Main Building, and Holly Hills Country Club. Jordan painted a mural for the Holiday Inn-Rivermont and, in 1968, completed a 4 × 20-foot mural for the Top of the 100 Club, for which he traveled to Louisiana and Arkansas and did extensive historical research in public libraries and private book collections. "A Mural of Memphis" depicts the history of the city from the era of the Chickasaw Indians and Hernando de Soto to the age of Boss Crump and Elvis Presley.

Known for his richly detailed paintings, Jordan gained national attention for works such as his 1964 "Birth of the Blues," considered by critics to be one of his best paintings. According to Bloomfield, Jordan "was the closest thing to the old masters that I've ever seen. He made a painting look alive." Although he painted portraits of celebrities such as Danny Thomas, Sammy Davis, Jr., and Tennessee Ernie Ford, he was noted primarily for his paintings of rural Blacks. When he was criticized for such works during the Black consciousness movement of the 1960s, the painter responded, "That's my heritage.

Hell, man, that's the South." One of his favorite paintings was "The Judgment Is Near," which depicts a woman looking disdainfully at a sinner. The artist explained with a laugh, "She's seeing old Dewitt, drunk and in the alley. You can just hear her saying...'I knew your parents, Dewitt.'" Three of his paintings—"Cotton Landing at Memphis," "Birth of the Blues," and "A Mural of Memphis"—were added to the First Tennessee Heritage Collection on December 11, 1985. Something of a Bohemian, Jordan liked to paint in the nude while drinking Scotch and listening to classical music. Once, some farmers caught him painting in the flesh and called the sheriff, who explained, "That's Dewitt. He's an artist. He's a little kooky." Then the sheriff bought three paintings, after telling Jordan, "I don't like your personality, but I like your painting." Believing that he would not become famous until after his death, his penchant for Scotch and pretty women led to an early demise. On October 9, 1977, Jordan was fatally shot by the brother of his girlfriend, Connie Gidwani, and left behind a wife, Janet Martindale Jordan, and their five children: Victor, Vincent, Eric, Anthony, and Cynthia.

Joysmith, Brenda (1952–) artist. She is a nationally acclaimed painter whose works have appeared on film and television stage sets, and have been included in individual and corporate collections. Born Brenda Joyce Smith on February 29, 1952, she was the seventh of Ada and Hamilton Smith's nine children. At Carnes Elementary School, she drew friends' portraits and sold handmade paper dolls for a quarter, and at Porter Junior High School, art teacher Santee Gholston introduced her to pastels and portraits when she was fourteen years old. After graduating from Booker T. Washington High School in 1970, she won a scholarship to the University of Chicago; there, she founded a fine arts club but developed an allergy to oil paint solvents, which led her back to pastels as her medium of choice. After receiving a bachelor's degree in 1974, she moved to the San Francisco area, lived with her sister and family, and worked as a part-time receptionist and substitute teacher while mastering her craft. In 1980, she opened a studio in her sister's garage and, since then, has worked full time as an artist.

For the next seven years, Brenda Joysmith (who combined her middle and last names into a professional pseudonym) worked steadily, producing pastel portraits of ordinary African Americans. In 1984, her family and friends in Memphis helped her to produce *Tapestry*, her first print folio of six portraits, including her signature piece, "Madonna," which depicts a woman in flowing white robes holding a baby. This most famous and best-selling of her portraits was on the walls of the Huxtables' living room in the television program, *The Cosby Show*. Other works of hers have appeared on the stage sets of *A Different World*, *The Jamie Foxx Show*, and *Everybody Hates Chris*, as well as in films such as *Philadelphia*, *The Preacher's Wife*, and *Kingdom Come*. In 1997, Joysmith underwent brain surgery and, after a difficult recovery, she and her husband, Robert Bain, decided to relocate to Memphis, where they bought a 6,400-square-foot, renovated warehouse in the South Main Art District.

In 2000, they opened the Joysmith Gallery and Studio on the first floor and converted the second floor into their living quarters, where she experiments in water-soluble oils, watercolors, acrylics, and three-dimensional clay. Although Joysmith's original paintings sell for thousands of dollars, she wants her work to be accessible to all art lovers, so her open-edition and limited edition prints are available at her gallery, through national distributors, and online. Her Black genre paintings are in the collections of celebrities such as Maya Angelou, George Benson, and Roberta Flack, as well as in the corporate collections of the National Council of Negro Women and the U.S. Embassy in Lesotho, South Africa. She has received awards from the Memphis City Schools, National Coalition of 100 Black Women, Delta Sigma Theta Alumnae Chapter, and many other organizations.

Kateo, Loretta Hicks (1914–2002), social worker. One of Memphis's pioneering social workers, "Loretta Kateo has molded and scolded thousands of young people since she became a social worker in 1939," according to an article in the *Memphis Press Scimitar*. She was born in Yazoo, Mississippi, on September 23, 1914, to Isaac Henry and Mamie Watts Jones. After graduating, in 1939, from LeMoyne College with an A.B. degree in sociology, she volunteered with Family Welfare in Memphis. Four years later, she received a master's degree in social work from Atlanta University and began a forty-year career with Family Service, where she was a casework supervisor. Concerned with the welfare of children, she had written her master's thesis on day care centers at a time when there were no public-funded centers or preschool facilities for African Americans in Memphis. In the early 1940s, she co-founded Orange Mound Day Nursery at 2415 Saratoga, the first facility built exclusively as a preschool program. She also served as a mental health consultant for the Memphis Early Childhood Development Center, resource instructor at LeMoyne-Owen College, and part-time social welfare instructor at Memphis State University. After her retirement from Family Service, she was a home-based counselor with Shelby County, CAA Headstart from 1984 to 1985.

Loretta Kateo was awarded a Ford Foundation grant in 1954 to study parenting skills at the University of Chicago and, in 1971, her article "What Is Monsarrat Street?" was published in *Highlights* magazine. She received awards from organizations such as the Memphis Branch YWCA, Memphis City Council, Shelby County Government, Tennessee Black Caucus, Tennessee House of Representatives, and National Association of Social Workers. Named Memphis Branch Social Worker of the Year as well as Outstanding Social Worker of America by the American Academy of Human Services, she was active in many organizations, including Friends of the Orpheum; LeMoyne-Owen

College Alumni Association; Pan Hellenic Society, which voted her Greek of the Year; and Zeta Phi Beta Sorority, Inc., which twice named her Soror of the Year. In 1981, she was designated Alumnus of the Year by LeMoyne-Owen College. Active in St. John Baptist Church, she sang in the choir and served as choir president. She and her husband, Karonto C. Kateo, had one daughter, Rosetta. Loretta Hicks Kateo died on February 20, 2002, and is buried in New Park Cemetery.

Kelley, Frances Burnett (1934–), singer, airline agent, television host, evangelist. A former television co-host and author of an inspirational memoir, she abandoned a glamorous life in show business to become an evangelist in the Church of God in Christ. Frances Burnett was born on April 4, 1934, but, when her mother became ill, she lived with her grandparents, Albert and Clara Connor. She attended Porter School and Booker T. Washington High School, where she was encouraged by an English teacher, Annette Hubbard Roberts. At seventeen, she began singing with a band, won a contest, and joined A. C. Williams's Teen Town Singers at radio station WDIA, before becoming an announcer on station WJAK in Jackson, Tennessee. After attending Lane College for two years, she went to Hot Springs, Arkansas, where an agent offered her a spot singing in Detroit nightclubs for $125 a week.

As an entertainer, Frances Burnett sang at the Apollo Theater, performed in London, recorded with Decca, opened for Billie Holiday, and sang with Dizzy Gillespie and Duke Ellington. She soon acquired a white Cadillac, designer gowns, and a Central Park apartment; eventually, she married her manager, George Kelley, and moved with him to Detroit, where he opened a nightclub. She was lonely and unhappy, however. Her marriage failed, she began drinking, and, finally, she attempted suicide. But in 1963, she walked into a little church and was saved by a minister who had been a heroin addict. In 1965, she returned to Memphis with her baby, George, and began to recover. She sold clothes at Goldsmith's for $47 a week and then obtained a job at American Airlines, where she was a ticket agent for twenty-seven years. In 1974, she was offered a position at WREG-TV Channel 3 as co-host of "Good Morning From Memphis." In the twelve years that she appeared on television, she interviewed many notables, but the most challenging was David Duke, wizard of the Ku Klux Klan.

Frances Kelley's memoir *Better Than I Was* recounts her development as an evangelist and inspirational speaker. A member of the Church of God in Christ, she has participated (since 1969) in a prison ministry at Shelby County Penal Farm. One of the highlights of her life was her May 1978 testimony before 52,000 people at the close of Billy Graham's Memphis Crusade, when she received a standing ovation. She has sponsored many crusades and revivals, and her ministry has led to her appointment as National Prayer Leader of COGIC, president of the State and Local Headquarters' Jurisdiction Inspirational Team, and member of the board of directors of the Charles Harrison Mason Bible College, Memphis Chapter. A Minority Scholarship Fund at Briarcrest Baptist School in Memphis was named in her honor. About her life, Frances Burnett Kelley says humbly, "I am just a sinner who was saved by grace."

King, Albert (1923–1992), guitarist, blues singer. Called the "Godfather of the Blues," he was one of the most influential bluesmen of the 1960s and '70s. He was born in Indianola, Mississippi, on April 17, 1923, but grew up in Forrest City and Osceola, Arkansas, where he listened to country blues. After moving to Memphis in the 1940s, he worked as a garage night manager for four years and learned to play the guitar by watching Beale Street musicians. He bought his first guitar for a dollar and twenty-five cents and a trumpet player taught him the keys, but he kept his day job—as a mechanic or truck driver or bulldoze operator—until he went on the road, where times were tough. "I've worked for a dollar and a half a night and a bowl of stew," he said. Sometimes, he had to pack a pistol, but not too many folk messed with Big Albert, who stood 6' 4" and weighed 260 pounds.

Albert King's early music reflected his Mississippi origin, particularly songs like "Drowning on Dry Land," which owed a lot to blues shouters like Big Joe Turner and Jimmy Witherspoon. When he moved North, however, his music became more urban; in fact, he is one of those credited with urbanizing the blues by merging the rough sound of Delta bottleneckers with the powerful city-sound of electric guitarists. After moving to East St. Louis, he recorded for Bobbin and, when King Records bought out Bobbin, he produced his first hit, "Don't Throw Your Love on Me So Strong." In 1965, he got his first break when a music promoter heard him playing in an after-hours club and booked him with Jimi Hendrix and Janis Joplin at San Francisco's famous Fillmore West auditorium. That gig led to a critically acclaimed album, *Live at Fillmore West and Fillmore East*, and it also brought him to the attention of producers at Stax, where he recorded his biggest hits: "Laundromat Blues," "Overall Junction," and "As Years Go Passing By." He also made some of his best albums, including *Blues Power*, *I'll Play the Blues for You*, and *Jammed Together*, with "Pops" Staples and Steve Cropper. After Stax closed, he performed in concerts and at jazz festivals throughout the country, and he stole the show at the 1970 Ann Arbor Blues Festival. Although he played for the Grammy Awards and was nominated twice for an award, the prize went, ironically, to his protégé, Stevie Ray Vaughn.

Big Albert moved back to Memphis in the late 1980s to play at Peabody Alley, becoming the first Black musician to play regularly at a downtown club. He was married to Glendle King of Lovejoy, Illinois, for many years, and they had three children: Evelyn, Gloria, and Donald. Albert King was planning to make a 1993 tour of Europe, when he died of a heart attack in Memphis on December 21, 1992, at age sixty-nine.

King, Riley "B. B." (1925–), guitarist, blues singer. Called the greatest living blues guitarist, King is noted for his biting lead guitar, passionate vocals, and gracious stage presence. The son of Albert and Nora Ella Pully King, he was born on September 16, 1925, on a cotton plantation between Ita Bena and Indianola, Mississippi. After his parents separated, he lived with his mother until her death when he was nine years old, and he began working as a farmhand in Indianola for $22.50 a week. Later, he went to live with his father and stepmother but was forbidden to sing the blues, which was considered Devil's music. Riley began singing gospel music in church and performed with groups such as the St. John Gospel Singers, but he was drawn to the blues. He heard the records of great bluesmen such as Blind Lemon Jefferson, Robert Johnson, and Sonny Boy Williamson on his aunt's Victrola and, later, he heard them in clubs such as Johnny Jones's Nightspot. Finally, his boss loaned him $30 to take music lessons and to order a guitar from the Sears and Roebuck catalog; soon he was playing and singing on street corners for a beer or tips, making more money than at his day job. After serving briefly in the Army, he visited Memphis, where he was captivated by the sophisticated music in Beale Street clubs.

In 1948, King went to Memphis and moved in with his cousin, Booker "Bukka" White, a blues artist living in the Orange Mound neighborhood. Bluesman Sonny Boy Williamson, who had a radio show on WDIA, was impressed with King's playing and offered him a radio show and a gig at Miss Annie's 16th Street Grill for $12 a night. A disk jockey at WDIA for four years, King became known as the "Beale Street Blues Boy," which was shortened to "Bee-Bee" and then to "B. B." After his recording of "Three O'Clock Blues" became a hit, he became widely known for his powerful vocals and first-finger vibrato guitar playing; by the mid-1950s, he was performing in 300 shows a year. Once, while playing in Arkansas, he ran back into a burning dance hall to retrieve his $60 guitar and almost lost his life. When he discovered that the arsonists were fighting over a woman named Lucille, he named his guitar Lucille to remind himself not to "do anything that foolish." The 1960s brought B. B. King fame, fortune, and maturity as a musician: in 1965, he released his first album *Live at the Regal* on the ABC label; performed at rock festivals with Led Zeppelin and Black Sabbath; played with rock musicians such as Jimi Hendrix and U2; played an all-night blues benefit for SCLC, after the assassination of Martin Luther King, Jr.; and, in 1969, released "The Thrill Is Gone," which won a Grammy.

In 1971, he co-founded the Foundation for the Advancement of Inmate Rehabilitation and Recreation (FAIRR), an organization to improve prison conditions. His albums *Live in Cook County Jail* (1971) and *Live at San Quentin* (1990) underscore his commitment to this work. B. B. King's music has brought him many honors: he has won four Grammy Awards, as well as Lifetime Achievement Awards from NARAS and the Songwriters Hall of Fame; he was inducted into the Rock and Roll Hall of Fame; he received a Presidential Medal of Freedom Award; he earned a star on Hollywood's Walk of Fame; and he received a lifetime achievement award from the Blues Foundation in 1997. Two restaurants bear his name: B. B. King's Memphis Blues Club and Restaurant on Beale Street opened in 1991, and B. B. King's Blues Club-L.A. opened in 1964. Married and divorced twice, he has fifteen children.

Kyles, Samuel Billy (1934–), clergyman, civil rights activist. One of Memphis's most dynamic pastors, he has been on the cutting edge of social and political change in the city. One of six boys, he was born in Shelby, Mississippi, on September 26, 1934, but the family moved to Chicago when his father, Joseph Henry Kyles, became pastor of Mt. Pleasant Baptist Church. His mother, Ludie Cameron Kyles, had a strong influence on her children by instilling self-confidence in them through prayers and precepts. Although Billy eventually completed Phillips Academy, a public high school, he dropped out at age sixteen, after the death of his father.

He attended Chicago's Northern Baptist Theological Seminary for several years, but was not comfortable with what he considered "White" theology. A conscientious objector, he refused induction into the Army during the Korean conflict and, later, became assistant pastor of Mount Pleasant and Tabernacle Baptist Churches in Chicago.

While in Memphis for a church convention, Kyles visited the newly organized Monumental Baptist Church, whose thirty-four members were meeting in Foote Homes Auditorium. He became the church's first pastor and commuted for a year, but finally moved to Memphis, in 1959, with his wife Gwendolyn and their two children. Under his leadership, the congregation acquired Wolfe Funeral Home at 50 South Parkway as its church home. Coming to Memphis at the beginning of the civil rights movement, he immediately took a leadership role in the struggle on the local and national levels. He led marches, boycotts, and demonstrations to desegregate city schools, downtown businesses, and public facilities; he protested police brutality and participated in the strikes of sanitation workers and bus drivers. Active in SCLC, he was a close associate and confidante of Martin Luther King, Jr., and Jesse Jackson, who headed SCLC's Operation Bread Basket. He invited King to dinner at his home on April 4, 1968, and was with King on the balcony of the Lorraine Hotel when the civil rights leader was assassinated. Reverend Kyles's church, now located at 704 South Parkway East, became the headquarters of PUSH (People United to Save Humanity) when he became executive director of the Memphis chapter.

Affiliated with the Progressive National Baptist Convention, S. B. Kyles has served on many boards and commissions. He was a member of the Tennessee Advisory Committee to the United States Civil Rights Commission and a former trustee of the Morehouse College School of Religion. In 1993, he spent two weeks in South Africa, where he was one of 650 representatives to an International Solidarity Conference in Johannesburg, and he returned to South Africa a year later to monitor the national elections. President Clinton appointed him to the twenty-member Advisory Commission on Religious Freedom Abroad and also to a seven-member panel at the White House Conference on Hate Crimes. He has four adult children—Dwain, Dwania, Drusheena, and Devin—from his first marriage. On June 7, 1986, his friend Jesse Jackson officiated at the marriage of S. B. Kyles and Aurelia Kennedy, former director of the National Association of Black Accountants, and they are the parents of Aurelia Belee Epernay, affectionately called "Epy."

Latting, Augustus Arvis "Doc" (1905–1975), attorney. Known as the "Dean of Black Memphis Lawyers," he was the first African American appointed to a major city board. He was born in Helena, Arkansas, on January 30, 1905, the youngest of Elizabeth and Mark Miller Latting's three children. After graduating from Elijah Miller High School, he earned a bachelor's degree from Fisk University and a law degree from Northwestern University. After serving for two years as acting dean and chair of the Department of Political Science and Economics at Jackson State College in Mississippi, he joined the faculty of LeMoyne College, where he taught political science. When Latting first moved to Memphis, he practiced in the offices of two distinguished attorneys, Benjamin F. Booth and William Foote, who bequeathed their law books to him.

A highly regarded attorney, Latting practiced law in Memphis for forty-one years, specializing in divorce, personal injury, and probate cases. Judge H. T. Lockard, a former student and intern of his, recalled, "He had his own style of practicing law, but if he couldn't get the settlement he wanted and had to bring suit, he was the *most difficult* to deal with. Lat was smart. He was bad!" In the 1940s and '50s, he handled several of Memphis' most sensational divorce cases and, according to Lockard, "whipped the socks off the opposition." Many of the young lawyers who emerged in the 1950s took lessons from the "dean" or observed his courtroom style; when they became involved in politics and civil rights, however, Latting supported their efforts but stayed out of the limelight.

A. A. Latting became the first Black to serve on a major board, when the mayor appointed him to the city's Civil Service Commission in 1964. That same year, he received a Congressional Certificate of Merit from the United States Congress for his work with the Selective Service System. In 1970, he was elected chairman of the City Civil Service Commission and became the first Black appointed to the board of directors of the Memphis and Shelby County Bar Association. A longtime member of Second Congregational Church, he received an award from the Men's Fellowship of the Church for his community service in the cause of human relations. He and his first wife, Thelma Taylor Latting, divorced about three years after the birth of their son, Arvis. He and his second wife, Marietta Ish Latting, were the parents of two daughters, Jean and Judith, who grew up in the family home at 1310 Quinn. A. A. Latting died on October 20, 1975.

Lawson, James Morris, Jr. "Jim" (1928–), clergyman, civil rights activist. Called the leading nonviolent theoretician of the civil rights movement by Martin Luther King, Jr., he became a force for change in Memphis during the 1960s. Born on September 22, 1928, in Uniontown, Ohio, he was one of ten children born to a Methodist minister from Canada and his Jamaica-born wife. After graduating from Washington High School in 1946, Lawson entered Baldwin

Wallace College in Ohio but received a two-year sentence in federal prison for refusing to fight in the Vietnam War. After spending thirteen months in prison, he returned to Baldwin Wallace to obtain a bachelor's degree in sociology. He then spent three years in India (1953–1956) as a missionary for the Methodist Board of Missions, working as the campus minister at Hislop College in Nagpur. There, he studied the teachings of Gandhi and read about the Montgomery Bus Boycott. Following a trip to Africa in 1956, he enrolled in the graduate school of theology at Oberlin College but, two years later, transferred to Vanderbilt University.

Lawson joined the Nashville civil rights movement, planning sit-ins, leading SCLC workshops, and helping to organize SNCC. He was arrested and expelled from Vanderbilt in what was called the "Lawson incident," but his expulsion was rescinded after faculty members threatened to resign. He transferred to Boston University, where he completed a master's in theology and then went to Shelbyville, Tennessee, to pastor Scott Methodist Church. On June 17, 1962, he became pastor of Centenary Methodist Church and plunged into Memphis's civil rights struggle, gaining a reputation as a brilliant strategist and an articulate spokesman. He chaired the strategy committee of the Committee on the Move for Equality, which shaped the 1968 sanitation workers' strike, and he was instrumental in bringing King to Memphis in support of the strike. He chaired the committee that planned the boycott of Memphis city schools in 1969, and he also helped organize the memorial march for King in April 1969. Actively involved in the antiwar movement, he made a trip to South Vietnam, Thailand, and Cambodia in 1965, under the auspices of a pacifist organization, which also sent him to Uruguay in 1966 to attend a workshop on nonviolence in Latin America. In 1972, he went to the Netherlands to chair a seminar on nonviolence, sponsored by the World Council of Churches.

Jim Lawson served as president of the Memphis Council on Human Relations and chairman of MAP South, an arm of the War on Poverty Committee. An unsuccessful candidate for the Memphis School Board, he was selected in 1973 to the fifteen-member National News Council. He has received many awards for his work in civil rights, including the Memphis Catholic Council of Human Relations Award, Russwurm Award from the National Newspaper Publishers Association, and Distinguished Alumnus Award from Boston University. James Lawson also left his mark on Centenary Methodist Church: he increased membership from 600 to 830, and the congregation acquired a larger church at 501 East McLemore. In June 1974, he became pastor of the 2,000-member Holman United Methodist Church, the largest Methodist church in Los Angeles. Still an activist, he served as president of the Los Angeles SCLC and was arrested in 1985 for praying for the homeless on the lawn of the White House. James Lawson returned to Memphis in 1986 to speak at a conference on nonviolence, in 1987 to participate in Centenary's 117th anniversary, and to lecture on civil rights at Rhodes College in 1988. He and his wife, Dorothy, have three sons: John, Morris, and Seth.

Lee, George Washington (1894–1976), orator, writer, insurance executive, political leader. An advocate of independence, race pride, and economic self-sufficiency, he was one of Memphis's most astute and eloquent political leaders for almost forty years. Born near Heathman, Mississippi, on January 4, 1894, Lee was the son of sharecroppers, George and Hattie Stringfellow Lee. Soon after his birth, his parents separated, so George and his older brother, Abner, were raised by their mother, who enrolled them in a one-room rural school. The family moved to Indianola, Mississippi, where eight-year-old George worked for a cotton planter and, later, became a drayman for a mercantile store. He entered Alcorn College, where he became an outstanding student and avid reader. In 1912, he joined his brother in Memphis, working as a bellhop at the Gayoso Hotel for five summers and returning to Alcorn each fall. When World War I erupted, the twenty-three-year-old Lee enlisted in the Army and was one of only a thousand college-educated Blacks admitted to a new training camp for officers. On October 14, 1917, he was commissioned as a lieutenant in the United States Army and was sent to France, where he received a citation for bravery in dislodging a German sniper.

On his return to Memphis, Lieutenant Lee, as he was called for the rest of his life, began selling industrial life policies for Mississippi Life Insurance Company. An outstanding salesman, he became vice president of the company and raised his annual income from $520 to $6,500 in four years. He was one of the founders of the National Negro Insurance Association, a trade organization. When Mississippi Life was sold to a White company, Lee persuaded all the Black agents to walk out, and he became manager of the local branch of the Black-owned Atlanta Life Insurance Company. Active in the community, he served as grand commissioner of the Improved Benevolent and Protective Order of Elks of the World, a Black fraternal organization. Known as the "Boswell of Beale Street," he wrote a novel, *Beale Street, Where the Blues Began* (1934), which became a Book-of-the-Month Club alternate selection. His second novel, *River George* (1937), describes a young Black man's search for racial justice, while *Beale Street Sundown* (1942) is a collection of short stories about Beale Street characters.

An eloquent orator and brilliant tactician, Lee rose quickly in local Republican party ranks, becoming a leader in Memphis's Lincoln League. A frequent visitor to the White House, he was a major player in national politics for over twenty years; in 1932, he was a Shelby County alternate to the Republican National Convention and, in 1952, he seconded Senator Robert Taft's nomination at the Chicago convention. He reached the zenith of his political career when he was credited with delivering Tennessee to Eisenhower in the 1956 presidential election, but he was not so fortunate in his personal life. Lee, who remained a bachelor for fifty-one years, lived with his mother until her death in 1939, but, in 1946, he married a divorcée, "Miss Bronze America of 1943." Within a short time, he filed for divorce and, after a long and bitter trial, obtained a divorce from Estella B. Lee on October 18, 1948. In his later years, he received many honors: he was commissioned a colonel on the staffs of two Tennessee governors; his portrait hangs in the rotunda of the state capital in Nashville; and a Memphis street and post office—the George W. Lee Station on Mississippi Boulevard—are named after him. At age eighty-two, he reentered politics in a race to become a statewide, at-large delegate pledged to support President Gerald Ford, but, on August 1, 1976, Lt. George W. Lee died following an automobile accident and is survived by a daughter, Gilda Lee Robinson.

Lee, Tom C. (1886–1952), sanitation worker. One of Memphis's most celebrated heroes, he saved thirty-two people from drowning in the Mississippi River. He was born in Hopefield, Arkansas, in 1886, but spent most of his life in Memphis. A handyman for the C. W. Hunter Company, he twice saved the life of his employer during his eighteen years with the company. On May 8, 1925, Tom Lee was heading back to Memphis alone in a twenty-eight-foot boat, the Zev, after taking Hunter to Helena, Arkansas. Suddenly, he saw a boat capsize. It was the M. E. Norman, a steamboat that had been chartered by the Engineers Club of Memphis for an excursion on the Mississippi River. The Norman was returning to Memphis with seventy-two passengers and crew members aboard when another steamer, the Choctaw, pulled ahead as it rounded a corner. The Norman struggled in the swift current and then capsized. Unable to swim, Lee made several trips to the sinking Norman, taking people aboard his wooden skiff and carrying them to a sandbar at the Coahoma Light Landing. After making a fire on shore, he helped survivors get to a house in the woods.

Tom Lee saved thirty-two people; seventeen others swam to safety; and twenty-three died. Memphians raised money to help him: the Engineers Club gave him $50 every Christmas and *The Commercial Appeal* raised $3,000 to buy him a new house at 923 N. Mansfield. The president of the *Memphis News-Scimitar* also introduced Lee to President Calvin Coolidge, who called him an "outstanding marine hero." After a sightseeing trip to the capitol, he was honored at a reception given by the Colored Tennessee Society of Washington. A swimming pool in North Memphis was dedicated to Lee on July 25, 1942, and he was given a job with the Memphis Sanitation Department in the 1930s. Two years after his death from cancer on April 1, 1952, Astor Park was renamed Tom Lee Park, and the inscription on the thirty-foot granite obelisk read: "Tom Lee Memorial. A very worthy Negro." A play, *This Medal Is For You*, based on his life, was presented at Sherwood Elementary School in 1983, and a new life-size bronze sculpture of Lee by artist David Alan Clark was dedicated in Tom Lee Park in 2006.

Lewis, Robert Stevenson (1883–1971), mortician, businessman, sports promoter. The founder of R. S. Lewis and Sons Funeral Home, he built the first Black-owned baseball stadium in the country. The son of Oscar and Ella Lewis, he was born in Memphis in 1883. After graduating from Fisk University, he became a cotton sampler with the Planters Compress Company and then went to work for his father, Oscar Lewis, who had co-founded Barnett and Lewis Funeral Home at Fourth and Beale in 1914. On September 29, 1915, Robert Lewis married Lilla Eugenia McDonald of Holly

Springs, Mississippi, and they had four children: Marjorie, Robert, Jr., Eloise, and Clarence. When his father died, "Bubba," as he was called by family and friends, took over the business and, in 1930, changed the name to R. S. Lewis and Company. In the 1920s, he and Bert Roddy owned and operated the Iroquois Café, a Beale Street restaurant, and he also built Lewis Park, a baseball stadium where legendary players such as Hank Aaron and Willie Mays got their start, and where local rallies, track meets, and football games were held. Built in the early 1920s, the stadium was located on the corner of Iowa Avenue and Lauderdale St. (now Crump Boulevard and South Lauderdale).

R. S. Lewis organized and managed the first Black professional baseball team in the city—the Memphis Red Sox, which belonged to the old Negro American League. He often traveled with the players in the team bus or accompanied them in a touring car with a running board. In 1927, he sold Lewis Park and the Memphis Red Sox to Dr. W. S. Martin and his brothers, who renamed it Martin Stadium. The stadium was demolished in 1961. A member of Collins Chapel C.M.E. Church, Lewis died on November 18, 1971, at age eighty-eight, and is buried in Elmwood Cemetery. On his death, the three-generation family business continued under the name R. S. Lewis & Sons Funeral Home, located at 374 Vance Avenue.

Lewis, Walter "Furry" (1893–1981), guitarist, blues singer. Walter Lewis was born in Greenwood, Mississippi, on March 6, 1893, a few months after his father had deserted the family. Six years later, the boy moved with his mother and two sisters to Memphis, where he learned to play the guitar and harmonica. As a youngster, he hung around Beale Street and began singing and playing with older musicians. He ran away from home to join a medicine show at age thirteen and spent several years hopping trains and riding the rails until he lost a leg in a train accident. After being fitted for a wooden leg in Memphis, he formed a jug band with other young men from North Memphis. In the 1920s, he began working in Beale Street clubs with musicians such as Gus Cannon, Will Shade, and Jim Jackson, his friend and mentor, whom he had met on the medicine show circuit. According to a blues historian, Lewis's "picking style owed something to both the banjo-picking styles prevalent on the medicine-show circuit and the more sophisticated approach of jazz-influenced guitar players." In spite of his versatility, he could not make a living as a musician, so, in 1923, he began working—for fifteen cents an hour—as a street cleaner with the Memphis Sanitation Department, a job that he held for forty-four years.

Furry—a name that he acquired because of his long, bushy hair—made his first recordings in 1927 with Vocalion Records of Chicago. In the next two years, he made 21 additional records, including unusual renditions of three folk ballads, "John Henry," "Cassie Jones," and "Stacko Lee," in which he humanized the mythological heroes. In his blues lyrics, set in the traditional twelve-bar frame, he fuses personal experiences with folk material from the Black oral tradition. Many of his recordings, such as "Joe Turner's Blues" and "Goin' to Brownsville," are Memphis blues standards, but Lewis also wrote the lyrics in such compositions as "I Will Turn Your Money Green." After his success in the 1920s, Furry lapsed into obscurity, until he was "rediscovered" forty years later by blues historian Sam Charters. He then became legendary, making hundreds of performances and recording several albums, including one for Folkways Records in 1959, a double album set in 1961 for Fantasy Records, and a collection of his early recordings, *Furry Lewis in His Prime, 1917–1928*, for Yazoo Records. He even made a movie, *W. W. and the Dixie Dance King*, when he was 81 years old. He was lionized by younger musicians for his humor, showmanship, and bottleneck style of guitar playing. When the Rolling Stones appeared at the Memphis Liberty Bowl, the band refused to go on until Furry performed. He lived in a three-room duplex at 811 Mosby, where he was injured in a fire just a month before his death on September 14, 1981. Furry Lewis was noted for his philosophic attitude and wry sense of humor.

Although he loved women—lots of them!—he never married. When asked why not, he explained with a laugh, "Why do I need a wife when my neighbor's got one."

Light, Joe Lewis (1934–2005), artist. The city's best-known vernacular artist, he gained a national reputation for his large, brightly colored creations. He was born in Dyersburg, Tennessee, on May 9, 1934, and dropped out of school in the eighth grade. When he was ten or eleven, he started "scribbling different types of pictures" at a friend's table and then sold painted signs to cafes for spending change—enough to buy a movie ticket. At seventeen, he enlisted in the Army but was discharged five months later, after injuring his arm. Thereafter, his luck went from bad to worse. Between age twenty-one and thirty-three, he was jailed three times: first, for stealing three chickens, then for robbing a warehouse, and finally for assaulting his father. He spent eight years in the Nashville penitentiary, converted to a self-taught form of Judaism, left prison in 1968, and moved immediately to Memphis. Without any formal training, the tall, lanky artist began creating colored signs, paintings, and sculptures on the front porch of his house in a rundown section of the Greenlaw neighborhood.

Using house paint on wood or cardboard, he created simple forms of birds, fish, humans, and paintings with titles such as "607 Looney Avenue," "Witch Doctor," and "God Is a Murderer," titles that underscore his commitment to the disadvantaged people of his neighborhood, his deeply held moral and religious beliefs, and his mission to change people's lives through his art. A product of the Black, Southern vernacular tradition, the loquacious artist painted stories and his green-white-gray signs offered advice: "Anybody that is lazy has no choice but to be a thief, liar and a bum." His talent was discovered by an Atlanta art collector who bought a Light piece for $300 and sold it in New York for $10,000. Exploitation by dealers and collectors persuaded Light to handle his own affairs, so he sold eight paintings—including one to the House of Blues restaurant chain for $4,000—after a photograph of his work appeared in the May 1997 issue of *Art in America* magazine.

Between his large family, ramshackle house on Looney, and unstable income, however, Light continued to struggle financially and had to file for bankruptcy four times, even as his work gained greater exposure. His signs and paintings were presented in three exhibitions at the Art Museum of the University of Memphis: "607 Looney Avenue: Joe Light/Mike Schmidt—A Collaboration" in 1997; "Noah's Art: Animals by Southern Self-Taught Artists," in 1998; and "Coming Home! Self-Taught Artists, the Bible and the American South" in 2004. Ten of his creations also appeared in the folk art exhibition, "Souls Grown Deep: African-American Vernacular Art of the South," during the 1996 summer Olympics. His work is represented in the collections of the Smithsonian Institution and the High Museum of Art in Atlanta, and some of his pieces are owned by Susan Sarandon, Tim Robbins, and Tommy Lee Jones. After the devastating loss of his wife, Rosie Lee Light, in February 2003, Joe Light died of colon cancer on August 6, 2005, leaving ten children, some with Old Testament names—Josephine, Rachel, Rebekah, Ceanndredel, Hosea, Mosea, Daniel, Elijah, Joe, Jr., and Genetta.

Lincoln, Charles Eric (1924–2000), writer, scholar, college professor. One of the leading scholars of Black history and religion, he graduated from LeMoyne College and lived for many years in Memphis. Born on June 23, 1924, in Athens, Georgia, he was raised by his grandparents, Mattie and Less Lincoln, who instilled in him the value of education and religion. While attending Trinity School, he scrubbed floors, picked cotton, and delivered laundry to help his grandparents. A serious student and an accomplished athlete in high school, he was nicknamed "Jazz Bird," for a mythological Greek javelin thrower, and "Lard" by football players because of his girth. At fifteen, with $50 in his pocket, he went to Chicago, where he stayed at the YMCA and attended evening classes at the University of Chicago. After two semesters, he transferred to LeMoyne College but left school to join the Navy, working for two years as a laboratory technician during World War II. In 1947, he was road manager for the Birmingham Black Barons, an old Negro League team. He married his LeMoyne sweetheart, and they had two children: Cedric and Joyce. After the war, he graduated from LeMoyne with a B.A. degree, the first of five degrees that he would receive, including a master's in religion from Fisk, a divinity degree from Chicago, a master's in education, and a doctorate in social ethics from Boston University, as well as three honorary degrees. After his divorce, he married New England Conservatory of Music student Lucy Cook, with whom he had two more children, Hillary and Less II.

C. Eric Lincoln wrote poetry, fiction, scholarly articles, and even country-western music but is best known for his books on history and religion. He authored twenty-two books, including the best-selling *The Black Muslims in America* (1961), which led to friendships with Malcolm X and Louis Farrakhan. Some of his other publications include *The Negro Pilgrimage in America* (1967), *Race, Religion, and the Continuing American Dilemma* (1984), and *The Black Church in the African-American Experience* (1990), written with a former student. He also published a novel, *The Avenue, Clayton City* (1988), which won the Lillian Smith Award for Best Southern Fiction and was optioned for a film. For thirty years, Dr. Lincoln taught at institutions such as Clark College, Fisk University, Columbia University, Union Theological Seminary, and the University of Ghana. In 1976, he went to Duke University, where he was named the William Rand Kenan Jr. Distinguished Professor of Religion and Culture in 1991. Although he retired in 1993, he continued to write, lecture, and serve as a media expert on religion and race relations. He donated his papers, including more than 5,000 items, to the Atlanta University

Center's Woodruff Library, and Clark Atlanta University established the C. Eric Lincoln Lectureship in Social Ethics in his honor. Professor Lincoln died in Durham, North Carolina, on May 14, 2000.

Lipscomb, Robert (1949–), corporate executive, city administrator. One of the most important "movers and shakers" in city government, he works effectively behind the scenes to deal with urban problems. One of nine children raised by a single mother, he was born on April 5, 1949, and moved with his mother, Willie Mae Lipscomb, and eight siblings from Crystal Springs, Mississippi, to Memphis in 1965. After graduating from Booker T. Washington High School in 1967, he entered LeMoyne-Owen College, where he was a baseball player, cross-country runner, and president of the Student Government Association in his senior year. After graduating from college in 1971, with a bachelor's degree in economics, he attended the University of Chicago Graduate School of Business, from which he received a master's in business administration in 1973. For two summers, he worked for Mobil Oil Company in Cicero, Illinois, and then became a cost accountant for DuPont in Memphis, from 1973 to 1978. Still with DuPont, he worked for six months in Deer Park, Texas, and, in August 1979, became senior financial analyst with Holiday Inns in Memphis before being promoted to manager of budgeting and capital expenditure analysis at the company.

Lipscomb started helping the residents of Walter Simmons Estates public housing project to build a park near Holiday Inn's corporate offices. In 1985, he founded and served as executive director of Memphis Partners, Incorporated, while working as manager of corporate accounting and budgeting for Holiday Corporation, one of the original sponsors of the program. He put together a volunteer network of area businesses, service organizations, and colleges to provide tutoring, job-readiness training, and job placement for hundreds of at-risk students every year. This program has graduated more than 300 students. In September 1989, in cooperation with the city, he launched a new program for high school students called Leaders of Tomorrow, patterned after Leadership Memphis. During the 1980s, the former college athlete also served as coach of the South Memphis Road Runners, a semipro baseball team. Described by colleagues as "hardworking, sincere, dedicated, and energetic," he became director of HCD (Memphis Housing and Community Development) on January 7, 1992, with responsibility for overseeing neighborhood revitalization projects.

Confessing that he is "a perfectionist and probably too much of a workaholic—a typical type-A personality," Robert Lipscomb returned to LeMoyne-Owen College, in September 1996, as chief operating officer and senior vice president of fiscal affairs and administration. In February 1999, he was appointed executive director of the Memphis Housing Authority, and, later that year, director of the Division of Housing and Community Development. He was also appointed chief financial officer for the City of Memphis in 2005, and, as head of both agencies, he has procured more than $125 million in competitive federal grants, developed the city's first strategic housing plan, created the RISE Foundation and The Renaissance Business Center, and initiated housing programs such as the Equity Fund, Housing Trust Fund, and Down Payment Assistance Program. Lipscomb received the prestigious Lewis Hine Award from the National Child Labor Commission and was named an Outstanding Young Tennessean by the Tennessee Jaycees in 1986 and 1988, respectively.

Little, James (1952–), painter. One of the most talented artists that the city has produced, he creates abstract paintings from a perspective that parallels the emotional intensity and intellectual depth of jazz. The son of Annie and Rogers Little, he was born in Memphis on July 21, 1952. In 1974, he received a bachelor's degree in fine arts from the Memphis Academy of Art and then entered Syracuse University College of Visual and Performing Arts as a Marion Jones Scholar and an Afro-American Studies Fellow. After acquiring an M.F.A. degree from Syracuse in 1976, he moved to New York but returned to Memphis to teach painting and drawing at the Memphis Academy of Art during the 1978 summer session. In the past two decades, Little has held four solo exhibitions in Manhattan: *Tondos and Ovals* at the June Kelly Gallery in 1990, *James Little: Ovals and Arbitration Paintings* at the Sid Deutsch Gallery in 1992, *Beyond Geometry: New Paintings* at L.I.C.K. Ltd. Fine Art in 2003, and *Reaching for the Sky* at G. R. N'Namdi Gallery in 2005. Since 1973, his work has also been exhibited in more than a hundred museums, galleries, and universities, including the Studio Museum of Harlem, Frans Halsmuseum in Holland, and the Smithsonian's Anacostia Museum. In Memphis, his paintings have been displayed at LeMoyne-Owen College, Memphis Brooks Museum of Art, Memphis Academy of Art, Alice Bingham Gallery, Southwestern University, Clough Hanson Gallery, and the University of Memphis, as well as at the Tennessee State Museum in an exhibit *The Tennessee Twelve: Contemporary Painting Today*.

Unlike other Memphis artists, whose expressionist paintings explore the Black Southern folk tradition, James Little's objective is "to return abstract painting to its rightful prominence at the forefront of contemporary American art." In 1979, he began experimenting with rubbings by tracing over man-hole covers with graphite and tracing paper to achieve distinctive patterns. In an untitled gouache, he used acrylic emulsion on Arches paper, and, more recently, he uses oil with wax, which adds body and depth to his paintings. According to an art critic, examples of Little's search for unexplored areas within the tradition of geometric abstraction are his canvases "False-Positive" and "The Siege," with their "jutting angular forms and acute angles set on a diagonal plane." Although Little says that, when he paints, he thinks of "art-based principles, not something social or ethnic," another critic insists that, although the painter does indeed deal with aesthetic issues such as color, texture, and composition, he also examines "issues of identity, race and spirituality." His paintings and exhibitions have been reviewed in articles and essays published by the *New York Times*, *Art in America*, and *The Village Voice*, and he is featured in *Contextures*, a publication about African American artists. He has also written many essays, including the catalog essay for the exhibition *Painted in New York City* for Hofstra University. Among his many awards and honors is the prestigious Jackson Pollock-Lee Krasner award in painting, in 2000–2001. James Little is married to Fatima Shaik, and they have three daughters.

Little, Vera (1929–), opera singer. One of the first African American opera singers to perform in Europe in the 1950s, Little became a leading mezzo-soprano at the West Berlin State Opera House in 1966. Born on October 12, 1929, she was one of the five children of the B. T. Littles. While a student at Manassas High School, from which she graduated in 1947, she began studying voice at the McCleave School of Music with Madame Florence McCleave, who had sung opera in Italy. On the advice of her voice teacher, Little continued her vocal studies at Talladega College in Alabama. After graduating from college, she moved to New York, where she washed dishes to earn money for voice lessons with Madame Covert. In 1955, she won a Fulbright Award for two years of study at the Paris Conservatory. She returned to Memphis in 1956 to sing at Manassas High School and, later that year, she gave a recital at the famed Mozarteum in Salzburg, where a critic wrote that Little had a "voice of magnificent quality and sweetness." After winning the Munchen Song Contest in 1958, she performed for the first time at the West Berlin Opera House in 1959, when she sang the lead role (as a guest) in *Carmen.*

Noted for her husky mezzo-soprano voice, Vera Little became a soloist with the West Berlin Opera House in 1961, a position that she held for several years. Since then, she has sung some forty opera roles throughout Europe, especially in Berlin, Munich, and Vienna. A statuesque woman of commanding presence, she has shared the stage with renown singers and conductors; she recorded *Walkure* with Birget Nilssen for Decca, and she performed in a Viennese production of *Falstaff,* conducted by Leonard Bernstein. Her success in Europe led to her first appearance with the Cosmopolitan Symphony Orchestra in New York, but in the 1950s and '60s there were few openings for Black singers in American opera companies. Vera Little now lives in Berlin with her husband, a geology professor, and spends her time teaching, playing the lottery, and writing poetry. She has published several books, including *My Life in Europe*; *Tears in My Eyes*, an anthology of poetry and prose; and *Touch of Warmth,* a collection of poetry and original songs. Her most recent publication is *The Lonely Priest and the Saturday Evening Eaters,* a collection of fifteen short stories and essays, written in English and German. In 1989, while in Memphis for the funeral of her sister, Helen Little, she sang at LeMoyne-Owen College.

Lockard, Hosea T. (1920–), attorney, judge. He is the first Black since Reconstruction to hold elective office in Shelby County government and the first to serve in the cabinet of a Tennessee governor. The oldest of Albert and Lucille Alston Lockard's six children, he was born on June 24, 1920. He grew up on a farm near Glimp, Tennessee, where his father put him to full-time work at age nine, delivering tomatoes to a canning factory in a mule-drawn wagon. He recalls that he worked five and a half days a week and went to church on Sundays. After attending LeMoyne College for two years, he was drafted into the U.S. Army Medical Corps in 1942. He served in Italy, France, Germany, and North Africa before his discharge in 1945. While completing his studies at LeMoyne, he did a summer internship in the office of Attorney A. A. Latting and then acquired a law degree from Lincoln University School of Law in 1948. On September 30, 1950, he married Wilhelmina Walker and, a year later, opened his law office in Memphis, where he became active in politics and civil rights. President of the Memphis Branch of the NAACP from 1953 to 1957, he also served as president of the Tennessee Conference of NAACP Branches from 1957 to 1962. He initiated suits that led to the desegregation of Memphis State University and the Memphis Transit System, and he joined in cases that resulted in the desegregation of Overton Park Zoo and Ellis Auditorium, as well as the Memphis airport and libraries.

In 1964, H. T. Lockard won a city-wide seat on the Shelby County Court (now the Shelby County Board of Commissioners) by a margin of only 267 votes. In the mid-1960s, he directed Program for Progress, a project to design a new form of government, which voters approved in 1966. Active in Democratic politics, he served as head of the Ninth District Democratic League, a Black political organization, and worked in the campaigns of Estes Kefauver, Edmund Orgill, and Ross Bass. After serving as co-chairman of Ellington's 1966 gubernatorial campaign, he was appointed one of four administrative assistants to the governor, becoming the first Black to hold a cabinet-level position in the Tennessee governor's office. After refusing appointment to the bench in 1968 and 1970, Lockard was appointed to succeed W. Otis Higgs, Jr., as Criminal Court judge of Division IV in 1975. He retired from the judgeship on August 31, 1994, after suffering a stroke. He has been active in many civic and professional organizations, including Alpha Phi Alpha Fraternity, Goodwill Boys Club, Beale Street National Historic Foundation, and the Shelby County and Missouri Bar Associations; he also served as president of the Ben F. Jones Chapter of the National Bar Association. His honors are many: an NAACP Merit Award in 1958, Bluff City Jaycees' "Man of the Year" award in 1964, and St. Paul Baptist Church's 103rd Anniversary of the Emancipation Proclamation Award in 1969. He has been married to Ida Walker Lockard since June 7, 1962, and they are active members of Metropolitan Baptist Church.

Love, John Robinson (1863–1937) postman, musician. In the early 1900s, this talented musician organized a band composed of African American postal employees. One of three children born to Sara Lanier Love and John Love, a brick mason and contractor, he was born in Memphis on May 1, 1863. Demonstrating an early aptitude for music, he played several instruments but preferred the cornet, and he became the featured soloist with various concert bands sponsored by Memphis fraternal organizations. Love organized the Mail Carriers Orchestra, which later became the Letter Carriers Band—the only one of its kind in the country. All the members, except for his wife who played the flute, were employees of the United States Post Office. They played at concerts, conventions, civic affairs, and government functions. The band traveled throughout the United States, Canada, and Mexico. In 1896, he married Annabelle Mosley, who was raised by an aunt, Belle Nevels, after her parents died in the yellow fever epidemics of 1878 and 1879. John Love worked for the post office for forty years, invested in real estate, and owned considerable property in Memphis and Chicago. A member of Second Congregational Church, he left a sizeable bequest to the church during the Depression, and this money was used to build a parish hall, later named "Love Hall" in his honor.

Lunceford, James Melvin "Jimmie" (1902–1947), bandleader, arranger, and instrumentalist. A former Memphis music teacher and football coach, Lunceford organized and led one of the most original and influential jazz bands of the 1930s. He was born in Fulton, Missouri, on June 6, 1902, but spent most of his childhood in Mississippi. He attended high school in Denver, Colorado, obtained a bachelor's degree in music from Fisk University in 1926, and later attended New York City College. A consummate musician, he mastered several instruments, including the flute, guitar, trombone, and saxophone, while playing with the bands of Elmer Snowden and Wilber Sweatment in the mid-1920s. It was in Memphis that Lunceford met his future wife, Rose Crystal Tullie, a teacher at Booker T. Washington High School. It was also in the Bluff City that he became a bandleader, while teaching music and coaching the football team at Manassas High School. In 1929, he organized a nine-piece band composed of students from Manassas and Fisk that broadcast on radio station WREC and performed in the summers of 1928 and 1929. The band cut its first record as the Chickasaw Syncopators in Dallas, in 1927, and Lunceford cut another record for Victor under his own name in 1930. After an engagement at New York's Lafayette Theatre, the group toured New England and had its big break in 1933, when the band was invited to play at and broadcast from Harlem's Cotton Club. The band appeared in the film *Blues in the Night* and toured Europe in 1937, but a second tour was canceled because of the war.

The Jimmie Lunceford Band earned a national reputation for its style and showmanship. Although the Lunceford sound was created, in part, by trumpeter Sy Oliver and pianist Ed Wilcox, who wrote original compositions, elaborate scores, and brilliant arrangements of popular songs such as "Swanee River" and "My Blue Heaven," it was Lunceford who conducted the band and created its distinctive flair. "Swing" was too limited a term to express the rhythm of his band, so one music historian called it "bounce," pointing out that "Lunceford's music was bouncing. It bounced on itself, from one rhythmic accent to the next..." He was a perfectionist and a strict disciplinarian, who required character, intelligence, and excellent musicianship of his band members. He was also quite a showman. Performances were described as visual and musical experiences: saxophones swung from side to side, trumpets were thrown and caught in unison, and trombones slid up and down together. Lunceford conducted with a long, white baton, while the musicians— among the best dressed in the business—took four different bows. Described as a tall, handsome man with a big smile, Lunceford left a rich legacy of recorded music, including such classics as "Uptown Blues," "Ain't She Sweet," and "Cheatin' on Me." Critics note that his band ranked with those of Duke Ellington, Count Basie, and Benny Goodman as one of the most important of the big jazz orchestras of the 1930s. While signing autographs in a music store, Jimmie Lunceford died of a heart attack on July 16, 1947, at age forty-five, and was buried in Elmwood Cemetery.

Lyke, James Patterson (1939–1992), clergyman, civil rights activist. The youngest bishop and one of only five Black bishops in the church, he was the only Black archbishop in the Roman Catholic Church at the time of his death. The youngest of the seven children of Amos Lyke, a factory worker, and Ora Sweet Lyke, a domestic, he was born in Chicago on February 18, 1939, and grew up in the Wentworth Housing Projects on the South Side. He attended McGosh Grammar School and Robert S. Abbot School, but his mother, who felt that he was not challenged in public school, worked as a laundress at St. George Catholic School to pay her son's tuition. After attending St. Benize High School for a year, he completed high school and a two-year liberal arts course at St. Joseph's Minor Seminary in Oakwood, Illinois in 1959. Lyke entered Lady of Angels House of Philosophy in Cleveland, where he received a bachelor's degree through Quincy College in 1963. In the summer of 1965, he went to Grambling State University in Louisiana as a Newman minister. A member of the Order of Franciscan Minors, Brother Seth, as he was called, was ordained on June 24, 1966, and received a Master of Divinity degree in theology in 1967. That same year, he became a teacher at Padua High School, a predominantly White school in Ohio. In Cleveland, he met and collaborated with Martin Luther King, Jr., whose gospel of social and economic justice attracted him to the civil rights movement. A member of SCLC, Lyke joined Operation Breadbasket, worked to desegregate Cleveland, and campaigned for Carl Stokes, Cleveland's first Black mayor. Deeply affected by King's assassination in 1968, he requested a transfer to Memphis.

In 1968, the Franciscan priest came to Memphis as associate pastor of St. Thomas Catholic Church, which later merged with St. Augustine Church. In January 1970, he was appointed pastor of St. Thomas, administrator of Father Bertrand School, and superior of San Franciscan Friary. He made the church visible in the Black community, introducing Black music into the liturgy, redecorating the church in liberation colors (red, green, and black), placing photographs of King and Malcolm X in the church, and installing two life-size paintings of St. Benedict the Black and St. Martin de Porres. An activist priest who "wore his blackness with a cloak of dignity," Father Lyke led his parishioners in civil rights protests, marches, and demonstrations to get Black representation on the Memphis School Board, to eliminate segregation at St. Joseph Catholic Hospital, and to unionize workers at St. Francis Hospital. Called "Father Jim" by all who knew him, the popular young priest was noted for his large Afro hair cut and gold lapel pin, depicting the clenched fist of the Black Power movement. A life member of the NAACP and a board member of the local branch, he chaired the NAACP's Police Committee and received a citation from the Afro-American Police Association for his service as co-founder and chaplain of the organization. He also served as chairman of MAP South and as a member of the board of the Memphis Health Center. Feeling that his work in the community had peaked, in 1977, Father Lyke left the city to become pastor of St. Benedict the Black Church and director of the Newman campus ministry at Grambling State University.

One of only 225 Black Catholic priests in the United States, Father Lyke was active in church affairs on the local and national levels. On August 1, 1979, he was appointed Auxiliary Bishop of Cleveland and Vicar of the Urban Region, becoming the youngest bishop in the country, the only Black bishop in the Midwest, and one of only five Black Catholic bishops in the country. On June 30, 1981, he was awarded a Ph.D. degree in theology from Union Graduate School and, on June 24, 1991, he was installed as archbishop of Atlanta. After a lengthy illness, Archbishop Lyke died in Atlanta on December 27, 1992. In his honor, an historical marker was placed at St. Thomas School, the Archbishop James P. Lyke Elementary School was dedicated in Cleveland in 1993, and Atlanta University's Newman House was named The Lyke House in September 1998.

Lynk, Miles Vandahurst (1871–1956), physician, lawyer, educator, writer. One of Memphis's pioneering physicians, he published the first Black medical journal in the country and founded a university that educated most of the city's Black doctors in the first quarter of the twentieth century. He was born on June 3, 1871, to former slaves John Henry and Mary Louis Lynk, who lived on a farm near Brownsville, Tennessee. His father died early, leaving a widow with five children—Hattie, Miles, John, William, and Augusta—to support on a fifty-acre farm. Determined to become a physician, Lynk attended a five-month rural school but learned more at home through extensive reading. At age eleven, he managed the family farm and, at thirteen, passed the county teachers' examination, although he was too young to teach. He studied advanced subjects under a tutor for a year and taught at a summer school in 1888 to earn money for medical school. The following year, he prepared for medical school under the direction of a Meharry-educated Brownsville physician, which enabled him to trim a year off of his professional education.

In 1889, the tall, slender young man entered Meharry Medical School as a second-year student because of high scores on his entrance examination. When he graduated from Meharry in 1991, at age nineteen—second in a class of thirteen—he opened an office in Jackson, Tennessee, where he built up a large and lucrative practice. A year later, he began publishing *The Medical and Surgical Observer*, the first Black medical journal in the country, which appeared monthly from December 1892 through January 1894. In the next 15 years, he also wrote books and published a magazine on Black history and culture, founded a publishing house to print those materials, obtained a law degree and founded a law school, and co-founded the National Medical Association, the first professional organization for African American physicians. Dr. Lynk's major achievement, however, is the founding of the University of West Tennessee, which trained medical professionals from around the country and abroad. The university, which first opened in Jackson, Tennessee, in 1900, was designed to educate physicians, dentists, pharmacists, nurses, and lawyers. The Lynks mortgaged their home to finance the school, which opened in a four-room building near Court Square with 30 students. The rapid growth of the school necessitated a move to an urban center that could provide better clinical facilities and a larger faculty, so in 1907, Lynk relocated UWT to Memphis. The students came from twenty-two states and six countries, including Liberia, Trinidad, the Philippines, Columbia, and Japan. In the twenty-three years of its existence, the university educated most of Memphis's early doctors and dentists, including Benjamin F. McCleave, William O. Speight, Ransom Q. Venson, Frank E. White, Isaac A. Watson, and others.

Dr. Lynk's writing spans half a century. His first book, *The Black Troopers or the Daring Deeds of the Negro Soldier in the*

Spanish-American War (1899), describes the heroism of soldiers in Cuba. He also published an anthology, *Afro-American School Speaker and Gems of Literature*, which includes an original six-act drama, "The Princess of Itah Island," the first play by a Black Memphian. At age eighty, he published his last work, *Sixty Years of Medicine or the Life and Times of Dr. Miles V. Lynk, An Autobiography* (1951). The multitalented doctor also found time to get married. On April 12, 1893, he wed Beebe Steven, a graduate of Lane College, who received a degree in pharmaceutic chemistry from the University of West Tennessee in 1903, and then joined the faculty. After her death on November 11, 1948, Dr. Lynk married Mrs. Ola Herin Moore on April 14, 1949. He died seven years later.

Maburn, Harold (1936–), jazz pianist, composer. A dynamic soloist and accompanist, he has performed throughout Europe and the United States with noted jazz artists and ensembles. Born in Memphis on March 30, 1936, he attended Manassas High School and taught himself to play the piano as a teenager. He admired the work of Memphis pianists Charles Thomas and Phineas Newborn, Jr., whose techniques have influenced his own style. About Newborn, he said, "When Phineas played, everything was at his command. I knew the first time I saw him I wanted to play like that. I also knew I had my work cut out for me." In 1954, Maburn left for Chicago, where he studied with Ahmad Jamal and played with the group MJT+3. In the late 1960s he cut an album, *Workin' and Wailin'*, for Prestige Records, which included compositions such as "Blues for Phineas" and "Strozier's Mode" that revealed his admiration for the work of other Memphis jazzmen. Later, he moved to New York to join Lionel Hampton. Donald Byrd, and Wes Montgomery with whom he toured Europe in 1965. A gentle, soft-spoken man of imposing stature—over six feet tall "with the build of an aging offensive lineman"—Maburn has gained the respect of jazz musicians and critics alike.

In the 1970s, Harold Maburn worked with Sarah Vaughn and Arthur Prysock; he also toured Japan with Billy Harper in 1971, and Europe with the George Coleman Octet in 1981. Stanley Cowell invited him to join the Piano Choir in the 1970s, and he was a member of James Williams's Contemporary Piano Ensemble in the 1990s. He participated with Memphians Williams, Newborn, and Charles Thomas in the "Memphis Piano Summit," held in December 1981. His talent and inventiveness are evident in *The Leading Man*, a Columbia album produced in 1995 by James Williams. This album, which is included in the "Legendary Pioneers of Jazz" series, is a testament to Maburn's stature as a jazz pianist and composer. Williams, a close friend, also produced Maburn's previous trio album *Straight Street*. He returned to Memphis on November 1, 1997, to participate, along with Williams, Mulgrew Miller, and Kirk Whalum in the Renaissance Gala at the Memphis Convention Center. Although he has lived in New York for the past thirty-five years, he acknowledges that his work is grounded in Memphis music. He said, "In Memphis we were all forced to play rhythm and blues. Even today, I consider myself a blues pianist who happens to understand jazz."

Martin, Reginald (1956–), professor, scholar, writer. Described as one of the hardest-working and most highly motivated academics of his generation, he has gained an international reputation for his teaching, writing, and research. The son of Alice and Philippe Martin, he was born in New Orleans on May 15, 1956, but was raised in Memphis by his great grandparents, Carrie and Lester Jackson, and his great-great-grandmother,

Lucinda Jones. He grew up on Forrest Avenue in the Binghamton neighborhood, where he attended Lester Elementary School and graduated from East High School. At age sixteen, he began boxing at the Fairgrounds and, although he was fast and targeted, he gave up the sport when the city recruited young prisoners from the local jail to enter the ring. Martin has five earned degrees, including a bachelor's in magazine journalism from Boston College, which he completed in two and a half years with honors; a master's with honors in American literature from Memphis State University, and a doctorate in English language and literature from the University of Tulsa. After receiving a doctorate in 1985, he came back to Memphis and later described "what a joy it was to return and put my Ph.D. in the hands of my great-grandmother." Although he was teaching and eventually acquired two more degrees—an M.F.A. in writing and an A.S. degree in general technology—he also helped care for his great-grandparents and his great-great-grandmother.

Dr. Martin has received offers from other institutions and has lectured or taught at universities such as Harvard, Pennsylvania, and Michigan State, but he has remained at the University of Memphis, where he became the youngest full professor in 1991. The recipient of a 1989 Ford Foundation postdoctoral fellowship to work at LeMoyne-Owen College, he became a special assistant to the president of U of M in 1991, and served as assistant to the president of Georgia State University on an American Council on Education Fellowship in 1992–1993. A professor of composition, he is former director of Professional Writing Programs and presently serves as coordinator of the African American Literature Program and chair of the Tenure and Promotion Committee in the English Department. A prolific poet, novelist, and literary critic, Martin has published articles and monographs, as well as authored, edited, or co-edited nine books, including the scholarly *Ishmael Reed and the New Black Aesthetic Critics*, *Everybody Knows What Time It Is* (novel), *Southern Secrets* (poetry), and three anthologies: *Dark Eros: Black Erotic Writing*, *A Deeper Shade of Sex: The Best in Black Erotic Writing*, and *Erotique Noire: Black Erotica*.

Twenty-two years ago, he founded Professional Communications Services, Ltd., Inc., a writing/editing firm, and he also operates reginaldmartinbooks, a publishing company that produced two volumes in 2006. Among his awards are the Russell W. Smith Award for Distinguished Teaching, Council of Arts and Sciences Distinguished Research Award, and College of Arts and Sciences Award for Distinguished Research. A member of the Leadership Memphis Class of 1991–1992, he was president of the Memphis Black Arts Alliance and board member of the Memphis Black Business Association, and he is presently board chairman of Youth Opportunity Memphis. The oldest of four siblings, he mentors students in the public schools, helps prospective writers, and works with neighborhood kids who "have no black males to look up to."

Martin, William S. (1879–1958), physician. He was the oldest of the legendary Martin brothers—medical pioneers, businessmen, and baseball team owners—who were known by their initials: physician W. S., pharmacist J. B. (1885–1973), physician A. T. (1886–1975), and dentist B. B. (1889–1976). William was born on August 9, 1879, attended LeMoyne Institute and Walden University in Nashville, graduated from Meharry, completed an internship at New York's Bellevue Hospital, and opened a medical practice in Memphis in 1907. A Shriner and a 33rd-degree Mason, he served as vice president of the Negro American Baseball League and president of the Bluff City Medical Society. In 1920, Dr. Martin became superintendent of Collins Chapel Hospital, where his wife, the former Eva Cartman, served as head nurse, and he was named staff president of the hospital in 1955, three years before his death.

In 1910, pharmacist J. B. Martin opened the South Memphis Drug Store at 907 Florida Avenue, and he later bought a funeral home and investment property. A Republican political leader, he was forced out of town in 1940, when a dispute with Democrat Edward "Boss" Crump resulted in harassment by Memphis policemen, who searched Martin's customers daily. The pharmacist turned the store over to his son, sold his interest in the Red Sox, and moved to Chicago, where he became a businessman and political leader. In 1942, he won the Republican nomination to the Cook County Commission and, in 1946, he was elected trustee of the Chicago Sanitation Department, the highest elective office held by a Black. While in office, he bought the Chicago American Giants and was president of the Negro American League. He and his wife, Lula, had two sons, William and J. B. Martin, Jr. Physician A. T. Martin was active in social and professional organizations; he worked with the Boy Scouts and was a member of the Bluff City Medical Society, The Memphians, Inc., and Mt. Olive C.M.E. Church. Three years after his wife's death, he died on November 4, 1975, and is buried in Elmwood Cemetery. The youngest of the brothers was B. B. Martin, who practiced dentistry in Memphis for over fifty years. A former Director of the Tri-State Bank, he was a member of the Top Hat and Tails Social Club and Collins Chapel C.M.E. Church. Dr. Martin died on his birthday in 1976, and was survived by a daughter, Claudia B. Aldridge of Buffalo, New York.

The Martin brothers—sons of the Lee M. Martins of Senatobia, Mississippi—all attended LeMoyne Institute, graduated from Meharry Medical School, and established practices or businesses in Memphis. They had a tightly knit family that also included their sister Hattie, who married Memphis physician Dr. A. L. Saunders. Two of the brothers lived next door to each other on South Parkway East: A. T. and his wife Valerie at no. 28, and divorcé B. B. at 26. Three of the brothers—W. S., A. T., and B. B.—built the Martin Medical Building on South Third near Beale Street, where they had their offices, a restaurant, barbershop, and large parking lot. Visitors to the building, where Jackie Robinson reportedly signed a contract to become the first Black player in the major leagues, included Satchell Paige, Joe Louis, and Roy Campanella. In 1927, the four brothers bought the Memphis Red Sox baseball team and Lewis Park, the first baseball stadium in the country owned by Blacks, which had been built by Memphis mortician Robert S. Lewis, and they renamed it Martin Stadium. B. B. served as general manager of the Red Sox for twenty years and is credited with selling several African American players to the major leagues and seven players to the minor leagues. Under J. B.'s direction, the team joined the Negro National League for six years, the Negro Southern League for two years, and was a charter member of the Negro American League, to which it belonged from 1937 to 1950, winning the NAL first-half championship in 1938. J. B. also operated a concession stand at the stadium and built a hotel next to the park.

Mason, Charles Harrison (1862–1961), evangelist, church founder, religious leader. The charismatic founder and Senior Bishop of the Church of God in Christ shaped a distinctly African American Pentecostal movement. Born a slave on September 8, 1862, on the Prior farm near Bartlett, Tennessee, he was the son of sharecroppers Eliza and Jerry Mason. Describing himself as a sickly child haunted by dreams and visions, he was healed in 1880 after experiencing a dramatic conversion when "the glory of God came down upon" him. When his parents, who were devout Baptists, moved to Arkansas in 1878, he worshiped with them in rural churches. With only a fourth grade education, he enrolled at Arkansas Baptist College around 1885 to become a better preacher but withdrew after only three months because he discovered that "there was no salvation in schools." Called to the ministry in his late twenties, Mason established his first church in a deserted cotton gin on the banks of a creek outside of Lexington, Mississippi. In the late 1890s, he organized the Church of God but changed the name to the Church of God in Christ in 1897. Persecuted for expounding a "radical" definition of holiness, he was ordered out of town, tossed into jail, and beaten by townsfolk. In 1906, he attended a revival in Los Angeles, where he received the Holy Ghost and accepted the doctrines of the Pentecostal denomination. When he moved to Memphis, he held all-night meetings in a small frame church on Wellington Street, where hundreds were attracted to his fervent services.

In 1907, Mason called a meeting to organize the first general assembly of the Church of God in Christ and was elected general overseer and chief apostle of the denomination. Bishop Mason began holding revivals in other parts of the country and, under his guidance, evangelists spread the holiness doctrine, so that, by 1917, there were congregations in several cities and some foreign countries. Presently, COGIC holds an annual twenty-one day convocation, which brings as many as 40,000 people to Memphis every November, and the Church's international headquarters was formerly located in the 300-room Chisca Hotel in downtown Memphis. When COGIC celebrated its 100th anniversary in Memphis in 1997, it was acknowledged as the country's largest Pentecostal church and its fastest-growing Protestant denomination, with more than five million members.

Success, however, did not come easy for the religious leader. The subject of federal surveillance and intimidation for his views on conscientious objection during World War I, Mason was arrested in 1918 for suspected collusion with the Germans and, in the 1950s, a cross was burned in front of the house that he bought in the all-White Glenview neighborhood. In spite of such persecution, the diminutive Mason, who was only 5' 4" tall and 120 pounds, continued to build his institution. In 1945, he dedicated Mason's Temple, built over a five-year period at a cost of $275,679, as the world headquarters of COGIC. At the time, Mason's Temple had the largest church auditorium in the city, as well as a barber shop, beauty shop, post office, cafeteria, nursery, and eight dormitory buildings It was in the Temple's 7,500-seat auditorium that Martin Luther King, Jr., delivered his fateful "I Have Been to the Mountaintop" speech on the night of April 3, 1968. In 1954, Bishop Mason also established Saints Junior College near Lexington, Mississippi.

Bishop C. H. Mason was an humble, soft-spoken man of great integrity and strength of character, who dressed simply and began his day with two hours of prayer. A mesmerizing preacher and an inspiring leader, he died in Detroit, Michigan, on November 17, 1961, at age ninety-nine. He is buried in a marble vault in the front lobby of Mason Temple. He and his first wife, Lelia Mason, had eight children and, after her death, he married Elsie Washington of Memphis. In 1983, *Lest We Forget*, a musical drama based on Bishop Mason's life, was performed in the auditorium of Dixon Myers Hall in Memphis.

Mathis, Verdell L. "Lefty" (1914–1998), baseball player. A star pitcher with the Memphis Red Sox, he was known as the best left-hand player in the Negro American League in the 1940s. Born in Crawfordsville, Arkansas, on November 18, 1914, he grew up in Memphis "just a couple of blocks from the ballpark." He attended Booker T. Washington High School and had only one year of semipro experience before joining the Red Sox, in 1940, as an outfielder and pitcher. He received advice on pitching from his boyhood hero, Satchel Paige, whom he eventually defeated in New Orleans, Kansas City, and Chicago on "Satchel Paige Day" in front of thirty thousand fans. In 1946, he toured with Satchel Paige's All-Stars against Bob Feller's All-Star team.

At the height of his career, he was the Red Sox's "main man"; he had his own bat boy and "could pitch a tantalizing ball so slow you could count the stitches." Mathis was known as a "Sunday pitcher," because only the best players in the league made the team on the highest-grossing day of the week. Although he won almost half of the Red Sox victories in 1945, he needed surgery after the season to remove bone chips from his left elbow, an operation that led to the short-circuiting of his career in 1950. He spent almost his entire ten-year career in baseball in Memphis, except for a season with the Philadelphia Stars in 1943. His highest salary with the Sox was $700 a month, with an extra $25 for Sunday double-headers, but he explained: "Sometimes we'd run out of eating money. We'd get $2 a day to eat on. And if we played a night game, we got an extra dollar to ride on." After the season was over, the "southpaw ace" played winter ball with Vargas in Puerto Rico and Tampico in Mexico, where he once defeated Mexico City in a doubleheader. After leaving baseball, he worked as a locker-room attendant at Colonial Country Club for fifteen years. In 1984, his friends gathered at Cade's Barbershop to pay tribute to a man who achieved fame in the days before Blacks could play in the major leagues. In 1989, he was among a group of Red Sox players invited to a reunion sponsored by the Atlanta Braves and Bell-South, when Hank Aaron presented each player with a legends watch. Mathis and other members of the Red Sox were also honored by an exhibit at the Memphis Pink Palace Museum in 1996, when the documentary *Black Diamonds, Blues City: Stories of the Memphis Red Sox* was released. Mathis and his wife Helen, who lived at 1888 Rile, had three daughters and a son: Helen, Jean, Ann, and Verdell L. Mathis, Jr. The "King of the Hill," as he was known at Martin Stadium, died of pneumonia in November 1998.

McCleave, Florence Cole Talbert (1890–1961), opera singer, music educator. A pioneer concert and operatic soprano, she was the first Black to perform the title role of Aida with a European opera company. She was born in Detroit, Michigan, on June 17, 1890, but her roots were in Tennessee, where her grandfather had been a slave. She grew up in a musical family; both her parents sang and her mother traveled with the famed Fisk Jubilee Singers. While she was in elementary school, her family moved to California and she graduated from the University of Southern California. At age fifteen, she went to see *Aida* and vowed, after seeing a White in the title role, that she would one day have the lead part. In 1916, she won first prize at Chicago Musical College and, in 1918, became the first African American to sing at the Aeolian Hall in New York. Later, she sang with the Chicago Symphony and performed with orchestras throughout the country. Although operatic roles for African Americans were scarce, Florence Talbert refused her promoters' suggestion that she pass as an Indian to obtain more opportunities. In the 1920s, she recorded with Harlem-based Black Swan Records, the first record company owned and operated by Blacks, which was founded by former Memphian Harry H. Pace. In 1925, she went to Rome for training, and she also studied and sang in France. On March 16, 1927, she became the first African American to perform at a major opera house, when she sang the title role in *Aida* with the Teatro Communale in Cosenza, Italy. Later, she taught at Tuskegee Institute, Rust College, Fisk University, and Bishop College.

After her August 27, 1930, marriage to Dr. Benjamin F. McCleave, a dentist and physician, she moved to Memphis, where she was called "Madame McCleave" because of her marital status and regal bearing. Marriage brought an end to her performances but not to her musical career; like other artists, she turned to teaching as an outlet for her talent. The first floor of her home on the corner of Vance and Danny Thomas became a doctor's office for her husband and a music studio for Madame McCleave, whose students included future opera singers Vera Little and Alpha Brawner. She founded the Memphis branch of the National Association of Negro Musicians and co-founded the

Memphis Music Association, which brought singers such as Marian Anderson and Roland Hayes to Memphis. On Sundays, she sang solos at the Christian Science Society Church, which she helped organize, and her column, "Observations," appeared weekly in the *Tri-State Defender*. A member of the Elite Club and state president of the Women's Medical Auxiliary, she became an honorary member of Delta Sigma Theta Sorority and composed the music for the Delta National Hymn. Madame Florence Talbert McCleave died at Collins Chapel Hospital on April 3, 1961.

McCray, Shirley Yvonne (1941–), educator, coach. Celebrated as the country's first female coach of an all-male football team, she was born in Chicago on November 17, 1941, but was raised in Memphis by her paternal grandmother, Clara Dean McCray. "Little Shirley" grew up on Cummings and South Parkway, where "Mamma" took in laundry to support them. At Hamilton School, she played basketball with the boys because there was no team for girls and every summer she visited her father, Walter McCray, in Chicago, where the former staff sergeant taught his daughter to repair cars and mow lawns. After graduating from Hamilton in 1959, she moved to Chicago, graduated from Wilson Junior College in 1962, and returned to Memphis to attend Memphis State University. At MSU she encountered racial prejudice, particularly in her efforts to participate in team sports. When she told the girls' basketball coach that she would bring the executive secretary of the NAACP to talk with her, she was permitted to join the team but could not travel out of town.

The first Black woman to play basketball for MSU, she received her bachelor's degree in 1967, and then taught at Riverview High School, where she organized track, volleyball, and basketball teams for girls. In 1970, she became the first Black teacher at Kingsbury

High School but was reassigned to Chickasaw Junior High School in 1973. Although she knew little about football, she became coach of the boys' football team and learned the game fast, becoming a winning coach and a national celebrity after her undefeated Chickasaw Chieftains became league champions in 1978 and '79. Articles on McCray appeared in local newspapers, and *Ebony* and *Jet* magazines; she was featured in a CBS television program; and she signed a movie contract for her story. When football was eliminated in junior high schools, she waged a four-year battle to reinstate the sport. In the meantime, she coached championship teams for the Memphis Park Commission, which named her 1982 "Coach of the Year." She became assistant coach at Lanier Junior High School in 1984, and junior varsity football coach at Booker T. Washington High School in 1986, but she was not accepted by her male counterparts. She fought back and received back pay and reinstatement at BTW, in a 1993 settlement. After retiring in 1997, she published *Coach McCray: The Inspiring Story of America's First Woman Coach of an All-Male Football Team*, written by Amos Jones, Jr.

Miller, Mulgrew (1955–), jazz pianist, composer. A superb technician who has synthesized the piano styles of the 1960s and '70s, he is acknowledged as one of the major figures in forging the contemporary jazz piano tradition. He was born in Greenwood, Mississippi, on August 13, 1955, and developed an early interest in music. At eight, he began taking piano lessons in classical music and, at fourteen, was playing in church, school bands, and local dance halls. His brother's collection of jazz music by Ahmad Jamal and Erroll Garner stimulated his interest in jazz and, after watching a television performance by Oscar Peterson, he decided to become a jazz musician. After graduating from high school, he attended Memphis State University, where he studied jazz theory, heard musicians such as Phineas Newborn, Jr., and met jazz pianist James Williams, who became his close friend and mentor. While attending MSU, he started playing in gospel and R&B groups in the city. Influenced by Herbie Hancock, Chick Corea, and McCoy Tyner, he developed a keyboard style that reflects his early exposure to blues and gospel, his training in classical music, and his knowledge of the modern jazz tradition.

Mulgrew Miller served a lengthy apprenticeship under several jazz masters. In the late 1970s, he toured with the Mercer Ellington band for three years and took his first trip to Europe. In the 1980s, he worked with Betty Carter before joining the Woody Shaw quintet for two years. He joined Art Blakey's Jazz Messengers in 1984, and, a year later, produced his debut album, *Keys to the City*, which includes four original compositions: the blues-based "Song for Darnell," named after his son; "Prometheus," inspired by a Greek myth; "Portrait of a Mountain"; and "Saud's Run," a tribute to McCoy Tyner. The album is dedicated to his wife Tanya and to "the great masters of the music," who inspired him. After leaving the Messengers, Miller joined Tony Williams's Quartet and accompanied Cassandra Wilson and Dianne Reeves in recording sessions. He has since organized his own trio and made several albums under his own name. One of his best albums is *Hand in Hand* (Novus, 1992), which includes some original compositions. With his trio—bassist Richie Goods and Memphis drummer Tony Reedus—he gave a concert at Memphis's Centenary United Methodist Church in 2001.

Mitchell, Willie (1928–), musician, bandleader, arranger, composer, producer. A musical genius and Memphis legend, he is credited with helping to create the Memphis sound. He was born on January 1, 1928, in Ashland, Mississippi, but moved with his parents to Shelby County in 1933. With his eight siblings, he grew up on Hamilton Street in the Orange Mound neighborhood not too far from the Defense Depot, where his father worked. Mitchell learned to play the trumpet at eight, mastered six instruments, played trumpet in his high school band, and led his own fourteen-piece band by age fourteen. After graduating from Melrose High School in 1947, he attended Rust College and then served in the Army from 1950 to 1954, before returning to Memphis to form a combo. By day, he worked as a pharmacy deliveryman and, later, for a slipcover company. By night, he played trumpet with his band, performing at private parties for luminaries like Elvis Presley and at local night spots such as Club Paradise and Currie's Club Tropicana.

In 1959, Mitchell joined Hi Records, where he produced such instrumentals as "20-75," "Everything Is Gonna Be Alright," and "Soul Serenade," a Top Ten R&B single and the last of his hits as a player. At first, he worked with instrumentalists and groups such as Ace Cannon and the Bill Black Combo, and then he produced hit singles with vocalists like O. V. Wright, Bobby "Blue" Bland, Otis Clay, and Ann Peebles, whose chart-climber "I Can't Stand the Rain" became her signature piece. In his fifteen years with Hi, Mitchell was a musician, producer, key composer, principal arranger, and vice president; and he took over the label when president Joe Cuoghi died in 1970. He was best known as an arranger and producer, with 28 gold and platinum hits to his credit for stars such as Ike and Tina Turner, Denise La Salle, and Al Green—his most famous artist—who cut twenty-two gold and platinum records between 1970 and 1976. Since 1980, he has recorded out of Royal Studios at 1320 South Lauderdale Street, a section of which was renamed Willie Mitchell Boulevard in 2004. His recent albums include *Soul Serenade: Best of Willie Mitchell* (1999); the double-disk anthology, *Poppa Willie: The Hi Years, 1962–1974*; and *It's What's Happenin'/ The Hit Sound of Willie Mitchell*. "Pops," as he is called, was awarded a Grammy in 1986, received the 1998 Memphis Sound Award at the Blues Ball, and was named a Living Legend by the Rhythm and Blues Foundation. He has served on the executive boards of the Memphis Music Foundation, Beale Street Foundation, and Tennessee Film, Tape, and Music Commission. He and his wife, Barbara Ann Mitchell, have two daughters.

Morris, Alma (1924–2008), barber, civic worker. One of the most diligent leaders in North Memphis, she has dedicated her life to helping others. She was born in York, Alabama, on September 23, 1924, to Lillie and Tommy J. Grades. She moved with her family to Memphis in 1936, and has been involved in community work since she was a child. A 1942 graduate of Manassas High School, she completed her education at Tyler Barber College. With her husband, Charlie Morris, she opened Morris Barber Shop in 1953; located at 1239 North Evergreen at Chelsea, their barbershop is a landmark of the North Memphis community. During the civil rights movement, she marched and supported Martin Luther King, Jr., and even went to jail with him. An early riser, her day is filled with work to help the poor, young, and elderly; she takes food to the hungry, helps people with their utility bills, drives youths to their jobs, organizes cleanup campaigns, visits prisoners, monitors police activity, and fights slum landlords who "need to be run out of our poor Black neighborhoods," she says.

In December 1967, Alma and Charlie Morris organized the Kennedy Democratic Organization, which conducts voter registration drives, supports political candidates, obtains summer jobs for young people, and locates housing for seniors. With a membership of approximately 150 and a regular attendance of 30 to 40 members, the KDC has hosted speakers such as Mayors Willie Herenton and A C Wharton, as well as Congressmen Harold Ford, Sr., and Jr. In the 1970s, she ran for the City Council and then, in 1987, was a candidate for at-large position 1 of the City Council. She lost both elections but filed lawsuits against Pat Vandershaff, alleging that the council member did not live in the city. In 1985, as president of the Memphis Area Clients Council, she accused the Memphis Area Legal Services Board of forcing the head of the organization to resign. A member of Corinthian Baptist Church, Mrs. Morris has served on the boards of the Memphis Branch of the NAACP, Southern Christian Leadership Council, North Memphis Action, War on Poverty, and City Beautiful. The first Black woman to desegregate the Greater Democratic Women's Club, she is past president of La-Rita Social Club and of Gay YWCA. Alma and Charlie Morris have raised three sons—Charles, Jr., Ronnie, and the late Anthony Morris—as well as several grandchildren.

Morris, Herman, Jr. (1951–), attorney, business executive. He is the first African American to serve as president of the Memphis Light, Gas and Water Division and the first to be elected president of the Memphis Chamber of Commerce. The son of Reba Garrett Morris and Herman Morris, he was born in Memphis on January 16, 1951. After graduating from the Memphis public schools, he entered Southwestern at Memphis, from which he received a bachelor's degree in economics in 1973. He financed his college education by working as a counselor at Dixie Homes Boys' Club and Porter Leath Children's Center. After receiving a degree from Vanderbilt University School of Law, in 1977, he became an associate attorney with Ratner and Sugarmon (1977–1982) and then joined two other attorneys to form Sugarmon, Salky & Morris (1982–1986), which he left to organize Herman Morris and Associates in 1986. He lost a runoff election for an at-large City Council seat in 1987, and, a year later, he and Elijah Noel, Jr., opened Morris and Noel at 88 Union Center.

Herman Morris, Jr., was appointed General Council of Memphis Light, Gas and Water Division in 1989, and, after serving as interim president for several months, was appointed president of the Division in July 1997, by Mayor W. W. Herenton. Noted for his savvy management skills, Morris was the first Black permanent president of the country's largest three-service, municipally owned utility company. After leaving MLGW, he became director of Memphis First Community Bank. In October 2007, after waging a vigorous campaign for mayor of the city, he was defeated by incumbent W. W. Herenton. Active in civic and professional organizations, Morris became the first African American to serve as chairman of the Memphis Area Chamber of Commerce in 1999. He has served as president of the Memphis Branch of the NAACP and of the Ben Jones Chapter of the National Bar Association; he has also been board chairman of Memphis Health Center, Inc., Dixie Homes Boys' Club, and the Shelby County Home Rule Charter Commission. Morris has been admitted to the bar of the U.S. Supreme Court, Sixth Circuit Court of Appeals, U.S. District Court, and Supreme Court of Tennessee. In 1998, he was selected Employee of the Year by the 3,000-member National Employee Services and Recreation Association. He married Brenda Partee, a physician, on October 4, 1980, and they have three children: Amanda, Patrick, and Geoffrey.

Muhammad, Talib-Karim (1937–1997), religious leader, city councilman. Called a "warrior for many," the former boxer and head of Memphis's Muslim community was a political activist. The son of Donna and Theodore Manuel, he was born Theodore Manuel, Jr., and grew up in South Memphis, where he attended La Rose Elementary School, Porter Junior High School, and Booker T. Washington High School. In 1959, he converted to

Islam under the influence of Philbert X, the brother of Malcolm X; changed his name to Talib-Karim; and added the surname Muhammad in 1985. A leader among mainstream Black Muslims, he eventually left the Muslims and joined Louis Farrakhan's Nation of Islam but became independent again in 1989. After opening a series of businesses in Oklahoma, in 1975, he moved to Detroit, where he became a social worker and taught at Wayne State Community College. Active in the civil rights movement, he marched in Selma with Dr. M. L. King and journeyed to Resurrection City.

In 1985, Muhammad returned to Memphis, where he founded and directed the Islamic Center of Memphis and served as chief executive officer of Muhammad Enterprises and chairman of the board of Muhammad Child Development Center. On November 17, 1988, he filed suit in U.S. District Court, challenging the election system that allowed at-large seats on the Memphis City Council, which he maintained was unfair to minority voters. His suit led to the abolition of city-wide council seats, when a U.S. District judge invalidated Memphis's twenty-nine-year-old electoral system in 1995. Although Muhammad wanted a council composed entirely of single-member districts, Memphis voters approved a compromise: seven single-member districts and two super districts, each of which covers half the city. In 1991, Muhammad became a candidate for city mayor at the African People's Convention but later withdrew from the race. Campaigning on a platform that stressed education and economic development, he was elected to District 8, a super district, in October 1994. Muhammad established the Tennessee Chapter of the International Pan African movement in 1994, and served as national president of the Pan African movement U.S.A. He also edited a newspaper, *The Independent News*, and hosted a talk show for WLOK Radio for two years. The Epsilon Phi Chapter of Omega Psi Phi Fraternity named him 1993 Citizen of the Year. He received an honorary Doctor of Law degree from the City University of Los Angeles, but when *The Commercial Appeal* refused to accord him the title of "Dr." because he did not have an earned doctorate, he changed his first name, legally, to "Dr." in March 1990. He and his wife, Maryum-Karim Muhammad, were the parents of three daughters, Sudah Karim, Ameenab Karim, Khalilah Kari, and three sons, Karim, Talib-Ibn Karim, and Hassan Karim. After a long struggle with cancer, Dr. Talib-Karim Muhammad died on March 9, 1997.

Nelson-West, Bennetta "Bennie" (1944–), artist, educator, arts administrator. A potter, sculptor, and founding director of the Memphis Black Arts Alliance, she believes that "artists have the power to make change." The daughter of educator Jeanette Brown Nelson and postman Benjamin H. Nelson, she was born in Memphis on October 19, 1944. As a child, she studied ballet, piano, and art at LeMoyne College, Melrose High School, and the YMCA, under "caring adults who nurtured [her] creativity and love of the arts." She attended her mother's Nelson's Kindergarten and several elementary schools, before graduating from Melrose High School in 1962. Bennie marched and picketed during the civil rights movement and was arrested in 1960 for going to the Memphis Zoo on a "Whites Only" day, so she was prepared to fight against gender oppression in college. At Tuskegee, one of her professors said, "Daughter, nobody's going to hire a colored girl to run a hotel and restaurant," when he discovered that she wanted to get a degree in institutional management so she could run her own hotel/restaurant/lounge. With a letter from Robert Snowden, for whom she had worked at the Chisca Plaza Hotel, she completed a degree in her chosen field but had to work as a dietitian in Detroit and California. In 1969, after receiving a master's degree in public health from Columbia, she worked in New Jersey but lived for a decade in New York City, where she became involved in the Black Arts movement; took classes in dance, writing, theater, and pottery; moonlighted at Bea's Cluttered Closet Antiques; and created her own studio and gallery—ClaySpirits. In preparation for a career change, Bennie studied arts management at the New School for Social Research.

Upon her return to Memphis in 1979 to care for her mother, Nelson became Community Services Coordinator for the Continuing Education Department of Shelby State Community College; created the CETA-Summer Youth Program, "Art...Serious Business"; organized the First National African American Crafts Conference & Jubilee (precursor to the National Black Arts Festival); and edited the symposium papers with artist/art historian Dr. David C. Driskell. The 1979 conference/jubilee laid the groundwork for the creation, three years later, of the Memphis Black Arts Alliance, an arts and cultural organization. Founder and director of the Alliance, Nelson also pursued two advanced degrees at Memphis State University in the 1980s: a doctorate in higher education and an executive master's in business administration. After a brief hiatus from the MBAA, she returned in 1994 to help create the FireHouse Community Arts Academy, Little Theater, and Gallery; VOICES AFIRE; and FireHouse Community Arts Festival at Soulsville U.S.A. Festival, as well as the fund-raising event, Memphis "Men Who Cook." Located in a restored 1912 fire station on Bellevue Avenue, the Alliance stages art exhibitions, musical concerts, dance performances, and dramatic presentations.

A 1982 Leadership Memphis alumna, Nelson-West serves on the Admissions Committee for Leadership Memphis Institute, is a member of the Directors Council of the National Guild of Community Schools of the Arts, and has served on the boards of Brooks Museum of Art, Memphis Convention & Visitors Bureau, and Memphis Chapter of the Association of Fundraising Professionals. The mother of three—Joshua Parks, Jacob Ford, and the late Sarah June Parks—she has been married to artist Leonard D. West since 1995.

Newborn, Phineas, Jr. (1932–1989), jazz pianist, composer. Called "the greatest living jazz pianist" by a critic, he won critical acclaim for his harmonic artistry and mastery of the keyboard. His parents, Phineas and Rosie Lee Murphy Newborn, moved to Memphis after their marriage, but their first child was born in Whiteville, Tennessee, on December 14, 1932. His family included gospel musicians, a church vocalist, drummer, bandleader, and guitarist. At age nine, Phineas began private piano lessons and attended La Rose Elementary School and Booker T. Washington High School, where he learned to play the tuba, trumpet, and French horn. He joined BTW's swing band, the Booker Teasers, and Manassas High School's Rhythm Bombers. On Sundays, he played the piano at Mt. Vernon Baptist Church, but on Saturday nights he joined the Finas Newborn Orchestra, with his father on drums, his brother on guitar and trombone, and Junior (Phineas) on piano, vibraharp, and trumpet. While in high school, he also played with Willie Mitchell's band at Danny's Club in West Memphis and with Tuff Green and the Rocketeers. In 1951, he entered Tennessee State College, where he majored in music and learned to play the baritone, tenor, and alto saxophones, but he was drafted in August 1953. After his discharge in 1955, the young pianist formed the Phineas Newborn, Jr. Quartet and recorded his first album, *Here Is Phineas*. Concerts, jazz festivals, and nightclub engagements at New York's Birdland and Café Bohemia followed his debut at Basin Street in May 1956.

An ambidextrous pianist, Phineas could play the melody with either hand or play an entire concert with his left hand, as one of his compositions, "Blues for the Left Hand Only," indicates. Said to have the fastest right hand since Art Tatum, he played intricate polyrhythms and contrapuntal harmonies. He was also a fine arranger and composer, who infused classical music with a gospel and blues beat to create a contemporary jazz concept. In 1957, he and Charlie Mingus played jazz while Langston Hughes read his poetry at the Village Vanguard, and they wrote the soundtrack for the John Cassavetes film, *Shadows*. His quartet toured with Count Basie, Sarah Vaughn, Billy Eckstein, and others to sell out crowds in the "Birdland Show of 1957," and, a year later, Phineas toured Europe. He recorded over a dozen albums, including *A World of Piano*, *The Newborn Touch*, and *Piano Artistry of Phineas Newborn*. In spite of the critical acclaim, his life was marked by tragedies: he was plagued by mental illness and hospitalizations, and his two marriages—to Dorothy Stewart Newborn and Aleista Newborn—ended in divorce. His 1975 Grammy-nominated album, *Solo Piano*, marked his comeback: in 1978, he opened at the Village Gate and, later, he toured Europe and performed at the Montreux Jazz Festival. He was honored at the United Music Heritage Awards Benefit, appeared in a homecoming concert with Memphis natives Mulgrew Miller and James Williams, and gave a final performance at the Memphis in May concert at the Overton Park Shell in 1989. A month later, on May 26, 1989, Phineas Newborn, Jr., died at age fifty-seven and is survived by two daughters, Shelly and Pamela Newborn and a son, Phineas Newborn III.

Olive, Benjamin Garfield, Jr. (1890–1980), philanthropist, businessman, insurance executive. One of Anna and Benjamin Olive's twelve children, he was born on February 21, 1890, in Lexington, Mississippi. After attending Alcorn AM&N College, he transferred, in 1907, to Tuskegee Institute, where he studied chemistry under George Washington Carver and worked as a night guard for Booker T. Washington to pay his way through college. After graduating from Tuskegee in 1910, he worked for eight years in his father's construction company, where he became a foreman and licensed bricklayer. In 1918, Olive became an insurance salesman and, for the next fourteen years, worked for several Black insurance companies, including Mississippi Life, North Carolina Mutual, Woodmen Union Life of Arkansas, and Century Life of Hot Springs, which he helped to organize. In 1932, he became first vice president and secretary of Universal

Life Insurance Company, and he helped make it the fourth-largest Black-owned insurance company in the country. In 1914, he wed Bessie L. Wright, who died in 1939. Later, he married Ida Mhoon, and they had a son, John Avery Olive, who died on June 12, 1977.

B. G. Olive, Jr., was a philanthropist who gave time and money to support organizations such as the Goodwill Boys Club, Urban League, Shelby United Neighbors, and Memphis Heart Association. Convinced that education would provide civic and economic advancement for Blacks, he and his wife paid the college tuition of more than twenty students; made donations to Meharry Medical College, Southern Christian College, Tougaloo College, Tuskegee Institute, and Tennessee A&I State College; and, in 1977, he gave an estimated $750,000 in stocks—the single largest gift from an individual—to LeMoyne-Owen College to provide scholarships for business majors. In recognition of his gift to the college, LeMoyne-Owen awarded him the Doctor of Humane Letters a year later. He supported the acquisition, preservation, and publication of historical material by Universal and spearheaded publication of the company's first Black Legacy Calendar in 1963. Active in professional organizations such as the National Business League, he served as president of the National Insurance Association. Although Olive retired from Universal in February 1980, he continued to serve as a consultant and member of the board of directors until his death on December 30, 1980, at age ninety.

Owen, Samuel Augustus (1886–1974), pastor, educator, religious leader. Called "the most accomplished Negro clergyman in Memphis history," he became a national leader in the Baptist Church. Born on July 21, 1886, in Haywood County, Tennessee, he was the son of former slaves, Fannie and Henry Clay Owen. Samuel Owen attended Roger Williams College in Nashville and then entered Morehouse

College but returned to Memphis because his father was dying. A scholarly minister with an advanced degree from the University of Chicago School of Divinity, he became the first president of Florida Memorial College and pastored several Baptist churches in Florida. In 1916, Owen married Mary Jane Wood of Alexandria, Virginia, who was a new teacher at the college. A year later, the couple moved to Nashville, where Owen was appointed president of Roger Williams College, a position that he held from 1920 to 1923.

On April 17, 1923, he was named pastor of Memphis's Metropolitan Baptist Church and immediately began a savings plan to build a new sanctuary, but the church lost $27,000 when the Solvent Savings Bank failed in 1927. Undaunted, Owen launched a campaign to raise funds and, on April 7, 1929, the church opened a $60,000 sanctuary. Under the leadership of its pastor, Metropolitan became one of the largest Black Baptist churches in the state, with a membership of about 1,000. Except for his service as an Army chaplain in World War II, Owen was pastor of Metropolitan for forty-nine years, missing only two Sundays because of illness. Reverend Owen became an outstanding church leader, making a pilgrimage to the Holy Land and attending international conventions in Africa, Germany, France, and Denmark. A moderator of the West Tennessee Baptist Missionary and Educational District Association from 1928 to 1961, he was elected president of the Tennessee Baptist Missionary and Educational Convention in 1936, and held the position for twenty-seven years.

In 1953, he was elected vice president at large of the National Baptist Convention, U.S.A., Inc. on a reform ticket. Because of the president's failure to reform the organization, Owen left the Convention in 1957 and helped organize the Progressive Baptist Convention. He served as president of the Interdenominational Ministers' Alliance, which named him "Minister of the Year" in 1953. In the 1950s, Owen was instrumental in the founding of a junior college in Memphis, when the Baptist State Convention paid $375,000 for property at the corner of Vance and Orleans. Over his protests, the trustees named the college after its founder, and S. A. Owen Junior

College opened with twenty-two students in 1954. The first chairman of the board of trustees, he continued in that position when Owen Junior College merged with LeMoyne College in 1968. Described as a man of "great personal charm and intelligent leadership," he retired from the pulpit on June 9, 1972, to devote more time to a church-supported foreign mission in Nigeria. S. A. Owen died in 1974.

Pace, Harry Herbert (1884–1943), editor, insurance executive, music publisher, attorney. The son of Nancy Francis Pace and Charles Pace, a blacksmith, he was born in Covington, Georgia, on January 6, 1884. His father died when he was an infant and he was raised by his mother. A precocious child, he finished elementary school at age twelve and, seven years later, graduated as valedictorian of his class at Atlanta University, where he was mentored by W. E. B. Du Bois. After brief stints as an Atlanta printer and as an instructor at Haines Institute in Augusta, Georgia, he was persuaded by Du Bois to join him and Ed Simon in publishing *The Moon Illustrated Weekly* in Memphis. Founded in 1905 and located at 197 Beale Avenue, with Pace as managing editor and Simon as publisher, it was the first illustrated African American journal. After the demise of the *Weekly*, Pace became professor of Latin and Greek at Lincoln University in Missouri at a salary of $110 a month. He returned to Memphis in 1907, when Milton L. Clay and R. R. Church offered him the position of cashier of the Solvent Savings Bank. Under his management, the bank's assets increased from approximately $50,000 in 1908 to $600,000 by the end of 1912. That same year, he met and collaborated with W. C. Handy in composing songs.

In 1913, H. H. Pace became secretary-treasurer of Standard Life Insurance Company in Atlanta and embarked on a career in the insurance business. On June 20, 1917, he married Ethlynde Bibb, and they had two children, Josephine and Harry Herbert, Jr. In 1920, he and Handy organized the Pace and Handy Music Company in New York but, when the partnership dissolved, Pace founded the Black Swan Phonograph Company, the first Black-owned record company. He resigned the presidency of the company in 1925, when he organized and became the first president of Northeastern Life Insurance Company in Newark, New Jersey. When he merged Northeastern with Supreme Life and Casualty of Columbus, Ohio, and Liberty Life Insurance Company of Chicago to form Supreme Liberty Life of Chicago, he headed the largest Black-owned company in the North in the 1930s. He realized his life-long ambition by entering law school in 1930, and, in 1933, he graduated fourth in a class of forty to receive the Doctor of Jurisprudence degree. He opened the Chicago law firm of Bibb, Tyree, and Pace in 1942.

Pace was active in civic, political, and professional organizations in Memphis, Atlanta, and Chicago. He founded the first Elk's Lodge in the city, Bluff City No. 96, and became grand secretary of this order at age twenty-four and grand exalted ruler at age twenty-seven, making him the only man ever to hold both offices. In 1911, he organized and became president of the Colored Citizens Association of Memphis, with Bert Roddy as secretary. He also served as secretary of the Republican Committee of Shelby County and as assistant secretary of the State Republican Committee. From 1917 to 1926, he was district grand treasurer of the Grand Lodge of Odd Fellows of Georgia and president of the National Negro Insurance Association from 1928 to 1929. In 1933, he was appointed to the advisory committee of the Secretary of Commerce, and in 1935, he was appointed assistant counsel for the Illinois Commerce Commission. He published a book of inspirational essays, *Beginning Again*, in 1934, a serial novel published by the Chicago *Defender*, and several books and pamphlets on insurance. Harry Herbert Pace died in 1943.

Patterson, Gilbert Earl (1939–2007), church leader. As Presiding Bishop of the Church of God in Christ, he founded one of Memphis's largest Black churches and organized a ministry that served the community. He was born in Humboldt, Tennessee, on September 22, 1939, to Mary and W. A. Patterson, Jr., but grew up in Memphis and moved to Detroit as a teenager. When he was only seventeen, he preached his first sermon at his father's Detroit church on January 22, 1957. He studied at the Detroit Bible Institute and, later, at LeMoyne College. In 1962, he returned to Memphis, where he was ordained an elder in the Church of God in Christ and became co-pastor, with his father, of Holy Temple COGIC on Wilson Street. In 1975, he left the Church of God in Christ and founded an independent Pentecostal church, Temple of Deliverance, which presently has one of the country's fastest growing congregations, with over 12,000 members and three facilities, including Temple of Deliverance downtown, Bountiful Blessings in Whitehaven, and a new 4,000-seat sanctuary behind Temple of Deliverance. Patterson remained outside of COGIC for thirteen years, but returned to the church to reclaim his name and heritage, because he came from a long line of Patterson preachers: his father, Bishop W. A. Patterson; his uncle, Bishop J. O. Patterson; and his cousin, Bishop J. O. Patterson, Jr.

Temple of Deliverance serves as the home base for Patterson's Bountiful Blessings Ministries (BBM), which has a hundred employees, a mailing list of over 100,000 donors, a preschool, Bible college, radio and television studios, bookstore, health center, family ministry, and prison ministry that serves the Criminal Justice Center and Penal Farm. Bishop Patterson was founder and president of BBM, as well as president and general manager of Memphis-based WBBP-1480, a gospel radio station with more than 100,000 daily listeners. A renowned speaker who delivered his messages without notes in a deep and resonant voice, he broadcast sermons weekly on BET and TBN cable networks, and he sold audio and videotapes of his sermons by the thousands. He was also publisher of *Bountiful Blessings Magazine* and a contributing writer to the *Spirit-Filled Life Bible*. He received an honorary doctorate from Oral Roberts University and serves as president of the Charles H. Mason Bible College of Tennessee Fourth Jurisdiction in Memphis.

In 2000, G. E. Patterson defeated incumbent Chandler D. Owens of Atlanta in a heated election to become presiding prelate and chief apostle of the Church of God in Christ, the largest Pentecostal denomination in the country, with six million members in fifty-four countries. Headquartered in Memphis, it is the sixth largest Christian church in the United States and is estimated to be the nation's largest African American denomination. In 2004, Patterson was reelected to a second four-year term as presiding bishop but announced in September 2005 that he had prostate cancer, to which he succumbed in March 2007. Later that year, a housing project, the Joseph A. Fowler Homes, was renamed G. E. Patterson Pointe in his honor. The bishop was married to Louise D. Patterson for more than thirty-five years.

Patterson, James Oglethorpe (1912–1989), clergyman, religious leader. As head of the nation's largest African American Holiness Body, he became an internationally acclaimed church leader. The son of William and Mollie Patterson, he was born in Derma, Mississippi, on July 21, 1912, and grew up in Derma; Heath, Arkansas; and Memphis, Tennessee. Although he attended public schools in Derma and Heath, most of his formal education was acquired in the Memphis school system and at Howe School of Religion. In 1935, he was ordained an elder and, a year later, he was sent to pastor a church in Gates, Tennessee. In the years that followed, he served a church in Brownsville, Tennessee; Homeland Church of God in Christ and Temple COGIC in Memphis; and Reid Temple in East Orange, New Jersey. For forty-eight years, he was senior pastor of Pentecostal Temple Institutional Church of God in Christ in Memphis. In 1955, he was appointed Bishop and Prelate of the Second Ecclesiastical Jurisdiction of Tennessee by Bishop Charles H. Mason. After Bishop Mason's death in 1961, Bishop Patterson also became general secretary, a member of the board of directors, and manager of the Church's publishing house.

At COGIC's sixty-first General Assembly in 1968, J. O. Patterson was elected the first presiding bishop of the Church of God in Christ, making him the spiritual leader of three and a half million church members. A year later, he became the jurisdictional bishop of the Headquarters Jurisdiction at Memphis, Tennessee. He founded the Charles Harrison Mason Seminary in Atlanta, C. H. Mason System of Bible Colleges, J. O. Patterson Fine Arts Department, and Historical Museum and Fine Arts Center. He founded and presided over the World Fellowship of Black Pentecostal Churches, enlarged the COGIC bookstore and publishing house, and organized the Charles Harrison Mason Foundation, as well as the Presiding Bishop's Benefit Fund to provide scholarships to students. Active in the Memphis community, he served on the boards of the Boys Club, Boy Scouts of America, Y.M.C.A., Rotary Club, Memphis Landmark Commission, Lorraine Historical Museum Commission, and Tri-State Bank of Memphis. He was also active in national organizations such as the Black Church Summit of the World Council of Churches and the Congress of National Black Churches.

Bishop Patterson acquired the 500-room Chisca Plaza Hotel through a donation by its owners, and that property became COGIC's national headquarters. Under his stewardship, the Church also acquired other valuable Memphis downtown property, which was used for its bookstore, publishing house, senior citizens' housing, and other philanthropic activities. In the twenty-one years of his leadership, Bishop Patterson increased church membership to four million in fifty states and forty-seven foreign countries, and he appointed more than 100 prelates to positions of authority. He received honorary degrees from several colleges and was named every year, beginning in 1975, in *Ebony* magazine's list of 100 Most Influential African American Leaders in America. He married Deborah Mason, the daughter of Bishop Charles H. Mason, and they had two children: James Oglethorpe, Jr., and Janet Laverne. Four years after Mrs. Patterson's death, he married Mary Peterson Peak.

Patton, Georgia E. L. (1864–1900), physician, medical missionary. The first African American woman licensed to practice medicine in Tennessee and the first to practice medicine in Memphis, she was a medical pioneer. She was born a slave on April 16, 1864, in Grundy County in southeast Tennessee, but little is known about her early life. When she was twenty-two years old, she entered Nashville's Central Tennessee College, and, after completing the senior normal course in 1890, she enrolled in the College's Meharry Medical Department. The first Black woman to graduate from the medical school, she also became the first Meharry graduate to serve as a missionary to Africa. Two months after her graduation and after an unsuccessful attempt to get the financial support of her church's missionary society, Patton became a self-supporting medical missionary to Liberia. When she set sail on April 5, 1893, she shared a cabin with former Memphian Ida B. Wells, a journalist and antilynching crusader. The two young women landed in Liverpool, England, on April 13, and, the following Saturday, Patton sailed for Liberia.

Although she worked with insufficient medical supplies, inadequate equipment, and poor operating facilities, she gained the confidence of the Liberians through her successful treatment of patients; she reported to her former dean at Meharry that she had lost only four of the 100 patients that she had treated.

Dr. Georgia Patton remained in Liberia only two years, however, because her health began to fail. In 1895, she opened a lucrative medical practice at 282 Second Street in downtown Memphis. On December 29, 1897, she married David W. Washington, who was born a slave at LaGrange, Tennessee, in 1852. The first Black hired as a letter carrier in Memphis, Washington, who was twelve years older than his wife, became a successful businessman and real estate owner. The couple's first child, Willie Patton Washington, was born on February 14, 1899, but died the same day. A second son, David W. Washington, was born on July 11, 1900, but died four months later. Georgia Patton Washington, who had contracted tuberculosis, was in poor health for several years and apparently gave up her medical practice in the late 1890s at the time of her children's births. On November 8, 1900, Dr. Patton died at age thirty-six and was funeralized at Centenary Methodist Episcopal Church two days later. She and her two sons are buried in Zion Cemetery, the oldest Black cemetery in Memphis.

"Pie Lady, The." See Sarah Clayborne.

Porter, David (1941–), musician, composer, producer, music publisher. A music impresario and creative wiz, he helped create the sound that made Memphis a soul music capital. Porter was born in Memphis on November 21, 1941. After graduating from Booker T. Washington High School in 1961, he and his friend Maurice White, who later founded Earth, Wind & Fire, started singing in gospel groups at Rose Hill Baptist Church. In the early 1960s, he sang at the Flamingo Room and at a few of Elvis Presley's parties, and he cut a couple of records on the Golden

Eagle and Savoy labels. With the encouragement of Estelle Axton, he began listening to music at Satellite Records, across the street from Big Star Grocery Store where he worked. When Satellite changed its name to Stax and its focus from country to soul music, he joined the company as its first staff writer and started singing with Booker T & the MGs. After persuading keyboardist Isaac Hayes to collaborate with him in writing music for Stax, the Porter/Hayes duo—with Porter composing the lyrics and Hayes writing the music—was on its way to fame and fortune. "Most of what we did was what we called head arranging," Porter explained. "We'd get into the room, hum the lines [and] peck them out on the piano."

In the 1960s, the dynamic duo composed over 200 songs for such Stax luminaries as Sam & Dave ("When Something Is Wrong with My Baby," "Soul Man," and "Hold On, I'm Comin"), Carla Thomas ("B-A-B-Y"), and Johnnie Taylor ("I Got to Love Somebody's Baby" and "I Had a Dream"). The team split around 1970, when Hayes's "Hot Buttered Soul" hit the top of the charts, and he decided to pursue a solo career. Porter, who remained with Stax in its declining years, made four solo records between 1970 and 1975 and took a behind-the-scenes role in Memphis's music industry. He served as president of the Memphis chapter of NARAS; opened a music club, Da Blues, at the Memphis/Shelby County Airport; became a partner in B. B. King's Blues Clubs; built a recording studio; started a label, Robosac Records; and continued composing music with other partners. Porter acknowledged that he made money, primarily during the 1990s, when rap and urban artists sampled his older hits. For example, in his Grammy-winning "Gettin' Jiggy Wit It," Will Smith sampled Porter's "Song and Dance"; and in her 1993 hit "Dreamlover," Mariah Carey sampled the tune "Blind Alley." A few years ago, Porter joined with two veterans of Stax to launch a new Memphis-based R&B label, International Pocket Records (IPR), which released its first CD, *He Did What!*, by Lyric, a female trio from Alabama.

Like music entrepreneur Quincy Jones, David Porter continues to push the envelope; he owns a producing company, publishing company, record label, media production office, and artist development complex. As a result, many awards have come his way: in 1996, he received an honorary brass note on Beale Street's Walk of Fame. In 1999, he and Hayes received Pioneer Awards from the Rhythm and Blues Foundation and, in 2005, they were inducted into the Songwriters Hall of Fame.

Price, Hollis Freeman (1904–1982), educator, college president. He served as president of LeMoyne (later, LeMoyne-Owen) College for twenty-seven years, leading the institution through a period of rapid growth and student unrest. The only son of an American Missionary Association school principal, he was born on June 29, 1904, on a farm outside of Capahosic, Virginia. One of the first African Americans to graduate from the Williston Academy in Massachusetts, he received a B.A. degree from Amherst College in 1927 and an M.A. degree in economics from Columbia University. In 1931, Price became a professor of economics at Tuskegee Institute and, three years later, married Althea Banks with whom he had a son, Hollis F. Price, Jr. Characterized as a "great and gifted teacher who had an uncanny ability to inspire his students," he was appointed dean of LeMoyne College in 1941, and two years later, he was appointed president of the college. While attending a banquet honoring him as Educator of the Year in November 1968, he learned that a student demonstration was taking place on the college campus, so he left the banquet and persuaded the students to end their demonstration. Under his leadership, college enrollment increased, the curriculum was strengthened, and the merger of LeMoyne and Owen Junior College was effected in 1968. He served the college with distinction until 1970, but took a leave of absence in 1954 to direct fund raising for the United Negro College Fund.

In 1957, Hollis F. Price directed the Rapid Social Change Study in Liberia for the World Council of Churches and the Phelps Stokes Fund; the following year, he traveled to Austria and Greece to participate in Rapid Social Change conferences. A humanitarian, noted for his integrity and sound judgment, he served on many boards and commissions, including the Tennessee Council on Human Relations, Tennessee Conference on Social Welfare, and Better Schools Committee. He was appointed one of two Black advisors to the Memphis Board of Education, following the 1969 NAACP-led boycott of public schools, and he served in that position for two years. After his retirement as president of LeMoyne-Owen College in 1970, he became director of Urban Affairs at WMC-TV. The recipient of honorary degrees from Brandeis University, Amherst College, and Southwestern at Memphis, Dr. Price was given awards by the Memphis Board of Education, Memphis Newspaper Guild, and Memphis Round Table of the National Conference of Christians and Jews. Called a "master bridge builder," he was the first male member of the Memphis chapter of the League of Women Voters and was one of the first three Blacks inducted into the Memphis Rotary Club. A longtime member of Second Congregational Church, he became the first Black national moderator of the United Church of Christ. After a lengthy illness, he died on November 6, 1982. A street adjacent to LeMoyne-Owen College was renamed in his honor and city officials declared February 7, 1983, "Dr. Hollis F. Price Day."

Riley, Larry (1952–1992), actor, director, composer. He achieved success on Broadway and in Hollywood but returned to Memphis often to direct plays in the city where his talent was first nurtured. The son of Corine Riley, he was born in Memphis on June 20, 1952, and grew up in the Orange Mound neighborhood. After graduating from Melrose High School, he attended Memphis State University and acquired a love of theater from drama professor Erma Clanton, who directed him in her long-running *Evening of Soul*. He performed on the Broadway stage during the 1970s and '80s, winning praise for his portrayal of the character named "Memphis" in the stage production and film version of *A Soldier's Story*. An accomplished singer and songwriter, he won the ASCAP award for Best Incidental Music and Best Newcoming Composer for the music that he wrote for *A Soldier's Story* (both the play and movie). He also wrote the musical score for the 1987 film *Blind Side* and the theme song for the HBO movie *Long Gone*, and scored some of the music for the television serial *Knot's Landing*.

As an actor, Riley had a magnetic stage presence; he brought intensity, integrity, and keen intelligence to his work. Perhaps best known for the role of Frank Williams in *Knot's Landing*, he made frequent trips to Memphis, where he gave generously of his time and talent: in 1987, he directed *Rosencrantz and Gildenstern Are Dead* at Memphis State University; in 1989, he participated in the 10th annual Handy Blues Awards; and he appeared later that year in *Heart Strings*, a theatrical production and fund-raiser for AIDS. His wife wrote, "Ironically, at the time Larry had no idea he was carrying the AIDS virus." He returned to Memphis, a year and a half later, to support one of Levi and Deborah Frazier's productions at the Blues City Cultural Center. He was married to Californian Nina Riley, an advocate for AIDS awareness, who wrote a touching memoir, "Look Homeward, Angel," for *Memphis* magazine in which she describes her husband's love of his hometown and their disappointment at the dearth of medical facilities in Memphis for the treatment of AIDS in the early 1990s. The Rileys decided to move to Memphis, but Larry became seriously ill at the airport on May 11, 1992, while awaiting a plane to bring him home. He entered the hospital and died in Burbank, California, on June 6, 1992, two weeks before his fortieth birthday.

Robinson, Kenneth Stanley (1954–), pastor, physician, medical educator, health official. A national authority on the development of community health and wellness programs through nonprofit organizations, he uses his training as a minister and physician to promote comprehensive approaches to public health. The son of James M. and Mary Frances Robinson, a school administrator and teacher, he was born in Nashville, Tennessee, on May 19, 1954. He discussed sermons at two, recited the *Gettysburg Address* at four, and took advanced placement classes in elementary school. At ten, he volunteered to work with handicapped children and, three years later, represented Tennessee at the Youth National Association for Mentally Retarded Children and was elected president of the organization at sixteen. In 1970, the American Foundation named him an Outstanding Teenager of America and, two years later, after appointment to the National Committee on Mental Retardation, he traveled to The Hague, Netherlands to address the International Conference on Social Welfare. After graduating as valedictorian from Pearl High School in 1971, he received a B.A., cum laude, from Harvard and an M.D. from the Harvard Medical School. Two days after graduating from medical school, Dr. Robinson married Marilynn Sasportas, a Harvard graduate with a master's in public health from Yale.

After completing an internship in Boston, Dr. Robinson joined the faculty of the Vanderbilt School of Medicine, while pursuing a master of divinity degree. He joined the African Methodist Episcopal Church, serving as pastor of St. Peter and Payne Chapel A.M.E. Churches in Nashville before accepting the pastorate, in 1991, of St. Andrew A.M.E. Church in Memphis. Under his leadership, the church has established a day care center, ministries for singles, mentors for youth, a food bank, a health center, and classes in sign language and Tae Kwon Do, as well as a summer program at its four-acre recreation and retreat center. Through partnerships with schools, foundations, and health care providers, his congregation has launched community programs dealing with issues such as alcohol and drug abuse. He is the founder and past president of The Works, Inc., organized to help the church's inner-city neighbors build affordable housing.

An academic physician, the Reverend Doctor Robinson served as assistant dean of Admissions and Student Affairs at the University of Tennessee College of Medicine before being named commissioner of the Tennessee Department of Health in 2003. In 1998, he was named one of the Robert Wood Johnson Foundation's ten outstanding community health leaders in America and, two years later, he was given the Community Builders Award by United Way of America. In 2005, he delivered the Robert H. Ebert Lecture at Harvard, reminding students that a medical degree carries a dual burden of entitlement and commitment. He and his wife have twins—Maisha and Nuriva—and Mrs. Robinson presently serves as vice president of St. Francis Hospital, as well as assistant pastor of St. Andrew.

Roddy, Bert Maynard (1886–1963), businessman. Founder of the first chain of Black-owned grocery stores in Memphis, Roddy was an innovative and progressive entrepreneur who was active in civic and political affairs. He was born on August 19, 1886, in Augusta, Arkansas, to Jerry and Harriette McKenny Roddy. The family, which included four daughters and a son, moved to Memphis, where young Bert enrolled in LeMoyne Normal School. After graduation, he became bookkeeper and, in 1914, cashier of the Solvent Savings Bank and Trust Company. In 1911, he co-founded, with Harry H. Pace and Robert Church, Jr., the Colored Citizens Association, which led a registration drive and lobbied to obtain park facilities, paved streets, and sprinkling service from the city government. Roddy was a life member of the National Negro Business League, and he helped organize the Three States Better Farming Association in 1917. With Robert Lewis, he opened the Iroquois Café on Beale Street; founded the Ten-Men Investment Club, which built the first Black-owned movie theater in Memphis; and helped organize the Negro Southern Baseball League, which operated in eight cities.

Bert Roddy was the first Black Memphian to consider organizing a branch of the NAACP in Memphis. In May 1914, he wrote the national office about establishing a chapter, but he received little support from local Blacks until violence broke out in the city in 1917. On June 17, soon after the burning of Eli Persons, Roddy held a meeting to organize the branch, and fifty-three people, primarily business and professional men, joined the NAACP. Subsequently, Roddy was elected the first president of the branch. During World War I, he was among race leaders who pledged to sell $174,823 in Thrift Stamps and to double their quota of $75,000 in the United War Work campaign. Committed to the political advancement of the race, he joined with other Black Memphians on February 2, 1916, to form the Lincoln League, a Black Republican organization, and he was elected treasurer of the League. Although he lost his campaign for the Tennessee State Senate on the Lincoln League ticket in the November 1916 election, he was a delegate to the League's first national convention in Chicago in 1920.

In 1918, he married a former LeMoyne classmate, Hannah Jefferson Wilson of Meridian, Mississippi, who taught in the Memphis public schools. The Roddys and their three children—Harriet, Gwendolyn, and Bert, Jr.—were members of Second Congregational Church, where he served as superintendent of the Sunday School. In 1918, he attended a meeting called by W. E. B. DuBois to discuss the "idea of co-operation among colored people" and, a year later, received a state charter to establish Roddy's Citizens' Co-operative Stores. Within a few months, he sold $10,000 in stock at

$10 a share and established five stores; by 1920, he operated fifteen neighborhood stores with several dozen employees and had a fleet of delivery trucks and more than 9,000 investors, who had bought stock. When debts became insurmountable, Roddy used his position as cashier of the Solvent Savings Bank to obtain an unsecured loan of $100,000 in a futile effort to keep the stores afloat, but the venture collapsed in 1922. Roddy then helped organize Supreme Life and Casualty Company of Ohio and, when the company (renamed Supreme Liberty Life Insurance Company) was relocated, Roddy moved his family to Chicago, where he became assistant agency officer of the company in 1931. He served in that position until poor health forced his retirement in 1957, and he died in March 1963.

Sawyer, Chew Cornelium (1918–1973), businessman, real estate developer. One of Memphis's most successful entrepreneurs in the 1950s and '60s, he founded four firms that provided economic opportunities for African Americans. Born on August 20, 1918, he was the son of Mrs. A. C. Sawyer, who lived at 843 Ioka Street. After graduating from Booker T. Washington High School, he attended LeMoyne College. A real estate developer who owned extensive property near the downtown area, he founded Sawyer Realty Company, located at 334–336 Vance Avenue, which later became Cornette Realty Company, Arnette Construction Company, Future Insurance Agency, and Sawyer Rental Agency. Through these companies, he built houses, churches, business offices, and apartment buildings for Blacks in the 1950s. In 1956, he founded and served as president of Mutual Federal Savings and Loan Association, the first Black-owned-and-managed savings and loan company in Tennessee. With assets of $779,846 in 1958 and $2,801,038 in 1969, the company provided loans, first mortgages, and home improvement loans for low- and middle-income families, thus helping to restore blighted neighborhoods. Sawyer financed and constructed the building at 588 Vance Avenue, where Mutual Federal was located; after the association closed, the building was bought by the Memphis Branch of the NAACP for its local headquarters.

Active in civic and community affairs, Sawyer was a life member of the NAACP and joined other prominent Black businessmen, such as Jesse H. Turner and A. Maceo Walker, who sat-in at downtown restaurants to end segregation. He was also prominent in social and fraternal organizations; he was a member of the Omega Psi Phi Fraternity and a charter member and president of the Top Hats and Tails, an organization of Black professional men. He and his wife, Helen Smith Sawyer, whom he married on October 5, 1942, often entertained in their South Parkway home and were noted for their annual Christmas party. Although the Sawyers had no children, he had a sister, Othella S. Shannon, principal of Georgia Avenue School, and two brothers, Windell S. Sawyer and Otho S. Sawyer, Jr., who worked with him in business. After a lengthy illness, he died in Memphis on September 23, 1973, and is buried in Elmwood Cemetery.

Scott, Joe Burt (1920–), baseball player. An outfielder and first baseman with the Memphis Red Sox, he was the first African American to play in Wrigley Field. One of four children, he was born in Memphis on October 2, 1920. As a child, he often received whippings for skipping Sunday school to play baseball on a vacant lot in South Memphis. His mother raised him, because his father, a shop-owning mechanic, deserted the family when his son was ten years old. At age sixteen, Joe moved to Chicago to live with an aunt and entered Tilden Technological High School, where he was named to the school's Hall of Fame several years later. An ambitious student and an all-round athlete, he played chess, baseball, and football, although he was the only Black on the team. After graduating from high school, he joined several semipro and industrial teams, and in the off-season he loaded beef onto boxcars.

The turning point in Scott's professional career came in 1939, when he joined Satchel Paige's team, played games abroad, and made several All-Star appearances. Between 1942 and 1945, he served in the Air Forces-Special Services, with the 345th Aviation Squadron. After his discharge, he played five years for the Memphis Red Sox in the Negro Leagues, batting .360 at the time, and he later played for the New York Black Yankees, Pittsburgh Crawfords, Dayton Kitty Hawks, Dizzy Dean All-Stars, Hot Spring Bathers, and Knoxville Smokies. Scott believes that many Negro League players could have made the major leagues if the color barrier, broken by Jackie Robinson in 1947, had been lifted earlier. At 5' 9", he was an undersized outfielder, but he could hit, run, and throw. John "Buck" O'Neil, a legendary first baseman recalled: "Joe was an outstanding player in a league of outstanding players." Scott had to give up spring training with the Philadelphia Athletics in 1950, after a bus wreck in Canada left him with a crushed disc. In 1956, when his playing days were over, he returned to Memphis and went into the trucking business for twenty-seven years. After retiring, he traveled a bit, played the dogs at Southland Greyhound Park, and took trips to Dodgers' games.

Settle, Josiah T. (1850–1915), attorney, state representative, district attorney, political leader. One of Memphis's best trained and most experienced early lawyers, he had lucrative practices in two states and became a powerful figure in Republican politics. One of the eight children of Nancy Graves, a slave, and Josiah Settle, a wealthy planter, he was born in 1850 in East Tennessee while his parents were traveling from North Carolina to Mississippi, where his father had bought a plantation. After freeing his common-law slave wife and their children, Josiah Settle moved his family to Hamilton, Ohio, in 1859, and joined them there at the beginning of the Civil War. His son attended school in Hamilton, entered Oberlin College in 1868, and transferred to Howard University the following year. In 1872, he was in Howard's first graduating class, and he went on to obtain a law degree from Howard three years later. While attending college and law school, he served as reading clerk of the House of Delegates, clerk for the Board of Public Works, member of the D.C. School Board, and clerk for the Board of Public Works. In 1875, Settle moved to Sardis, Mississippi, where he practiced law for ten years and became active in state and national politics. The youngest member of the delegation, he represented Mississippi at the 1876 Republican National Convention, where he seconded the nomination for vice president of the United States; he also served that year as a presidential elector at large. Although he lost an earlier election for district attorney of the Twelfth Judicial District of Mississippi, the charismatic politician was elected by a margin of 1,200 votes to the Mississippi House of Representatives in 1883.

Two years later, Josiah T. Settle moved to Memphis, where he was appointed assistant attorney general of the Criminal Court of Shelby County. The presiding judge of the court attested to Settle's integrity, character, "manly courtesy," and "exemplary professional deportment." After two years on the bench, Settle returned to private practice, where he earned a reputation as an astute lawyer and gifted orator. One of his most celebrated cases challenged the state law mandating segregation on street cars. In 1905, he and Attorney Benjamin F. Booth represented Mary Morrison, who refused to accept a seat in the segregated section of the street car. Although $5,000 was raised to argue the case before the State Supreme Court, the judge ruled in favor of the state law. Indicative of his legal ability, J. T. Settle passed the bar in the

District of Columbia, Mississippi, Tennessee, and several other Southern states, and he was admitted to practice before the United States Supreme Court on April 20, 1906. He continued to play an active role in Republican politics, serving as Tennessee delegate to the Republican National Convention in 1892, alternate delegate in 1896, and delegate from the state at large to the conventions of 1900, 1904, and 1912. On March 20, 1890, Settle married Fannie McCullough, director of music at LeMoyne Normal Institute, and they had two sons: Josiah T. Settle, Jr., and Francis McCullough Settle, who followed their father into the legal profession. The Settles belonged to Emmanuel Episcopal Church and lived in a two-story, Victorian house on South Orleans Street. Josiah T. Settle died in 1915, at age sixty-four.

Shaw, Edward (1818–1891) editor, lawyer, businessman, city official. The first Black Tennessean to run for the United States Congress, he was a militant political leader during Reconstruction. Born free in Kentucky, he boasted that he did not participate in the Civil War because it was "a white man's fight" and there were no promotions for colored soldiers. Shaw moved to Memphis in 1867, opened a saloon near Beale Street, and became active in Black organizations such as the Sons of Ham, Independent Order of Pole Bearers, and Negro Mutual Protection Organization. Considered one of the city's first Black militants, he was thrown out of the smoking car on the Memphis and Ohio Railroad in January 1868, and, later that year, he and other Black leaders returned fire after they were shot at by members of the Ku Klux Klan. Called "one of two great Negro orators of the South," he urged former slaves to exercise their rights: to register, vote, and elect Black candidates to office. In 1869, Shaw ran unsuccessfully for the Shelby County Commission and, although he was a Republican, he campaigned as an independent for the U.S. Congress in 1870, because he was disenchanted by the racial prejudice of local

Republicans. He campaigned against a White Republican, whom he accused of receiving a $5,000 bribe from the Memphis Street Railway Company and, although Shaw received less than 200 votes, he prevented his opponent from winning the election and demonstrated to White Republicans that they could not take Black political support for granted.

In 1872, Edward Shaw won election to the Memphis City Council and pressured city officials to hire African American teachers in Memphis city schools; two years later, he was elected wharfmaster, the highest paying job in city government. When the State Convention of Colored Men convened in Nashville in 1874, the delegates elected him chairman of the convention. Under his leadership, the convention urged passage of the Civil Rights Bill, opposed discrimination in jury selection, and questioned the constitutionality of laws forbidding interracial marriages. When segregationists claimed that a civil rights bill would lead to intermarriage, Shaw responded that White men had been practicing equality in Black bedrooms for a long time. Noted for his biting humor, he told a gathering of Blacks, "They say, 'Oh! You want to marry our daughters.' From the looks of this congregation it seems that one could hardly marry any other than their daughters!"

In June 1874, Shaw, who owned and edited the *Memphis Weekly Planet* was elected president of the convention of colored editors in Cincinnati, and he was selected to accompany Ulysses S. Grant on a visit to LeMoyne Normal Institute and Beale Street Baptist Church when the former general visited Memphis on April 14, 1880. From 1881 until his death, Shaw was listed in the city directory as a lawyer with an office at 83 DeSoto and a residence at 421 Clay. On April 18, 1887, Ida B. Wells, a militant Memphis teacher, wrote in her diary, "The dignified patriarchal & stern demeanor and bearing of Mr. Shaw—show that the men of the race who do think are endeavoring to put their thoughts in action…to inspire those who do not think." Four years later, on March 21, 1891, Edward Shaw died of pneumonia at age sixty-three.

Shaw, Lily Patricia Walker "Pat" (1939–1985), civic worker, businesswoman, insurance executive. The first woman to head a major American life insurance company and the first woman president of the National Insurance Association, she was one of the country's top women executives. The daughter of Antonio Maceo and Harriet Ish Walker, she was born in Little Rock, Arkansas, on July 26, 1939. She attended the Memphis public schools before entering Oakwood School in Poughkeepsie, New York, from which she graduated in 1956. While in college, "Pat" or "Lily Pat," as she was called, worked in the summers as an accounting trainee at Tri-State Bank and as a clerk in the underwriting department at Universal Life Insurance Company. After receiving the B.A. degree, cum laude, from Fisk University in 1961, she took graduate courses in business administration at the University of Chicago and University of Tennessee Graduate School of Social Work, and she received a teaching certificate from Tennessee State University's Graduate School of Education. From 1961 to 1962, Walker was a social worker in Chicago. She married Harold R. Shaw on June 17, 1961, and returned to Memphis, where she was a welfare worker before joining Universal as a keypunch operator in 1966. Although her father was president of the company that was founded by her grandfather, Dr. Joseph E. Walker, Shaw had to work her way up through the ranks for seventeen years, but she pointed out that "moving step by step through the company has been the most important learning experience of my life." In 1981, she was appointed executive vice president in charge of developing new market thrusts.

On February 14, 1983, Patricia Walker Shaw was elected president and chief executive officer of Universal Life Insurance Company, succeeding her father as head of the fourth largest Black-owned insurance company in the nation. Then, the company had thirty-six branch offices, assets of more than $62 million, and more than $610 million of insurance in force. Continuing a family tradition of leadership in business and public service, Shaw was elected president of the National Insurance Association and was the first African American to serve on the board of Memphis Light, Gas and Water Division. In 1981, she was elected vice chairman of the Division, which named the Patricia Walker-Shaw Water Pumping Station in her memory. She served on the State Commission on Minority Economic Development and as Chairman of the Board of the Memphis Branch of the Federal Reserve Bank of St. Louis. She was on the boards of the Memphis Development Foundation, Economic Club of Memphis, and Memphis-Plough Community Foundation. A member of Leadership Memphis and past president of Memphis in May, Shaw was a director of the Memphis Area Chamber of Commerce and a member of the YWCA, NAACP, and PUSH. Her awards included the American Black Achievement Award from *Ebony* magazine, Par Excellence Award from Operation PUSH, and the 1980 "Outstanding Black Woman Award" from Moolah Court #22. In 1983, she was one of twelve women in the nation to receive the Candace Award for "extraordinary achievements by Black women" from the National Coalition of 100 Black Women. After a long illness, Patricia Walker Shaw died in Memphis on June 30, 1985, leaving her husband and their son, Harold Shaw, Jr.

Shaw, Lucy Mae Yates (1947–), nurse, teacher, hospital administrator. She was the first woman and first African American to serve as chief operating officer of the Regional Medical Center (The Med). One of the seven children of John and Sadie Shell Yates, she was born in Memphis on September 11, 1947. At age nine, she began cleaning house for a teacher and, later, clerking at Witherspoon Sundry and A. Schwab Dry

Goods Store. Her father, a former riverboat cook and Beale Street café owner, died when she was fourteen. After attending Leath, Porter, and Father Bertrand Schools, she graduated from Zion Benton Township High School in Illinois. Yates went to Memphis State University for a year and then moved to Gary, where she lived with an aunt and worked as a medical assistant for a doctor. While pursuing a nursing degree at Purdue University, she married Harold Witherspoon and they had two children. She worked as a practical nurse for two years, divorced, and in 1974, returned to Memphis, where she taught health occupations at Hamilton and Carver High Schools and worked part time as a nurse at Baptist Memorial Hospital. She eventually married Harold Shaw and they are the parents of three children: Harold Witherspoon, Darryl Michael Shaw, and Harold Shaw, Jr.

By 1985, Lucy Shaw had acquired an M.A. in nursing and an M.B.A. in professional resource development from Memphis State University. She had also advanced rapidly as a nursing administrator at Baptist Hospital; she was promoted from clinical coordinator to evening house supervisor, and from day administrator to assistant director of nursing. When she became associate director of nursing in 1982, she was the highest ranking Black in management at Baptist Hospital. Four years later, she became vice president of nursing at The Med and, in 1988, was promoted to chief operating officer. In 1990, she became president and chief executive officer of The Med, a 550-bed, nonprofit hospital with 2,800 employees and an annual budget of $200 million. A highly professional executive, she made significant improvements to the hospital, changing the image of the hospital, improving relations with the staff, and changing the working relationship with the University of Tennessee. One of the leading hospital administrators in the country, Lucy Shaw testified before Congress and achieved national acclaim for her service at The Med. She was a member of the executive committee of the National Association of Public Hospitals and of the Picker/Commonwealth Hospital Task Force, and became president and chair of the Tennessee Public and Teaching Hospitals Association. Her colleagues were stunned, therefore, when Shaw resigned from The Med in February 1994.

Shaw formerly served on the Advisory Board to The Federal Reserve Bank of St. Louis; the boards of the Memphis Area Health Industry Council, Free the Children's Executive Committee, and Girl Scout Women's Network; and the board of directors of the National Bank of Commerce and trustee board of the University of Tennessee. In 1991, she was elected president of the Memphis in May International Festival, which led to her appointment as Honorary Consul of New Zealand. Her resignation from The Med signaled an important shift in Shaw's personal and professional life. She and her late husband belonged to The Church at Memphis, an assembly of Seventh Day Christians. Now a medical missionary, she is a consultant, founding president of Common Denominator, Inc., and author of *The Brickmakers' Journal: Surviving in the Flesh: Thriving in the Spirit*, a journal and workbook of biblical quotations, inspirational messages, and exercises.

Smith, Maxine Atkins (1929–), educator, administrator, civil rights activist. Acknowledged as one of the most influential people in Memphis, she served for many years as executive secretary of the Memphis Branch of the NAACP and as a member of the Memphis Board of Education. She was born in Memphis on October 31, 1929, the youngest child of Georgia Rounds Atkins and Joseph P. Atkins, a postman. After her father's death, when she was nine year old, she and her two siblings were raised by their mother, who worked at Metropolitan Baptist Church. Maxine entered public school in the third grade and graduated, at age fifteen, from Booker T. Washington High School. After receiving a bachelor's degree from Spelman College in 1949 and a master's from Middlebury College in 1950, she taught French at Prairie View College and Florida A&M University. In 1953, she married Vasco A. Smith, Jr., a dentist, and moved with him to Scott Air Force Base.

On their return to Memphis, she taught at LeMoyne College for a year, until the birth of their son, Vasco A. "Smitty" Smith III on December 25, 1956.

When Maxine Smith and a friend were denied admission to all-White Memphis State University in 1957, she began a life-long battle against racial discrimination. Between 1957 and 1962, she volunteered with the Memphis Branch of the NAACP, serving as a member of the executive board, membership chairman, director of voter registration, and coordinator of the 1960 sit-in movement. In 1962, she was named executive secretary of the branch, which by 1975 had become the largest in the South. Under her leadership, the organization received the Thalheimer Award, given to the most outstanding branch in the country, 31 out of 32 years. In 1961, she helped escort thirteen Black children to four formerly all-White schools; a year later, she helped desegregate another school when she took her son to the first grade at Peabody Elementary School. She organized an eighteen-month boycott of downtown stores, supported the sanitation workers' strike in 1967, and led a series of Black Monday demonstrations against the Memphis Board of Education in 1969. Smith was personally involved in every phase of Memphis's civil rights movement. A friend of Martin Luther King, Jr., since their college days in the 1940s, Smith and her husband joined King and other leaders in the 1963 March on Washington and she was with Medgar Evers just before his assassination on June 12, 1963.

In 1971, Smith was elected to the board of Memphis City Schools, the seventh largest school system in the country, and she served as board president in 1991–1992. The subject of a 1972 WMC-TV documentary, *Maxine*, she was honored at the NAACP's Fourth Annual Testimonial Banquet in 1974, and was voted the Black Memphis Leader who has "the power to influence the goals and actions of the most people" in a 1977 *Commercial Appeal* survey. Among her more than 160 awards and citations are the 1975 American Civil Liberties Union Bill of Rights Award, 1993 Lifetime Achievement Award from the University of Memphis Black Students Association, 1997 Richard R. Green Award for outstanding contributions to urban education, and the National Civil Rights Museum's 2003 Freedom Award, which she shared with former president Bill Clinton. Although she resigned from the School Board in 1995 and from directorship of the Memphis Branch of the NAACP in 1996, she served on the Tennessee Board of Regents until 2006 and remains on the national board of the NAACP. The recipient of honorary degrees from LeMoyne-Owen College and Spelman College, she is the subject of a 2007 biography, *Maxine Smith's Unwilling Pupils: Lessons Learned in Memphis's Civil Rights Classroom.*

Smith, Otis Milton (1922–1994), attorney, corporate officer, state supreme court justice. He was the first Black appointed to the Michigan Supreme Court and the first Black corporate officer of General Motors Corporation. Born in Memphis on February 20, 1922, he was the son of Eva Willoughby Smith of Natchez, Mississippi, and Samuel McCullough Williamson, founder of a Memphis mortgage company. He and his older brother, Hamilton, were raised by their mother, who worked as a domestic during the Depression. After graduating as class salutatorian from Carnes Grammar School, he entered Manassas High School but dropped out for a year. In 1939, Smith graduated from Booker T. Washington High School, where he excelled, winning a letter in football, serving as senior class president, editing the student newspaper and yearbook, and joining several clubs. While working as a porter in Nashville to save money for college, he became active in the NAACP, wrote for a Black newspaper, and joined the Nashville Suitcase Theatre. After a year at Fisk, Smith—now 6' 4" and 180 pounds—became a noncommissioned officer in the Air Force, assigned to the 477th Bombardment Group. After his honorable discharge in 1946, he attended Syracuse University and then obtained a law degree from Catholic University.

On December 29, 1949, during his last year in law school, he married Mavis Clare Livingston, and they had four sons—Vincent, Raymond, Anthony, and Steven. After graduating from law school in 1950, he joined the offices of Dudley Mallory in Flint, Michigan. A respected attorney, Smith rose rapidly in his profession, serving as Chairman of the Michigan Public Service Commission from 1957 to 1959, auditor general of Michigan from 1959 to 1961, and justice of the Supreme Court of Michigan from 1961 through 1966. Moving into the corporate world in the mid-1960s, he joined the legal staff of General Motors, serving in several positions from attorney-in-charge of Appellate and Administrative Practice to General Council. Otis Smith was vice president of the company, when he retired from General Motors Corporation on April 1, 1984. His taped memoirs formed the basis of a posthumous autobiography, *Looking Beyond Race: The Life of Otis Milton Smith* (Great Lakes Books, 2000), co-edited by Mary M. Stolberg. His concern for others also motivated Justice Smith's service on the boards of civic and professional organizations, including the Detroit Symphony Orchestra, Henry Ford Health Systems, Administrative Conference of the United States, Kroger Company, and Detroit Edison Company. He received honorary Doctor of Law degrees from eight universities, including Catholic University of America, Morgan State University, Southwestern at Memphis, and the University of Michigan. Justice Otis M. Smith died of cancer on June 29, 1994, at age seventy-two.

Smith, Vasco Albert, Jr. (1920–), dentist, county commissioner, civil rights activist. A pioneer in the struggle for civil rights, Smith has had a long and distinguished career in public service. The son of Florence E. Smith and the Reverend Vasco A. Smith, he was born in Harvard, Arkansas, on August 24, 1920, and grew up in Memphis at 350 East Georgia Avenue. After graduating from Booker T. Washington High School in 1937, he received the B.S. degree from LeMoyne College in 1941. He took menial jobs to pay his college and dental school tuition: he was a busboy at the B & W Cafeteria for $2.50 a week, waited tables at the Memphis Country Club, worked at American Finishing Company, and was a machinist at Frisco Railroad Shop. At Meharry Medical College, from which he received the D.D.S. degree in 1945, he was inducted into two national and international honors societies. When he took his state board examination at the University of Tennessee Dental School, he and the three other Blacks were seated in a segregated section "where their patients would be more at ease." In spite of such indignities, he served his country as an enlisted man in the Second World War and as an officer in the Korean War from 1953 to '55. He first opened an office in Dyersburg, Tennessee but, later, moved his practice to Memphis. In 1953, he married Maxine Atkins, and they have a son, Vasco A. "Smitty" Smith III, who is also a dentist.

When Vasco and Maxine Smith returned to Memphis in 1955, after he had completed his tour of duty in the Air Force, they came back to a totally segregated city and became active in voter registration, political campaigns, and the civil rights struggle, working as volunteers with the Shelby County Democratic Club, Democratic Voters' Council, and Memphis Branch of the NAACP. With other activists, he joined the attack against institutional segregation that was launched by the Memphis Branch of the NAACP in the 1950s and '60s; he helped develop strategy, raised money, picketed, and sat-in to end segregation in schools and public facilities; and he was arrested five times while participating in the freedom movement. In 1973, Dr. Smith was elected to the Shelby County Commission and served for 21 years, until his retirement on August 31, 1994. During his tenure on the Commission, he introduced or supported legislation to create a County Equal Employment Opportunity Office, build a $60 million city hospital, improve nursing facilities for the poor and elderly, improve public housing for the poor, and establish services for the elderly. As a member of the Charter Commission, he helped create opportunities for Black representation in government.

A jazz buff, Smith is a member of the Memphis Jazz Society, taught a course in jazz at Shelby State Community College, and has an awesome collection of records, tapes, and compact disks, many by Memphis musicians. A Renaissance man, he plays contract bridge, swims up to forty laps a day, and specializes in growing tropical plants. In recognition of his outstanding service to the community, he has received many citations and awards, including a Civil Rights Award from the National Dental Association and a Doctor of Humane Letters from the Tennessee Baptist Theological Seminary. In spite of his many achievements, Vasco A. Smith, Jr., returns often to the poor neighborhood where he grew up to remind himself that "but for the grace of God."

Spillers, Hortense J. (1942–), writer, literary critic, college professor. A nationally acclaimed scholar of African American literature, she has won awards and fellowships for her creative and scholarly writing. A native Memphian, she was born on April 24, 1942, to Evelyn Taylor Spillers and Curtis Spillers, Sr. She lived in the family home in Orange Mound and attended St. John Missionary Baptist Church, co-founded by her maternal grandfather, Robert Taylor. After graduating from Melrose High School in 1960, Spillers entered Bennett College but transferred after a year to Memphis State University, from which she received a bachelor's degree in English in 1964 and a master's in 1965. In 1973, while completing a dissertation on the rhetoric of Black sermons, she received a joint appointment in English and Black Studies at Wellesley College and, a year later, she was awarded a Ph.D. degree by Brandeis University. One of few Blacks on the faculty of Wellesley, she was denied tenure in spite of positive reports by outside referees, so in 1979, she joined the faculty of the University of Nebraska but took a leave in 1980 to accept a Rockefeller Fellowship. On June 15, 1980, Dr. Spillers married Michael McLoughlin, but the marriage ended in divorce three years later. From 1981 to 1987, she taught at Haverford College, where she became an associate professor with tenure in 1982. A Fellow at Cornell's Society for the Humanities in 1987, she joined the English faculty as a full professor a year later. Between 1990 and 1993, she taught at Emory University and was a 1991–1992 Fellow at the prestigious National Humanities Center in North Carolina before returning to Cornell in 1993. She took a leave from the University in 1996–1997 to join the Center for Advanced Studies in the Behavioral Sciences at Stanford and, in 1998, she was named the Goldwin Smith Professor of American Studies at Cornell.

Dr. Hortense Spillers' scholarly articles on African American writers have appeared in journals such as *Diacritics*, *Mississippi Quarterly* and *New Centennial Review*. One of her essays, "Martin Luther King's Pulpit Style," won the *Black Scholar*'s prize for 1971, and another, "All the Things You Could Be By Now if Sigmund Freud's Wife Was Your Mother: Psychoanalysis and Race" appeared in *Critical Inquiry* and *Boundary II*. She has edited or co-edited the following books: *Conjuring: Black Women, Fiction, and Literary Tradition* (1985), *Comparative American Identities: Race, Sex, and Nationality in the Modern Text* (1991), and *The Norton Anthology of African American Literature* (1997). She has authored *Black, White, and in Color: Essays on American Literature and Culture* (2003). Also a creative writer, Spillers has a novel in progress and has published several award-winning short stories, including "Isom," which won the National Award for Excellence in Fiction and Belles Lettres in 1975. On November 12, 1997, she gave the Fagin Lecture, "Historical Revision and Cultural Memory," at LeMoyne-Owen College. Dr. Spillers joined the English faculty at Vanderbilt University in July, 2006, as the Gertrude Conaway Vanderbilt chair in English.

Steinberg, Martha Jean (1930–2000), evangelist, broadcaster, businesswoman. Known as "The Queen" because of her charisma, good looks, and regal bearing, she was a pioneering deejay in Memphis and Detroit, as well as a station owner and philanthropist. Born in Memphis on September 9, 1930, to Florence and Virgil Jones, she graduated from St. Augustine High School in 1948, and, six years later, became one the first Black women hired as a deejay at Radio Station WDIA. The only woman among such noted broadcasters as Rufus Thomas, Nat D. Williams, and A. C. Williams, Martha Jean anchored "Nite Spot" from 9:00 to 9:30. Along with co-worker Mark Stansbury, she started the first sock hops or platter parties at Foote Homes Auditorium. In 1963, after almost ten years at WDIA, Steinberg moved to Michigan, where she became a legendary evangelist and businesswoman in a career that spanned almost four decades. She started at WCHB in Inkster, Michigan in 1963, but, after three years, moved to Radio Station WJLB in Detroit. In the late 1960s, a friend appropriated her Memphis deejay title, "Premium Stuff," for a record company that had a ten-record life span. The tracks were cut in Memphis by noted music producer Willie Mitchell.

During the urban riots that struck Detroit and other cities in 1967, Steinberg remained on the radio for forty-eight hours straight, urging citizens to stay off the streets, and her actions were credited with quelling the disturbance. Later that year, in cooperation with the Detroit Police Department, she created the "Buzz the Fuzz" program, which gained national attention for its effectiveness. A founding member of WQHB, she bought the station in 1998, through her Queen Broadcast Corporation, and expanded its gospel, blues, talk, and preaching format. An astute businesswoman with a larger-than-life personality, Steinberg served as president and general manager of the station, which was sold after her death for over $4 million. "The

Queen" was also an evangelist and ordained minister, who founded the Order of the Fishermen Ministry in 1975, and the Queen's Home of Love Church. As an evangelist, she gave the opening prayer at a session of the U.S. House of Representatives in 1993. She was also noted for her philanthropy: one of her organizations, "The Forgotten People," helped blue-collar workers develop positive thinking, self-esteem, and self-sufficiency, and she established the Rosa Parks Trust Fund in 1994, to cover the living expenses of the "Mother of the civil rights movement." Martha Jean Steinberg received many awards and tributes. The staff and readers of the *Detroit Free Press* recommended her as the "Michiganian of the Year," and she was named to the Michigan Women's Hall of Fame in 1998. She was also inducted into the Deejay's Radio Exhibit at the Rock and Roll Hall of Fame in Cleveland, Ohio. Martha Jean Steinberg died unexpectedly on January 29, 2000, and a memorial musical tribute, sponsored by the St. Augustine Class of 1948 and Radio Station WDIA, was held in her honor at St. Augustine Church. She and her former husband, musician Luther Steinberg, had three daughters: Diane, Sandra Kay, and Trienere.

Stevens, Rochelle (1966–), athlete, businesswoman. A world-class athlete, she won a silver medal at the 1992 Olympics in Barcelona and was an Olympic gold medalist in the women's 400-meter relay in 1996. Born in Memphis on September 8, 1966, she is the daughter of Beatrice Holloway, a former track star at Barret's Chapel High School. At age twelve, Rochelle started running track for the Memphis Recreation Department and became one of the best 800-meter runners for her age group in the country. In 1984, she graduated from Melrose High School, where she was an 800-meter runner with a best of 2:11:01, and where she also played the clarinet, drums, and guitar. After winning state titles in the 400- and 200-meter competitions, she attended Morgan State University, where she majored in telecommunications and sales, made the Dean's List, and won the 1988 NCAA 400-meter outdoor championship in her senior year. Although Nike became her sponsor, she was disappointed on placing fifth in the 1988 women's 400-meter race at the U.S. Olympic Track and Field trials in Indianapolis, so she quit track for almost six months and started working at a Memphis portrait studio. Her mother, who had won a track scholarship to Tennessee State University but became pregnant with Rochelle in her freshman year, encouraged her daughter to resume training and became her coach in 1991. When Rochelle's sister, Catherine Holloway, died of a brain tumor, the young track star promised that she would win a medal for her at the Olympics in Barcelona. In 1992—at age twenty-five, standing 5' 8" and weighing 125 pounds—she had the fastest 400-meter time of any American and was ranked number three in the world.

Rochelle Stevens received a medal in every meet she entered until 1993, when she had a series of physical setbacks, including a pulled hamstring and broken jaw, but she came back strong in 1998 to place second in the nation. With few corporate sponsorships, she survived financially through fees obtained from European appearances. For several summers, she sponsored the Rochelle Stevens Invitational Track Meet in Memphis, which drew 2,000 student athletes from ten states. Between 1994 and 1997, she operated the Golden Falls Ballroom, a 3,000-square-foot facility in Southeast Memphis, which catered events for churches, businesses, and social clubs. In 1999, the young entrepreneur opened Rochelle's Health and Wellness Center, which offers skin care, body wraps, and weight loss treatments. The former athlete is also a spokesperson for Posner cosmetics, a registered agent with the Canadian Football League, and a soloist at her mother's church, Word of Life Holiness Church of God.

Stuart, Merah Stevens (1878–1946), author, businessman, insurance executive. One of the city's pioneering Black businessmen, he wrote a definitive and scholarly history of the insurance industry. Born on June 27, 1878 on the Stampley plantation in rural Mississippi, he was the son of Henrietta, the daughter of slaves, and Blount W. Stuart, a plantation owner. For ten years, he attended a one-room rural school that was cold and uncomfortable, and where children sat near the stove in one-hour shifts. With the $20 that he made from cultivating two acres of farmland, he entered Alcorn College and supplemented his tuition by milking cows, cleaning the mess hall, working in the college shoe store, and stuffing mattresses with straw. In his early teens, he married Emma Stewart and they had seven children. After teaching in Wilkerson County for $28 a month, he obtained a position at The Town School in Centerville for $35 a month. Eddie P. Jones, a prominent member of the Odd Fellows, persuaded Stuart to become president of the Eddie P. Jones Institute, but Stuart resigned after a disagreement over policy to become a teller with the Delta Penny Bank.

In 1906, M. S. Stuart became cashier of the American Trust and Savings Bank of Jackson, Mississippi, but, when he discovered that the capital was insufficient to generate a profit, he recommended that the company be liquidated and that the debtors and stockholders be paid. In 1910, he became a railway postal clerk but, six months later, he began investigating fraudulent claims for several Mississippi fraternal orders. Between 1914 and 1923, he served as general manager of the Industrial Department of Mississippi Life Insurance Company in Indianola; during that period, the company's income increased from $60,000 to $1,200,000. In 1924, he and a partner organized the Stuart-Anderson Debit Agency, which operated under the charter of the Southern Life Insurance Company (a White company) in Arkansas, Mississippi, and Texas. The company earned a profit of $43,000, with $10,000 going to each partner. When Mississippi Life was acquired by Universal Life Insurance Company, Stuart was elected vice president and general manager of Universal in September 1926, and in 1937, he was appointed vice president and director of government relations, in charge of the technical and social security department.

One of the organizers of the National Negro Insurance Association, he served as president for two terms. When he was elected historian of the organization in 1934, he wrote *An Economic Detour: A History of Insurance in the Lives of American Negroes*, which has been described as a rich source of information on the insurance industry. Like so many pioneering businessmen of his generation, Stuart did not complete high school, but he reveals in his writing a profound knowledge of economics, business, and finance. An active member of the community, he served as president of the local NAACP, helped raise money for the YWCA, and was on the Steering Committee of the National Negro Business League. He and his second wife, Evelyn Crouch Stuart, and their daughter Clivetta lived on Neptune Street, before moving to a house that he built on Adelaide Street. A grocery and café were located on the first floor of the building, while the family lived in a second-floor apartment. M. S. Stuart died of a heart attack in his office on May 1, 1946, at age sixty-eight.

Stuckey, Elma Johnson (1907–1988), poet. Called one of the "authentic American poets of our century," she drew on the rich cultural tradition of the Delta to write original works of art. The granddaughter of former slaves, she was born in Memphis on March 15, 1907 into a family that included eleven children. She grew up listening to the stories and folk tales of ex-slaves in her North Memphis neighborhood, and she began writing poetry at age eleven. Elma Johnson attended Manassas High School—built on land that was donated by her grandfather Spencer Johnson—during the 1920s. After graduating as valedictorian of her class, she earned a teaching certificate from Lane College and then taught in a rural school, before returning to Memphis as the head teacher in a nursery school. She also worked at Firestone Rubber Company, Three Sisters, the Tea Room, and Johnny Mills Restaurant on Beale Street. Elma Stuckey recited poems such as "Trumpet," "His Hands," and "Daylight Saving Time" in over a hundred Memphis churches, and she published some of her poems in *The Commercial Appeal*, *Memphis Press Scimitar*, and other local papers. Later, her poems appeared in journals such as *Freedomways*, *The Journal of Black Poetry*, and *Black American Literature Forum*. In 1945, she and her husband, Ples Stuckey, a former waiter at the Claridge and Peabody Hotels, moved to Chicago in search of greater opportunities for their two children, Jean and Sterling. In Chicago, the Stuckeys moved near the Pill Hill neighborhood, where they were visited by writers such as Sterling Brown and Paul Robeson. After studying for a short time at Roosevelt University, Elma Stuckey worked as a hat checker at Harding's Restaurant and became a supervisor at the Illinois Department of Labor.

After an early retirement, Stuckey began to write full time. At age sixty-nine, she published *The Big Gate* (1976), with an introduction by literary critic Stephen Henderson. The collection includes many poems about slavery that were inspired by her reading of African American history and, especially, by the stories that she heard as a child in Memphis. A second volume, *The Collected Poems of Elma Stuckey*, which includes the long narrative poem "Ribbons and Lace," about a former slave named Aint Rachel, appeared in 1987. In his introduction, Memphian E. D. Hirsch, Jr., wrote that this collection captures "the entire odyssey of blacks in America." Stuckey's work gained national attention after she was interviewed by Studs Terkel on radio station WFMT in Chicago, appeared on Grace Cavalieri's "The Poet and The Poem" for National Public Radio, and gave readings at the University of California at Berkeley, as well as at Harvard,

Cornell, and Stanford Universities. A writer-in-residence at St. Mary's College and the University of Illinois, Stuckey was also a gifted performer with a wicked sense of humor, who delighted young family members with her dramatizations, in costume, of her folk poetry. In 1989, the Memphis Black Writers' Workshop held a conference in her honor at LeMoyne-Owen College. Her poems have been anthologized in several collections, including *Homespun Images: An Anthology of Memphis Artists and Writers* and *Trouble the Water: 250 Years of African-American Poetry*. On September 25, 1988, Elma Stuckey died of a heart attack while in Washington, D.C., to make a recording of her poetry for the Smithsonian Institution. Her papers are in the archives of the Chicago Historical Society.

Stuckey, Ples Sterling (1932–), activist, scholar, college professor. A leading historian and interpreter of the African American experience, he pioneered the interdisciplinary study of slavery in numerous articles and books. The son of Elma Johnson Stuckey and Ples Stuckey, he was born in Memphis on March 2, 1932. Stuckey has deep roots in North Memphis: he attended Manassas Elementary School; his great-grandfather, Spencer Thomas Johnson, donated the land for Manassas; his family, including his sister Jean, worshiped at Collins Chapel C.M.E. Church; his uncles worked at Firestone; and his mother wrote poems about former slaves who lived in their neighborhood. In 1945, the Stuckeys moved to Chicago, where visitors such as Sterling Brown, Maragaret Burroughs, and Paul Robeson kindled young Sterling's life-long interest in African American culture and history. After receiving a bachelor's degree in political science from Northwestern University in 1955, he taught at an elementary school for two years and then at Chicago's Wendell Phillips High School for six years.

In the early 1960s, Sterling Stuckey became actively involved in the civil rights movement: he co-founded and chaired Chicago's Emergency Relief Committee, which sent food and clothing to Tennessee's Fayette and Haywood Counties; chaired the Chicago Freedom Rider Committee; served as Mid-Western Regional Director of CORE; and co-chaired the Chicago youth wing of A. Philip Randolph's March on Washington for Jobs and Freedom Now. When the segregated public schools were boycotted in 1964, he taught Black history courses in Chicago's Freedom Schools, and, later, served as a consultant to National Public Radio, when NPR and the Smithsonian produced a series of programs on sacred music of the civil rights movement. His participation in the Black liberation movement of the 1960s was intrinsic to his development as a scholar and humanist. In 1965, he returned to Northwestern University, where he earned a master's and doctorate in history and served as a professor of history from 1971 to 1989. In 1989, Dr. Stuckey joined the faculty of the University of California-Riverside, where he held the presidential chair and was distinguished professor of history. On his retirement in 2004, a conference, "Africans, Culture, and Intellectuals in North America: P. Sterling Stuckey and the Folk," celebrated his intellectual legacy, and selected papers from the conference were published in a special issue of *The Journal of African American History* in fall 2006.

A consummate writer and scholar, Professor Stuckey has published numerous reviews, book chapters, and articles such as the groundbreaking essay, "Through the Prism of Folklore: The Black Ethos in Slavery," which has been reprinted nineteen times. His books include *Slave Culture: Nationalist Theory and the Foundations of Black America*, which examines the significance of art forms such as the Ring Shout; *Going Through the Storm: The Influence of African American Art in History*, a collection of essays on African American intellectual and cultural history; and *African Culture and Melville's Art: The Creative Process in Benito Cereno and Moby Dick*, which explores Black motifs in Melville's writing. He also co-authored *The Ideological Origins of Black Nationalism*, as well as two textbooks, *Call to Freedom* and *The American Nation*. His current projects include research on the life and work of Paul Robeson and an extended study of slave dance, tentatively titled *The Fires of Creation: The Ring Shout and the Formation of Culture*. Stuckey was a Senior Fellow at the Smithsonian Institution and at the Humanities Research Institute, University of California, Irvine; he was also a Rockefeller Foundation Resident Fellow at the Center for Black Music Research and a Fellow at the Center for Advanced Study in the Behavioral Sciences at Stanford University on three separate occasions. Dr. Stuckey and his wife, Harriette Coggs Stuckey, endowed two studies at Stanford's Center for Advanced Study in the Behavioral Sciences in honor of his mother, Elma Stuckey, and his great-aunt, Vivian E. Johnson Cook, a Baltimore educator and civic leader.

Sugarmon, Russell Bertram, Jr. (1929–), attorney, state representative, judge. One of the first Blacks to seek a major post in city government in the 1950s, he became a civil rights attorney, member of Memphis's first integrated law firm, and city judge. Born on May 11, 1929, to Russell and Lessye Hank Sugarmon, he grew up in South Memphis, where he attended Co-Operative Grammar School and, in 1946, graduated from Booker T. Washington High School at age fifteen. After a year at Morehouse College, he transferred to Rutgers University, from which he received an A.B. degree in political science in 1950. At Rutgers, he earned four varsity letters, including one as a defensive line backer on the light weight football team, and joined Alpha Phi Alpha Fraternity, the first Black fraternity or sorority in New Jersey. In 1953, he received an LL.D. degree from Harvard Law School and, later, completed a year's study at Boston University's Graduate School of Finance. After attaining the rank of corporal in the Adjutant General Corps of the U.S. Army, he received a letter of commendation for his nine-month tour of duty in Japan. On his discharge in 1955, he married Miriam DeCosta of Orangeburg, South Carolina, and they have four children: Tarik, Elena, Erika, and Monique.

In 1956, the couple moved to Memphis, where attorney Sugarmon opened a law office in the Mutual Federal Savings & Loan Association building and became active in politics and the civil rights movement. He ran in the August 20, 1959, election for commissioner of Public Works on the Volunteer Ticket, along with Benjamin Hooks, Roy Love, and Henry Bunton, but he finished second behind William W. Farris, when Whites united in opposition to his candidacy. A member of the NAACP and 14th Ward Civic Club, he helped to revitalize the Shelby County Democratic Club and served as its executive director; he also co-founded the Tennessee Voters' Council, the first state-wide political organization of Blacks in the country. Sugarmon was known as an astute political strategist, who used bloc voting and other techniques to back political candidates, particularly those endorsed by the Shelby County Democratic Club. Active in the campaigns of John F. Kennedy and Estes Kefauver, he was a key strategist in Vasco A. Smith's 1973 race to become the first Black elected to the Shelby County Commission. Although Sugarmon lost his bid for the Tennessee State Senate in 1964, he was elected to the state Democratic Party Executive Committee and, eleven years later, the Committee elected him as National Democratic Committeeman from Tennessee. In 1966, he won election to the Tennessee House District 11 seat, when he garnered 5,927 votes against N. J. Ford's 1,458. He served two one-year terms in the House before losing to Alvin King in 1968, by a vote of 2,713 to 2,044.

In 1967, he was a founding partner with three other attorneys in the formation of Ratner, Sugarmon, Lucas & Willis, which broke professional barriers to become the first integrated law firm in the city and state. The firm became Ratner, Sugarmon & Lucas in the 1970s. When the firm of Ratner & Sugarmon dissolved in 1982, three attorneys, including Irvin Salky and Herman Morris, formed Sugarmon,

Salky & Morris. He served as referee in the Memphis Juvenile Court system from 1976 to 1987. During his thirty-one years as a trial lawyer, he was introduced to the United States Supreme Court and represented the NAACP on several major desegregation cases, including the county school case and the airport restaurant case. In 1987, by a vote of ten to one, he was elected by the County Board of Commissioners to fill the unexpired term as General Sessions Court Judge for Division Four, when that seat was vacated because of the conviction of the former judge, Ira Murphy. In 2007, he received the Arthur S. Holmon Lifetime Achievement Award, given by the University of Memphis's Black Student Association. He ran successfully for reelection in 1990 and again in 1998, without opposition. His first marriage ended in divorce and, in 1967, he married Regina Spence, a former Head Start administrator, with two daughters, Tina and Carol.

Swingler, Lewis Ossie (1906–1962), journalist, editor. One of the most important and outspoken newspapermen in the city for two and a half decades, he helped shape public opinion in the pages of the *Memphis World* and the *Tri-State Defender*. He was born in Crittendon County, Arkansas, and grew up in Tulsa, Oklahoma, where he attended public school and graduated from Booker T. Washington High School. After receiving a B.A. degree with a certificate in journalism from the University of Nebraska, Swingler moved to Memphis in 1931 to edit the *Memphis World*. Drafted into the U.S. Army as a corporal in World War II, he was stationed at Fort Benning, Georgia, where he edited *The Bayonet*, an Army newspaper. When he was discharged, he led a successful campaign to force the Memphis Police Department to hire Black policemen in 1948. After resigning from the editorship of the *World*, he published the first issue of the

Tri-State Defender on November 3, 1951. One of the founders of the paper, he served as editor-in-chief of the weekly until 1955, when he was succeeded by L. Alex Wilson. Under Swingler's stewardship, the paper helped develop Black civic and political consciousness in the years preceding the civil rights movement. The paper published weekly columns on religion and golf by Bishop A. B. McEwen and Dr. H. H. Johnson, cultural and social news by Madame Florence McCleave and Addie Jones, and editorials by Dr. R. Q. Venson and Nat D. Williams.

A quiet, soft-spoken man, Swingler served for a short time as executive secretary of the Abe Scharff Branch of the YMCA and then started his own paper, *The Mid-South Times*, but it soon folded because he was unable to get financial backing. Later, he edited the Memphis edition of the *Kansas City Call* and the *Times-Herald* but then turned to teaching. He taught for a while in Marked Tree, Arkansas, before joining the faculty of Mound Bayou High School, where he taught history and social sciences from 1960 to 1961. For many years, he edited the *Sphinx*, the official organ of Alpha Phi Alpha fraternity, to which he belonged. A charter member of the Negro Newspaper Publishers' Association, he was active in the Urban League, Family Service, and YMCA. He also served as public relations director of the Negro Tri-State Fair and as trustee of the First Baptist Church on Lauderdale. His wife was the former Edna House, a teacher at Riverview Elementary School. Lewis O. Swingler died on September 27, 1962, at age fifty-six, and is buried in National Cemetery. At the time of his death, he was writing a history of Mound Bayou, an all-Black town in Mississippi.

Talbert, Florence Cole. See Florence Cole Talbert McCleave.

Taylor, Cora Price (1885–1932), educator. A legendary teacher and principal who inspired generations of young people, she devoted her life to the educational needs of African American youth. The daughter of the John Prices, she was born in Mississippi on May 7, 1885, and moved with her parents to Memphis, where she married Anneil Taylor. A teacher from the age of sixteen, she held positions at the Virginia Avenue School in Memphis and the Spring Hill County School in Raleigh. In 1909, she replaced Rose Washington Foote as principal of Manassas Street School, which was a part of the county school system until 1930. In 1915, she raised funds to purchase land across from the school, on which a sixteen-room stucco building was constructed in 1918. Three years later, Mrs. Taylor again sought financial aid from school patrons, and, with the help of students and neighborhood men, a two-story frame building was erected. With support from the Rosenwald Fund, Manassas acquired a library, librarian, chemistry and physics laboratories, and more machines for the home economics department. Manassas had its first high school graduating class in 1924, when it was also rated as the largest Rosenwald school in the world. Competitive sports, such as baseball, basketball, and football were added to the school's program in 1924–1925. Cora P. Taylor personally brought bricks from Millington to build a school auditorium in 1927, but, two years later, she was forced to retire because of poor health. She died at her McDowell Street home on March 28, 1932, and her funeral was held in the Manassas auditorium. In 1941, a 24" × 26" bronze plaque was placed at the entrance to the auditorium, which was named in her honor.

Taylor, Lonzie Odie (1900–1977), photographer, minister. One of Memphis's most important photographers in the second quarter of the twentieth century, he documented the lives of ordinary Black people within the context of the social and religious activities that defined them. Born in Osceola, Arkansas, in 1900, he moved to Memphis at age fifteen, when his mother became caretaker of Pilgrim's Rest Baptist Church. At an early age, he was called to the ministry and was ordained at age twenty-three. After serving as pastor of Pilgrim's Rest for a short time, he accepted the pastorate of First Baptist Church on Broad Avenue. In September 1928, he married Blanche Johnson, a teacher from Jericho, Arkansas. Soon after his marriage, the self-taught photographer began taking portraits in his East Hyde Park home, as well as photographs of social events such as weddings, funerals, birthday parties, church programs, and school functions. He also found other ways to supplement his income; he repaired small appliances and sold his homemade candy in a little shop on Eldridge Street. In 1931, he became pastor of Olivet Baptist Church, which had the largest Black congregation in Memphis, and he erected an educational building, paid off the mortgage, and increased the membership. He was noted throughout the city for his dynamic, humorous, and thought-provoking sermons, built around simple metaphors such as brooms and pencils. When he left Olivet in 1956 because of poor health, he founded the Greater Hyde Park Baptist Church with just seventeen members, and served as pastor until his retirement in 1967.

During the 1940s and '50s, L. O. Taylor continued to expand his photography business. He built a darkroom on the second floor of his Hunter Street home and created a studio on the first floor, with a portrait backdrop hanging between the living and dining rooms. Most of his income came from portraits, family photographs, and reproductions of old prints. He began to make 16mm films of neighborhood people and events such as national Baptist conventions, which he would show in churches—while providing commentaries—so that people could see themselves in action. Interested in all types of documentation and creative expression, he wrote a book of poems and essays, and he made 78 rpm audio disc recordings of sermons, choir concerts, and radio programs. Like photographers James Van Der Zee and Gordon Parks, Taylor depicted the beauty, vitality, and dignity of Black folk: mechanics, preachers, shop owners, church ladies, handymen, and hairdressers. After his death in 1977, the Center for Southern Folklore bought the L. O. Taylor Collection, which includes 30,000 feet of color and black and white film, 5,000 nitrate and safety negatives, 500 prints, and 100 home-cut 78 rpm discs. In 1980, the Center produced an exhibit, "Taylor Made Pictures," which includes thirty-five of his photographs, and in 1989, Memphis filmmaker Lynne Sachs produced a documentary film, *Sermons and Sacred Pictures: The Life and Work of Reverend L. O. Taylor*, which was screened throughout the country and in several foreign countries.

Terrell, Mary Church (1863–1954), educator, writer, clubwoman. A national leader who championed rights for women and Blacks, she was a founder of the National Association of Colored Women and a charter member of the NAACP. Born in Memphis on September 23, 1863, she was the oldest child of Louisa Ayers Church, owner of a hair salon, and Robert Reed Church, a businessman. At an early age, "Mollie," as she was called, was sent to the Model School at Antioch College in Yellow Springs, Ohio. Two years later, she entered the public schools in Yellow Springs and, in 1879, graduated from a high school in Oberlin, Ohio. At Oberlin College, she took the four-year "gentleman's course" in the classics instead of the two-year "literary course" for female students. After graduating from Oberlin in 1884, Mollie Church began teaching at Wilberforce College in Ohio and, two years later, became a teacher at the Colored High School in Washington, D.C. She received a master's degree from Oberlin in 1888, and, at the invitation of her father, spent two years traveling and studying in Europe. On October 18, 1891, she married Robert Heberton Terrell, who had degrees from Harvard and Howard University Law School. After three miscarriages, she gave birth to Phillis in 1898, and, in 1905, she and her husband adopted her brother's daughter, Mary.

In 1892, Mary Church Terrell founded the Colored Women's League, which merged with the National Federation of Afro-American Women in 1896, to form the National Federation of Colored Women, with Terrell as its first president. On November 22, 1897, she spoke at Collins Chapel C.M.E. Church in Memphis on "The Life and Character of Harriet Beecher Stowe." Terrell was the first African American woman appointed to the District of Columbia Board of Education, serving from 1895 to 1901 and from 1906 to 1911. She became one of the charter members of the NAACP when, in 1909, she signed the "Call" that led to the founding of the organization. A dynamic lecturer, she addressed the 1904 Berlin International Congress of Women in German, French, and English; spoke at the 1919 International League for Peace and Freedom in Zurich; and addressed the World Fellowship of Faiths in London in 1937. A gifted writer who first used the pen name Euphemia Kirk, Terrell wrote diaries in French and German; published articles in newspapers, magazines, and journals; and wrote an autobiography, *A Colored Woman in a White World* (1940), with a preface by H. G. Wells.

She remained active in civil rights causes throughout her life. In 1946, at age eighty-three, she began a three-year battle to gain readmission to the Washington branch of the American Association of University Women; backed by the national organization, she was eventually reinstated in spite of adverse court rulings. In 1949, she was elected chair of the Coordinating Committee for the Enforcement of District of Columbia Anti-Discrimination Laws, which effected the desegregation of public facilities in the nation's capital. At age eighty-nine, Terrell led a picket line to demand desegregation of Thompson's Restaurant in Washington and then testified before the Supreme Court in the Coordinating Committee's suit against the restaurant. Later, she led a crusade to free Rosa Ingram and her sons, Black sharecroppers sentenced to death; she spoke on their behalf at the United Nations and went to Georgia to seek a pardon from the governor. Mary Church Terrell died in Annapolis, Maryland, on July 24, 1954, at age ninety.

Thomas, Carla (1942–), vocalist. Known as the "Queen of Memphis Soul," she became one of the biggest stars at Stax Records The daughter of Lorene and Rufus Thomas, she was born on December 21, 1942, in a Foote Homes apartment and spent her early childhood in public housing. She grew up in a family of musicians that included her father, a singer, performer, and disk jockey; a brother, who is a composer and arranger; and a sister who is also a vocalist. As an adolescent, Carla sang in the choir at the Memphis church pastored by Reverend C. L. Franklin, Aretha Franklin's father. When she was ten, she joined WDIA's Teen-Town Singers, led by A. C. Williams, although she was four years below the required age, and she performed with the group for eight years. After graduating from Hamilton High School, where she was named Football Queen and "most talented girl," she received a bachelor's degree with a minor in speech and drama and a 3.7 grade point average from Tennessee A&I State University. She also began study toward a master's degree in English at Howard University.

Rufus Thomas was a major influence in Carla's musical career. In 1960, the father-daughter team recorded a duet, "Cause I Love You," that became a Southern hit, and in 1961, one of her compositions, "Gee Whiz (Look in His Eyes)" became the first Memphis soul record to gain national prominence when it made the Top Ten in both the R&B and Pop categories. Credited with the voice that launched Stax, she gave the company its first top-selling hit with "Cause I Love You" and its first million-dollar seller with "Gee Whiz," which was followed by another smash record, "B-A-B-Y." Between 1961 and 1971, she had twenty-two singles on national charts, including "I'll Bring It on Home to You" and "Let Me Be Good to You," and her duets with Otis Redding on the album *King and Queen* were critically acclaimed. In the 1970s, the pop diva undertook several military tours for servicemen in the Southeast area, and she received a USO plaque as the favorite American singer by U.S. Forces in Vietnam. When she and her father spent three weeks performing at military bases in Europe in the early 1980s, Rufus commented: "We don't get to work together too often, but when we do it's a blast."

Carla Thomas has performed in nightclubs and music festivals; she has appeared in movies and on television programs; she has made commercials and given concerts. For example, she performed at the Stax/Volt Revue in London, Monterey Pops Festival, Bag O' Nails Club in Great Britain, New York's Village Gate, and Royal Box at the Hotel Americana. She appeared on television in *Dial M for Music* and in several movies and documentaries, including *Wattstax* in 1973, and *Only the Strong Survive* in 2002. After spending eight years in Los Angeles and seven in Washington, D.C., she returned to her hometown in the late 1980s, where she has continued to sing and also to tutor for the Memphis Literacy Council. The city has honored the Queen of Soul: in 1993, she received the Pioneer Award by the Rhythm and Blues Foundation, and the Stax Historical Preservation Commission honored her at its 9th Annual Dr. Martin Luther King Jr. / Stax Musical Explosion on April 5, 1998 at the Black Diamond Club on Beale Street.

Thomas, Rufus (1917–2001), singer, entertainer, disk jockey. In a career that spanned more than seventy years, this legendary performer, affectionately known as "The World's Oldest Teenager," helped shape Memphis music in the twentieth Century. He was born on March 26, 1917, in Cayce, Mississippi, but soon moved with his family to Memphis, where he started singing at Booker T. Washington High School. His professional career began in the 1930s, when he joined traveling vaudeville shows such as The Rabbit Foot Minstrels, Georgia Dixon Traveling Show, and Royal American Tent Shows. On the tent circuit, he tap-danced and performed comedy routines with Robert "Bones" Couch under the name "Rufus and Bones." Back in Memphis in the 1940s, he hosted talent shows at Beale Street's Palace Theater and spun records on radio station WDIA, where local musicians such as B. B. King, Ike Turner, Junior Parker, and Bobby "Blue" Bland were featured. In the 1940s, he and his wife, C. Lorene Thomas, had three children—Marvell, Carla, and Vaneese—all of whom became noted musicians.

Rufus Thomas launched his singing career in 1953, when his recording, "Bear Cat," became the first national hit for Sam Phillips's Memphis Recording Studio, which later became Sun Records. In 1959, Rufus and his daughter Carla recorded the scintillating duet "Cause I Love You," for Satellite Records, which became Stax in 1961. In his decade and a half with Stax, Rufus recorded a series of Top Five R&B hits that include "Walking the Dog," "Do the Funky Chicken," and "The Breakdown." In 1973, he performed in the Wattstax concert at the LA Forum. He also appeared in many documentaries on the history of blues and rock, and made cameo appearances in several films, including *Mystery Train*, *Cookie's Fortune* and *A Family Thing*. In 1997, he gave three concerts at the Olympics in Atlanta, and for several years he hosted Beale Street's New Year's celebration. He often performed at the annual Sweet Soul Music Festival in Poretta Terme, Italy, where the Italians named a park after him.

Rufus had a dynamic performance style that was accentuated by his flamboyant outfits—loud shirts, Bermuda shorts, and flowing capes—that were the height of funky fashion. All decked out to the nines, he would laugh and say, "Look at me, man, ain't I clean!" When he was honored by the Rock and Roll Hall of Fame in 1992, he sang "Dust My Broom" at the ceremony, backed up by a band that included Johnny Cash, Keith Richards, and The Isley Brothers. Awarded the W. C. Handy/Howlin' Wolf Award at the Chicago Blues Festival for "Outstanding Blues Performer," he also received three lifetime achievement awards from Wings of Change, the Beale Street Merchants Association, and the American Society of Composers, Authors and Publishers. When he died on December 15, 2001, the beloved entertainer was honored by a motorcade down Beale Street, a funeral service attended by over 2,500 and broadcast live on WDIA, and tributes by musicians and officials such as Isaac Hayes, B. B. King, Kirk Whalum, Rev. Dwight "Gatemouth" Moore, and Mayor W. W. Herenton.

Thomas, Sheree Renée (1972–), writer, editor, publisher. Called "a hip mama, writer, southern girl, and bibliophile," this award-winning poet, novelist, and anthologist is making a name for herself in the literary world. The daughter of Jacqueline Denise Thomas and Eddie Larry Thomas, she was born in Memphis on September 30, 1972. She and her two brothers grew up in a house filled with spoken and written words. "I was the kind of kid that if you wanted to punish me, you had to keep me out of my room and away from a book." Her love of writing and storytelling was stimulated by two of her grandparents—her father's mother, Willie Walton, and her mother's father, Ezekiel Wade. She explains, "I tell stories the way my grandfather told me stories on the porch, the way my grandmother told me stories while she was fixing another kick ass meal." At Sheffield High School, she was valedictorian of the class of 1991, and at Rhodes College she was a history major who studied the art of Toulouse-Lautrec in France and contributed to the college newspaper, *The Sou'wester*. After leaving

Rhodes in 1995, she moved to New York City to pursue a career in writing and publishing.

Sheree Thomas's novel-in-progress, *Bonecarver*, received the 2003 Ledig House/LEF Foundation Prize for Fiction, her poetry was nominated for the Rhysling Award by the Science Fiction Poetry Association, and her work received honorable mention in the *Year's Best Fantasy & Horror*, 16th and 17th annual editions. She is co-publisher of the literary journal, *Anansi: Fiction of the African Diaspora* and published *Scarab*, a limited edition of handmade, Coptic-bound anthologies. As an editor, she is best known for her series of science fiction anthologies, including her groundbreaking collection, *Dark Matter: A Century of Speculative Fiction from the African Diaspora*, which won the 2001 World Fantasy Award and Black Writers Alliance's Gold Pen Award; it was a *Washington Post* Editor's "Rave," was named a *New York Times* Notable Book of the Year, as well as an Amazon.com "Essential Book." The second volume in the series, *Dark Matter: Reading the Bones*, was awarded the 2005 World Fantasy Award, and Thomas is currently editing a third volume, tentatively titled *Dark Matter: Africa Rising*.

Her poetry and fiction have appeared in anthologies, magazines, and literary journals such as *Essence*, *Mojo: Conjure Stories*, *Bum Rush the Page: A Def Poetry Jam*, and Ishmael Reed's *Konch*; and she recently published an essay in *Callaloo* that pays tribute to Octavia E. Butler and to her own Memphis roots. The founder of Wanganegresse Press, Thomas—who "still talks and walks like a Memphian in Manhattan," according to one critic—is a Cave Canem Fellow, New York Foundation of the Arts Fellow, and Clarion West graduate. Thomas conducts writing workshops and teaches fiction at the Frederick Douglass Creative Arts Center in Manhattan. Her creative work and support of other writers emerge from her belief that "our culture is legitimate, is valid, is important, should be cherished and continued and I think our language, Blackspeak is what I call it, is a part of that." She shares these values with her two daughters: Jacqueline, a junior high school student, and nine-year-old Jada.

Thornton, Matthew (1873–1963), mail carrier. Known as the "Mayor of Beale Street," he was one of the first African Americans employed by the Memphis Post Office as a special delivery mail carrier. The son of former slaves, he was born on May 18, 1873, on a farm in West Point, Mississippi and came to Memphis at age fourteen. In the early 1900s, he organized the Matthew Thornton Knights of Pythias Band, the first recognized Black brass band in Memphis. Thornton, who is credited with bringing W. C. Handy to Memphis, as well as George W. Henderson, founder of Henderson Business College, began working as a special delivery mail carrier for the post office in 1928. In 1938, he won the campaign for "Mayor of Beale Street," sponsored by the *Memphis World* newspaper, polling 12,000 of the 33,000 votes cast. This was an honorary position that carried such ceremonial duties as greeting distinguished guests and serving as the official spokesman for the "street where the blues began."

The Mayor—noted for his dark glasses, heavy cane, high wing collar, and wide cravat adorned with a diamond stickpin—took his duties seriously. During World War II, he became an honorary Navy recruiter and sold thousands of dollars in war bonds; established safety councils in Black schools; organized the Harmony Club; persuaded Kroger's to hire clerks, butchers, and managers in Black neighborhoods; and, in 1957, opened the Memphis Hall of Fame in Church's Park Auditorium. In 1943, at age seventy, he was honored at Booker T. Washington High School for fifty years of service to the community. On his eighty-second birthday, in 1955, he was given a reception at LeMoyne College and received $400 to attend a birthday banquet for his friend W. C. Handy in New York. In 1962, he was honored on his eighty-ninth birthday and given $175 in gifts. He and his wife, who lived at 1187 South Wellington, had three sons: Matthew, Jr., Haywood, and Powers. The Mayor died on September 9, 1963, at age ninety.

Toles, Elizabeth (1920–), educator, pastor, prophetess. Called one of the outstanding psychic minds in the country by *Ebony* magazine and the *National Enquirer*, she has appeared on radio and television talk shows to make her annual predictions. The daughter of Estelle and George Toles, she was born in Memphis on August 5, 1920, and she and her two siblings grew up on Texas Street in South Memphis. After her mother's death, when she was only three months old, she was raised by an aunt, Lillie Countis, who discovered her gift of prophecy and encouraged her to use it. After graduating from Booker T. Washington High School in 1938, and from LeMoyne College in 1942, she became a teacher with the Memphis Public Schools and spent thirty-two years in the profession before retiring in 1975. She often used her gift of clairvoyance in the classroom to determine the strengths and weaknesses of her students, and the principal of Georgia Elementary School, where she taught fourth grade, frequently asked her help in finding lost items and evaluating school records.

For the past four decades, Toles has made predictions of local and national events, based on the visions that she receives at midnight on New Year's Eve. She explains: "The way that I do this list is I begin to pray at midnight just as the New Year is beginning. I pray to God to give me these predictions, and He does. Then I write them down." From her home office at 2356 Malone Street, she counsels clients three days a week, explaining that she uses her talent to help clients locate lost articles, lost loves, and lost hope. She rose to national fame with the claim that she predicted the assassinations of John F. Kennedy and Martin Luther King, as well as the resignation of President Nixon. Called a "doer, not a talker," Mrs. Toles helped organize the South Memphis Law & Order Club and served as its president for over a year. In 1969, she donated part of a commercial building at 1277 Mississippi Boulevard to the Memphis Police Department to use as a community service center. Although she attended

Salem Gilfield Baptist Church for many years, she now pastors the Good Fellowship Church at 3311 Kimball Street. A member of Beta Eta Chapter of Phi Delta Kappa Sorority, which she has served as Basileus and Senior Advisor, she was appointed national chaplain at the sorority's 1991 conclave. She is also chaplain of the Memphis Section of the National Council of Negro Women and was the only woman executive board member of the "Give Me a Chance Ministry" at Oral Roberts University. She has received many honors and awards, including the 1991 Sojourner Truth Service Award from the National Association of Negro Business and Professional Women's Club, an Outstanding Achievement Award from the governor of Tennessee, and a Lifetime of Achievement Award from *Memphis Woman* magazine in 2000.

Turner, Elaine Lee (1944–) educator, businesswoman, civil rights activist. The owner and co-founder of Heritage Tours, Inc., she is committed to preserving the history and cultural heritage of African Americans. One of the fourteen children of Alversa Williams Lee and Robert Edward Lee, she was born on June 12, 1944, and grew up in North Memphis, where she attended Carnes Elementary School and graduated from Manassas High School in 1962. In the summer of 1960, while still in high school, Elaine joined her older sister, Ernestine, a LeMoyne College student, and other siblings in sit-ins at lunch counters and other public facilities. She was jailed three times during the civil rights movement, while nine of her sisters and brothers also participated in student protests and demonstrations. The Lee children had grown up in a home where African American history and culture were taught through family stories passed down from one generation to the next. Their mother told them about her father who was born in Henning, Tennessee, the birthplace of Alex Haley. Although born a slave, Mrs. Lee's father was a courageous landowner, who demanded respect and stood up for himself. He talked about his mother and grandmother, who came from South Carolina, and about Mandi, his earliest-known ancestor, who was stolen from Africa about 1810. Such stories instilled pride in the children and a determination to participate in the movement.

Elaine Lee began teaching in September 1966, soon after graduating from LeMoyne College with a bachelor's degree in English. After marriage to Melvin Turner, the births of their four children—Melvin II, Alana, Kamilah, and Kevin—and thirteen years of teaching, she decided to leave the classroom to raise her children. In 1983, she and her sister, Joan Lee Nelson, founded Heritage Tours, Inc., which organizes individual and group tours to historic sites, such as Beale Street, the National Civil Rights Museum, and First Baptist Beale Street Church. In connection with their business, the two sisters have initiated several special projects: they were instrumental in erecting a monument to enslaved Africans in Elmwood Cemetery and they operate the W. C. Handy House Museum, which is on their tour. Their biggest project has been their work in the restoration and management of the Slavehaven Underground Railroad Museum/ Jacob Burkle Estate. One of the few way stations for escaped slaves located in the South, it has been transformed into a private, nonprofit museum through small grants and funds acquired from the city. The unassuming and soft-spoken Elaine Lee Turner explains the motivation behind her work in this way: "I believe knowledge of history makes us all more tolerant of one another."

Turner, Jesse Hosea (1919–1989), banker, accountant, county commissioner, civil rights leader. One of the main strategists for the NAACP during the civil rights movement, Turner shaped the economic and political direction of this community for four decades. He was born in Longview, Mississippi, on September 14, 1919, the third of eleven children born to Martha Turner, a teacher, and Reverend O. J. Turner, a Baptist minister. The Turners moved to West

Point, Mississippi, where their children were educated in private, church schools. Jesse was awarded an athletic scholarship to LeMoyne College, where he played football and received a bachelor's degree in mathematics with honors. In 1941, he was drafted into the Army as a private and was sent to a school for cooks, although his entrance scores were very high. After appealing his status, he was sent to officer's training school and was commissioned as a second lieutenant. Although he became a captain, he was arrested seven times in Memphis for "impersonating an officer." A member of the 758th Tank Battalion, the first Black tank unit in the Army, Turner was awarded the Bronze Star for bravery in Italy during the Second World War.

Turner moved to Memphis in 1947, after receiving a master's degree in business administration from the University of Chicago. When he took the Certified Public Accountant's examination in 1948, there were fewer than ten Black CPAs in the country. He planned to open his own accounting firm but was persuaded to become an officer of the Tri-State Bank, which had opened in 1946. Under his forty-year stewardship, the bank became one of the best regulated and most stable institutions in the community. He also opened and operated a public accounting firm, was a member of the American Institute of Certified Public Accountants, and served as president of the National Bankers Association. Meanwhile, he continued the campaign against racial discrimination that he had launched in the military. In 1957, he filed the first lawsuit to end segregation in Shelby County, when he brought suit against the public library after being refused service at the Peabody Library. He was also a plaintiff in suits to desegregate Dobbs House and the University of Tennessee. In 1960, he was arrested after joining eleven other Memphians in the city's first sit-in demonstration. Known as "Mr. NAACP," Turner served as president and chairman of the executive board of the Memphis branch of the NAACP from 1957 to 1968. Also active with the national organization, Turner was a member of the national board of the NAACP, president of the National Housing Corporation, trustee of the Special Contributions Fund, and national treasurer from 1972 until his death in 1989.

Active in voter registration drives and campaigns for public office, Turner took on a second career in politics and government service. When he was elected to the Shelby County Democratic Executive Committee in 1960, he became the first Black elected to such an office since Reconstruction. He served on the Program of Progress Charter Commission, which drew up Memphis's mayor-council charter in the 1960s. In 1964, he was elected as a delegate to the State Constitutional Convention, and the governor appointed him to serve on the Tax Study Commission in 1966. Turner was one of the first Blacks elected to the Shelby County Quarterly Court (now the Shelby County Commission) in 1966, and he soon became one of its most respected members. Chairman of the Commission from 1983 to 1984 and chair of the budget committee for many years, he was recognized as one of the city's top experts in governmental finance. He turned down an appointment to the State Banking Commission, when it was offered to him by Governor Ned McWherter. Turner was committed to his family, church, and community. A longtime member of Metropolitan Baptist Church, he taught Sunday School and chaired the trustee board. He and his wife, the former Allegra Will, married on June 25, 1949, and raised their five children—Jesse, Jr., Ray, Eric, Frances, and Lisa—in their modest home at 1278 Gill Avenue. After his death on April 14, 1989, a park at the corner of Bellevue and South Parkway was named in his honor.

Urevbu, Ephraim Muvire (1955–), artist, gallery owner. A Nigerian artist who has lived in Memphis for twenty-five years, he was commissioned to paint the Memphis in May poster in 1989. Born in Warri, an oil town on western Nigeria's Atlantic coast, he excelled at science and art as a child, so his parents, Eunice Okorare and Samuel

Urevbu, encouraged him to become a doctor. He remained in medical school for just one semester, however, because he could not tolerate the sight of blood. Without telling his parents, he entered the Yaba College of Technology in Lagos, Nigeria, where he received an associate's degree in art. After graduating from Yaba, he worked with the Nigerian television network, taught art in a secondary school, worked at the National Arts Theater, and sold his paintings. In 1979, Urevbu moved to New York to continue his education, but he was not happy there, so he relocated to Memphis. After entering the Memphis College of Art, he transferred to Memphis State University, from which he received a bachelor's in fine arts in 1983, and a master's degree in 1987.

When Memphis honored Kenya in 1989, the Nigerian artist was commissioned to create the Memphis in May poster, a work entitled "Drums Echo Back to Back." He was also commissioned to create official posters for the Del Ray Arts Festival and Las Olas Arts Festival in Florida. "The Village" was used as the cover of *Social Psychology—Understanding Human Interaction* and several of his works presently adorn the walls of the Memphis International Airport. Signed and numbered prints, such as "The Market Place" featuring two African women against a colorful background, were available at the Memphis Black Arts Alliance's 1990 "Salute the Arts" program. His large, colorful paintings have been exhibited in Atlanta, Chicago, New York, Memphis, and Miami, and one of his paintings was featured in the Memphis Arts Council's 1988–1989 calendar. He explains, however, that his works, which he describes as "exaggerated abstractions on large canvases," are not the type that most Memphis galleries are able to sell. Undaunted by local aesthetics, Ephraim Urevbu opened his own studio, The Village Art Gallery, Inc., in 1990, but was evicted by Beale Street Management Company for nonpayment of the $30-per-month association dues. The artist replied that the association benefits Beale Street clubs and not retail establishments. In 1994, he relocated his gallery to an old 5,000-square-foot warehouse at 410 South Main Street, where he can work on four or five pieces at the same time.

Venson, Ethyl Belle Horton (1909–1998), administrator, civic leader. The first Black woman appointed to the Memphis Housing Authority Board, she worked to provide economic and cultural opportunities for African Americans. Born on January 1, 1909, she was the oldest of six children. Her mother, who moved to Memphis from Eads, and her father, who had an ice and coal business, lived at 409 Ayers. She attended Carnes Elementary School and graduated from LeMoyne College. Her first job was as a dental assistant making $5.00 a week, until Dr. R. Q. Venson offered her $7.00 to work for him. In 1934, Ethyl Horton and Ransom Q. Venson were married and, a year later, they co-founded the Cotton Makers' Jubilee, after a young relative complained that "all the Negroes were horses" in the Cotton Carnival parade. Mrs. Venson became the Jubilee's first queen, and the next year, she and her husband invited W. C. Handy and the Paul Whiteman Orchestra to perform. Although activists picketed the Jubilee in the 1960s, claiming that it was an imitation of the segregated Memphis Cotton Carnival, Ethyl Venson did not give in to pressure. In 1981, the Jubilee joined the Cotton Carnival as a grand krewe and, eleven years later, the renamed Carnival Memphis combined its parade with the Jubilee.

On November 15, 1966, Ethyl H. Venson became the first Black and the first woman appointed to the Memphis Housing Authority Board. Maintaining that public housing should be built in all areas of the city, she advocated slum clearance and low-rent housing for the poor. On March 20, 1972, she was unanimously elected chair of the MHA Board; after serving on the board for seventeen years, she resigned because of a conflict of interest and joined the Memphis Community Relations Commission. In 1972, the governor appointed her to the State Commission on the Status of Women. Active in efforts to preserve historical landmarks, she supported the Beale Street Urban Renewal Project. After the death of her husband in 1970, she continued to volunteer with the Memphis Red Cross, Mental Health Association, Memphis Heart Association, and Shelby County Department of Welfare. She also worked with the Memphis Urban League, serving as president of the League's Guild and as acting executive director. For years she worked as a volunteer member of the Memphis Ecumenical Children's Association to build a residential program for abused and neglected children, and she was president of MECA in 1978, when it opened Dogwood Village, now Youth Villages. She chaired the Community Action Program, was a charter member of the Liberty Bowl Festival, and was a member of the Memphis War on Poverty Committee and the board of governors of the Girls Club, as well as an active member of St. John Baptist Church. After several strokes, Ethyl H. Venson died on January 20, 1998, and is survived by a daughter, Pamela Ann. After her death, the Memphis Urban League established a scholarship fund in her memory and she received, posthumously, the Frances M. Hassell Prayer of Service Award during the Tennessee Black Heritage Celebration.

Wade, Theo (1906–1980), disk jockey, gospel vocalist and manager. In a career that spanned half a century, he developed radio programs and sponsored events to promote gospel music in Memphis. The son of Sarah and Charles Wade, he was born on April 30, 1906, in Palestine, Arkansas. Wade began his musical career in the 1930s, when he joined the Spirit of

Memphis Quartet, which received its training from gospel singer Queen C. Anderson. A talented first tenor, he also served as business manager and, eventually, president of the group, with the responsibility of organizing recording sessions and appearances throughout the area. A former member of the quartet recalled: "In 1939, we all decided we would quit our jobs and start traveling. It was tough on us when we started. We went hungry a lot of days, but we made it."

After twenty-five years with the Spirit of Memphis, Wade went to work for radio station WDIA in 1954, and created such programs as "Delta Melodies," " Hallelujah Jubilee," and "Temple Time," featuring gospel groups that often waited in line to be heard live on the air. He earned the nickname Brother Theo "Bless My Bones" Wade because that is what he would say between records. Noted for his jokes and good humor, he kept his audience in stitches with such wake-up calls as this one: "All right, my overweight sisters, set up and get to packing all that meat in them girdles." His humor, affability, and style made him one of WDIA's top salesmen, a radio personality who could sell everything from flour and syrup to Icy Hot.

The "Grand Old Papa" of gospel music was also an astute businessman, who filled Mason's Temple and other churches with nationally-recognized gospel groups such as the Soul Stirrers, Swan Silvertones, Dixie Hummingbirds, and Caravans—groups that included future stars Lou Rawls, Sam Cooke, Johnny Taylor, Joe Hinton, and others. He and his wife also established a family business, "The House of Hits," on Cooper Street. Theo Wade was the first WDIA Goodwill bus driver. After finishing his early morning program, he picked up handicapped children and took them to Keel Avenue School for Handicapped Children. A member of the station's Goodwill Fund Board, he determined policy for the fund's operation. A devout Christian, he belonged to Mt. Olive C.M.E. Cathedral, where he was a steward. In 1979, he was honored by the Memphis Gospel Association, which he had served as president, and on February 1, 1980, at a "Tribute to Gospel Music" held at the Coliseum, Wade was named "Dean of Gospel Music" in the Mid-South. He died three weeks later, on February 21, 1980, and is survived by his wife, Essie Mae Wade, and two sons: Emmett Warren Wade and Theo Bernard Wade, Jr., who, like his father, became a gospel disk jockey at radio station KWAM.

Walker, Antonio Maceo (1909–1994), banker, insurance executive, community leader. One of the city's most accomplished businessmen, Walker built two financial institutions that have served the community for over half a century. He was born in Indianola, Mississippi, on June 7, 1909, to Dr. Joseph Edison Walker and his wife Lelia O'Neal Walker. When he was thirteen, he moved with his family to Memphis, where he attended LeMoyne High School. He received a bachelor's degree in business administration from Fisk University in 1930, a master's in business from New York University in 1932, and another master's in actuarial science from the University of Michigan in 1935, at a time when there were no other Black actuaries in Tennessee. In the summer, he sold insurance and, later, joined the audit department of Universal Life Insurance Company, where he was elected to the board of directors in 1935. With his father, he founded Tri-State Bank, one of the oldest and largest Black banks in the country. After serving as vice president, he was elected president of the bank in August 1958, and was chairman of the board until his death. He also served as president of Memphis Mortgage Guarantee Company, founded by C. C. Sawyer.

After the death of his father in 1952, Walker became president of Universal, the largest Black business in Memphis, and he was elected chairman of the board in 1959. Although Universal had $10 million in assets and $83 million worth of insurance in force in 1952, the company grew rapidly under his leadership; he expanded the sales force, invested in bonds, and made mortgage loans for homes and churches. He also spearheaded the acquisition of other insurance companies: Excelsior Life of Dallas (1958), Louisiana Life of New Orleans (1961), Richmond Beneficial Life (1965), Afro-American Texas Debits (1975), and Union Protective of Memphis (1980). Universal also financed the construction of three low-income housing projects: Riverview Homes, built in 1951; the 700-unit J. E. Walker Housing Projects, constructed in 1953; and the 200-unit Elliston Heights apartments, erected in 1956. In 1983, he turned the presidency of the company over to his daughter, Patricia Walker Shaw, but, on her death in 1985, he resumed office. A year later, he engineered the $1.2-million purchase of Security Life Insurance Company of the South in Jackson, Mississippi.

Maceo Walker was a member of the board of directors of the Abe Scharff Branch of the YMCA, Memphis Chamber of Commerce, Shelby United Neighbors, and United Negro College Fund. He also served as vice president of the Memphis Chamber of Commerce and as president and vice president of the National Insurance Association. Chairman of the Trustee Board of the Mississippi Boulevard Christian Church, he was honored in 1983 as one of the two living founders of the Church. A leader in political and civil rights activities, Walker headed a committee that paid tuition for the first group of Black students to attend Memphis State University. In 1961, he was appointed to the Memphis Transit Authority Board by Mayor Henry Loeb. Maceo Walker received many honors and awards, including honorary degrees from Morehouse College, Fisk University, and Wilberforce University. He represented the U.S. government at the American Exhibition in Mali in 1964; President Lyndon B. Johnson appointed him to the National Citizens Committee in 1965; and President Jimmy Carter named him to the White House Conference on Small Business in 1979. He was named by *Ebony* magazine as one of the 100 most influential Blacks in the United States, and on September 30, 1974, the Memphis City Council changed the name of Driver Place to A. Maceo Walker Drive. He and his wife, Harriette Lucille Ish Walker, whom in married in 1938, had three children: Lily Patricia Walker Shaw, Antonio M. Walker, Jr., and Harriette Lucille "Candy"

Walker. Following the death of his first wife, he married Charlestine Miles in 1990. After a long illness, A. Maceo Walker died in Memphis on June 8, 1994, the day after his eighty-fifth birthday.

Walker, Joseph Edison (1880–1958), physician, banker, insurance executive. Although he was born into poverty, he founded two financial institutions and became one of the wealthiest and most respected businessmen in Memphis. The son of George and Patsy Wheeler Walker was born in a cabin near Tillman, Mississippi, on March 31, 1880. He worked on the farm and attended a rural school in Claiborne County before entering Alcorn A&M College at age seventeen. Walker worked on the college farm and taught in the summer to pay his way through Alcorn, from which he graduated in 1903. In April 1906, he graduated from medical school and, a month later, married Lelia O'Neal, a Tougaloo College student, described as "the belle and sweetheart of Sunflower County." Dr. Walker opened his medical practice in a small office in Indianola, Mississippi, where he often had to operate on kitchen tables by lamplight or travel by horse and buggy to deliver babies. He became president of Delta Penny Savings Bank, the first Black bank in Mississippi and, in 1909, helped organize Mississippi Life Insurance Company. Under his presidency, the income of Mississippi Life increased from $201,168 to $943,671, and the company paid dividends of $185 to stockholders. In 1920, Mississippi Life was relocated to Memphis, but Walker resigned from the company in February 1923 and chartered Universal Life Insurance Company on March 15 of that year. Universal started to expand: in 1924, it opened offices in Missouri; in 1925, it moved into Texas; in 1926, it acquired Mississippi Life Insurance Company for $156,000; and, in 1932, it bought the assets of Woodman Union Life Insurance Company. In

1925, the company was relocated from a small, one-story, wooden building at Beale and Hernando to a two-story brick building on Hernando and, in 1940, the company was moved to a large, three-story building at 408 Linden. Designed and built by a Black architectural firm in Nashville, the building cost $500,000.

Despite the failure of two Black Memphis banks, J. E. Walker wanted to open a bank, so his son sold stocks and, within a month, had raised $45,000. After acquiring the balance of the capital, Dr. Walker opened the Tri-State Bank of Memphis on December 16, 1946. Ironically, the bank was located at 392 Beale Street, the site of the failed Solvent Savings Bank. Within two years, the bank had deposits of over $1,000,000 and assets of $1,500,000. Walker was active in political, religious, and professional organizations. In 1926, he helped organize the Negro Chamber of Commerce and, in 1932, he co-founded the Community Welfare League, which became the Memphis Urban League. He was elected president of the National Negro Insurance Association and the National Negro Business League, and he served on the trustee boards of Jarvis Christian College and LeMoyne College. During World War II, when Universal bought $200,000 in U.S. Savings Bonds, he was National Chairman of the War Bonds Savings Club. One of the founders of the Mississippi Boulevard Christian Church, he was a delegate to the World's Convention of Disciples of Christ in England in 1935. A Republican in his early years, he co-founded and served as president of the Shelby County Democrats. After his failure to win election to the Memphis Board of Education in 1951, Walker organized the Nonpartisan Voters' Registration Club, which increased Black voter registration from 7,500 to 35,000. Listed as one of the top ten most powerful Negroes in America by *Our World* and *Jet* magazines, he is also included in *Who's Who in Colored America*.

The Walkers had two children: Johnetta Elmo and A. Maceo Walker. After the death of his wife in 1954, he married Louise O'Riley, a teacher, in November 1957. On July 28, 1958, Dr. Joseph E. Walker was fatally shot by Judge W. "Hamp" Hamilton, a mentally disturbed acquaintance.

Walter, Ronald Anderson "Ron" (1949–), historian, librarian, business executive. A fourth-generation Memphian, he is the son of Estelle Anderson Walter and Norris O. Walter, a supervisor at Bethesda Medical Center in Washington, D.C. He was born on September 23, 1949, and grew up in the family home at 838 Ioka. After attending Florida Elementary School, he completed a year at Carver High School and two years at Porter Junior High School. In 1967, he graduated in the top 1% of his class at Booker T. Washington High School and then entered Clark University in Massachusetts, from which he received a bachelor's degree in chemistry in 1971. Three years later, he was awarded a master's degree in library science by Case Western Reserve University. For two years, he worked at the Memphis/Shelby County Library, first, at the Main Library and, later, as chief of the popular book section of the Cossitt-Goodwyn Library. In 1977, Walter became chief administrative officer to U.S. Representative Harold Ford, with the responsibility of coordinating operations in the congressman's Memphis and Washington offices. He resigned that position in 1980 to join the Memphis Light, Gas and Water Division, serving as assistant to the president, director of personnel, and, finally, vice president of customer relations. In 1987, he joined the staff of WREG-TV, where he became executive vice president and station manager, and president and general manager of the station in 2004.

Ron Walter's interest in local history led to the taping of a series of interviews with prominent Black Memphians, such as Nat D. Williams, Blair T. Hunt, and Fred Hutchins, during his employment with the library. With support from the Links and funding from the Tennessee Bicentennial Commission, he and Ben Head organized "Memphis Historical Perspectives in Black," which documents the contributions of African Americans. Walter also wrote a weekly column on Black Memphians for *The Commercial Appeal* and co-authored *Nineteenth-Century Memphians of Color* with Roberta Church. His friendship and collaboration with Miss Church led to his selection as chair of the Friends of the Robert R. Churches. He played a major role in the renovation of Church's Park, following his 1986 appointment as chair of the Church's Park Restoration Committee. The first Black to serve on the Tennessee Historical Commission, he is also a member of the Shelby County Historical Committee and the West Tennessee Historical Society, and he has been instrumental in erecting historical markers to commemorate individuals, organizations, and institutions of historical significance.

Ron Walter served as president of the Kiwanis Club of Memphis and vice president of the executive board of the Memphis Branch of the NAACP; a member of the boards of trustees of LeMoyne-Owen College and Clark University; and board member of the Chickasaw Council of the Boy Scouts, Boys Club of Memphis, Memphis Arts Council, Salvation Army, and Mid-South Chapter of the American Red Cross. In 2004, he became the first African American inducted into the Descendants of Early Settlers of Shelby County. Less well known, perhaps, is his devotion to elderly Memphians, particularly childless widows who have depended on him for care and administrative assistance in their later years. While a bachelor, Ron Walter and his mother hosted an annual Christmas party at their home on Ioka Street. On June 12, 1987, he married Marianne Savare, a city school teacher, in an elaborate ceremony at the Orpheum Theater, and the Walters are the parents of three children: Arianne, Ronald, Jr., and Jon.

Washington, David Whittier (1852–1932), postman, businessman. The first Black mail carrier hired by the U.S. Postal Service in Memphis, he amassed a small fortune in real estate. Born a slave on the Cassett plantation near LaGrange, Tennessee, he moved to Memphis after the Civil War. Washington worked as a bootblack before his appointment as a postal carrier in July 1872, a position that he held for forty-six years, until his retirement in 1918. A thrifty man and an astute businessman, he became a stockholder in the Solvent Savings Bank and Trust Company, a Black bank that opened on Beale Street in 1906. Like other former slaves who acquired some education and employment during Reconstruction, he worked to improve the social, cultural, and economic conditions of his community. Motivated by race pride, he joined the Committee for Civil Rights in 1883, and became president of the Whittier Historical Association. Inspired by his religious faith, he contributed to LeMoyne Normal Institute, which he had once attended; helped finance the Old Folks and Orphans Home on Hernando Road; and made interest-free loans to the indigent. A member of the Odd Fellows, he organized the Afro-American Hall Company and served, in 1892, as sergeant-at-arms of the National Association of Postal Workers.

An ordained minister, Washington was active throughout his adult life in the Avery Chapel A.M.E. Church, serving for forty years as director of the choir and for forty-five years as superintendent of the Sunday School. For many years, he held the office of president of the Interdenominational Sunday School Society. After the death of his first wife, Esther Horton Washington, he married Georgia E. L. Patton, a physician and former medical missionary to Liberia, on December 29, 1897. Their two sons—Willie Patton Washington, born on February 14, 1899, and David W. Washington, born on July 11, 1900—died soon after their births, and Geogia Patton Washington died on November 8, 1900, at age thirty-six. In 1908, the widower married Effie Victoria Hayes, a school teacher in Arlington, Tennessee. David W. Washington died on December 22, 1932, leaving an estate estimated at $250,000 to his widow and five children: Emma Dorcas, David Whittier, Esther Victoria, Ruth Louise, and Paul Hayes. His real estate holdings included four brick buildings on

Main Street, a house on Elliston Avenue, a house and lot on Linden Avenue, 55 acres on Ball Avenue, and a 30-acre lot at Hernando and Elliston. According to his friend and attorney B. F. Booth, Washington once had $50,000 in the bank and refused an offer of $125,000 for his Main Street property, which he later mortgaged to finance the education of his five children in northern schools.

Weathers, Luke J. (1921?–), pilot, air traffic controller. One of the famed Tuskegee Airmen, Weathers shot down two German fighter planes in one day during World War II, as a member of the 332nd Fighter Group. Born in Grenada, Mississippi, he moved to Memphis as a baby and graduated from Booker T. Washington High School in 1939. He attended Xavier University and Lane College, and he completed all degree requirements except the thesis for a master's from Tennessee State University. In 1942, two years after President Franklin D. Roosevelt ordered the U.S. Army Corps to build an all-Negro flying unit, Weathers joined a small group of select Black men who were being trained to become pilots at Tuskegee Institute, and he received his wings in 1943. He flew numerous missions with "The Redtails," the famous all-Black unit that fought fascism abroad and racial prejudice at home; he belonged to the only U.S. Fighter Group in World War II that could claim to have never lost a bomber in its care. Captain Weathers received the Distinguished Flying Cross and an Air Medal with seven clusters after flying 112 combat missions over Europe and North Africa, shooting down four and a half planes, and destroying twelve planes on the ground. He spent twenty-three years in the military, including more than three years of active duty and almost twenty years in the Air Force Reserves.

When the city designated June 25, 1945, as "Captain Luke Weathers Day," the distinguished serviceman became the first Black in Memphis history to receive such an honor. The day began with a lunch at Foote Homes, the sale of $50,000 in war bonds, and a parade down Beale Street at 6:00 p.m. Weathers, who had single-engine, commercial, and instrument ratings and who had flown multi-engines and jet planes, founded the Weathers-Jerry Flying School in Jackson, Tennessee, where he trained many Mid-South pilots between 1946 and 1953. He operated a public relations firm and worked for the school system before becoming an air traffic control specialist with the FAA, briefing pilots and preparing flight plans. After twenty-nine years with the FAA, he retired to his home in Arlington, Virginia, where he became a consultant to foreign countries and began an autobiography, *Beale Street Eagle: Portrait of a Tuskegee Airman.* In 1991, he returned to Memphis for the funeral of his mother, Jessie Weathers Bradford. Now divorced and living in Arizona, he raised five children, including Luke J. Weathers, Jr., who worked for the postal service in Memphis.

Wells, Ida Bell (1862–1931), journalist, suffragist, antilynching crusader. A militant advocate of equal rights for Blacks and women, Wells used the pen and the podium in the struggle for equality. The oldest of eight children, she was born in Holly Springs, Mississippi, on July 16, 1862, to slave parents, Elizabeth "Lizzie" Warrenton and James "Jim" Wells. She attended Rust University until the deaths of her parents and brother in the yellow fever epidemic of 1878. Orphaned at age sixteen, Wells kept her family together by teaching in a rural school for $25.00 a month. In 1880, she moved to Tennessee to teach in Shelby County until she obtained a position with the Memphis public schools in 1884. In May of that year, she was forcibly removed from a train after refusing to move to a segregated coach, so she sued the Chesapeake, Ohio and Southwestern Railroad. Although the Circuit

Court ruled in her favor, the decision was reversed by the Tennessee Supreme Court in 1887. That event motivated her to write articles about her experience and launched Wells on a career in journalism. In 1889, she bought a one-third interest in the *Memphis Free Speech and Headlight*, and became editor, two years later, after being fired by the school board for attacking segregated schools.

When three prominent Black grocers were lynched at the "Curve" of Mississippi and Walker Avenue, Wells wrote fiery editorials urging Blacks to leave Memphis. She maintained that lynching was a ruse to eliminate prosperous Blacks and that the charge of rape was used to justify violence against Negroes. She even suggested that White women were sexually attracted to Black men, so a "committee of leading citizens" threatened her life and destroyed her newspaper office. Wells then moved to New York, bought an interest in the *New York Age*, and began an antilynching campaign. She lectured, published articles, and wrote pamphlets such as *Southern Horrors: Lynch Law in All Its Phases* (1892) and *A Red Record: Tabulated Statistics and Alleged Causes of Lynching in the United States, 1892, 1893, and 1894* (1895). She also toured Great Britain in 1893 and 1894, lectured on lynching, and wrote a column, "Ida B. Wells Abroad," for the Chicago *Inter-Ocean*. On June 27, 1895, Ida B. Wells married Ferdinand L. Barnette, an attorney and founder of the *Chicago Conservator*. A widower with two sons, he had four children with his new wife: Charles Aked, Herman Kohlsaat, Ida B. Wells, Jr., and Alfreda M. Barnett.

After a brief hiatus from public life following the birth of her second child, Wells-Barnett resumed her activities with increased vigor: she met with President William McKinley to urge passage of a federal law against lynching and she signed the call for a conference that led to the formation of the National Association for the Advancement of Colored People. She became increasingly controversial, however, because of her radical views, support of Marcus Garvey, and criticism of other Black leaders. In 1910, she founded the Negro Fellowship League in Chicago and, when financial support waned, she donated her salary as an adult probation officer. An advocate of women's rights, Wells-Barnett was one of the founders of the National Association of Colored Women and the Alpha Suffrage Club, which sent her as a delegate to the National American Woman Suffrage Association's parade in Washington, D.C. In 1918, she wrote articles on the East St. Louis, Illinois race riot for the *Chicago Defender* and, in 1922, she investigated the indictment for murder of twelve innocent farmers in Elaine, Arkansas. Afterwards, she published *The Arkansas Race Riot* (1922) in which she reported the results of her investigation. She was an accomplished journalist, essayist, and diarist, whose autobiography, *Crusade for Justice*, was edited and published posthumously in 1970 by her daughter, Alfreda M. Duster. Ida B. Wells-Barnett died in Chicago on March 26, 1931, at age sixty-nine.

Wells, Junior. See Amos Blackmore.

Whalum, Kirk Wendell (1958–), composer, jazz musician. An internationally acclaimed saxophonist, Whalum plays and composes music that is deeply rooted in the blues and gospel idioms. The son of Helen and Kenneth T. Whalum, a former Memphis city councilman and pastor of Olivet Baptist Church, he was born in Memphis on July 11, 1958. He grew up in his father's church, playing the saxophone and traveling with the choir during vacations. After graduating from Melrose High School, where he was "Mr. Melrose," he entered Texas Southern University and received a bachelor's in music performance in 1981. While a student at TSU, he organized the Kirk Whalum Band and, in 1981, formed a five-man band, the Kirk Whalum Group, a progressive jazz ensemble that played jazz, rock, and gospel music. Proficient on the flute as well as the tenor and soprano saxophones, he remained in Houston for twelve years, working in R&B bands such as Bubba Thomas and the Lightmen. Many of his early compositions are dedicated to family members: "Cuz" for his younger brother; "Ms. Helen," inspired by his mother; and "Styne," dedicated to his wife. He and Rubystyne Payne Whalum, who have four children, started dating at Central High School, when he was fifteen and she was fourteen. Deeply religious, he has composed songs such as "Seeing Him As He Is," which are influenced by the gospel music that he heard in church. He cut his first album, *Floppy Disk*, for Columbia in 1985, and his 1988 *And You Know That* topped the Billboard jazz charts for six weeks. In 1993, he recorded a solo album, *Caché*, a mix of jazz fusion and urban, contemporary sounds. Moving freely from jazz to blues to gospel to contemporary music in his releases—*In This Life* (1995) and *Colors* (1997)—he continues to expand his musical palette.

Among his many Memphis gigs is his performance on November 1, 1997, at the Renaissance Gala, a benefit for LeMoyne-Owen College, when he joined other Memphis jazz greats, James Williams and Mulgrew Miller, in a spirited and soulful session. In January 1993, Whalum played at President Clinton's inauguration, in Quincy Jones's all-star saxophone section, which included David Sanborn, Grover Washington, and Kenny G. Later that year, he took his family to live in Paris for a year because he wanted his children to learn French. Throughout the 1990s, he toured with the Kirk Whalum Band and joined Whitney Houston on tour, playing the tenor saxophone on her "I Will Always Love You," the biggest selling single in history at that point. He has also worked with Luther Vandross and Barbra Streisand, and he appeared with Streisand in the movie *The Prince of Tides*. In 2006, he moved back to Memphis to become artist-in-residence at Stax Soulsville U.S.A.

Whalum, Wendell Phillips (1931–1987), musician, composer, arranger, choir director, college professor. A legendary director of the Morehouse College Glee Club, he won international acclaim as an educator and musician. The third of the five children of H. David and

Thelma Twigg Whalum, he was born in Memphis on September 4, 1931. He grew up in a deeply religious and musical family: his father belonged to Avery Chapel A.M.E. Church, where he sang in the choir, and his mother, a public school music teacher, was organist and music director of Metropolitan Baptist Church. With roots planted in the Black Church, young Wendell played the piano at Avery Chapel, Central Baptist Church, and Providence A.M.E. Church. In 1948, he graduated from Booker T. Washington High School, where he was in the band and glee club, and he went on to Morehouse College, from which he received a B.A. degree in 1952. After acquiring an M.A. degree from Columbia University in 1953, he began teaching music at his alma mater, where he became director of the glee club. Whalum spent his entire professional career of thirty-four years at Morehouse, serving as professor, director of the band and glee club, chairman of the Music Department, and Fuller E. Calloway Professor of Music.

Throughout his life, Wendell Whalum strived to achieve excellence in his field. In 1965, he received a doctorate from the University of Iowa and he was a Danforth Fellow and recipient of a Merrill Faculty Travel-Study Grant Abroad, which took him to Germany for additional study. He took the glee club on a State Department tour of Ethiopia, Ghana, Nigeria, Senegal, and Uganda; he directed the choir at the inauguration of President Jimmy Carter; and he trained the chorus for the world premiere of the opera *Treemonisha*. Dr. Whalum also directed the Atlanta University Center Community Chorus and co-directed the Morehouse-Spelman Chorus; he was the organist-choirmaster of Providence, Ebenezer, and Friendship Baptist Churches, and of Allen Temple A.M.E. Church; and he conducted the Atlanta Symphony Orchestra at the Lincoln and Kennedy Centers. He returned to Memphis every year with the Morehouse College

Choir to give a concert for Metropolitan's Rebecca Club, to which his mother had belonged.

Whalum was a scholar who belonged to eighteen professional organizations and learned societies, including Phi Beta Kappa, National Humanities Faculty, and National Society of Literature and the Arts. He was also a member of cultural organizations such as the Atlanta Opera Company and Scott Joplin Foundation. In recognition of his achievements, he was awarded an honorary doctorate by the University of Haiti in 1968, and the Wendell P. Whalum Organ in Morehouse's chapel was dedicated to him in 1982. Wendell P. Whalum died in June 1987, and is survived by his wife, Clarie Guy-Whalum and a son, Wendell P. Whalum, Jr.

Wharton, A C, Jr. (1945–), attorney, law professor, county mayor. The first African American elected mayor of Shelby County, he is one of the most respected members of the legal profession. He was born on August 17, 1945 in Lebanon, Tennessee, one of the five children of Mary and A. C. Wharton, owner of Wharton General Store in the rural section of Wilson County. While attending the segregated Wilson County Training School, A C (the letters are his name) witnessed a racial incident—the beating of a Black man by a policeman—that led him into law. He received a scholarship to Tennessee State University, from which he received a B.S. degree with honors in political science in 1966. After graduation, he participated in a summer program for prospective lawyers at Harvard University, where he met Ruby Roy, and they married after she finished law school at Boston College. In 1971, he graduated with honors from The University of Mississippi Law School, which proved that he could excel even in a racially charged atmosphere. For two years, A C and Ruby Wharton worked in Washington, D.C., before moving to Memphis, where he became executive director of Memphis Area Legal Services.

Over the next thirty years, A C held many positions in the legal profession, from investigator for the E.E.O.C. to chief public defender for Memphis and Shelby County. As public defender, he had to assure that poor people accused of crimes had legal representation, and he criticized overcrowding in the Shelby County Jail, claiming that inmates' cases moved too slowly to indictment and trial. Licensed to practice law in both Tennessee and Mississippi, Wharton was a member of the Tennessee Criminal Justice Commission as well as attorney for the Lawyers Committee for Civil Rights Under Law. In 1974, he became the first Black professor of law at The University of Mississippi, and remained on the faculty until 1999. With his wife, he established the law firm of Wharton & Wharton & Associates and built up a successful criminal defense practice representing such high-profile clients as W. W. Herenton, John Ford, and Michael Hooks, Sr.

Respected for his honesty, charisma. and political acumen, Wharton has become increasingly involved in local and state politics. He managed two of Herenton's successful mayoral campaigns and served as an adviser to Al Gore in his bid for the presidency. Finally, in 2002, he threw his hat into the race for county mayor. With 62% of the vote and substantial support across party and racial lines, A C Wharton was elected mayor of Shelby County, a victory that he attributes to "determination, luck, and the belief of others [in him]." As mayor, his goals have included streamlining county government, managing the county's debt, hiring qualified people, instituting a performance-based management system, and improving growth and development strategies. His service to the community reaches into other areas: he served on the boards of Methodist-Le Bonheur Hospital and the Tennessee Higher Education Commission, and he was also chairman of the board for Methodist Healthcare. A C Wharton and his wife, Attorney Ruby Roy Wharton, have three sons—A C III, Andre Courtney, and Alexander Conrad—and they have helped to raise three other young men: Tavarski, Daniel, and Monte.

White, Augustus A. III (1936–), physician, surgeon, professor of medicine. One of the foremost orthopedic surgeons in the world, he has specialized in back pain, fracture healing, and care of the spine. He was born in Memphis on June 4, 1936, the son of Augustus White, Jr., a physician, and Vivian Dandridge White. After his father's death when he was eight years old, he was raised by his mother, a teacher and librarian in the Memphis public schools. He left Memphis at age thirteen to attend Northfield Mount Hermon, a New England preparatory school for boys. His experiences with sports injuries on the football field at Brown University, where he was a star athlete and outstanding scholar, kindled his interest in orthopedics. After graduating from Brown in 1957, he attended Stanford University Medical School, where he developed a research interest in the complex problems of back pain. In 1961, he became the first African American to receive a medical degree from Stanford. Afterwards, he completed an internship at the University of Michigan Hospital and at Presbyterian Medical Center in San Francisco, and then he entered the Yale Medical Center, in 1963, to do a residency in orthopedics

Dr. White earned a Bronze Star and worked as a volunteer in a leper colony, while serving a one-year tour of duty in Vietnam as a captain in the U.S. Army Medical Corps in 1966. After completing a doctorate in orthopedic biomechanics at Sweden's Karolinska Institute, he became a professor of orthopedic surgery at Yale Medical School and director of the Engineering Laboratory for Musculoskeletal Disease, which he helped to found. Later, he became professor of Orthopedic Surgery Technology and Orthopedic Surgeon-in-Chief at Beth Israel Hospital, and he co-founded Beth Israel Hospital's Orthopedic Biomechanics Laboratory. His interest in health care management motivated him to complete the Advanced Management Program at Harvard Business School, where his classmates selected him to deliver a commencement address. A professor of orthopedic surgery at Harvard Medical School and the Ellen and Melvin Gordon Professor of Medical Education, he returned to Memphis on October 24, 1996, as the University of Tennessee-Memphis James H. Horner Distinguished Visiting Professor.

Dr. White is a prolific researcher and writer: he has authored or co-authored more than 175 articles, published *The Clinical Biomechanics of the Spine*, co-edited *Symposium on Idiopathic Low Back Pain*, and written *Your Aching Back: A Doctor's Guide to Relief* and *Clinical Biomechanics of the Spine*. As a scholar and surgeon, he has earned many awards, including an honorary Doctor of Humane Letters from the University of New Haven, Martin Luther King Jr. Medical Achievement Award, and the Jaycees' "Ten Outstanding Young Men" award. A founding member and past president of the Cervical Spine Research Society, he is also a member of the American Orthopaedic Association, American Academy of Orthopaedic Surgeons, Orthopaedic Research Society, Scoliosis Research Society, International Society for the Study of Lumbar Spine, and American Orthopaedic Society for Sports Medicine. Augustus A. White is married to Anita Ottemo, and they are the parents of three daughters: Alissa, Atina, and Annica.

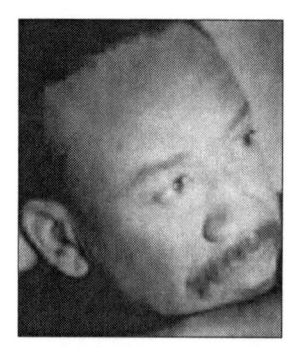

White, Maurice (1941–), vocalist, composer, producer, bandleader. Song-writing legend and founder of Earth Wind & Fire, he has produced albums for some outstanding singers. Born in Memphis's LeMoyne Gardens Housing Project on December 19, 1941, he was raised by his grandmother, who exposed him to Black church music. At six, he began singing gospel music in church and had his first secular gig at Porter Elementary School playing with Booker T. Jones, who later formed Booker T. & the MGs. After finishing

Porter Junior High School, White entered Booker T. Washington High School, where he played with a jazz combo and marching band. According to White, band director Walter Martin, Jr., was a decisive factor in his formation as a drummer; Martin, who recognized the boy's talent but realized that his family was poor, bought him his first set of drums. After graduating from high school in 1962, White moved to Chicago, where he attended Crane Junior College and the Chicago Conservatory of Music, and was a drummer for Etta James, Little Milton, Howlin' Wolf, and others. From 1966 to 1969, he toured with the Ramsey Lewis Trio and then formed a group, Salty Peppers, which included his younger brother, Verdine, a Hamilton High School graduate.

In 1970, Maurice White organized Earth, Wind & Fire, serving as its percussionist, songwriter, and lead vocalist. The group performed for thirteen years, producing fifteen hit singles and twenty-six gold and platinum albums, before disbanding in 1983. The members of EW&F reunited in 1988 to do a "Touch the World" tour and, when they performed in Memphis, they were backed up by members of the Hillcrest Choir. White, who produced four platinum albums for EW&F, became successful in his own right, garnering seven Grammys, recording seven double platinum albums, and producing albums for Barbra Streisand and Neil Diamond.

Although he lives in Los Angeles, White returns often to Memphis because, as he explains: "To come home, to know that people care… it's beautiful, and I love it and I love Memphis." In 1974, he performed with Earth, Wind & Fire at the Memphis Auditorium and, in 1978, he appeared at the Mid-South Coliseum when EW&F did a 50-city tour. He returned again in 1986, to start a music production company, Memphis Mecca, with songwriter David Porter, with whom he had attended high school. Recently, he collaborated with Maurice Hines in creating *Hot Feet*, an $8-million musical that premiered on Broadway in 2006. White wrote six new songs for the show, an urban version of Hans Christian Andersen's fairy tale "The Red Shoes," which features jazz, hip-hop, and krumping.

Whittaker, John W. II (1902–1996), musician, educator. One of Memphis's most dedicated music educators, he taught generations of students to value the arts. He was born in Russellville, Kentucky, and demonstrated a talent for music at an early age. With a music scholarship to Fisk University, he joined the Men's Glee Club and traveled throughout the United States and Europe with the renowned Fisk Jubilee Singers. While in college, he played jazz—a life-long interest—and befriended Jimmie Lunceford, the acclaimed jazzman and band director who once taught at Manassas High School. After receiving bachelor's and master's degrees from Fisk, with a major in French and minor in English, he began teaching. During the 1930s, he taught English and French at Avery Institute, a private elementary and secondary school in Charleston, South Carolina, which was founded after the Civil War by the American Missionary Association. A gifted tenor, pianist, and arranger, "Prof," as his students called him, directed the high school choir and often invited students and teachers to his faculty quarters to hear him play jazz. In 1932, under his direction, the Avery octette became the first African American group to perform on a Charleston radio program. In 1936, he married Louise Borden, who had three children—George, Thelma, and Betty—from a former marriage, and they lived in a large apartment on Spring Street, where they entertained and became actively involved in the social and cultural life of the African American community. Later, they had a son, John W. Whittaker III.

The Whittakers moved to Memphis in 1939, when he was appointed choir director and professor of music at LeMoyne College, and his wife became secretary to the dean. A gentleman par excellence, whose imposing stature belied his quiet, unassuming manner, he was adored by the students to whom he taught French, English, and music appreciation. His teaching extended beyond the classroom and onto the stage, when he invited singers such as Leontyne Price, Grace Bumbry, and William Warfield to perform at the college. Soon after his arrival in Memphis, John Whittaker joined Metropolitan Baptist Church, where he directed the sanctuary choir, conducted an annual performance of Handel's *Messiah*, and served as minister of music until his retirement in 1978. In addition to his work at Metropolitan and LeMoyne, he gave private piano lessons, hosted "The Symphony of the Air" on WLOK Radio, organized a glee club at the Abe Scharff YMCA, directed the LeMoyne College Alumni chorus, served on the board of the Memphis Youth Symphony, and played a tough game of checkers. Even in retirement, he remained actively engaged in the arts, spending long hours reading, listening to music, and organizing his extensive record collection. "Pop" Whittaker, as he was affectionately known, died at Fort Walton Beach, Florida, on January 19, 1996.

Wilbun, Shepperson A. "Shep" (1925–1991), attorney, judge. The first Black assistant city attorney and the first Black city court judge, he distinguished himself in the 1960s and '70s as a civil rights attorney. He was born in Helena, Arkansas, on October 24, 1925, and graduated from Little Rock's Philander Smith College. After receiving a law degree in 1948 from Howard University School of Law, he taught for two years and served as acting head of the Department of Business Administration at Sam Houston College in Austin, Texas. In 1949, he opened a private practice in Helena, Arkansas, and, in 1955, he moved to Memphis, where he practiced law at 334 Vance Avenue. During the civil rights movement, he defended demonstrators and student protestors who defied the segregation laws in Memphis, and he ran unsuccessfully, in 1958 and again in 1966, for the state legislature. From 1964 to 1973, he was an assistant city attorney, as well as a part-time prosecutor for the Alcohol Commission. In 1973, upon the nomination of Mayor Wyeth Chandler, he became judge of the newly created 5th Division of City Court, a position that he held for five years.

In March 1978, Governor Ray Blanton appointed him to fill an unexpired term as Circuit Court Judge, Division 5, and Wilbun was elected to the position without opposition the following August. After twelve years on the bench, he was defeated by Judge Kay Robilio. A quiet and unassuming man, he was given high marks for his fairness, performance, and attendance record by lawyers who presented cases in his court. An active member of his profession, Judge Wilbun was a member of the American Bar Association, Tennessee Bar Association, Memphis and Shelby County Bar Association, and American Judicature Society, as well as a co-founder of the Ben F. Jones Chapter of the National Bar Association. He was a trustee and devoted member of Mt. Olive C.M.E. Cathedral. He and his wife, Rubye K. Wilbun, had two sons, Gary and "Shep," Jr., a former city councilman and Juvenile Court judge. S. A. Wilbun died in November 1991.

Wilburn, Emma Currin Barbee (1875–1937), businesswoman. Described as a "vital force in the business, civic, and social life of Memphis and the Mid-South," she became one of the largest property owners in Shelby County. One of Harriet and Hudson Currin's thirteen children, Emma was born in Lauderdale County, Tennessee, in 1875. Before she turned twenty-five, she lost two husbands and was left with four children to support. In the late 1890s, Wilburn opened a small hotel in Halls, Tennessee, and then moved to Memphis in search of greater opportunities. After working for Zion Cemetery Company, which operated the oldest Black cemetery in the city, she bought Carson Funeral Company, located at Georgia and South Orleans, in 1914. Six years later, she moved the Emma Wilburn Funeral Home to a larger facility at 913 Mississippi Boulevard. The attractive matron could often be seen, dressed in an elegant riding habit and mounted on a graceful white horse, leading funeral processions through the city to the cemetery. With a talent for business, she bought additional property in the city and acquired another funeral home in Dyersburg, Tennessee. In January 1933, she leased her Memphis establishment to National Burial Association and, two months later, bought the seventy-five-acre New Park Cemetery in South Memphis. Wilburn held annual memorial services at the cemetery, and New Park soon became one of the finest burial sites in the country.

Emma Currin Wilburn taught her children—Hudson, Sadie, Minnie, and Cutis—the funeral trade and encouraged them to go into business. After working as an embalmer at Campbell & Wiggins, Hudson Barbee, her oldest son, founded Barbee Casket Company, which became a successful operation. With her mother's support, Cutis, Wilburn's youngest daughter, opened the Cutis Thomas Funeral Home on South Lauderdale. When Minnie and her husband, Johnson Rideout, opened Rideout Funeral Home in Los Angeles in 1935, her mother bought an airplane ticket to attend the grand opening. Alleging that Blacks could not travel from Memphis on American Airlines, local officials tried to revoke her ticket, but Wilburn wired the airline's headquarters in Chicago to protest. She won a victory for others when she became the first African American woman to fly from Memphis on American Airlines. Two years later, on April 13, 1937, Emma Currin Wilburn died at her home on Horn Lake Road.

Williams, Eddie N. (1932–), administrator. Known as one of the most influential Blacks in American politics, he served for thirty-two years as president of the Joint Center for Political and Economic Studies. Born on August 18, 1932, he was the only child of Ed and Georgia Lee Barr Williams. His mother was a maid at the Hotel Gayoso, and his father was a piano player on Mississippi River boats, as well as the choir director and pianist at Mount Zion Baptist Church. After the death of his father when he was five, Eddie was raised by his mother in North Memphis's Hyde Park neighborhood. Following his graduation from Manassas High School, where he developed an interest in journalism, he entered the University of Illinois on an ROTC scholarship, worked as a summer intern at the *Tri-State Defender* in Chicago, and graduated in 1956, with a degree in journalism. He served for two years in the U.S. Army before entering the newspaper business; when he was refused a job at the *Champaign-Urbana Courier* because of his race, he accepted a position with an African American paper, *The Atlanta World*. After winning a congressional fellowship in 1958, Williams went to Washington, D.C. to work for Senator Hubert H. Humprey and the U.S. Senate Committee on Foreign Relations. At the time, Louis Martin, publisher of the *Chicago Defender*, was serving on President Kennedy's transition team and offered Williams a job as a Foreign Service reserve officer with the State Department.

During the thirty-two years that he served as president and CEO of the Joint Center for Political and Economic Studies, an organization that provides data for politicians and others in the public policy arena, he developed the Center into a 43-employee organization with an annual budget of 5.46 million. Under his leadership, the Center received a multiyear grant of $7 million from the W. K. Kellogg Foundation to create a Health Policy Institute. After he retired from the Center in 2005, Williams accepted the vice chairmanship of the Black Leadership Forum and he has established a consulting firm, Eddie Williams and Associates. He has earned many awards, including a "Genius Grant" of $330,00 from the MacArthur Foundation in 1988, and he was one of six inductees into the 2000–2001 Memphis City Schools Alumni Hall of Fame. His wife, Jearline Franklin Williams, whom he married on July 17, 1981, is a former deputy city administrator for Washington, D.C., and the Williamses are the parents of three children: Larry, Traci, and Terrence.

Williams, James (1951–2004), composer, jazz pianist. Acclaimed as one of the most creative pianist in contemporary jazz, Williams has underscored Memphis's rich jazz tradition. Born in Memphis on March 8, 1951, he began playing gospel music at Eastern Star Baptist Church, to which his family belonged. At thirteen, he started piano lessons and, later, helped organize a band at Central High School. At Memphis State University, he gained a foundation in classical music but gravitated toward jazz through his study of theory and interest in the music of jazzmen like Miles Davis and John Coltrane. While at MSU, he and his quintet won two national collegiate jazz festivals and performed in the 1973 Newport Jazz Festival. After graduating from MSU in 1974, with a degree in music education, he cut his first album, *Flying Colors*, with instrumentation by three other Memphians. From 1972 to 1977, he taught at Boston's Berklee College of Music and in September 1977, he performed at the Beale Street Music Arts Forum. In the late 1970s, Williams joined Art Blakey and the Jazz Messengers as pianist and composer, adding compositions such as "Stretchin'" to the group's repertoire.

James Williams performed at the Variety Inn on Highland in 1980, and returned to Memphis, a year later, to participate in Memphis State's Visiting Artist Series, when he received the second Alumni Achievement Award. In 1981, he presented the "Memphis Piano Summit," in Boston and Memphis, with a quartet of Memphis jazz pianists: Williams, Phineas Newborn, Jr., Harold Mabern, and Charles Thomas. He explained, "Memphis pianists have a certain down-home feeling to their playing—a warmth—[and they are] technically above average." That piano legacy is evident in two of his albums—*The Memphis Convention* and *The Memphis Piano Convention*—and his indebtedness to Newborn is expressed in *Four Pianos for Phineas*, recorded after his mentor's death in 1989. He also wrote the liner notes to a Newborn reissue and led a national tour, "Four for Phineas," featuring Memphians Williams, Mabern, Mulgrew Miller, and Donald Brown. A more recent album, *James Williams Meets the Saxophone Masters*, also features jazz musicians from the Bluff City.

According to critics, Williams's piano style is characterized by a "strong sense of swing and high-stepping verve with a solid command of the technical side of music." Accompanied by Bill Easley and Wynton Marsalis, he returned to Memphis in December 1986, to perform at the Varsity Inn and at Upstairs at the Square. He organized the Contemporary Piano Ensemble with Miller and Mabern in 1993, and offered free concerts at the National Civil Rights Museum. After having taught at Dartmouth, Harvard, and The New England Conservatory, he was appointed director of jazz studies at William Peterson University in 1999. James Williams died of cancer on July 26, 2004, at age fifty-three.

Williams, Nathaniel Dowde "Nat D." (1907–1983), educator, journalist, editor, entertainer, broadcaster. Called the "Voice of Beale Street," the multitalented Nat D. was one of the most important cultural activists in Memphis from the 1930s through the '60s. The son of Albert and Hattie (Momma Hat) Williams and the grandson of slaves, he was born on Beale Street on October 19, 1907. After graduating from Kortrecht School, he attended Howard University and received bachelor's and master's degrees from Tennessee A&I State University. At Booker T. Washington, where he taught American history for forty-three years, he was known as the "Black Genius of the Mid-South. For years, he "bootlegged" Black history, introducing students to Black Studies before that subject gained acceptance. Described as a great teacher and thinker by his colleagues, he instilled independence of thought, strength of character, and race pride in his students. Gifted with a prodigious memory, he served as editor of the *Oracle,* the Omega Psi Phi Fraternity magazine, and wrote columns for Black newspapers such as the *Chicago Defender,* *Pittsburgh Courier,* and *Tri-State Defender.* As editor of the *Memphis World* for more than thirty years, he wrote a weekly column, "Down on Beale," about Blacks in the city. In 1935, Nat assisted Dr. and Mrs. R. Q. Venson with the Cotton Makers' Jubilee and also started Amateur Night at the Palace Theatre.

Known as the "Granddaddy of Black Jocks," Nat D. became the South's first Black disk jockey in 1948, when he was hired by WDIA. He said that he was so nervous that he couldn't stop laughing, and that laugh, his thick glasses, pipe, and dark complexion became his trademarks. He had two radio shows, five days a week: "Coffee Club" at 6:30 a.m., before school started, and "Tan Town Jamboree" at 4:00 p.m., as well as a three-hour program on Saturdays and his award-winning public forum, "Brown America Speaks," on Sunday afternoons. Nat created opportunities in radio for others. He put Maurice "Hot Rod" Hulburt, A. C. "Moohah" Williams, and Cleo "Bless My Bones" Wade on the air; he gave Rufus Thomas and B. B. King their start; and he introduced Elvis Presley to Black music. Williams also encouraged students and professionals to perform in shows that he produced: Amateur Night, Jubilect, Goodwill Revue, Starlight Revue, and the Booker T. Washington Ballet. Perhaps more than any other single individual in the entertainment business, he was instrumental in the fusion of musical styles that produced the "Memphis Sound." A devout man, he read the Bible daily, taught a Sunday School class, sang in the Sanctuary Choir, and attended St. John Baptist Church for over fifty years. He and his wife, the former Lucille Butler, had three daughters—Natolyn, Naomi, who became a noted vocalist, and Shirley Jean. After suffering a stroke in

1972, Nathaniel D. Williams retired from teaching and broadcasting and died, at age seventy-six, on October 27, 1983. A year later, Channel 3 staged a five-part series, "A Tribute to Nat D. Williams," which included a benefit concert at the Orpheum Theater.

Williamson, Juanita V. (1917–1993), educator, linguist. Named Distinguished Service Professor at LeMoyne-Owen College in 1977, she served the college for more than forty years. Born in Shelby, Mississippi, on January 18, 1917, to John M. and Alice McAllister Williamson, she attended the Memphis City Schools and graduated from Booker T. Washington, where she demonstrated an early aptitude for language. After receiving the B.A. degree in English and Romance languages from LeMoyne in 1938, she acquired an M.A. degree in English literature from Atlanta University in 1948, and a Ph.D. degree in linguistics from the University of Michigan in 1961, becoming one of the first Black women in Memphis to earn a doctorate. Dr. Williamson joined the faculty of LeMoyne College in 1947, eventually becoming professor of English and chair of the Humanities Division. Her publications, including *A Various Language* (1971), co-authored with Virginia M. Burke, a monograph, "A Phonological and Morphological Study of the Speech of the Negro in Memphis, Tennessee," and articles such as "A Look at Black English," earned her a national reputation as a linguist.

Dr. Williamson received grants from the Rockefeller and Ford Foundations, American Council of Learned Societies, and United Negro College Fund to study Black speech patterns in the South. She served as a consultant or visiting professor at numerous universities, including Atlanta University, Princeton University, Rhodes College, Stanford University, and others. Active in local cultural and service organizations such as the YWCA, United Way, Girl Scouts of America, and League of Women Voters, she also participated in professional organizations, including the National Council for Teachers of English, American Dialect Society, Modern Language Association, and College Language Association. She died in Memphis on August 8, 1993. The Juanita Williamson Academic Excellence Award at LeMoyne-Owen College is named in her honor; it is given annually to a student whose scholastic performance enhances the College's academic environment.

Williamson, Kenneth (1955–1988), artist, entrepreneur. The first Black to win the Memphis in May Fine Arts Poster Contest, he transformed images and symbols of Memphis life into works of art. One of seven children, he was born on August 4, 1955, to Vassar M. and James Critten, but he took the surname of his stepfather. He grew up in North Memphis and, after graduating from Manassas High School, where he began formal art training under Walter Guy, he attended the Memphis Art Academy from 1973 to 1976. Because his family had limited resources, he rode a bicycle to school rather than let his mother pay his car fare. In 1975, several of his paintings toured the United States and Europe as part of the American Telephone and Telegraph Company's Traveling Exhibition. While at the Academy, he opened the Mona Lisa Art Studio at 1331 Union and sold portraits of Elvis Presley, Isaac Hayes, Al Green, and Harold Ford to pay his way through college. When the demand for his work increased, he began selling limited edition prints for as much as $500. Within a short time, he sold 100 sets of limited edition prints of paintings such as "Cotton Field Memories," "Replica of the Past—Beale Street," and "The Barn," his most famous work until 1988. Exhibitions of his work were held locally at the Peabody Hotel, Christian Brothers College, and LeMoyne-Owen

College, and he developed a marketing strategy to promote his work through large billboards featuring full-color replicas of his paintings.

With other investors, Williamson organized Medical Arts Limited to market a series of prints, an exclusive edition limited to only 300 hand-signed and numbered prints in *The Great Men of Medicine Series*. As an artist, he achieved acclaim for his painting "London on the Mississippi," which won the 1988 Memphis in May Fine Arts Poster Contest, and which created a sensation in the artistic community because of his iconoclastic rendering of the London skyline. The painting depicts historic landmarks—Memphis's Hernando DeSoto Bridge and London's Big Ben Clock and Houses of Parliament—against a dark blue, surrealistic cityscape. Completed in only two weeks, it exemplifies the conceptual depth, skilled craftsmanship, and attention to detail that the painter brought to his work. Described by an artist friend as a "brilliant strategist, sharp thinker, and spiffy dresser," he collected oriental rugs, fine antiques, and vintage cars, which he sold through his company, Williamson Enterprises, Antiques and Collectibles. An ordained Baptist minister and a gifted musician, he attracted people from all walks of life, including physicians, musicians, and downtown businessmen. There was also a dark side to this complex man, whom other artists described as elusive and guarded, a man whose "life was shrouded in secrecy." He married Elena DeCosta Sugarmon, a high school Spanish teacher, on August 1, 1985, and they had two children: Kenneth Toriano and Angelique Nicole, who was born six months after her father's death. Kenneth Williamson was found shot to death on June 15, 1988, in Martin Luther King Jr. Riverside Park.

Willis, Archie Walter, Jr. (1925–1988), attorney, state legislator, businessman, mortgage banker. The first Black elected to the Tennessee State Legislature since Reconstruction and the first to run for mayor of Memphis, Willis was considered one of the city's most powerful Black political leaders in the 1960s. The oldest of the three children of Mamie Camack Willis and A. W. Willis, first vice president of Universal Life Insurance Company, he was born on March 16, 1925, in Birmingham, Alabama. The family later moved to Memphis, where he attended La Rose Elementary School and Booker T. Washington High School. After a year at Tuskegee Institute, he entered Talladega College but was drafted into the United States Army before he could graduate. When he was discharged, he returned to Talladega and received a bachelor's degree in political science in 1950. In 1949, he married Annie Irving of Columbus, Mississippi, and they had five children: Rosalyn, Michael (Menelik Fombi), Archie III, Stephanie, and Marc. After completing his degree at the University of Wisconsin Law School in 1953, Willis returned to Memphis and began practicing law. As a legal counsel for the NAACP, he filed the 1960 landmark suit that led to the desegregation of Memphis City Schools and, when James Meredith applied for admission to the University of Mississippi in 1961, Willis was the attorney of record. In 1967, he co-founded Ratner, Sugarmon, Lucas, and Willis, the first integrated law firm in Memphis and one of the first in the South.

A. W. Willis became active in politics in the mid-1950s, working in voter registration drives, campaigning for Black candidates, and helping to reorganize the Shelby County Democratic Club. After an unsuccessful race for the Shelby County Quarterly Court in 1960, he won election to the Tennessee General Assembly in 1964, becoming the first African American elected to that body since 1886. As a legislator, he introduced a bill to make congressional redistricting more equitable, a bill that would facilitate the election of Blacks to Congress. In 1966, he was elected to a second term in the legislature and, a year later, he became the first Black to run for mayor of Memphis. Although he lost that race, as well as his bid for a third term in the

General Assembly, he was most effective working behind the scenes. An astute political strategist who was described as a "near genius in organization," he was instrumental in the elections of local and national figures such as J. O. Patterson, Jr., William Morris, W. Otis Higgs, Harold Ford, Ned McWherter, and John F. Kennedy.

In 1955, Willis co-founded and served as executive vice president and secretary of Mutual Federal Savings and Loan Association, the first S & L owned and operated by Blacks in the South. Thirteen years later, he was one of the founders of the nationally franchised Mahalia Jackson's Chicken Systems. Around 1966, he co-founded and served as president of Supreme Mortgage and Realty Company, the first Black-owned mortgage company in the South. Among the many properties that he developed were Mallory Heights School Housing Project, Durango Subdivision in Westwood, four buildings in the Beale Street Historic District, and the Adler Hotel on Main Street, where Supreme was located. Willis worked to revitalize inner-city housing, promoting Shelby County's Homebuyer's Revolving Loan Fund for low and moderate income first-time buyers and working to secure funding for the Tennessee Housing Development Agency. He also played a decisive role in obtaining funding for the $8.8-million National Civil Rights Museum, and he worked to develop Beale Street as a Black cultural center. Former chairman of the Tennessee Human Rights Commission, he was a member of the Chamber of Commerce, Shelby County Housing Task Force, Shelby County Culture of Poverty Task Force, Center City Revenue Finance Corporation, and State Racing Commission, to which Governor Ned McWherter appointed him in 1987.

In November 28, 1989, a testimonial dinner in his honor was held at the Peabody Hotel, and, in December 1987, the Auction Avenue Bridge connecting Memphis and Mud Island was renamed the A. W. Willis, Jr. Bridge in recognition of his commitment to downtown development. A member of Pentecostal Temple Institutional Church of God in Christ, he served as legal counsel to the Church and negotiated the acquisition of the Chisca Hotel and other downtown properties for COGIC. After a three-year struggle with cancer, A. W. Willis, Jr., died on July 14, 1988, and is survived by his second wife, Miriam DeCosta-Willis, whom he married in 1972. On the day of his funeral, flags at all city facilities were flown at half-staff.

Wilson, Lucious Alexander (1909–1960), journalist, newspaper editor. During the civil rights movement, he used his position as editor of the city's major Black newspaper to raise political consciousness and protest institutional racism. Born in Yalaha, Florida, on March 30, 1909, he was the eldest of the seven children of James and Luetta Wilson. After receiving a bachelor's degree from Florida A&M University in 1937, he studied journalism at Lincoln University and pursued graduate work at the University of Wisconsin and Roosevelt College. From 1937 to 1938, he served as principal of Lake County Training School in Leesburg, Florida, and became publisher of the *Leesburg Herald*. Wilson was named principal of Washington High School in Fort St. Joe, Florida, in 1941 and, two years later, he joined the United States Marine Corps, serving from 1943 to 1945. After his discharge, he became a full-time journalist, working on the staffs of three Black newspapers; he was managing editor of the *Norfolk Journal and Guide* and *Detroit Tribune* and became editor of the *Ohio State News* in 1949. L. Alex Wilson joined the *Defender* publications in 1949, the year in which he won the Wendell Wilkie Award for best feature writing for two articles: "What Causes Crime" and "The Making of a Killer." A year later, he won the Page One Award for "Ladies of the Night." The *Chicago Defender* and the National Newspaper Publishers Association sent him to Korea in 1950 as a United Nations war correspondent.

When the *Tri-State Defender* began publication on November 3, 1951, the editor asked Wilson to join the paper as executive editor and general manager. Under the leadership of L. O. Swingler and

Wilson, the Memphis newspaper helped to develop Black civic and political consciousness at the onset of the civil rights movement in the 1950s. When Swingler left the *Tri-State Defender* in 1955, Wilson became editor-in-chief and shaped the direction of the newspaper during a critical period. He wrote front-page articles on racial discrimination and police brutality, which led to changes in the racial climate of the city. Wilson also championed voting rights for Blacks and endorsed progressive political leaders against their conservative, states-rights opponents. The *Defender's* endorsement of Edmund Orgill, for example, was instrumental in the mayoral candidate's defeat of Watkins Overton, a product of the Crump machine. Wilson took on other local issues such as racial discrimination at the Peabody Hotel and *The Commercial Appeal's* refusal to capitalize *Negro* or to give titles (Mr. or Mrs.) to Blacks; he wrote articles in support of the boycotts and mass rallies that the Black community waged against the Peabody and *The Commercial*. Wilson covered all the major civil rights events in the Mid-South, including the lynching of Emmett Till in 1955, Montgomery bus boycott in 1956, and the integration of Little Rock's Central High School in 1957. His exhaustive on-site investigation of the Till lynching offered, according to one account, "the most complete coverage of the case of any daily or weekly publication in the nation." It was, however, his coverage of the desegregation of Central High School that cast him into the national spotlight. In 1957, Wilson made repeated trips to Little Rock, Arkansas, where he worked closely with Daisy Bates, president of the Little Rock NAACP, and her husband L. C. Bates, editor of the *Arkansas State Press*. On the day when the nine Black students entered the high school, Wilson and two other Black journalists were viciously attacked by an angry mob of Whites. Wilson's courage and dignity in the face of violence brought him the respect and admiration of people throughout the country.

In June 1956, Wilson married Emogene Watkins, a public school teacher, and they had a daughter, Karen Rose Wilson. He also had a son, Bertram Wilson, from his prior marriage to Naomi Wilson. In 1959, he became editor of the *Chicago Daily Defender* and moved with his family to Chicago. After a short illness, precipitated by the Little Rock beating, L. Alex Wilson died in Chicago on October 11, 1960, and was buried in Elmwood Cemetery.

Winchester, Marie Louise Amarante Loiselle "Mary" (1800?–1839), wife of Memphis's first mayor. In his *History of Memphis and the Old Times Papers*, James D. Davis describes the bride of Marcus Brutus Winchester (1796–1856), who served as Memphis's first mayor from 1827 to 1829, as a "beautiful French quadroon girl," whom he calls "Mary" (in quotation marks). He claims that she had been the mistress of the future senator from Missouri, Thomas Hart Benton, who moved from Tennessee to Missouri in 1815, but historical evidence does not support Davis's claim. In St. Louis, Benton lived next door to Victoire Loisel—identified as a mulatto by the letter "m"—who had a daughter named Marie Louise Amarante Loisel. Tradition has it that on April 21, 1819, she was traveling with Benton—an older, father figure—on a steamboat, when she met Winchester. He was a prosperous businessman, who opened Memphis's first store, became the town's first postmaster, and owned a lucrative ferry business on the Mississippi River. In spite of their racial differences, the lovers were well matched; Marcus was well read, fluent in French, and cultured (a member of the Thespian Society, he performed in *She Stoops to Conquer*); Marie had studied in France, according to one source, and was said to be one of the best educated women in the Mississippi Valley. In spite of his attraction to a woman of African descent, the mayor, like Thomas Jefferson, was a slaveowner; in 1842, he sold ten of his slaves, among whom was Limus, his ferryboat operator.

It is believed that Marie and Marcus were married in 1824. According to Davis, Winchester "took 'Mary' to Louisiana, where the law permitted intermarriage of the races, and there formally married her," although the union was probably not legal in Tennessee because of its antimiscegenation laws. By 1827, the couple had baptized a son in St. Louis and Mrs. Winchester had moved to Memphis, where she bought a house on the corner of Jackson and Main Streets, near where the Pyramid now stands. The Winchesters had eight children, including Laura, Robert (named after Robert Dale Owen), Frances (named after Frances Wright), Louis, Selima, Loizelle (Marie's family name), Valeria, and Lisida, who were recorded as non-White in the 1830 census. Although most White Memphians shunned the mayor's wife, the Winchesters enjoyed the company of cosmopolitan freethinkers such as Scottish-born Robert Dale Owen (1801–1877) and Frances "Fanny" Wright (1795–1852), who believed in socialism, abolition of slavery, universal suffrage, birth control, and sexual freedom. Wright founded Nashoba, a cooperative community outside of Memphis that welcomed runaway slaves, and her sister Camille bought a house next to the Winchesters.

By 1837, Marcus Winchester was beset by financial problems that were exacerbated by his marriage to a "free person of color." Although the union had been tolerated by early Memphians, fear of slave uprisings created a climate of racial intolerance throughout the South. As a result, the Memphis City Council introduced an ordinance, in 1837, against "citizens keeping colored wives," an obvious move against Winchester, who was the only citizen (as far as is known) with a colored wife. Winchester then moved his family, including his wife and their eight children, to a tract of land, Muscogee Camp, that he owned outside of Memphis. The 1840 census recorded Marcus Winchester living with his eight children—now identified as White—at Muscogee Camp. No adult female appeared in the census, because Marie Louise Amarante Loiselle Winchester had died on August 19, 1839.

Withers, Dedrick "Teddy" (1952–1996), businessman, state legislator. He made history in 1974 when, at age twenty-two, he became the youngest legislator elected to the Tennessee House of Representatives. One of the eight children of Ernest C. and Dorothy Mae Curry Withers, he was born on February 5, 1952. He received a B.S. degree in criminal justice from Tennessee State University. In 1974, he defeated the incumbent state legislator in an upset victory to represent District 85 in the State House. Reelected to that position four times, he introduced legislation to improve roads and to establish the Tennessee Institute for African Affairs, the first bureau of its kind in the United States. A respected legislator, he chaired the Law Enforcement and Criminal Justice sub-committee and was a member of the House Ways and Means Committee. In 1975, he was a candidate in the first campaign to elect a mayor of Shelby County. When he lost reelection to the House in 1984, he became a pioneer in promoting trade relations between the United States and African countries. One of his dreams was a world trade center in Memphis that would include personnel from African countries. The concept of the pyramid as a Memphis landmark was his idea, because he wanted to build a pyramid-shaped structure to house the World Trade Center. When he brought the late President Siaka Stevens of Sierra Leone to Memphis in 1985 and former President Dawda Jawara of Gambia here in 1993, he became the only local politician to host two foreign heads of state.

In 1993, Withers traveled to Lisbon, Portugal, to receive the first license granted to an African American by the World Trade Centers Association. That same year, he headed a delegation to the second African/African-American Summit in Libreville, Gabon (Central Africa), where he met with heads of many African states. The month-long trade mission that began in London and ended in Johannesburg, South Africa was filmed by a news team from Black Entertainment Television (BET). Withers received the Southwest Jaycee's Outstanding Statesman Award in 1978, was named "One of America's New Outstanding Black Leaders" by *Ebony* magazine, and was listed in David Broder's *American Future Leaders*. Active in many professional organizations, he chaired the International Affairs Committee of the National Black Caucus of State Legislators. Teddy Withers died on May 17, 1996, at age forty-four. The following year, he was honored by Tennessee House Joint Resolution 36, filed by Representative Barbara Collins, who had worked with him as a co-convener of the African-American Peoples Convention Organization in 1991. The AAPO, which was chaired and co-founded by Withers, was instrumental in the election of Memphis's first Black mayor. In December 1997, the Memphis City Council designated a portion of Horn Lake Road as Dedrick "Teddy" Withers Parkway.

Withers, Ernest C. (1922–2007), businessman, photojournalist. Called one of the most important American photographers of the twentieth Century, he has documented the history and culture of Memphis and the Mid-South for over fifty years. He was born to Pearl and Earl Withers, a postal employee, on August 7, 1922, and grew up in the family home at 1062 N. Manassas with his two sisters and three brothers. Called "Duke" because of his prowess on Manassas High School's football team, he became hooked on photography as a student. A year after his 1941 graduation from Manassas, he married his high school sweetheart, Dorothy Mae Curry. When Withers was drafted into the U.S. Army in 1943, he was sent to photography school at Camp Sutton, joined the staff of the base newspaper, *Carry All*, and became a documentary photographer for the Corps of Engineers. After his discharge in 1946, he worked as a referee and umpire for the Bluff City Coaches and Officials Association. Two year later, he became one of Memphis's first Black policemen, when he and eight other African American men graduated from the Police Academy, but he was dismissed from the force three years later, after arresting a bootlegger who had police protection.

Ernest Withers opened his first photography studio in 1946 at 651–653 Firestone. He began working as a news photographer, covering stories for the *Memphis World* and *Tri-State Defender*, and as a commercial photographer, shooting funerals, weddings, and special events. Called Memphis's greatest living "natural" historian because he covered some of the most significant events of the civil rights movement, he photographed the trial of Emmett Till's murderers, Montgomery Bus Boycott, desegregation of Little Rock schools, Memphis Sanitation Strike, and the aftermath of Martin Luther King's assassination. Following Medgar Evers' funeral in 1963, he was beaten and arrested but explained, "I never was a militant, but all my life I had a protest mentality, just a different way of looking at things." He has photographed national icons such as Paul Robeson, Mahalia Jackson, and Thurgood Marshall, and his photographs have appeared in publications such as *Time*, *Newsweek*, *Ebony*, *Jet*, *New York Times*, and *The Washington Post*.

First Tennessee Bank presented an exhibit, "Ernest Withers: Reflections in History" in its Heritage Gallery in 1991, and, four years later, a traveling exhibit of 120 of his photographs, "Let Us March On: Selected Civil Rights Photographs, 1955–1968," was organized by the Massachusetts College of Art. The National Civil Rights Museum presented "Pilgrimage to Memphis," an exhibit of his photographs, to commemorate the 30th anniversary of the death of Dr. Martin Luther King, Jr., in April 1998. Among his many honors, he and his wife were invited by President Jimmy Carter to attend a black tie dinner at the White House in 1977, and he has awards from the Mallory Knights, Memphis Chapter of the National Business League, and the local chapter of the National Council of Christians and Jews. He was the 1968 National News Association's Best Photographer of the Year; in 1998, he was inducted into the Black Press Hall of Fame; and the building at 333 Beale Street was renamed the Ernest C. Withers, Sr. Building. The recipient of two honorary degrees, he was recognized as a 2000 Who's Who Among African Americans. A family man, Withers and his wife of sixty-five years raised their eight children—a daughter and seven sons—at their home at 480 W. Brooks Road and sent all of them to college. Soon after the city-wide celebration of his 85th birthday in Memphis's Hall of Mayors, he had a stroke and died on October 15, 2007. His life was commemorated by a New Orleans-style procession down Beale Street, led by the Rudy Williams Band.

Woodruff, Georgia Rodgers (1906–1981), singer. Called the "Memphis Songbird," she appeared with the Dixie Jubilee Singers in King Vidor's movie *Hallelulah!*, shot on location in Memphis in 1928. Born in Memphis on January 9, 1906, she was the daughter of Ruby Louvenia Washington Rodgers and Reverend Tyson Dock Rodgers. She grew up in North Memphis and attended Grant Elementary School, Kortrecht High School, and LeMoyne Normal School. In 1928, soon after her April 6, 1927, marriage to William Oscar Woodruff, opportunity knocked on her door. Eva Jessye, musical director of *Hallelujah!*, arrived in Memphis and asked a railroad porter if he knew a good singer, because one of the sopranos in the Dixie Jubilee Singers refused to come South. At the porter's suggestion, Jessye went to Central Baptist Church, where she met Woodruff, who was hired as lead soprano. *Hallelujah!* made movie history because it was the first all-Black musical and the first sound film to use an all-Black cast. The movie was filmed in Lenow Alley, a bayou near LeMoyne Gardens housing project, about two blocks from where Woodruff lived. Memphis extras were used in the street and bayou scenes, and two young boys—Milton Dickerson and Robert "Bones" Couch—appeared in the film after they were discovered dancing for pennies at the Peabody. When shooting was completed, Woodruff accompanied the cast to Hollywood, where the interior shots were filmed and the soundtrack was recorded. She completed *Hallelujah!*, which was released in 1929, and sang the background for another film, *Babes of*

Dixie, in 1930. After a brief return to Memphis, she joined Jessye and the Dixie Jubilee Singers in New York for a concert tour.

When her husband, who worked for the Illinois Central Railroad, refused to transfer to New York, Woodruff chose marriage and motherhood over fame and fortune. After a few months in New York, she returned to Memphis and gave birth to a daughter ten months later. She became close friends with the legendary Lucie Campbell, choir director at Central Baptist Church; Campbell would come in early on Sundays and hum a new composition that Woodruff would sing at the morning service. Although she appeared with gospel singers and composers such as Mahalia Jackson and William H. Brewster, Woodruff often wondered what her life would have been like if she had stayed in Hollywood or New York and accepted the offers of Eva Jessye, who became musical director of *Porgy and Bess*. Georgia Woodruff died on January 2, 1981, and her daughter, Rubye Woodruff Carter, donated the *Hallelujah!* collection of eighty-seven photographs and other mementoes, including letters and newspaper clippings, to the Memphis and Shelby County Room of the public library in June 1983.

Yates, Albert Carl "Tutt" (1941–), educator. Vice president of one institution and president of another, he became one of only a few Black presidents of a major research institution in the country. Born on September 29, 1941, he was one of the seven children of John Yates, a riverboat cook, and Sadie Yates, a housewife. His parents, who owned Yates Good Eats Café near the corner of Third and Beale, instilled in their children the value of education and hard work. Albert was a busboy at the Peabody, shined shoes and delivered *The Commercial Appeal* on his bicycle, and was as an orderly at John Gaston Hospital, working the 3-to-11 shift. He entered Booker T. Washington High School in 1955, but was expelled in the eleventh grade after failing most of his courses because he "wanted to fit in with the cool students." After graduating in 1959, he attended Fisk for a year, completed a stint in the Navy, and, in 1965, graduated magna cum laude from Memphis State University with a double major in chemistry and mathematics. He received a doctorate in theoretical chemical physics from Indiana University in 1968, accepted a fellowship at the University of Southern California, returned to Indiana University as a member of the chemistry faculty, and later taught for several years at the University of Cincinnati, where he was named vice president and dean of graduate studies and research in the mid-1970s. He also completed the Institute for Educational Management at the Harvard School of Business.

In 1981, Albert C. Yates became executive vice president and provost of Washington State University in Pullman, Washington. Faced with a tough economy and a tight budget, he had to downsize the university by reducing departments, eliminating programs, and weeding out nonproductive faculty. In 1990, he was named president of Colorado State University and Chancellor of the Colorado State System. Within ten years, he had increased annual private support from $8 to more than $40 million and led the university to enhanced national stature as one of the country's top 100 universities. Twenty-five years after his graduation, he gave the commencement address at Memphis State University in the Mid-South Coliseum. Dr. Yates returns often to his hometown to visit friends and family, including his sister, Lucy Yates Shaw, former CEO of The Med. In 1998, he attended his high school reunion and, a year later, returned to cheer on his Colorado State University Rams when they played Southern Mississippi in the Liberty Bowl. On his return to Memphis in 2003 for the AXA Liberty Bowl game, he was the guest of honor at a brunch and reunion of BTW graduates. Mayor W. W. Herenton, class of 1958, said: "He excelled at all the hard subjects. I was a guy who did well in school, but Albert Yates, Man, he was brilliant."

Dr. Yates has garnered numerous awards, including honorary doctoral degrees from the University of Denver, Colorado School of Mines, and Myongji University in Seoul, Korea; the 1992 Distinguished Alumni Award from the University of Memphis; and nomination to the Memphis City Schools Alumni Hall of Fame. In 2001, the state of Colorado celebrated Albert C. Yates Day and, a year later, Yates was given the "Citizen of the West" award. In honor of the educator who described mathematics as "the language of science," the Albert C. Yates Endowed Chair in Mathematics at Colorado State University was funded in 2003, through a $1.5 million gift from the Bohemian Foundation. On April 24, 2003, Albert C. Yates Hall, a chemistry-biosciences building, was dedicated "in tribute to his thirteen-year leadership of the university, enduring commitment to excellence in teaching and research, and appreciation for the importance of science in higher education."

OTHER NOTABLES

Alexander, John Marshall "Johnny Ace" (1930–1955). The talented young pianist had a program on WDIA, played with the bands of Joe Hill Lewis and B. B. King, made several recordings, and organized his own band before losing at Russian Roulette at age twenty-five.

Arnold, John Richard, Jr. (1912–1977). He established Arnold and Associates Advertising Agency, the second oldest Black advertising agency in the United States, which had accounts with Hart's Bakery and Southland Greyhound Park.

Bailey, Africa. Born a slave in Mississippi, Bailey was freed by the Union Army in 1863, and pressed into military service during the Civil War. He organized one of Memphis's first Baptist churches in a rudimentary shelter at the corner of Florida and Broadway Streets in South Memphis, but by 1867, the 242-member church was located in a substantial frame building.

Balfour, Thelma (1949–). For seven years, she was a marketing specialist for Memphis in May and has been a freelance writer for *Newsweek, USA Today, Essence*, and other publications. An astrologist for over twenty years, she is the author of *Black Sun Signs: An African-American Guide to the Zodiac* (1996) and *Black Love Signs: An Astrological Guide to Passion, Romance, and Relationships for African Americans* (1999).

Bolton, Julian (1949–). In 1982, he won election to District 2, Position 2 of the Shelby County Commission and was elected chairman pro tempore of the Commission in 1984. He resigned the post in 2006 to run for the 9th District U.S. House position vacated by Harold Ford, Jr. but lost in the primary.

Bowles, Charles R. (1860–1928). A skilled blacksmith, he worked for the James and Graham Wagon Company for more than thirty years. In the 1800s, he served with the Tennessee Rifles, an organization of Black men who patrolled Memphis streets during the yellow fever epidemics. In the 1920s, he was a court crier for the federal court in Memphis.

Branch, Ben F. (1927–). A musician and businessman, he was president of the country's first Black-owned soft drink company, Dr. Branch Products in Chicago. He was scheduled to perform with his orchestra at an SCLC function the evening that Dr. Martin L. King was assassinated.

Brooks, Henri E. (1949–). A state legislator since 1992, she has served as vice-chair of the House Government Operations Committee. One of the most visible legislators, she was elected chair of the Tennessee Black Caucus of the State Legislature in 1999. In the 2006 Democratic primary, she lost by thirty votes her bid for the State Senate District 29 seat vacated by John Ford.

Brown, Edgar Milton Lewis (1905–1949). A talented composer, arranger, and jazz musician, he played in Beale Street clubs, belonged to one of the first Memphis bands to record music, and traveled with the Rabbit Foot Minstrels Touring Show from 1941 to 1949.

Brown, Marjorie Lee (1914–1979). One of the first two Black women to earn a Ph.D. in mathematics from the University of Michigan, she received the first North Carolina Council of Teachers of Mathematics Award for "Excellence in Mathematics Education."

Burchett, A. Sidney J. (1862–1916). One of the city's early Black physicians, he was born in Mason, Tennessee, and moved to Memphis after graduation from Meharry Medical College in 1884. He opened an office on Main Street, where he built up a lucrative medical practice.

Burchett, Katie H. Known as Mme. Burchett, she received her training in St. Louis and Chicago. "The Pioneer of Beauty Shops" owned Burchett's Beauty Shop, one of the largest in the country, and Burchett's Beauty College and Laboratories at 201 Hernando Street, where she manufactured all of her beauty products.

Carter, Sandy Southern (1855–1922). One of the city's first Black attorneys, he served as assistant foreman of the folding room of the U.S. House of Representatives in Washington from 1882 to 1884. He was a self-educated man, who read law, completed a legal apprenticeship under two Memphis lawyers, passed the Tennessee bar exam, and opened a law office on North Main.

Cash, Henry (1907–1980). An educator and sports promoter, he served from 1963 to 1968 as principal of Hamilton High School. He was co-founder and president of the Tri-State Amateur Boxing Association, and had a boxing ring in the basement of his house. From the 1930s to early 1950s, he sponsored boxing matches in Church's Park and Auditorium on Beale Street.

Chism, Ray (1941–). He and his brothers founded a chain of grocery stores, with Ray serving as president. They built their first store, a 3,000-square-foot market in southwest Memphis in 1976, and, two years later, opened a 15,000-square-foot supermarket. In 1990, they had about $15 million in annual sales and more than 200 employees.

Chism, Sidney (1940–). The former president of Memphis Teamsters local 1196 and vice president of Teamsters Joint Council No. 87, he was chairman of the Shelby County Democratic Party and representative to the State Executive Committee of the Tennessee Democratic Party.

Clay, M. L. (1866–?). He became a feed and grain merchant, third vice president of the Solvent Savings Bank & Trust Company, and owner of a well-equipped barbershop, with fixtures such as individual wash stands and white enamel chairs, as well as a bathroom and large poolroom.

Cottrell, T. C. (?–1899). A graduate of Meharry Medical School, he moved to Memphis in 1884, where he opened a private practice. In 1889, he became secretary and dean of the short-lived Hannibal Medical College.

Crawford, Robert. He was one of twelve African Americans hired as firemen in 1955, and he was stationed at Fire Station #8 at Mississippi and Crump Boulevard. He was finally promoted to lieutenant in December 1969, and later became the first Black deputy director of the department.

Delk, Fannie Mitchell (1933–1989). A Memphis City Schools teacher and professor of English at LeMoyne-Owen College, she was a Ford Foundation Fellow and a consultant to The Writing Place. In 1980, she co-founded the Memphis Black Writers Workshop and co-edited *Homespun Images: An Anthology of Black Memphis Writers and Artists*.

Dinkins, Charles L. (1920–1996). He came to Memphis in 1959 as the second president of Owen College and, when it merged with LeMoyne College, he was named director of development. Between 1968 and 1994, he was pastor of First Baptist Church Lauderdale and, as urban affairs officer for National Bank of Commerce, he was involved in minority business development.

Dortch-Okara, Barbara A. (1949–). With degrees from Brandeis and Boston College Law School, she was associate general counsel of the Massachusetts Port Authority, assistant general counsel for the Massachusetts Bay Transportation Authority, attorney-advisor with the Office of the Regional Solicitor of the U.S. Department of the Interior, and assistant corporation counsel for Boston.

Duncan, Alice Faye (1967–). A school librarian and author of children's books, she conducts writing workshops for adults and teenagers and has written five books, including *Willie Jerome, Christmas Song, Honey Baby Sugar Child*, and the award-winning *National Civil Rights Museum Celebrates Everyday People*.

Ellison, H. C. (1871–?). One of the city's earliest Black contractors, he was born in Georgia and, in 1896, moved to Memphis, where he built many homes, schools, and churches, including Mt. Olive C.M.E. and Metropolitan Baptist Churches, and the Masonic Temple Building on Hernando, which became the headquarters of Universal Life Insurance Company and the local branch of the NAACP.

Elmore, Anthony C. "Amp" (1954–). A five-time world super heavyweight kickboxing champion, he wrote, directed, produced, and starred in the 1989 semiautobiographical film *Iron Thunder*, which traced the life of a kickboxing champion. He presently owns a carpet company, and he and his Ethiopian wife live in a 5,400-square-foot, all-African house in Orange Mound.

Exum, John Madison (1909–?). A leader in the Christian Methodist Episcopal church for more than 40 years, he was editor of the *Christian Index* and bishop of the First Episcopal District, covering Arkansas and Tennessee, before becoming C.M.E. bishop of Africa.

Flagg, Thomas (1930–). A pianist with degrees from Columbia University and the Juliard School, he has taught music for more than thirty-five years, headed a department at Howard University, and given piano concerts throughout the country.

Foote, William Henry (1876–1937). A graduate of LeMoyne Normal Institute, he became a teacher and a postal worker. After earning a law degree through correspondence courses, he became legal advisor to the Universal Life Insurance Company in 1927.

Ford, Fred (1930–1999). A blues/jazz/R&B fixture, this saxophonist helped shape the Memphis Sound, playing in the bands of Onzie Horne and Bill Harvey. He performed with B. B. King, Jerry Lee Lewis, Big Mama Thornton, and Honeymoon Garner for over five decades, and he produced the Vanilla album for Cybill Shepard and the come-back album for Phineas Newborn.

Ford, James W. (?–2001). A physician, minister, politician, and funeral director, he was elected to District 3, Position 3 of the Memphis City Council, had a private practice in ophthalmology, pastored Fellowship Baptist Church, and was director of N. J. Ford & Sons Funeral Home.

Ford, John Newton (1942–). A funeral director and insurance agent, he served on the Memphis City Council from 1971 to 1979, was elected to the State Senate in 1974, became Speaker pro tempore of the Tennessee General Assembly in 1986, and was elected General Sessions Court Clerk in 1992. In 2005, he was forced to resign from the Senate after being indicted for bribery following the Tennessee Waltz sting operation.

Forest, Earl Lacy (1927–2003). A singer and drummer, he was one of the legendary "Beale Streeters," which included Bobby Bland, Johnny Ace, Junior Parker, and Rosco Gordon. He also wrote songs, such as "Next Time You See Me" for Bland, Parker, Little Milton, and others.

Frazier, Deborah Glass (1950–). An actor, director, and playwright, she co-founded the Blues City Cultural Center with her husband, Levi Frazier. As program director of the BCCC, she created the Trolley Stop Creative Arts Camp for children; wrote *Knight Song*, based on the life and poetry of Etheridge Knight; and co-wrote and produced *Peace in the House*, a play on violence.

Gholson, James (1944–). With a bachelor's degree in music from Michigan State University and a master's and doctorate from Catholic University, he is a clarinet professor in the Music Department at the University of Memphis. For more than two decades, he has been the principal clarinetist with the Memphis Symphony Orchestra.

Gibson, Walter W. (1907–?). As professor of biology and chairman of the Division of Natural Sciences at LeMoyne-Owen College, he prepared hundreds of students for careers in medicine, research, and teaching. The Gibson-Orgill Science and Mathematics Center is named for him.

Gillis, Clarence (1882–1943). With his brothers Andrew and Cornelius, he opened a grocery store on Polk Street, another store on Kansas Street, as well as a furniture store and twenty-eight-room hotel on Beale Street.

Gladney, Alexander (1914–1988). A noted civic leader in the Douglass Community, he was a founder of the Shelby County Democratic Club and president of the North Memphis Voters' League. He retired after twenty-seven years with International Harvester.

Golden, Joan Elizabeth Williams (1937–2007). Known as the "Golden Girl," she became a radio personality in 1963, and was the popular host of a morning gospel show on radio station WLOK. She was also a talented pianist who served as an accompanist for the Gospel Messengers.

Graves, William (1936–). Since 1982, he has served as presiding bishop of the First Episcopal District of the C.M.E. Church, which includes more than 100 churches in Tennessee and Arkansas. He is also on the board of trustees of the Memphis Theological Seminary and chairman of the board of John Madison Exum Towers.

Gray, L. LaSimba (1946–). The former pastor of St. Mark Missionary Baptist Church, he has served as senior pastor of New Sardis

Baptist Church since 1993. One of the city's activist clergymen, he is also president of the Memphis chapter of the Rainbow PUSH coalition.

Green, Herman (1930–). Head of Jazz Studies at LeMoyne-Owen College, the saxophonist played in Lionel Hampton's band and has performed with John Coltrane and Miles Davis, as well as Memphis legends Rufus Thomas and Isaac Hayes. Among his CDs are *Who IS Herman Green?* and *Inspiration: Family and Friends.*

Green, Reuben H. (1934–2008). A graduate of Bishop College, Oberlin Graduate School of Theology, Iliff School of Theology, and Vanderbilt University Divinity School, he has pastored Central Baptist Church since 1968, and was professor of philosophy and religion at Owen College and LeMoyne-Owen College until his retirement in 2005.

Hairston, Jacob Christopher (1858–1946). A Virginia native, he opened a medical practice in Memphis in 1888, after graduating from Meharry Medical College. He was a professor of diseases of women and abdominal surgery at the University of West Tennessee and, at the turn of the century, he opened the first infirmary for Blacks in his home on Orleans Street.

Hardin, George E. (1934–). A photographer and journalist, he was executive editor of the *Tri-State Defender*, copy editor for *The Commercial Appeal*, staff writer for *Mid-South Magazine*, acting manager of the *Norfolk Journal & Guide*, public information officer at N. C. Central University at Durham, and public relations officer at MHA.

Hayes, Thomas H., Jr. (1902–1982). Owner and president of T. H. Hayes & Sons Funeral Homes, founded by his father, he was co-owner of the Queen Ann Hotel, and co-founder and vice president of Union Protective Life Insurance Company. He also owned and operated the Birmingham Black Barons baseball club from 1939 to 1951.

Hayes, James Ashton (1885–1961). In 1923, he moved to Memphis, where he became principal of Douglass School, football coach at Booker T. Washington High School, and principal of Manassas

High School for twenty-three years. Under his leadership, Manassas became the first accredited high school for Blacks in Shelby County and part of the Memphis City School system in 1930.

Haynes, William Joseph, Jr. (1949–). The first Black U.S. District Judge for the Middle District of Tennessee, he worked in the Tennessee State Attorney General's office and was deputy attorney general for Antitrust and Consumer Protection. He later became special deputy for Litigation and was appointed magistrate judge of the Middle District.

Hobson, Louis B. (?–1990). Known as a "master educator," he taught at Howe-Roger Williams College and Greenwood School. He served as principal of Lester Grade School from 1949 to 1953 and of Manassas High School from 1953 until his retirement in 1974.

Hooks, Michael. A real estate appraiser and president of Michael A. Hooks & Associates, he was elected to District 4 of the City Council in 1979, and was chosen chairman of the Council in 1987. He became the first Black elected Shelby County Property Assessor, but his career ended when he pled guilty to a charge of extortion and received a sentence of twenty-six months.

Houston, Earline (1945–1986). The first Black woman to graduate from the University of Tennessee College of Medicine, she became superintendent of the Philadelphia State Hospital at Byberry and medical director of the Philadelphia Child Guidance Clinic.

Hulbert, James Alexander (1906–?). In 1951, he was appointed the first Black publicist at the United States Information Service Center in Paris and, five years later, he was transferred to the ISC office in East Pakistan (now Bangladesh). He also founded a library, taught prospective librarians at Dacca University Center, and published *An Introduction to Library Service*.

Hulburt, Maurice, Jr. "Hot Rod" (1916–1996). One of four original disc jockeys on WDIA's "Good Will Review," he created "The Deejay from Outer Space." In 1951, the "bald-headed prince" left

WDIA for Baltimore's WITH, where he launched a program called "Commander Hot Rod and the Rocket Ship." Ray Charles wrote the song "Hot Rod" in his honor.

Irving, Ernest Walker (1869–1944). After graduating from Meharry Medical College in 1897, he opened a practice in Memphis, where he became an expert in treating victims of industrial accidents and represented the Continental Casualty Company in reviewing damage suits.

Jacocks, Kendrick (1971–). A graduate of the University of Illinois at Urbana-Champaign where he studied with singer Mignon Dunn, he is a noted tenor who has performed in Canada, Spain, Mexico, and Germany; given concerts at The Beethoven Club; made radio appearances; and sung with Opera Memphis and the Illinois Opera Theater.

Johnson, Jerry C. (1919–). The men's basketball coach at LeMoyne-Owen College from 1959 to 2005, he had the most victories of any active NCAA Division II coach in forty-five seasons, and was the coach with the second most victories in that division's history. He retired with five SIAC Championships, the 1975 National Division III Championship, and four titles in the former Volunteer State Athletic Conference.

Johnson, Lawrence E. (1941–). Owner and president of the largest Black real estate company in Memphis, he has almost forty-five years' experience in the business. After forming Johnson & Bowser Real Estate Company in 1976, he founded Lawrence Johnson Realtors of Memphis, in 1985. He was president of the National Association of Real Estate Brokers, a Black organization.

Jones, Andrewnetta Hawkins (1934–1998). With a degree in medical technology, she served as acting chief medical technologist at E. H. Crump Hospital. She was the first administrator of Shelby County's Equal Opportunity Compliance office, helped train Community Action Agency staffs in eight Southern states, and was branch executive at the Sarah Brown YWCA.

Jones, John Eddie (1943–). A medical photographer for the University of Tennessee Center for the Health Sciences for twenty-six years, he is on the faculty of Southwest Tennessee Community College. He made documentary films on blues artists Monroe Jackson and James "Son" Thomas and produced a multimedia exhibit, *Dewitt Jordan: A Delta Genius*.

Jones, Rufus E. (1940–). With a degree in business administration from Michigan State University, he became president of GRID, Inc., Jones Big Star Supermarket in 1968. In 1981, Jones was elected to the Tennessee General Assembly.

Jones, Robert Townsend, Jr. (1948–). A documentary photographer, he studied art at Booker T. Washington High School, graphic art at Shelby State Community College, and photography at the Memphis Academy of Arts. His photographic collections, such as *Southern Rhythms*, capture the strength and dignity of Blacks in the Mississippi Delta and in his North Memphis neighborhood.

Jones-Bolden, Elizabeth (1890–2006). In August 2006, at age 116, she became the oldest person in the world. Born to former slaves, Amber and Annie Jones, this Memphian left six generations, including two surviving children, 40 grandchildren, 75 great-grandchildren, 150 great-great-grandchildren, 230 great-great-great-grandchildren, and 75 great-great-great-great-grandchildren.

Kirby, Edward "Prince Gabe" (1930–1987). A guitarist and saxophonist, he organized a band, "Prince Gabe and the Millionaires," which toured Europe in the 1980s. He released an album, *Memories of Beale Street*, and published a book, *From Africa to Beale Street*.

Kittrell, A. N. (1875–1952). An ordained minister, businessman, and physician, he moved to Memphis in 1905, and opened a medical office on Beale Street, between Second and Third. He helped organize the Bluff City Medical Society, was a member of the National Medical Association and Lincoln League, and was one of the first directors of the Tri-State Bank of Memphis.

Kneeland, Francis M. "Fanny" (?–1936). An 1898 honors graduate of Meharry Medical College, she was one of the city's first Black women physicians as well as a faculty member and director of nursing at the University of West Tennessee Medical School. She also served as principal of Melrose School at the turn of the century and worked as a truant officer in the 1930s.

Laws, Erma Lee (1930–). Called "a legend in her own time," she taught at Georgia Avenue and Westwood Elementary Schools, testified for the NAACP Defense Fund during the civil rights movement, and served as press coordinator during the Sanitation Strike. She began as a columnist for the *Tri-State Defender* in 1951, and was appointed senior staff member in 1976. She was active in organizations such as the JUGS and, in 1956, founded the Coettes, a girls' social club.

Locke, Walter Alonzo (1874–1947). Born in Tennessee, he was raised in Illinois, where he went into the hotel business at age thirteen. He moved to Memphis in 1906, and worked at the Gayoso Hotel for nineteen years before becoming headwaiter at the Peabody Hotel. He served many celebrities, including Sarah Bernhardt, Theodore Roosevelt, and Eleanor Roosevelt. Alonzo Locke Elementary School is named for him.

Lofton, Fred C. (1928–). The former chaplain and professor of religion at Owen College was pastor of Metropolitan Baptist Church from 1972 to 2001, and president of the Progressive National Baptist Convention, which honored him with the "2006 Preacher of the Year Award." He has written, co-authored, or edited several books, including *Help Me Somebody*, *A Crying Shepherd* and *The Almighty Troubleth Me*, a collection of sermons.

Love, Roy (1906?–1976). The pastor of Mt. Nebo Baptist Church, he ran for the Memphis School Board in 1955, with the support of the Ministers and Citizens League. In 1959, he ran again for the school board on the Volunteer Ticket, but he lost his bid for public office both times. When the civil rights movement began in the 1950s, he supported the struggle.

Martin, J. C. (1865–?). A prominent minister, he became pastor of Collins Chapel C.M.E. Church in 1901, as well as a delegate to the Ecumenical Conference in London, and, four years later, he was appointed Presiding Elder of the South Memphis District. A prosperous businessman and land owner, he was elected president of the Solvent Savings Bank & Trust Company in 1911.

Miller, Clifford Dewitt (1912–1997). His first business was Clifford's Barbecue Barn in North Memphis. Later, he operated Bluff City Cab Company, owned three night clubs and the Orleans Hotel, and was part owner of Busy Bee and United Cab Companies. After moving to Las Vegas in 1979, he worked in public relations for Las Vegas Downs, a dog track.

Miller, Gene "Bowlegs" (1934–1988). He was a trumpet player and record producer who began his career on Beale Street and was one of the original "Memphis Horns." The southern record promoter for Island and CBS Records, he discovered Ann Peebles, launched Peabo Bryson's career, and performed with such musical legends as Aretha Franklin, Otis Redding, and B. B. King.

Mitchell, Andrew "Sunbeam" (1906–1989). For twenty years, he owned and operated Club Paradise at 645 East Georgia, where he booked soul and R&B legends such as Count Basie, Nancy Wilson, and Ike and Tina Turner. An entertainment entrepreneur, the "Godfather of Beale Street" also owned and operated Club Handy, Club Ebony, and Earnestine's Grill, which helped put Beale Street and Memphis music on the map.

Moody, Naomi (1949–). A blues and jazz singer who has performed on radio and television, she played the title role of Bess in the Houston Grand Opera's 1977 production of *Porgy and Bess*, and she headlined the *Spectacle American* at the Olympia Theater in Paris. She also sang at the Zurich Opera Festival in Switzerland and at La

Scala Opera House in Milan, and for two years she performed in *Sophisticated Ladies* on Broadway.

Moore, Luke C. (1924–1994). He was assistant U.S. attorney and, later, chief of the Superior Court Division of the U.S. Attorney's Office, before President Kennedy appointed him U.S. Marshal for the District in 1962. The first African American to hold that office since Frederick Douglass's appointment in 1827, he served on the Superior Court for more than twenty-two years.

Moore, Robert (1886–1957). A graduate of LeMoyne College and Meharry Medical School, he opened a medical office on Mississippi Boulevard, where he practiced medicine for more than forty years.

Moten, Wendy (1965–). An R&B singer, she was born in Memphis, where she attended Overton High School and the University of Memphis. After performing at a New York benefit concert, she signed with EMI/ERG, released a debut album, *Wendy Moten*, and backed Michael Bolton on tour. Among her other albums are *Time for Change* and *Life's What You Make It*.

Nelson, Ford. One of WDIA's pioneering Black broadcasters, he started with a fifteen-minute R&B show called "Let's Have Some Fun" and moved to a quarter-hour gospel show before joining the radio station full time in 1950. An early pianist for B. B. King, he also worked as a reporter for the *Tri-State Defender* and as an announcer for the Memphis Public Library's radio station WYPL.

Netters, James L. (1927–). The pastor of Mount Vernon Baptist Church since 1956, he was a city school teacher, an administrative assistant to Mayor Wyeth Chandler, and one of the first Blacks elected to the City Council, District 6. A civic leader who was active in the civil rights movement, he was one of two men arrested for sitting in the front of a segregated bus.

Nightingale, Taylor. In the 1880s, he became pastor of the First (Beale Street Baptist) Church at 169 Beale. Active in Republican politics, he was defeated in his campaign for the school board in the city elections on January 7, 1886, and intended to contest the election on the grounds of fraud. A journalist, he also co-founded the *Free Speech and Headlight*, with which Ida B. Wells was later affiliated.

Norment, Lynn (1952–). As a journalist for *The Commercial Appeal*, she won several awards for her investigative reporting. In 1977, she became assistant editor of *Ebony*, the largest Black-owned publication in the world, and she presently serves as senior editor and member of the editorial board. She has written feature stories on Anita Baker, Bill Cosby, Spike Lee, and Jesse Jackson, as well as articles on religion, relationships, and social issues.

Norris, Isham F. A Republican, he was one of the first Blacks to serve in the Tennessee General Assembly, representing Shelby County for two terms: 1881 to 1883 and 1891 to 1893. He was a prosperous entrepreneur, who operated a coal and wood business in 1885 and a grocery store from 1885 to 1891. After a dispute with some Whites over his grocery store, he and his family were threatened and had to leave Memphis suddenly at night.

Palmer, Vicki Gilmore (1953–). A former loan officer at First Tennessee Bank and manager of corporate finance at Federal Express, she became fund manager at Coca-Cola in Atlanta, before joining Coca-Cola Enterprises, where she serves as corporate vice president and treasurer.

Parker, Johnice (1952–). A specialist in visual and graphic arts, she was assistant professor of art at LeMoyne-Owen College and assistant director of the Memphis Black Arts Alliance. Now living in Dallas, she is a freelance artist whose paintings have appeared on television and movie sets, including *The Cosby Show* and *Waiting to Exhale*. She has received many awards, and her work has been exhibited in Denver, Memphis, Washington, and other cities.

Patterson, James Oglethorpe, Jr. Now a bishop in the Church of God in Christ and pastor of Pentecostal Temple Institutional of God in Christ, he was one of the first Blacks elected to the Memphis City

Council and was in the State Senate from 1967 to 1976. While serving as council chairman, he became acting mayor of Memphis, after a special election in 1982, becoming the first Black mayor of the city.

Pearson, Tony "Jet Man" (1957–). Between 1977 and 1994, this professional body builder won or placed high in more than sixty competitions, gaining titles such as Mr. World, Mr. America, Mr. Universe, and World Pro Champ. He has appeared on *Good Morning America*, *NBC Sportsworld*, and *Soul Train*, and he was featured in *Sports Illustrated*, *Iron Man*, and *Muscle and Fitness* magazines. An advocate of health and fitness, he is a personal trainer and nutrition consultant.

Peebles, Ann (1947–). A legendary Memphis singer, she set the stage on fire with her hit "I Can't Stand the Rain" at a hometown performance in the 1990s, when she and her band performed the title cut from her CD *Fill This World With Love*. According to one critic, "Peebles has got a 90s thing going that's a must see."

Pinkston, Greene Fort (1876–1963). He came from a land-owning family near Forest, Mississippi and he eventually acquired over 300 acres of farm land in Cordova. A graduate of Meharry Medical School, he moved to Memphis in 1895, and practiced medicine for more than fifty-five years in Memphis and Cordova. Several of his nine children and twenty-six grandchildren became dentists, physicians, lawyers, and educators.

Reed, Edward W. The first African American board-certified general surgeon in Memphis and the first to serve on the faculty of the UT-Memphis Department of Surgery, he was board chairman of The Regional Medical Center and served on the boards of Meharry Medical College and St. Jude Children's Research Hospital. Before his retirement from private practice, he was active at eight hospitals in the Memphis area.

Richardson, Scovel (1912–1982). A distinguished jurist, he served as senior attorney in the Office of Price Administration, dean of the

Lincoln University Law School, judge of the United States Court of International Trade, presiding judge of the Third Division of the Customs Court, and he was the first Black appointed to the United States Board of Parole in Washington.

Roulhac, Christopher Maxwell (1885–1965). A practicing physician in Memphis for fifty-five years, he was on the faculty of the University of West Tennessee Medical College, as well as school physician for athletic programs at Father Bertrand High School, Booker T. Washington High School, and LeMoyne College. He was president of the Bluff City Medical Association and on the boards of Owen College, Abe Scharff YMCA, and Union Protective Life Insurance Co.

Salley, Vivian H. H. A former executive director of the Sarah Brown Branch of the YWCA, she served as president of the Tennessee Baptist Missionary and Educational Women's Convention and state director of Christian Education for the Tennessee B. M. and E. Convention.

Sanford, J. W., Jr. (1862–?). One of the city's earliest Black contractors, he constructed buildings throughout the tri-state area and became one of the largest property owners in Memphis, with 33 pieces of property in the city and 300 acres on President's Island; 170 acres of farm land in Covington; 120 acres in Jericho, Arkansas; and 540 acres in Terrell, Arkansas—for a total of 1,130 acres of the best farm land in the South, valued in 1911 at $100,000.

Savage, Fred (1835–1910). The first Black elected to the city school board in the 1880s, he was defeated in his campaign for reelection to the board (School Visitors) in the city election on January 7, 1886. He was a shoemaker with Zellner and Company.

Scott, J. Jay (1860–?). A former teacher, college chaplain, and pastor of a Congregational church, he was the only African American officer in the Third Alabama Regiment of Spanish-American Volunteers. After moving to Memphis, he and his brother, H. Wayman Wilkerson, established the Scott, Wilkerson & Scott Undertaking Company. In 1910, he was elected president of the Fraternal Savings Bank & Trust Company.

Searcy, Thomas Jefferson (1852–1912). President of the Baptist State Convention of Tennessee and vice president of the National Baptist Convention, the former slave served as pastor of Metropolitan Baptist Church for many years. He was secretary of Mt. Carmel Cemetery Company and owned property in Memphis as well as 100 acres of land on President's Island.

Sengstacke, Whittier Alexander (1916–1996). A member of the National Newspaper Publishers Association, he came to Memphis in 1959 as publisher of the *Tri-State Defender*, a position that he held until 1974. His uncle founded the *Chicago Defender* in 1905, and Sengstacke Enterprises eventually owned newspapers in Chicago, Detroit, Pittsburgh, and Memphis.

Sexton, Katie Harris (1910–1970). One of the most active leaders in the Klondike community, she helped found the Kennedy Democratic Organization and she belonged to more than twenty organizations, including the Klondike Civic Club, Memphis and Shelby County Council of Civic Clubs, Shelby County Democratic Club, and Memphis Branch of the NAACP. In the late 1960s, the Katie Sexton Community Center at 1335 Brown Street was established in her honor.

Shelby, Charles H. (1872–1958). Although he had to work his way through college, he graduated with honors from Meharry Medical College in 1901, after which he returned to Memphis to practice medicine. Active in civic and social affairs, he served on the executive committee of the Memphis Branch of the NAACP.

Smith, Carl Williams. An originator of the "Memphis Sound," he produced and wrote hits such as "Rescue Me," "(Your Love Keeps Lifting Me) Higher and Higher," "We the People," "I Want to Get Funky," and "We're Gonna Make It" for Stax Records.

Smith, Harold E., Jr. (?–1993). During World War II, he was one of the Tuskegee Airmen, a group of Black pilots who were trained to accompany fighter aircraft. A member of the 477th Bomber Group, he attained the rank of captain and served as co-pilot of "Chappie" James, a four-star general. After the war, he moved to California and became principal of Oxnard High School.

Steinberg, Luther (1930–1999). He organized the Luther Steinberg Orchestra, the first Black band to appear on Memphis television in 1952. The group included three of his brothers, as well as Phineas Newborn, Herman Green, Fred Ford, and others. Although known primarily as a trumpeter, the talented musician also played the piano, composed music, and arranged scores for musicians such as Bobby "Blue" Bland and B. B. King.

Steven, Callie L. (1926–). A former principal of Melrose Elementary and Florida Elementary Schools, she served as assistant superintendent for curriculum and instruction, as well as district superintendent, North Area, District I, in the Memphis City Schools.

Stewart-Watson, Carlota (1900–). With an M.A. degree from the University of Michigan, she was the first certified school counselor in the Memphis City School System, retiring as director of guidance at Booker T. Washington High School in 1972, after fifty-four years of service.

Stotts, Carl Wesley (1933–1997). One of the first Blacks hired by the Memphis Fire Department in 1955, he served as a fireman for forty years. He filed a class-action suit that led to a 1980 consent decree that forced the fire department to promote more Black firemen. While fighting a fire in 1973, he almost died in a freak explosion and eventually died of work-related disabilities.

Strong, Harry L. (1921–2000). He worked at the Veterans Administration Medical Center for forty-two years. In 1951, he organized a male choral group at the Mallory Air Force Depot, which led to the formation of the Mallory Knights Charitable Organization, Inc.

Through the efforts of the Knights, a monument to Martin Luther King was erected on Mid-America Mall and a park was renamed Martin Luther King, Jr. Riverside Park.

Terrell, Cleveland Augustus (1866–1943). After graduating from Meharry Medical College, he moved to Memphis and, with his nephew, Dr. L. G. Patterson, opened the Terrell-Patterson Infirmary at 159 Beale. Later, the two physicians and Dr. Augustus A. White opened a hospital at 698 Williams St., which became the Jane Terrell Memorial Hospital, with Dr. Terrell as director. The hospital became the major source of health care for African Americans in Memphis.

Thomas, Marvell (1941–). A musician, arranger, composer, and music producer, he has led bands, conducted music business seminars, appeared in movies, organized the annual Sweet Soul Music Festival in Italy, and founded a publishing company and a production company, which offers technical support to musicians. With his wife, he also formed the Rufus Thomas Scholarship Fund to assist talented youngsters with limited means to prepare for careers in the music industry.

Venson, Ransom Q. (1895–1970). One of the city's early dentists, he served as president of the National Dental Association. A lieutenant in World War I, he helped found American Legion Post # 27, was a delegate to the first American Legion Convention, and was the first Black to represent Tennessee at the National Legion Convention in 1931. With his wife Ethel, he co-founded the Cotton Makers' Jubilee.

Vinson, Mose (1917–2002). One of the last practitioners of barrel house blues piano, he released his first CD, *Mose Vinson: Piano Man*, in 1997, and he had a weekly gig at the Center for Southern Folklore on Beale Street. He once worked as a clean-up man and part-time pianist at Sun Studios, where Sam Phillips recorded him on the piano in 1954.

Waller, Eugene (1924–1995). Known as the "Prince of Peace," he was pastor of Cummings Street Baptist Church for many years, and he also pastored Mt. Zion, New Zion, Pleasant Grove, and Early Grove Baptist Churches. During his fifty-year ministry, he lectured at the Memphis Theological Seminary, Vanderbilt Divinity School, and Tennessee Baptist Congress.

Weathers, Ann Dilworth Lawrence (1922–1988). An educator for forty-one years, she taught at Florida Street, Kansas Street, Macon, and Rozelle Schools. She was well known for her selfless service on behalf of the NAACP, LeMoyne-Owen College, United Negro College Fund, and Mississippi Boulevard Christian Church, which named a scholarship in her honor. She received many awards, including an honorary doctorate from the Tennessee School of Religion.

Wells, Cornell L. (1914–1993). The first African American assistant superintendent for Shelby County, he was a pioneer in North Shelby County education for almost 47 years, serving as a teacher, administrator, and assistant superintendent of special services. He graduated from LeMoyne College and received a master's degree from Tennessee A&I State University.

Westbrooks, Logan H. A former record producer, who served as Midwest regional promoter for Mercury Records and director of special markets for CBS Records, he co-founded Soul Train Records; launched his own company, Source Records; and became vice president and general manager of *Black Radio Exclusive*. The author of *The Anatomy of a Record Company*, he was a million-dollar real estate entrepreneur before becoming an elder in the Church of God in Christ.

Whalum, Hugh David (1890–1947). One of Universal Life Insurance Company's first district managers, he co-founded Union Protective Life Assurance Company, which had more than $500,000 in assets at the time of his death.

Whalum, Kenneth Twigg (1934–2007). The former director of personnel for the Memphis Post Office and director of employee relations for the Post Office's Southern Region, he served as a city councilman from 1988 to 1996 and as pastor of Olivet Baptist Church from 1969 to 1999. A Memphis city street, Rev. Kenneth T. Whalum Boulevard, was named after him, and in 2007, a post office on South Third St. was renamed "The Kenneth T. Whalum Sr. Post Office Building."

Wharton, Ruby R. (1943–). The first African American woman to practice law in Memphis since the nineteenth century, she is a principal with The Wharton Firm, which she co-founded in 1980 with her husband, A C Wharton. She serves on the board of commissioners of the Memphis-Shelby County Airport Authority and is on the board of directors of the Memphis Symphony.

Wigley, Mattie (1919–1996). The "Queen of Gospel" was a contralto who was known for her dynamic singing style. She was president of the Music Department of Headquarters Jurisdiction, national first vice president of the Music Department, and president of the Deborah Mason Patterson Memorial Choir. A licensed missionary, Madame Wigley was a member of the trustee board of Pentecostal Temple Institutional Church of God in Christ.

Williams, A. C. He taught at Manassas High School in the late 1940s and early '50s and worked part-time as a disc jockey and in community relations at WDIA Radio Station, where he organized the Teen Town Singers with Katherine Rivers. Among the singers were Carla Thomas, Marvel Thomas, and Spencer Wiggins.

Williams, A. McEwen (1894–1991). A minister and educator, he did graduate work at Union Theological Seminary and Columbia University. After several years as a minister in Canada, he became dean of Rogers Williams College and of Howe Institute, as well as president of Henderson Business College from 1940 to 1960. For fifty-eight years, he served as pastor of St. John Baptist Church.

Williams, R. Earl (1920–1955). After learning photography in the Navy, he opened a studio in Memphis in the mid-1940s. His clients included the *Memphis World*, *Tri-State Defender* and *Memphis*

Press-Scimitar newspapers, as well as the Cotton Makers' Jubilee and the Church of God in Christ.

Willis, Archie Walter. He began his career in insurance as an agent for Mississippi Life, before becoming a special ordinary agent for North Carolina Mutual Life. In 1923, he joined Universal Life Insurance Company, and was eventually elected first vice president of Universal.

Wilson, Ruby. Known as the Queen of Beale Street, this Memphis blues legend has recorded over ten albums and has performed with singers such as B. B. King, Isaac Hayes, Ray Charles, and Willie Nelson. She has also had cameo roles in several films, including *Cookie's Fortune*, *The Chamber*, *The Client*, and *Black Snake Moan*.

Woodson, Benjamin Franklin (1844–1912). He was an attorney, contractor, and customs surveyor whose grandfather was reportedly the son of Sally Hemings, a slave, and Thomas Jefferson. He attended Wilberforce College, studied law, and was admitted to the Ohio bar in 1879. Two years later, he moved to Memphis, where he became deputy surveyor of customs in 1886, but he later abandoned law to become a contractor and cabinet maker.

Appendix A

Chronology by Birth Dates

1796	Harris, Joseph "FreeJoe"
1800?	Winchester, Marie Louise Amarante Loiselle "Mary"
1802	Henderson, Morris
1814	Clouston, Joseph
1818?	Shaw, Edward
1839	Church, Robert Reed
1847	Cassels, Thomas Frank
1850	Settle, Josiah T.
1852	Hooks, Julia Ann Britton
	Washington, David Whittier
1856	Broughton, Virginia E. Walker
1858	Booth, Benjamin Franklin
1862	Mason, Charles Harrison
	Wells, Ida Bell
1863	Love, John Robinson
	Terrell, Mary Church
1864	Patton, Georgia E. L.
1867	Fuller, Thomas Oscar
	Hamilton, Green Polonius
1868	Hayes, Thomas Henry
1871	Brown, Lawyer Edward
	Byas, Andrew D.
	Lynk, Miles Vandahurst
1872	Griggs, Sutton Elbert
1873	Handy, William Christopher
	Thornton, Matthew
1875	Griggs, Emma J. Williams
	Wilburn, Emma Currin Barbee

1878	Stuart, Merah Stevens
1879	Martin, William S.
1880	Walker, Joseph Edison
1883	Cannon, Gus
	Lewis, Robert Stevenson
1884	Pace, Harry Herbert
1885	Campbell, Lucie Eddie
	Church, Robert Reed, Jr.
	Taylor, Cora Price
1886	Lee, Tom C.
	Owen, Samuel Augustus
	Roddy, Bert Maynard
1888	Henderson, George W.
	Hunt, Blair Theodore, Jr.
	Hutchins, Fred Lew
1889	Cook, Vivian E. Johnson
1890	McCleave, Florence Cole Talbert
	Olive, Benjamin Garfield, Jr.
1893	Lewis, Walter "Furry"
1894	Lee, George Washington
1895	Hunter, Alberta
1896	Hulbert, Maurice "Fess"
1897	Brewster, William Herbert
	Douglas, Lizzie "Memphis Minnie"
	Falls, Montee Therese Norman
1898	Armstrong, Lillian Hardin "Lil"
	Bisson, Wheelock Alexander
	Branch, Addison A.
1900	Taylor, Lonzie Odie
1902	Bailey, William C. "Buster"
	Bodden, Ira Swithin
	Lunceford, James Melvin "Jimmie"
	Whittaker, John W. II
1903	Bunton, Henry C.
1904	Price, Hollis Freeman
1905	Latting, Augustus Arvis "Doc"

Chronology by Birth Dates

1906	Cochran, Flora Cole
	Swingler, Lewis Ossie
	Wade, Theo
	Woodruff, Georgia Rodgers
1907	Stuckey, Elma Johnson
	Williams, Nathaniel Dowde "Nat D."
1908	Cleaves, Irene Curtis
1909	Venson, Ethyl Belle Horton
	Walker, Antonio Maceo
	Wilson, Lucious Alexander
1912	Carter, Marlin "Pee Wee"
	Patterson, James Oglethorpe
1914	Church, Sara Roberta
	Ford, Newton Jackson
	Kateo, Loretta Hicks
	Mathis, Verdell L. "Lefty"
1915	Chatman, Peter II "Memphis Slim"
	Holloway, George
1916	Calloway, DeVerne Lee
	Crenshaw, Cornelia
1917	Thomas, Rufus
	Williamson, Juanita V.
1918	Boyd, Robert Richard "Bob"
	Clark, LeRoy D.
	Sawyer, Chew Cornelium
1919	Turner, Jesse Hosea
1920	Bankhead, Daniel Robert "Dan"
	Lockard, Hosea T.
	Scott, Joe Burt
	Smith, Vasco Albert, Jr.
	Toles, Elizabeth
1921	Brandon, Otha
	Weathers, Luke J.
1922	Hyter, James A.
	Smith, Otis Milton
	Withers, Ernest C.

1923	Horne, Onzie O.
	King, Albert
1924	Jones, Thomas Oliver
	Lincoln, Charles Eric
	Morris, Alma
1925	Evers, O. Z.
	Hassell, Frances Massey
	Hooks, Benjamin Lawson
	King, Riley "B. B."
	Wilbun, Shepperson A. "Shep"
	Willis, Archie Walter, Jr.
1927	Criss, William "Sonny"
1928	Lawson, James Morris, Jr. "Jim"
	Mitchell, Willie
1929	Brawner, Clara Arena
	Horton, Odell
	Little, Vera
	Smith, Maxine Atkins
1930	Bland, Bobby "Blue"
	Champion, Charles
	Jones, Velma Lois
	Steinberg, Martha Jean
1931	Whalum, Wendell Phillips
1932	Bridges, Josephine Valeria Johnson "Jo"
	Newborn, Phineas, Jr.
	Stuckey, Ples Sterling
	Williams, Eddie N.
1933	Cleaborn, Edward O.
	Jordan, Dewitt W., Jr.
1934	Blackmore, Amos (a.k.a. Junior Wells)
	Crawford, Bennie Ross "Hank"
	Davis, Fred
	Hayden, Frank, Jr.
	Kyles, Samuel Billy
	Light, Joe Lewis

Chronology by Birth Dates

1936	Barry, Marion Shepilov, Jr.
	Gilliam, Dorothy Butler
	Hoskins, Ollie Braxton "Nightingale"
	Maburn, Harold
	White, Augustus A. III
1937	Blackmon, Joyce McAnulty
	Brewer, Harper
	Freeman, Morgan
	Gayles, Gloria Jean Wade
	Muhammad, Talib-Karim
1938	Alston, Bettye J. Harris
	Green, Mildred Denby
	Hedgeman, Lulah McEwen
	Johnican, Minerva
1939	Brown, George Henry, Jr.
	Cantrell, Anderson
	Crawford, Alvin Howell
	Lyke, James Patterson
	Patterson, Gilbert E.
	Shaw, Lily Patricia Walker "Pat"
1940	Bailey, Walter Lee, Jr.
	Herenton, Willie Wilbert.
	Hunt, George
1941	Bailey, D'Army
	Banks, Frank
	Hayes, Isaac
	McCray, Shirley Yvonne
	Porter, David
	White, Maurice
	Yates, Albert Carl "Tutt"
1942	Franklin, Aretha
	Hampton, Luther
	Spillers, Hortense J.
	Thomas, Carla
1943	Gilliam, Herman Arthur, Jr. "Art"

1944	Nelson-West, Bennetta "Bennie"
	Turner, Elaine Lee
1945	Wharton, A C, Jr.
	Cobb, Joyce
	Coleman, Veronica Freeman
	DeBerry, Lois M.
	Ford, Harold Eugene
1946	Blackfoot, J. "Foot"
	Green, Leorns "Al"
	Guy-Sheftall, Beverly
1947	Brown, Joe
	Shaw, Lucy Mae Yates
1948	Buckley, Harriet Ann
	Dotson, Phillip Randolph "Phil"
	Jones, Fred, Jr.
1949	Harvey, Peggy Ann Prater
	Lipscomb, Robert
	Walter, Ronald Anderson "Ron"
1950	Familoni, Jumi Olajumoke
	Flowers, Arthur R.
	Jackson, Alvin O'Neal
1951	Bryce, Harry A.
	Donald, Bernice Bowen
	Finch, Larry
	Frazier, Levi, Jr.
	Morris, Herman, Jr.
	Williams, James
1952	Crossley, Callie
	Joysmith, Brenda
	Little, James
	Riley, Larry
	Withers, Dedrick "Teddy"
1953	Albert, Laurence
	Conley, Larry

Chronology by Birth Dates

1954	Brown, Donald
	Robinson, Kenneth Stanley
1955	Miller, Mulgrew
	Urevbu, Ephraim Muvire
	Williamson, Kenneth
1956	Johnson, Jason Miccolo
	Martin, Reginald
1957	Henry, Wiley, Jr.
1958	Familoni, Jumi Olajumoke
1958	Whalum, Kirk Wendell
1961	Dickey, Eric Jerome
1963	Draper, O'Landa
1964	Chisholm, Bridget
1966	Stevens, Rochelle
1970	Ford, Harold Eugene, Jr.
1971	Hardaway, Anfernee Deon "Penny"
1972	Thomas, Sheree Renée

Appendix B

Occupations

Accountants

Banks, Frank
Brandon, Otha Leon
Turner, Jesse Hosea

Actors

Freeman, Morgan
Riley, Larry
Woodruff, Georgia Rodgers

Administrators

Blackmon, Joyce McAnulty
Harvey, Peggy Ann Prater
Lipscomb, Robert
Morris, Herman, Jr.
Nelson-West, Bennetta "Bennie"
Shaw, Lucy Mae Yates
Smith, Otis Milton
Walter, Ronald Anderson "Ron"
Williams, Eddie N.

Artists

Buckley, Harriet Ann
Dotson, Phillip Randolph "Phil"
Hampton, Luther

Hayden, Frank, Jr.
Henry, Wiley, Jr.
Hunt, George
Jordan, Dewitt W., Jr.
Joysmith, Brenda
Light, Joe Lewis
Urevbu, Ephraim Muvire
Williamson, Kenneth

ATHLETES

Bankhead, Daniel Robert "Dan"
Boyd, Robert Richard "Bob"
Carter, Marlin "Pee Wee"
Finch, Larry
Hardaway, Anfernee Deon "Penny"
McCray, Shirley Yvonne
Mathis, Verdell L. "Lefty"
Scott, Joe Burt
Stevens, Rochelle

ATTORNEYS

Bailey, D'Army
Bailey, Walter Lee, Jr.
Booth, Benjamin Franklin
Brown, George Henry, Jr.
Brown, Joe
Cassels, Thomas Frank
Coleman, Veronica Freeman
Donald, Bernice Bowen
Hooks, Benjamin Lawson
Horton, Odell
Latting, Augustus Arvis "Doc"
Lockard, Hosea T.

Lynk, Miles Vandahurst
Morris, Herman, Jr.
Settle, Josiah T.
Smith, Otis Milton
Sugarmon, Russell Bertram, Jr.
Wharton, A C, Jr.
Wilbun, Shepperson A. "Shep"
Willis, Archie Walter, Jr.

BANKERS

Church, Robert Reed, Jr.
Pace, Harry Herbert
Turner, Jesse Hosea
Walker, Antonio Maceo

BARBERS

Clouston, Joseph
Morris, Alma
Shaw, Edward

BROADCASTERS

Brown, Joe
Crossley, Callie
Gilliam, Herman Arthur, Jr. "Art"
Steinberg, Martha Jean
Wade, Theo
Williams, Nathaniel Dowde "Nat D."

BUSINESSMEN AND WOMEN

Banks, Frank
Bodden, Ira Swithin
Brandon, Otha Leon

Bridges, Josephine Valeria Johnson "Jo"
Champion, Charles
Chisholm, Bridget
Church, Robert Reed
Church, Robert Reed, Jr.
Clayborne, Beverly Sarah "The Pie Lady"
Cleaves, Irene Curtis
Clouston, Joseph
Cochran, Flora Cole
Davis, Fred
Evers, O. Z.
Familoni, Jumi Olajumoke
Ford, Newton Jackson
Gilliam, Herman Arthur, Jr. "Art"
Harris, Joseph "FreeJoe"
Hassell, Frances Massey
Hayes, Thomas Henry
Henderson, George W.
Horne, Onzie O.
Johnican, Minerva
Jones, Fred
Lee, George Washington
Mitchell, Willie
Morris, Alma
Roddy, Bert Maynard
Sawyer, Chew Cornelium
Shaw, Edward
Shaw, Lily Patricia Walker "Pat"
Steinberg, Martha Jean
Stevens, Rochelle
Stuart, Merah Stevens
Turner, Elaine Lee
Turner, Jesse Hosea
Walker, Antonio Maceo

Walker, Joseph Edison
Wilburn, Emma Currin Barbee
Willis, Archie Walter, Jr.

Civic Leaders

Branch, Addison A.
Church, Robert Reed, Jr.
Clark, Leroy D.
Crenshaw, Cornelia
Evers, O. Z.
Holloway, George
Hooks, Julia Ann Britton
Kyles, Samuel Billy
Lawson, James Morris, Jr. "Jim"
Lipscomb, Robert
Lyke, James Patterson
Morris, Alma
Price, Hollis Freeman
Shaw, Edward
Terrell, Mary Church
Turner, Elaine Lee
Venson, Ethyl Belle Horton
Wells, Ida Bell

Clerics and Evangelists

Alston, Bettye J. Harris
Brewster, William Herbert
Bunton, Henry C.
Falls, Montee Therese Norman
Fuller, Thomas Oscar
Griggs, Sutton Elbert
Harris, Joseph "FreeJoe"
Henderson, Morris

Hooks, Benjamin Lawson
Hunt, Blair Theodore, Jr.
Jackson, Alvin O'Neal
Kelley, Frances Burnett
Kyles, Samuel Billy
Lawson, James Morris, Jr. "Jim"
Lyke, James Patterson
Mason, Charles Harrison
Muhammad, Talib-Karim
Owen, Samuel Augustus
Patterson, Gilbert E.
Patterson, James Oglethorpe
Robinson, Kenneth Stanley
Steinberg, Martha Jean
Toles, Elizabeth

Educators

Blackmon, Joyce McAnulty
Branch, Addison A.
Brewer, Harper
Bridges, Josephine Valeria Johnson "Jo"
Broughton, Virginia E. Walker
Brown, Donald
Brown, Lawyer Edward
Campbell, Lucie Eddie
Cook, Vivian E. Johnson
Crawford, Alvin Howell
Deberry, Lois
Dotson, Phillip Randolph "Phil"
Falls, Montee Therese Norman
Flowers, Arthur R.
Fuller, Thomas Oscar
Gayles, Gloria Jean Wade
Green, Mildred Denby

Griggs, Emma J. Williams
Guy-Sheftall, Beverly
Hamilton, Green Polonius
Hayden, Frank, Jr.
Hedgeman, Lulah McEwen
Henderson, George W.
Herenton, Willie Wilbert
Hooks, Julia Ann Britton
Horne, Onzie O.
Hunt, Blair Theodore, Jr.
Hunt, George
Johnican, Minerva
Jones, Velma Lois
Lincoln, Charles Eric
Lunceford, James Melvin "Jimmie"
Lynk, Miles Vandahurst
Martin, Reginald
McCray, Shirley Yvonne
Price, Hollis Freeman
Spillers, Hortense J.
Stuckey, Ples Sterling
Taylor, Cora Price
Terrell, Mary Church
Toles, Elizabeth
Wells, Ida Bell
Whalum, Wendell Phillips
Whittaker, John W. II
Williams, Nathaniel Dowde "Nat D."
Williamson, Juanita V.
Yates, Albert Carl "Tutt"

ENTERTAINERS

Hulbert, Maurice "Fess"
Kelley, Frances Burnett

Thomas, Rufus
Williams, Nathaniel Dowde "Nat D."
Woodruff, Georgia Rodgers

Insurance Professionals

Davis, Fred
Hassell, Frances Massey
Horne, Onzie O.
Lee, George Washington
Olive, Benjamin Garfield, Jr.
Pace, Harry Herbert
Shaw, Lily Patricia Walker "Pat"
Stuart, Merah Stevens
Walker, Joseph Edison
Walker, Antonio Maceo

Journalists

Conley, Larry
Crossley, Callie
Gilliam, Dorothy Butler
Henry, Wiley, Jr.
Shaw, Edward
Swingler, Lewis Ossie
Wells, Ida Bell
Wilson, Lucious Alexander

Labor Leaders

Clark, Leroy D.
Holloway, George L.
Jones, Thomas Oliver

MILITARY PERSONNEL

Cleaborn, Edward O.
Lee, George Washington
Weathers, Luke J.

MORTICIANS

Ford, Newton Jackson
Hayes, Thomas Henry
Lewis, Robert Stevenson
Wilburn, Emma Currin Barbee

MUSICIANS AND COMPOSERS

Albert, Laurence
Armstrong, Lillian Hardin "Lil"
Bailey, William C. "Buster"
Blackfoot, J. "Foot"
Blackmore, Amos (a.k.a. Junior Wells)
Bland, Bobby "Blue"
Brewster, William Herbert
Brown, Donald
Campbell, Lucie Eddie
Cannon, Gus
Chatman, Peter II "Memphis Slim"
Cobb, Joyce
Crawford, Bennie Ross "Hank"
Criss, William "Sonny"
Douglas, Lizzie "Memphis Minnie"
Draper, O'Landa
Green, Leorns "Al"
Green, Mildred Denby

Handy, William Christopher
Hayes, Isaac
Hedgeman, Lulah McEwen
Hooks, Julia A. Britton
Horne, Onzie O.
Hoskins, Ollie Braxton "Nightingale"
Hunter, Alberta
Hyter, James A.
King, Albert
King, Riley "B. B."
Lewis, Walter "Furry"
Little, Vera
Love, John Robinson
Lunceford, James Melvin "Jimmie"
Maburn, Harold
McCleave, Florence Cole Talbert
Miller, Mulgrew
Newborn, Phineas, Jr.
Porter, David
Thomas, Carla
Thomas, Rufus
Whalum, Kirk Wendell
Whalum, Wendell Phillips
White, Maurice
Whittaker, John W. II
Williams, James
Woodruff, Georgia Rodgers

Photographers

Cantrell, Anderson
Johnson, Jason Miccolo
Taylor, Lonzie Odie
Withers, Ernest C.

Physicians, Dentists, and Health Professionals

Alston, Bettye J. Harris
Bisson, Wheelock Alexander
Brawner, Clara Arena
Byas, Andrew D.
Champion, Charles
Crawford, Alvin Howell
Lynk, Miles Vandahurst
Martin, William S.
Patton, Georgia E. L.
Robinson, Kenneth Stanley
Shaw, Lucy Mae Yates
Smith, Vasco Albert, Jr.
Walker, Joseph Edison
White, Augustus A. III

Political Leaders

Bailey, Walter Lee, Jr.
Barry, Marion Shepilov, Jr.
Brewer, Harper
Calloway, DeVerne Lee
Cassels, Thomas Frank
Church, Robert Reed, Jr.
Clouston, Joseph
Davis, Fred
Deberry, Lois
Evers, O. Z.
Ford, Harold Eugene
Ford, Harold Eugene, Jr.
Johnican, Minerva
Lee, George Washington
Morris, Alma
Muhammad, Talib-Karim

Shaw, Edward
Smith, Maxine Atkins
Smith, Vasco Albert, Jr.
Turner, Jesse Hosea
Wharton, A C, Jr.
Withers, Dedrick "Teddy"

Postal Employees

Evers, O. Z.
Hutchins, Fred Lew
Love, John Robinson
Thornton, Matthew
Washington, David Whittier

Sanitation Workers

Jones, Thomas Oliver
Lee, Tom C.
Lewis, Walter "Furry"

Social Workers

Kateo, Loretta Hicks

Tailors

Bodden, Ira Swithin

Writers

Broughton, Virginia E. Walker
Church, Sara Roberta
Dickey, Eric Jerome
Flowers, Arthur R.

Frazier, Levi
Fuller, Thomas Oscar
Gayles, Gloria Jean Wade
Griggs, Sutton Elbert
Guy-Sheftall, Beverly
Hamilton, Green Polonius
Hutchins, Fred
Lincoln, Charles Eric
Lynk, Miles Vandahurst
Martin, Reginald
Spillers, Hortense J.
Stuart, Merah Stevens
Stuckey, Elma
Stuckey, Ples Sterling
Thomas, Sheree Renée
Walter, Ronald Anderson "Ron"
Wells, Ida Bell

Selected Bibliography

Andrews, William L., and Frances Smith Foster, eds. *Oxford Companion to African American Literature.* New York: Oxford University Press, 1997.

Bailey, D'Army. *Mine Eyes Have Seen: Dr. Martin Luther King Jr.'s Final Journey.* Ed. David Lyons. Memphis: Towery Publishing, Inc., 1993.

Barlow, William. *"Looking Up at Down": The Emergence of Blues Culture.* Philadelphia: Temple University Press, 1989.

Beale Street USA: Where the Blues Began. Blues Unlimited: Bexhill-on-Sea, Sussex, 1997.

Bernhardt, Clyde E. B. *I Remember: Eighty Years of Black Entertainment, Big Bands, and the Blues: An Autobiography.* Philadelphia: University of Philadelphia Press, 1986.

Bigelow, Barbara Carlisle, and L. Mpho Mabunda, eds. *Contemporary Black Biography: Profiles from the International Black Community.* vols. 2, 7, 8. Detroit: Gale Research, Inc., 1992, 1994, 1995.

Bond, Beverly G., and Jansaan Sherman. *Beale Street.* Arcadia: Mt. Pleasant, SC, 2007.

Booth, Mary E., with Yuvonne C. Brooks. *B. F. Booth: The Legacy.* Tempe, AZ: M. R. Booth, 2001.

Bowman, Bob M. J. *Soulsville U.S.A.: The Story of Stax Records.* New York: Schermer Books, 1997.

Boyer, Horace Clarence. *How Sweet the Sound: The Golden Age of Gospel.* Washington: Elliott & Clark Publishing, 1995.

Burkett, Randall K., et al., eds. *Black Biography, 1790–1950.* Alexandria, VA: Chadwyck-Healy. 3 vols., 1991.

Carr, Ian, et al. *Jazz: The Rough Guide.* London: Rough Guides, Ltd., 1995.

Cartwright, Joseph H. *The Triumph of Jim Crow: Tennessee Race Relations in the 1880s.* Knoxville: University of Tennessee Press, 1976.

Charters, Samuel. *The Legacy of the Blues.* New York: Da Capo Press, 1977.

Chilton, John. *Who's Who of Jazz: Storyville to Swing Street*. London: The Bloomsbury Book Shop, 1970.

Church, Annette E., and Roberta Church. *The Robert R. Churches of Memphis: A Father and Son Who Achieved in Spite of Race*. Ann Arbor: Edwards Bros., 1974.

Church, Roberta, and Ronald Walter. *Nineteenth Century Memphis Families of Color, 1850–1900*. Ed. Charles W. Crawford. Memphis: By Authors, 1987.

City Directory of 1941.

A Classified Directory of Memphis and Shelby County. Memphis: Negro Chamber of Commerce, 1900.

Crawford, Charles W. *Yesterday's Memphis*. Miami: E. A. Seemann Publishing Co., 1976.

Daniels, Jeremy. *Anfernee Hardaway*. New York: Chelsea House Publishers, 1996.

DeCosta-Willis, Miriam. "The History of Beale Street, 1850 to 1950." In *Feasibility of the Beale Street Cultural Center, Memphis, Tennessee*, vol. 2 Washington, DC: Match Institution, 1973.

———. "Ida B. Wells's Diary: A Narrative of the Black Community of Memphis in the 1880s." *West Tennessee Historical Society Papers* 45 (December): 35–47.

———, ed. *The Memphis Diary of Ida B. Wells*. Boston: Beacon Press, 1995.

DeCosta-Willis, Miriam, Fannie Delk, and Philip Dotson, eds. *Homespun Images: An Anthology of Black Memphis Writers and Artists*. Memphis: LeMoyne-Owen College, 1989.

Duster, Alfreda M., ed. *Crusade for Justice: The Autobiography of Ida B. Wells*. Chicago: University of Chicago Press, 1970.

Erlewine, Michael, ed., with Ron Wynn. *All Music Guide to Jazz*. San Francisco: Miller Freeman Books, 1996.

Feather, Leonard. *The Encyclopedia of Jazz*. New York: Horizon Press, 1955.

Findlay, Stephen Morrison. *Memphis, Historical Perspectives in Black*. Memphis: Memphis/Shelby County Public Library and Information Center, 1975.

Franklin, Aretha, and David Ritz. *Aretha: From These Roots*. New York: Villard Books, 1999.

Selected Bibliography

Fuller, Thomas Oscar. *History of the Negro Baptists of Tennessee*. Memphis. The Author, 1936.

———. *Pictorial History of the American Negro*. Memphis. The Author, 1933.

———. *Twenty Years in Public Life, 1890–1910*. Nashville: National Baptist Publishing Board, 1910.

———. *The Story of the Church Life Among Negroes in Memphis, Tennessee, for Students and Workers*. Memphis: The Author, 1938.

Garon, Paul, and Beth Garon. *Woman with Guitar: Memphis Minnie's Blues*. New York: Da Capo Press, 1992.

Gottlieb, Robert. *Reading Jazz: A Gathering of Autobiography, Reportage, and Criticism from 1919 to Now*. New York: Pantheon Books, 1996.

Hamilton, G. P. *Beacon Lights of the Race*. Memphis: E. H. Clarke, 1911.

———. *The Bright Side of Memphis*. Memphis: The Author, 1908.

———. *Booker T. Washington High School: Retrospective Prospective, from 1889 to 1927*. Memphis: The Author, 1927.

Haley, James T. *Afro-American Encyclopedia*. n. p. 1895.

———. *Sparkling Gems of Race Knowledge Worth Reading*. Nashville: J. T. Haley & Co., 1897.

Handy, William C. *Father of the Blues: An Autobiography*. Ed. Arna Bontemps. New York: Macmillan Co., 1941.

Harkins, John E. *Metropolis of the American Nile: An Illustrated History of Memphis and Shelby County*. Woodland Hill, CA: Windson, 1982.

Harris, Sheldon. *Blues Who's Who: A Biographical Dictionary of Blues Singers*. New York: Da Capo Press, 1981.

Hawkins, Walter L. *African American Biographies: Profiles of 332 Current Men and Women*. Jefferson, NC: McFarland & Co., 1994.

———. *African American Biographies: Profiles of 558 Current Men and Women*. Jefferson, NC: McFarland & Co., 1992.

Heilbut, Anthony. *The Gospel Sound: Good News and Bad Times*. New York: Limelight Editions, 1985.

Herzhaft, Gerard. *Encyclopedia of the Blues*. Trans. Brigitte Debord. Fayetteville: University of Arkansas Press, 1987.

Hine, Darlene Clark, ed. *Black Women in America: An Historical Encyclopedia.* 2 vols. Brooklyn: Carlson Publishing Inc., 1993.

Historic Black Memphians. Memphis: Memphis Pink Palace Museum Foundation, c. 1970.

Hogan, Lawrence D. *Shades of Glory: The Negro Leagues and the Story of African American Baseball.* Washington, DC: National Geographic Society, 2006.

Honey, Michael K. *Black Workers Remember: An Oral History of Segregation, Unionism, and the Freedom Struggle.* Berkeley: University of California Press, 1999.

———. *Going Down Jericho Road: The Memphis Strike, Martin Luther King's Last Campaign.* New York: W. W. Norton & Co., 2007

———. *Southern Labor and Black Civil Rights: Organizing Memphis Workers.* Urbana: University of Illinois Press, 1993.

Hooks, Benjamin L., with Jerry Guess. *The March for Civil Rights: The Benjamin Hooks Story.* Chicago: American Bar Association, 2003.

Hoppe, Sherry L., and Bruce W. Speck. *Maxine Smith's Unwilling Pupils: Lessons Learned in Memphis's Civil Rights Classroom.* Knoxville: The University of Tennessee Press, 2007.

Hunt, George, and Lonnie Wilson. *25 Black Afro-American Artist[s] of Memphis, Tennessee.* Memphis: Art/Serious Business, Shelby State Community College, 1985.

Hunt, Marsha. *Repossessing Ernestine: A Granddaughter Uncovers the Secret History of Her American Family.* New York: HarperCollins Publishers, 1996.

Hutchins, Fred L. *Sketch History of Second Congregational Church Centennial 1868–1968.* Memphis: Johnson Printery, 1968.

———. *What Happened in Memphis.* Memphis: The Author, 1965.

Johnson, Thomas J. *From the Driftwood of Bayou Pierre.* Louisville: Dunne, 1949.

Jones, Addie D. *Portrait of a Ghetto School.* New York: Vantage Press, 1973.

Kelley, Frances Burnett. *Better Than I Was.* Nashville: T. Nelson, 1979.

———. *Here Am I, Send Me: The Dramatic Story of Presiding Bishop J. O. Patterson, Challenging and Bold Leader of the Church of God in Christ.* Memphis: Church of God in Christ Publishing House, 1970.

Selected Bibliography

Lacey, Ernest Edward. *FreeJoe*. Memphis: FreeJoe Enterprises, 1996.

Lamon, Lester C. *Black Tennesseans, 1900–1930*. Knoxville: University of Tennessee Press, 1977.

———. *Blacks in Tennessee, 1791–1970*. Knoxville: University of Tennessee Press, 1981.

LaPointe, Patricia M. *From Saddlebags to Science: A Century of Health Care in Memphis, 1830–1930*. Memphis: The Health Science Museum Foundation of the Memphis and Shelby County Medical Society and Auxiliary, 1984.

Lee, George W. *Beale Street: Where the Blues Began*. College Park, MD: McGrath Publishing Co., 1969.

Lewis, Selma S., and Marjean G. Kremer. *The Angel of Beale Street: A Biography of Julia Ann Hooks*. Memphis: St. Luke's, 1986.

Little, Vera. *Tears in My Eyes*. New York: Vantage Press, 1978.

Litwack, Leon F. *Trouble in Mind: Black Southerners in the Age of Jim Crow*. New York: Alfred A. Knopf, 1998.

Logan, Rayford W., and Michael R. Winston, eds. *Dictionary of American Negro Biography*. NewYork: W. W. Norton and Co., 1982.

Lornell, Kip. *Happy in the Service of the Lord: African-American Sacred Vocal Harmony Quartets in Memphis*. Knoxville: University of Tennessee Press, 1995.

Lovett, Bobby Lee. *The Civil Rights Movement in Tennessee: A Narrative History*. Knoxville: University of Tennessee Press, 2005.

Lovett, Bobby L., and Linda T. Wynn, eds. *Profiles of African Americans in Tennessee*. Nashville: Annual Local Conference on Afro-American Culture and History, 1996.

Lynk, M. V. *Sixty Years of Medicine or The Life and Times of Dr. Miles V. Lynk, An Autobiography*. Memphis: The Twentieth Century Press, 1931.

Magness, Perre. *Elmwood 2002: In the Shadows of the Elms*. Memphis: Elmwood Cemetery, 2001.

Margolies, Jacob. *The Negro Leagues: The Story of Black Baseball*. New York: Franklin Watts, 1993.

McCray, Shirley Yvonne, with Amos Jones, Jr. *Coach McCray: The Inspiring Story of America's First Woman Coach of an All-Male Football Team*. Nashville: Bethlehem Book Publishers, Inc., 1997.

McKee, Margaret, and Fred Chisenhall. *Beale Black & Blue: Life and Music on Black America's Main Street.* Baton Rouge: Louisiana State University Press, 1981.

Milton, Gloria Brown. "Blacks in Memphis, Tennessee, 1920–1955: A Historical Study." Ph.D. dissertation, Washington State University, 1982.

Moffit, Larry, and Jonathan Kronstadt. *Crossing the Line: Black Major Leaguers, 1947–1959.* Iowa City: University of Iowa P, 1994.

Mooney, Chase C. *Slavery in Tennessee.* Bloomington: Indiana University Press, 1957.

Nager, Larry. *Memphis Beat: The Lives and Times of America's Musical Crossroads.* New York: St. Martin's, 1998.

Negro Year Book and Directory. Memphis: Negro Chamber of Commerce, 1900.

Newborn, Calvin. *As Quiet as It's Kept!: The Genius of Phineas Newborn, Jr.* Memphis: The Author, 1996.

Patterson, Caleb Perry. *The Negro in Tennessee, 1790–1865.* Austin: University of Texas Press, 1922.

Patterson, J. O., German R. Ross, and Julia Mason Atkins, eds. *History and Formative Years of the Church of God in Christ with Excerpts from the Life and Works of Its Founder—Bishop C. H. Mason.* Memphis: Church of God in Christ Publishing House, 1969.

Petterson, Robert. *Only the Ball Was White: A History of Legendary Black [Baseball] Players.* Englewood Cliffs: Prentice-Hall, 1970.

Piazza, Tom. *Blues Up and Down: Jazz in Our Time.* New York: St. Martin's, 1997.

Pohlmann, Marcus D., and Michael P. Kirby. *Racial Politics at the Crossroads: Memphis Elects Dr. W. W. Herenton.* Knoxville: University of Tennessee Press, 1996.

Reagon, Bernice Johnson. *We'll Understand It Better By and By: Pioneering African American Gospel Composers.* Washington: Smithsonian Press, 1992.

Riley, James A. *The Biographical Encyclopedia of the Negro Baseball Leagues.* New York: Carroll and Graf Publishers, Inc. 1994.

Sawyer, Charles. *The Arrival of B. B. King.* New York: Da Capo Press, 1980.

Shepperd, Gladys Byram. *Mary Church Terrell, Respectable Person*. Baltimore: Human Relations Press, 1954.

Smith, Jessie Carney, ed. *Notable Black American Women*. Detroit: Gale Research Inc., 1992.

Smith, Otis Milton, and Mary M. Stolberg. *Looking Beyond Race: The Life of Otis Milton Smith*. Detroit: Wayne State Press, 2000.

Southern, Eileen. *The Music of Black Americans: A History*. New York: Norton, 1983.

Stuart, M. S. *An Economic Detour: A History of Insurance in the Lives of American Negroes*. New York: Wendell Malliet and Co., 1940.

Taylor, Alrutheus Ambush. *The Negro in Tennessee, 1865–1880*. Washington, DC: The Associated Publishers, Inc., 1941.

Taylor, Frank C., with Gerald Cook. *Alberta Hunter: A Celebration in Blues*. New York: McGraw-Hill Book Co., 1987.

Terrell, Mary Church. *A Colored Woman in a White World*. Washington, DC: National Association of Colored Women's Clubs, 1968.

Tucker, David M. *Black Pastors & Leaders: The Memphis Clergy, 1819–1972*. Memphis: Memphis State University Press, 1975.

―――. *Lieutenant Lee of Beale Street*. Nashville: Vanderbilt University Press, 1971.

Turner, Allegra W. *Except By Grace: The Life of Jesse H. Turner*. 2003

Walk, Joe. *A History of African-Americans in Memphis Government*. Memphis: By Author, 1996.

Walker, Charles. *Miss Lucie*. Nashville: Townsend Press, 1993.

Walker, Randolph Meade. *The Metamorphosis of Sutton E. Griggs: The Transition from Black Radical to Conservative, 1913–1933*. Memphis: The Author, 1990.

Webb, Arthur L. *Index to the 1830, 1840, 1850 and 1860 Censuses Indicating Free African Americans in Shelby County*. Memphis: Author, 1990.

White, Augustus A. *Your Aching Back: A Doctor's Guide to Relief*. New York: Bantam Books, 1983.

Who's Who Among African Americans. New York: Gale Research, Inc., 1996.

Who's Who in Colored America: A Biographical Dictionary of Notable Living Persons of African Descent. New York: Who's Who in Colored America Corp., 1927.

Who's Who of American Women: A Biographical Dictionary of Notable Living American Women. Chicago: Marquis Who's Who, 1959.

Who's Who of the Colored Race: A General Biographical Dictionary of Men and Women of African Descent. Detroit: Gale Research Co., 1976.

ARTICLES

Church, Roberta. "Mary Church Terrell." *Homespun Images.* Memphis: LeMoyne-Owen College, 1989. 46–48.

DeCosta-Willis, Miriam. "Between a Rock and a Hard Place: Black Culture in Memphis During the Fifties." *Memphis, 1948–1958.* Memphis: Memphis Brooks Museum of Art, 1986.

"The Football Coach Is a Lady." *Ebony* 34 (December 1978): 115–122.

Green, Mildred D. "A Matter of Fact: Selected Black Memphis Musicians, 1950–1980." *Homespun Images.* Memphis: LeMoyne-Owen College, 1989. 67–71.

Hankins, Eddie. "Rufus!" *Memphis* 22 (October 1997): 38–39, 128.

Hardin, George E. "A Son of Tennessee in the Service of His Faith: A Profile of W. Herbert Brewster." *Homespun Images.* Memphis: LeMoyne-Owen College, 1989. 82–85.

Hassell, Frances M. "Linked Lives: Glimpses of Selected Personalities." *Homespun Images.* Memphis: LeMoyne-Owen College, 1989. 49–56.

Herrington, Chris. "Freeman in Memphis." *The Memphis Flyer* (27 March–2 April 2003): 16–17, 35.

Jackson, David Earl. "Hank Crawford Comes Home…" *Tri-State Defender* Section 1B. (23–27 August 1997).

Lollar, Michael. "Bright Eyes: The Life and Hard Times of Phineas Newborn Jr." *The Commercial Appeal.* Mid-South Section 25 (October 1987): 6–11.

McCall, Nathan. "Universal Life's Policy for Growth." *Black Enterprise* (June 1987): 232–36.

Magness, Perre. "Lunceford Band Among Bounciest." *The Commercial Appeal.* Section CC (17 July 1997): 2.

Matthews, Timothy Lee. "An Interview with Carla Thomas: Touching Base with Her Roots." *Homespun Images*. Memphis: LeMoyne-Owen College, 1989. 72–79.

"The Power of an Image: A Salute to African American Artists." Exhibition Program. Gallery Three Five O and MLGW (February 1993).

Qualls, J. Winfield. "The Beginnings and Early History of LeMoyne School at Memphis, 1871–1874." *West Tennessee Historical Society Papers* 7 (1953): 5–37.

Sampson, Tom. "The Gospel According to O'Landa." *Memphis* 19 (May 1994): 26–32, 73–75.

Savitt, Todd L. "A Journal of Our Own": *The Medical and Surgical Observer* at the Beginnings of an African-American Medical Profession in Late 19th-Century America." *Journal of the National Medical Association* 88 no. 1 (1996): 52–60 and no. 2 (1996): 115–22.

Waller, Robert L. "Now Whatcha Bet?: A Profile of Nathaniel D. Williams." *Homespun Images*. Memphis: LeMoyne-Owen College, 1989. 57–59.

Walters, Ron. "Black Memphis Leaders." *Homespun Images*. Memphis: LeMoyne-Owen College, 1989. 42–45.

———. "Memphis' Black Pioneers." *Homespun Images*. Memphis: LeMoyne-Owen College, 1989. 40–41.

Wilson, John S. "Celebrating Lunceford, A Big-Band Master." *The New York Times*.

Unpublished Manuscripts

Brewster, William Herbert. "Autobiography." n.d.

Smith, Otis Milton. "The 'Memoirs' of Otis Milton Smith." 20 February 1922–29 June 1994. [36 transcribed tapes].

Programs

Funeral program, William Herbert Brewster, Sr. (Memphis), October 20, 1987.

Funeral program, Peter "Memphis Slim" Chatman, (Memphis), March 4, 1988.

Funeral program, Fannie Mitchell Delk, (Memphis), August 28, 1989.

Funeral program, Juanita V. Williamson, (Memphis), August 14, 1993.

DISCOGRAPHY

Allen, Perry "Nite Owl." *Phineas Newborn, Jr. / Solo Piano.* New York: Atlantic Recording Corporation. 1975.

Brooks, Michael. "Album Notes." *John Kirby, Boss of the Bass.* New York: Columbia Records. CG 33557, 1975.

Dance, Stanley. "Album Notes." *Lunceford Special.* New York: Columbia Records. CS 9515.

Gerber, Alain. "Album Notes." *Jimmie Lunceford 2 "Harlem Shout" (1935–1936).* Universal City, California: MCA Records, Inc., (Jazz Heritage Series Vol. 6) MCA-1305, 1980.

Koenk, Lester. "Album Notes." *The Great Jazz Piano of Phineas Newborn Jr.* Los Angeles: Contemporary Records, Inc. M 3611, 1963.

Norman, Ray. *Jimmie Lunceford and His Orchestra 1940.* Atlanta: Circle Records. CLP-11, 1981.

Wein, George. "Album Notes." *Here Is Phineas: The Piano Artistry of Phineas Newborn Jr.* New York: Atlantic Recording Corporation. Atlantic 1235, 1956.

Photo Credits

Photographs are courtesy of the following sources.

Albert, Laurence: *Tri-State Defender.*
Alston, Bettye J. Harris: Courtesy of Alston.
Armstrong, Lillian Hardin "Lil": findagrave.com.
Bailey, D'Army: *Tri-State Defender.*
Bailey, Walter Lee, Jr.: Hooks Brothers Photographers. *Tri-State Defender.*
Bankhead, Daniel Robert "Dan": findagrave.com.
Banks, Frank: The African American History Calendar Partnership.
Barry, Marion Shepilov, Jr.: Courtesy of Barry's office.
Bisson, Wheelock Alexander: 1943 Board of Directors, Memphis Branch YMCA. Memphis and Shelby County Room, Memphis Public Library & Information Center.
Blackfoot, J. "Foot": *Tri-State Defender.*
Blackmon, Joyce McAnulty: Courtesy of Blackmon.
Blackmore, Amos (a.k.a. Junior Wells): Courtesy of Vincent at fufustew.wordpress.com.
Bland, Bobby "Blue": Stax Museum of American Soul Music.
Bodden, Ira Swithin: Courtesy of Frankie Bodden.
Booth, Benjamin Franklin: *The Bright Side of Memphis.*
Boyd, Robert Richard "Bob": findagrave.com.
Branch, Addison A.: The African American History Calendar Partnership.
Brandon, Otha Leon: LeMoyne-Owen College. *Columns.*
Brawner, Clara Arena: Spelman College Archives.
Brewer, Harper: Courtesy of Peggy Brewer.
Brewster, William Herbert: findagrave.com.
Bridges, Josephine Valeria Johnson "Jo": Courtesy of Kim Bridges.
Broughton, Virginia E. Walker: *Sparkling Gems of Race Pride.*

Brown, Donald: Courtesy of Brown.
Brown, George Henry, Jr.: *Tri-State Defender.*
Brown, Joe: *Tri-State Defender.*
Brown, Lawyer Edward: 1943 Board of Directors, Memphis Branch YMCA. Memphis and Shelby County Room, Memphis Public Library & Information Center.
Bryce, Harry A.: *The Commercial Appeal.*
Buckley, Harriet Ann: Courtesy of Buckley.
Bunton, Henry C.: Steve Zweig & Sons Photographers. *Tri-State Defender.*
Byas, Andrew D.: The African American History Calendar Partnership.
Calloway, Deverne Lee: The African American History Calendar Partnership.
Campbell, Lucie Eddie: Hooks Brothers Photographers.
Cannon, Gus: Leonard D. West, photographer. Harry E. Godwin Collection. Center for Southern Folklore Archives.
Cantrell, Anderson: *Tri-State Defender.*
Cassels, Thomas Frank: TSLA Collection.
Champion, Charles: *Tri-State Defender.*
Chatman, Peter II "Memphis Slim": Judy Peiser, photographer. Center for Southern Folklore Archives.
Chisholm, Bridget: Courtesy of Chisholm.
Church, Robert Reed: *The Robert R. Churches of Memphis.*
Church, Robert Reed, Jr.: Collection of Gilda Lee Robinson. Memphis and Shelby County Room, Memphis Public Library & Information Center.
Church, Sara Roberta: The Sara Church Collection. Memphis and Shelby County Room, Memphis Public Library & Information Center.
Clark, LeRoy D.: Memphis Branch NAACP.
Clayborne, Beverly Sarah "The Pie Lady": *Tri-State Defender.*
Cleaborn, Edward O.: *Memphis Press-Scimitar.*
Cleaves, Irene Curtis: Courtesy of Bernice Martin.
Cobb, Joyce: Courtesy of Cobb.

Cochran, Flora Cole: Courtesy of Joyce C. Foster.
Coleman, Veronica Freeman: *Tri-State Defender.*
Conley, Larry: Renee Hannans. *Atlanta Journal-Constitution.*
Cook, Vivian E. Johnson: Vivian Johnson Cook Papers. Moorland-Spingarn Research Center, Howard University.
Crawford, Alvin Howell: Courtesy of Crawford.
Crawford, Bennie Ross "Hank": George Hardin Photographer. Courtesy of Hardin.
Crenshaw, Cornelia: *The Commercial Appeal.*
Criss, William "Sonny": Courtesy of Vasco A. Smith.
Crossley, Callie: *Tri-State Defender.*
Davis, Fred: Courtesy of Davis.
DeBerry, Lois: *Tri-State Defender.*
Dickey, Eric Jerome: Courtesy of Jamon McEwan, Karibu Books.
Donald, Bernice Bowen: Memphis and Shelby County Room, Memphis Public Library & Information Center.
Dotson, Phillip Randolph "Phil": LeMoyne-Owen College. *Columns,* 1981.
Douglas, Lizzie "Memphis Minnie": *Woman With Guitar: Memphis Minnie's Blues.*
Draper, O'Landa: The African American History Calendar Partnership.
Evers, O. Z.: *Tri-State Defender.*
Falls, Montee Therese Norman: Courtesy of Mildred Davis.
Familoni, Jumi Olajumoke: *Memphis.*
Finch, Larry: *Tri-State Defender.*
Flowers, Arthur R.: Courtesy of Flowers.
Ford, Harold Eugene: John Landrigen, photographer. *Tri-State Defender.*
Ford, Harold Eugene, Jr.: Courtesy of Ford.
Ford, Newton Jackson: The African American History Calendar Partnership.
Frazier, Levi: Courtesy of Frazier.
Freeman, Morgan: Memphis Black Arts Alliance.
Fuller, Thomas Oscar: Hooks Brothers Photographers. *Historic Black Memphians.*

Gayles, Gloria Jean Wade: Jerry Siegel, photographer. Courtesy of Gayles.
Gilliam, Dorothy Butler: Courtesy of Gilliam.
Gilliam, Herman Arthur, Jr. "Art": *Tri-State Defender*.
Green, Leorns "Al": *Tri-State Defender*.
Green, Mildred Denby: *The Commercial Appeal*.
Griggs, Emma J. Williams: *City Directory of 1941*. Memphis and Shelby County Room, Memphis Public Library & Information Center.
Griggs, Sutton Elbert: *Sermons, Addresses, and Reminiscences and Important Correspondence*.
Guy-Sheftall, Beverly: Courtesy of Guy-Sheftall.
Hamilton, Green Polonius: *The Bright Side of Memphis*.
Hampton, Luther: Memphis Black Arts Alliance.
Handy, William Christopher: *Tri-State Defender*.
Hardaway, Anfernee Deon "Penny": Courtesy of Randy Wade.
Harvey, Peggy Ann Prater: Courtesy of Toni Harvey.
Hassell, Frances Massey: *Tri-State Defender*.
Hayden, Frank, Jr.: Courtesy of Claudia Hayden.
Hayes, Isaac: Stax Museum of American Soul Music.
Hayes, Thomas Henry: *The Bright Side of Memphis*.
Hedgeman, Lulah McEwen: *The Commercial Appeal*.
Henderson, George W.: *City Directory of 1941*. Memphis and Shelby County Room, Memphis Public Library & Information Center.
Henry, Wiley, Jr.: *Tri-State Defender*.
Herenton, Willie Wilbert: *Tri-State Defender*.
Holloway, George L.: *Tri-State Defender*.
Hooks, Benjamin Lawson: Hooks Brothers Photographers. *Tri-State Defender*.
Hooks, Julia Ann Britton: Hooks Brothers Photographers. *Historic Black Memphians*.
Horne, Onzie O.: Hooks Brothers Photographers. Courtesy of Onzie Horne, Jr.
Horton, Odell: *Tri-State Defender*.
Hoskins, Ollie Braxton "Nightingale": Copyright Makoto Takahashi. Courtesy of Takahashi.

Hulbert, Maurice "Fess": *Tri-State Defender*.
Hunt, Blair Theodore, Jr.: 1943 Board of Directors, Memphis Branch YMCA. Memphis and Shelby County Room, Memphis Public Library & Information Center.
Hunt, George: Courtesy of Hunt.
Hunter, Alberta: The African American History Calendar Partnership.
Hutchins, Fred Lew: *Tri-State Defender*.
Jackson, Alvin O'Neal: Courtesy of Jackson.
Johnican, Minerva: *Tri-State Defender*.
Johnson, Jason Miccolo: *Tri-State Defender*. Copyright 1994. Permission of Johnson.
Jones, Fred, Jr.: *Tri-State Defender*.
Jones, Thomas Oliver: Ernest Withers Photographer. *Tri-State Defender*.
Jones, Velma Lois: *Tri-State Defender*.
Jordan, Dewitt W., Jr.: *Dewitt Jordan: A Delta Genius*. Courtesy of Eddie Jones.
Joysmith, Brenda: Courtesy of Joysmith.
Kateo, Loretta Hicks: Courtesy of Rosetta H. Peterson.
Kelley, Frances Burnett: *Tri-State Defender*.
King, Albert: *Tri-State Defender*.
King, Riley "B. B.": The African American History Calendar Partnership.
Kyles, Samuel Billy: *Tri-State Defender*.
Latting, Augustus Arvis "Doc": The African American History Calendar Partnership.
Lawson, James Morris, Jr. "Jim": George Hardin Photographer. Courtesy of Hardin.
Lee, George Washington: Hooks Brothers Photographers. *Historic Black Memphians*.
Lewis, Robert Stevenson: Ernest Withers Photographer. Courtesy of R. S. Lewis, Jr.
Lewis, Walter "Furry": *Beale Black & Blue*.
Light, Joe Lewis: *The Commercial Appeal*.

Lincoln, Charles Eric: J. Markatos, photographer. *The Avenue Clayton City*.
Lipscomb, Robert: Courtesy of Lipscomb.
Little, James: Courtesy of Little.
Little, Vera: "Between a Rock and a Hard Place".
Lockard, Hosea T.: Memphis and Shelby County Room, Memphis Public Library & Information Center.
Love, John Robinson: *The Bright Side of Memphis*.
Lunceford, James Melvin "Jimmie": James Kriegsmann, photographer. Maurice "Fess" Hulbert Collection. Center for Southern Folklore Archives.
Lyke, James Patterson: Courtesy of Erma Laws.
Lynk, Miles Vandahurst: Memphis and Shelby County Room, Memphis Public Library & Information Center.
Martin, Reginald: *Tri-State Defender*.
Martin, William S.: Hooks Brothers Photographers. Memphis and Shelby County Room, Memphis Public Library & Information Center.
Mason, Charles Harrison: Hooks Brothers Photographers. *Historic Black Memphians*.
McCleave, Florence Cole Talbert: Hooks Brothers Photographers. *Historic Black Memphians*.
McCray, Shirley Yvonne: *Tri-State Defender*.
Miller, Mulgrew: Dr. Jazz, photographer. *All About Jazz*.
Mitchell, Willie: *Tri-State Defender*.
Morris, Alma: *Tri-State Defender*.
Morris, Herman, Jr.: The African American History Calendar Partnership.
Muhammad, Talib-Karim: *Tri-State Defender*.
Nelson-West, Bennetta: *Tri-State Defender*.
Newborn, Phineas, Jr.: Alan Ulmer, photographer. Courtesy of Irvin Salky.
Olive, Benjamin Garfield, Jr.: Hooks Brothers Photographers.
Owen, Samuel Augustus: Hooks Brothers Photographers. *Historic Black Memphians*.

Pace, Harry Herbert: *An Economic Detour*.
Patterson, Gilbert E.: *Tri-State Defender*.
Patterson, James Oglethorpe: *Tri-State Defender*.
Patton, Georgia E. L.: Miriam DeCosta-Willis Collection. Memphis and Shelby County Room, Memphis Public Library & Information Center.
Porter, David: Stax Museum of American Soul Music.
Price, Hollis Freeman: LeMoyne-Owen College. 1960 *Columns*.
Riley, Larry: Memphis Black Arts Alliance.
Robinson, Kenneth Stanley: *Tri-State Defender*.
Roddy, Bert Maynard: Hooks Brothers Photographers. Memphis and Shelby County Room, Memphis Public Library & Information Center.
Sawyer, Chew Cornelium: Hooks Brothers Photographers. A. W. Willis Collection. Memphis and Shelby County Room, Memphis Public Library & Information Center.
Scott, Joe Burt: Thomas Busler. *The Commercial Appeal*.
Settle, Josiah T.: Roberta Church Collection. Memphis and Shelby County Room, Memphis Public Library & Information Center.
Shaw, Lily Patricia Walker "Pat": The African American History Calendar Partnership.
Shaw, Lucy Mae Yates: *Tri-State Defender*.
Smith, Maxine Atkins: Courtesy of Vasco A. Smith III.
Smith, Otis Milton: Courtesy of Hamilton Smith.
Smith, Vasco A., Sr.: Courtesy of Vasco A. Smith III.
Spillers, Hortense J.: Lou Outlaw, photographer. Courtesy of Outlaw.
Steinberg, Martha Jean: *Tri-State Defender*.
Stevens, Rochelle: *The Commercial Appeal*.
Stuart, Merah Stevens: *An Economic Detour*.
Stuckey, Elma Johnson: Courtesy of Sterling Stuckey.
Stuckey, Ples Sterling: Courtesy of Stuckey.
Sugarmon, Russell Bertram, Jr.: Courtesy of Sugarmon.
Swingler, Lewis Ossie: *Tri-State Defender*.
Taylor, Cora Price: *Portrait of a Ghetto School*.
Taylor, Lonzie Odie: L. O. Taylor Collection. Center for Southern Folklore.

Terrell, Mary Church: *A Colored Woman in a White World*.
Thomas, Carla: Stax Museum of American Soul Music.
Thomas, Rufus: Stax Museum of American Soul Music.
Thomas, Sheree Renée: Courtesy of Thomas.
Thornton, Matthew: *City Directory of 1941*. Memphis & Shelby County Room, Memphis Public Library & Information Center.
Toles, Elizabeth: *The Commercial Appeal*.
Turner, Elaine Lee: *Tri-State Defender*.
Turner, Jesse Hosea: *Tri-State Defender*.
Urevbu, Ephraim Muvire: Courtesy of Urevbu.
Venson, Ethyl Belle Horton: *Tri-State Defender*.
Wade, Theo: Stax Museum of American Soul Music.
Walker, Antonio Maceo: The African American History Calendar Partnership.
Walker, Joseph Edison: Hooks Brothers Photographers. *Historic Black Memphians*.
Walter, Ronald Anderson "Ron": *Tri-State Defender*.
Washington, David Whittier: *The Bright Side of Memphis*. Memphis and Shelby County Room, Memphis Public Library & Informaton Center.
Whalum, Kirk Wendell: *Tri-State Defender*.
Whalum, Wendell Phillips: Courtesy of Morehouse College Archives.
Wharton, A C, Jr.: *Tri-State Defender*.
White, Augustus A. III: Bachrach Photography. Courtesy of White.
White, Maurice: *mauricewhite.com*.
Whittaker, John W. II: *Tri-State Defender*.
Wilbun, Shepperson A. "Shep": *Tri-State Defender*.
Wilburn, Emma Currin Barbee: The African American History Calendar Partnership.
Williams, Eddie N.: Bachrach Photography. Courtesy of Williams.
Williams, James: *The Commercial Appeal*.
Williamson, Juanita V.: LeMoyne-Owen College. *Columns*.
Williamson, Kenneth: Courtesy of Elena Williams.
Willis, Archie Walter, Jr.: *The Commercial Appeal*.
Wilson, Lucious Alexander: Courtesy of Emogene Wilson.

Withers, Dedrick "Teddy": Ernest C. Withers Photographer. *Tri-State Defender*.

Withers, Ernest C.: Ernest C. Withers Photographer. *Tri-State Defender*.

Woodruff, Georgia Rodgers: The Hallelujah Collection. Memphis and Shelby County Room, Memphis Public Library & Information Center.

Yates, Albert Carl "Tutt": Courtesy of Yates.

Index

Alcorn College, 213, 254, 290, 320
Alpha Phi Alpha Fraternity, 177, 226, 295, 298
American Federation of State, County and Municipal Employees (AFSCME), 84, 172, 196–197
American Missionary Association, 46, 265, 336
Arkansas, 3, 34, 38, 52, 63–64, 76, 85, 92, 116–117, 140, 150, 180, 184–185, 199, 203–204, 207, 209, 214, 238, 240, 254, 260, 269, 277, 283, 290, 297–300, 316, 328, 337, 350, 365, 367, 377
Atlanta Life Insurance Company, 12, 189, 213
Atlanta University, 147, 202, 220–221, 231, 257, 330, 344
Avery Chapel A.M.E. Church, 7, 9, 324, 330

Banks, Finley, White and Company, 16, 30
Beale Street Baptist Church (First Church), 7, 9, 80, 166, 276, 311, 374
Beale Street, 8–10, 12, 40–42, 69, 76–77, 80–81, 84, 88, 90, 92, 101, 103, 111–113, 122, 130, 150, 152, 162, 166–167, 174–178, 180–181, 184, 188, 204, 206–207, 213, 216–217, 226, 237, 247, 265, 270, 275,

Beale Street (*continued*)
279, 292, 304–306, 308, 311, 314–316, 321, 324, 326, 342, 345, 348, 355–356, 362–363, 366–367, 371, 373, 380, 383
Beale Street Music Festival, 103, 184
Binghamton, 76, 117, 235
Black Business Association, 38, 140, 195, 236
Black Enterprise, 110–111, 194
Black Swan Records, 242, 258
Blues City Cultural Center, 62, 95, 267, 367
Bluff City Medical Society, 49, 236–237, 371
Booker T. Washington High School, 11, 32, 66, 68, 88, 134–135, 149, 169, 173, 182, 189, 194, 200, 203, 221, 228, 240, 244, 249, 253, 263, 271, 280, 282–283, 295, 297, 304, 308–309, 322, 325, 330, 335, 347, 358, 368, 371, 377, 379
Brown v. Board of Education of Topeka, 13

Carnes Elementary School (Carnes Avenue Grammar School), 34, 200, 282, 310, 315
Carver High School, 57, 193, 279, 322
Centenary United Methodist Church, 189, 211–212, 245
Central Baptist Church, 167, 330, 356–357, 368

Central High School, 104, 329, 341, 350
Chickasaw, 1–2, 127, 199, 228, 244, 323
Church of God in Christ (COGIC), 9, 115, 203–204, 238–239, 259–261, 348, 375, 382–383
Church's Park and Auditorium, 9, 308, 323, 363
Civil Rights Bill, 5, 276
civil rights movement, 13, 46, 104, 111, 116, 135, 172, 184, 196, 208, 210–211, 230, 247, 250–251, 281, 288, 294, 296, 298, 310–311, 337, 349–350, 355, 372–374
Civil War, 4, 7, 79–80, 126, 132–133, 167, 274–275, 323, 336, 361, 372
Club Paradise, 100, 180, 246, 373
Collins Chapel C.M.E. Church, 7, 9, 172, 185, 216, 237, 293, 302, 373
Collins Chapel Hospital, 11, 144, 236, 243
Colored Benevolent Society, 7, 163, 175, 324
Commercial Appeal, 25, 139, 168, 215, 250, 292, 322, 350, 357, 368, 375
Congress of Racial Equality (CORE), 67, 117, 294
Cooke, Sam, 140, 317
Cotton Makers' Jubilee, 8, 166, 315, 380, 383
Council of Civic Clubs, 14, 46, 378
Crump, Edward H. "Boss," 12–13, 82, 134, 151, 176, 182, 199, 237, 350

Delta Sigma Theta Sorority, 54, 67, 84, 143, 201, 243
Depression, 10, 13, 40, 42, 70, 82, 227, 282

Ebony, 38, 67, 71, 83, 109–110, 124, 194, 244, 262, 278, 309, 319, 353, 355, 375
Elks, 177, 181, 213, 258
Elmwood Cemetery, 42, 73, 216, 229, 237, 272, 311, 351
Emma Wilburn Funeral Home, 10, 339
Emmanuel Episcopal Church, 42, 275
Essence, 96, 110, 307, 362
Evers, Medgar, 46, 281, 355

Father Bertrand High School, 155–156, 230, 279, 377
Federal Express Corporation, 17, 94, 108, 375
First Baptist Church Lauderdale, 133, 298, 364
Fisk Jubilee Singers, 242, 336
Fisk University, 6, 32, 50, 54, 60, 164, 174, 209, 215, 220, 228, 242, 277, 318–319, 336
Foote Homes, 135, 208, 287, 303, 326
Forrest, Nathan Bedford, 3–4
Fraternal Bank and Trust Company, 9–10, 378

Geeter High School, 118, 123, 126, 176
Georgia Avenue School, 192, 272, 309, 372
Gilliam Communications, Inc., 16, 139

Index

Grammy Awards, 39, 57, 115, 164, 205, 207
Great Migration, 5, 122

Hamilton High School, 19, 30, 106, 149, 164, 192, 243, 303, 335, 363
Handy Park, W. C., 152, 181
Harlem, 23, 36, 111, 122, 181, 186, 223, 242
Henderson Business College, 165–166, 308, 382
Hernando Street, 9–10, 175, 321, 325, 363, 365
Holly Springs, Mississippi, 43, 53, 79, 326
Hooks Brothers Photographers, 10, 175
Hooks Cottage School, 6, 175, 187
Howard University, 57, 93, 97, 124, 135, 179, 193, 274, 302–303, 318, 337, 342
Howe Institute, 51, 134, 162, 266, 382
Hyde Park, 300, 340

Indianola, Mississippi, 10, 190, 204, 206, 212, 290, 318, 320
Iroquois Café, 10, 216, 270

Jackson, Jesse, 46, 54, 84, 375
Jackson, Tennessee, 203, 232, 326
Jet, 71, 137, 244, 321, 355
Joysmith Gallery and Studio, 17, 201
jug bands, 8, 70, 113, 217

Kennedy Democratic Organization, 247, 378
King, Martin Luther, Jr., 14, 25–26, 47, 49, 60, 121, 124,

King, Martin Luther, Jr. (*continued*) 127, 143, 149, 184, 196, 208, 210, 230, 240, 247, 281, 304, 309, 334, 346, 355, 380
Klondyke, 37, 51, 171
Knights of Pythias, 44, 61, 308
Korean War, 87, 186, 284
Kortrecht School, 61, 68, 117, 148–149, 182, 342, 356
Ku Klux Klan, 5, 204, 275

Lane College, 58, 157, 233, 292, 325
LaRose Elementary School, 25, 57, 61, 249, 347
Lauderdale St., South, 74, 88, 144, 146, 163, 175–176, 181, 189, 196, 216, 246, 298, 338–339
Leadership Memphis, 22, 94, 156, 222, 236, 252, 278
LeMoyne Gardens Housing Project, 35, 334
LeMoyne Normal School, 6, 269, 324, 356, 366
LeMoyne-Owen College (LeMoyne College), xv, xx, 30, 32, 37, 46–47, 62–63, 66, 71, 79, 101, 106, 111, 135, 139–140, 142, 149, 169, 173–174, 176, 178–179, 188, 198, 202–203, 209, 219–223, 225, 235, 251, 255, 257, 259, 265–266, 271, 281–282, 284, 286, 293, 308–312, 315, 321, 323, 329, 336–337, 344–346, 364, 367–368, 370, 374–375, 377, 381
Lewis Park, 10, 216, 238
Lincoln League, 12–14, 81, 163, 213, 270, 371

Linden Avenue, 10, 114, 166, 321, 325
Links, Inc., 38, 79, 322
Loeb, Henry, 178, 196
lynching, 5, 187, 262, 326–327, 350

Malcolm X, 220, 230, 250
Manassas High School, 48, 53, 95–96, 100, 105, 126, 147, 160, 171, 176, 198, 224, 228, 233, 247, 253, 282, 292–293, 299, 310, 336, 340, 345, 354, 368–369, 382
Martin Medical Building, 10, 237
Martin Stadium, 10, 216, 238, 241
Masons, 7, 174, 176–177
Meharry Medical College, 6, 34, 49, 60, 65–66, 284, 363, 368, 372, 376, 378, 380
Melrose Elementary and High School, 21, 34, 50, 98, 120, 164, 246, 251, 266, 285, 288, 328, 372, 379
Memphis Academy of Art (Memphis College of Art, Memphis Art Academy), 58, 63, 150, 168, 223, 314, 345, 371
Memphis Arts Council, 112, 156, 184, 314, 323
Memphis Black Arts Alliance, xx, 168, 185, 236, 251–252, 314, 375
Memphis Black Writers' Workshop, 293, 364
Memphis Board of Education, 14, 58, 156, 266, 280–281, 302, 321, 377
Memphis Brooks Museum of Art, 50, 63, 79, 143, 150, 223, 252

Memphis Chamber of Commerce, 81, 158, 248, 319
Memphis City Council, 3, 5, 90, 105–106, 112, 192, 198, 202, 250, 276, 319, 352, 354, 366
Memphis Free Speech and Headlight, 7, 9
Memphis in May International Festival, 38, 58, 112, 184–185, 188, 254, 270, 278, 280, 313–314, 345–346, 362
Memphis Light, Gas and Water Division (MLGW), 16, 36, 101–102, 155–156, 248, 278, 322
Memphis Red Sox, 10, 28, 44, 72, 216, 238, 240–241, 272–273
Memphis Sound, 160, 245–246, 343, 366, 378
Memphis Symphony Orchestra, 20, 115, 367
Memphis Theological Seminary, 21, 49, 112, 367, 381
Memphis Urban League, 42, 168, 183, 298, 316, 321
Memphis World, 297, 308, 343, 355, 382
Memphis/Shelby County Public Library, 13, 188, 322, 374
Metropolitan Baptist Church, 9, 73, 227, 256, 280, 313, 330–331, 337, 365, 372, 374, 378
Millington, Tennessee, 44, 66, 101, 114, 142, 299
Mississippi Boulevard Christian Church, 37, 165, 190–192, 319–320, 381
Mississippi Boulevard, 48, 61, 89, 188, 214, 309, 327, 339, 364

Mississippi Delta, 89, 113, 122, 205, 213, 291, 317, 371
Mississippi Life Insurance Company, 10, 254, 290–291, 320
Mississippi River, 1, 3, 34, 214, 339, 351
Montgomery Bus Boycott, 13, 104, 211, 350, 355
Morehouse College, 19, 178, 182, 209, 255, 295, 319, 329–330
Mound Bayou, Mississippi, 48, 298
Mt. Olive C.M.E. Church (Cathedral), 237, 317, 338, 365
Mutual Federal Savings and Loan Association, 16, 173, 271, 296, 348

Nashville, Tennessee, 20, 32, 50, 54, 60, 66, 69, 73, 90–91, 100, 121, 134, 144–146, 165, 168, 182, 185, 199, 211, 214, 218, 236, 255–256, 262, 268, 276, 282, 321
National Academy of Recording Arts and Sciences (NARAS), Memphis Chapter of, 41, 91, 115, 161, 164, 207, 264
National Association for the Advancement of Colored People (NAACP), 13–14, 27, 32, 38, 46, 51, 54, 58, 67, 81–82, 85, 106, 109, 127, 132, 134, 156, 161, 163, 172–175, 177, 186, 195, 198, 226–227, 230, 243, 248–249, 266, 270, 272, 278, 280, 282, 284, 291, 296–297, 301–302, 311–313, 323, 327, 347, 350, 365, 372, 378, 381

National Baptist Convention, 55, 69, 135, 145, 209, 256, 378
National Bar Association, Ben F. Jones Chapter, 74, 174, 227, 249, 338
National Business League, Memphis Chapter, 48, 51, 255, 355
National Cemetery, 88, 93, 197, 298
National Civil Rights Museum, 25, 92, 156, 168, 174, 282, 311, 342, 348, 355, 365
National Council of Negro Women, 67, 201, 311
National Medical Association, 11, 35, 49, 99, 371
National Negro Business League, 270, 291, 320
National (Negro) Insurance Association, xvii, 158, 255, 277, 291, 319
Negro American League, 45, 72, 216, 238, 240, 272
Negro Business League, 93, 237, 291
New Daisy Theater, 130, 177
New Park Cemetery, 10, 339
North Carolina Mutual Life Insurance Company, 35, 254, 383

Oberlin College, 6, 73, 81, 83, 211, 274, 301, 368
Odd Fellows, 7, 258, 290, 324
Old Folks and Orphans Home, 7, 163, 175, 324
Olivet Baptist Church, 300, 328, 382
Omega Psi Phi Fraternity, 47, 250, 272, 343
Opera Memphis, 20, 189, 370

Orange Mound, 21, 34, 106, 119, 163, 202, 206, 245, 266, 285, 365
Overton High School, 115, 164, 374
Owen College (S. A. Owen Junior College), 142, 183, 256–257, 265, 364, 368, 372, 377

Paige, Satchel, 28, 240, 273
Palace Theater, 8, 40, 100, 177, 305
Parkway, South, 91, 177, 208, 237, 243, 272, 313
Peabody Hotel, 31, 126, 182, 292, 345, 348, 350, 356–357, 372
Pentecostal Temple Institutional Church of God in Christ, 261, 348, 375, 382
People United to Save Humanity (PUSH), 54, 208, 278, 368
Plessy v. Ferguson, 8, 12
Pole Bearers, 7, 275
Porter Junior High School, 61, 182, 194, 203, 249
Presley, Elvis, 53, 75, 199, 246, 263, 343, 345

Reconstruction, 5, 14, 177, 225, 275, 313, 324, 346
Redding, Otis, 36, 141, 160, 304, 373
Regional Medical Center (The Med), 17, 21, 278–280, 358, 376
Rhodes College (Southwestern at Memphis), 50, 129–130, 170, 212, 248, 266, 283, 306
Rhythm and Blues Foundation, 41, 246, 304
Rock and Roll Hall of Fame, 41, 141, 185, 207, 305

Roger Williams College, 52, 134, 144, 149, 165, 182, 255–256, 369
Rust College, 47, 65, 68, 189, 242, 246

Sanitation Workers' Strike, 25–26, 106, 172, 196, 211, 227, 355, 372
Second Congregational Church, 47, 61, 74, 188, 210, 266, 270
Shelby County, 15, 25, 42, 59, 65–66, 73, 79, 82–83, 86, 118, 126, 154–155, 173, 188, 192, 202, 258, 326, 331–332, 338, 353, 369, 375, 381
Shelby County Commission, 5, 26, 191, 275, 284, 296, 313, 362
Shelby County Criminal Court, 14, 178
Shelby County Democratic Club, 14, 26, 284, 296, 320, 347, 367, 378
Shelby County Quarterly Court, 14, 313, 347
Shelby State Community College (Southwest Tennessee Community College), 110, 119, 158, 252, 285, 371
Solvent Savings Bank and Trust Company, 9, 80, 256–257, 269, 271, 321, 324, 364, 373
Soulsville U.S.A., 79, 252, 329
Southern Christian Leadership Conference (SCLC), 65, 129, 172, 207–208, 211–212, 230, 362
Southern Heritage Classic, 16, 194–195
Southern Nonviolent Coordinating Committee (SNCC), 32, 211

Index

Southern University, 24–25, 159
Spelman College, 48, 62, 135, 147, 280, 282
St. Augustine Church, 230, 288
St. Augustine High School, 158, 287–288
St. John Baptist Church, 203, 316, 343, 382
Stax Records (Museum and Music Academy), xx, 36, 53–54, 70, 91, 111, 160, 170, 177, 179, 194, 205, 264, 303–305, 329, 378
Supreme Mortgage and Realty Company, 16, 348

Tabernacle Baptist Church, 9, 11, 141, 144, 146–147, 208
Talladega College, 135, 225, 347
Teen Town Singers, 203, 303, 382
Tennessee A&I State University, 53, 90, 123, 127, 157–158, 192, 195, 277, 303, 325, 331, 352
Tennessee Black Caucus of the State Legislature, 50, 202, 362
Tennessee General Assembly, 5, 14, 50, 73, 123, 347–348, 352, 366, 371, 375
Tougaloo College, 38, 45–46, 149, 183, 255, 320
Tri-State Bank of Memphis, 10, 14, 16, 30, 119, 174, 261, 277, 312, 318, 321, 371
Tri-State Defender, xvi, xix, 71, 137, 168, 243, 297–298, 343, 349–350, 355, 368, 372, 374, 378, 382
Tri-State Fair, 183, 298
Tuskegee Institute, 41–42, 47, 171, 242, 255, 265, 325, 347

Union Protective Life Insurance Company, 16, 368, 377, 381
United States Congress, 1, 5, 25, 43, 123, 127, 210, 275
United States Supreme Court, 8, 297
Universal Life Insurance Company, 10, 16, 44, 65, 138–139, 157, 254–255, 277, 291, 318–320, 347, 365–366, 381, 383
University of Memphis (Memphis State University), 21, 37, 56, 63, 91, 94–96, 105, 109–110, 119, 121, 130, 139, 153, 164, 169, 171, 174, 189, 192–194, 219, 223, 226, 235, 243–244, 252, 266–267, 279, 281, 285, 314, 319, 341, 358–359, 367, 374
University of Mississippi, 111, 132, 137, 347
University of Tennessee, 17, 32, 47, 56, 98, 116, 156, 178, 277, 279–280, 284, 312, 334, 369, 371
University of West Tennessee, 11, 232, 368, 372, 377
Urban League, 177, 183, 255, 298, 316, 321

Vance Avenue, 92, 101–102, 216, 271–272, 337
Vaudeville, 80, 186, 305
Vietnam, 26, 121–122, 211, 304, 334
Volunteer Ticket, 15, 296, 372

Walker Avenue, 24, 89, 144, 158, 327
Waters, Muddy, 39, 76, 91, 114

WDIA Radio, 40, 52, 114, 176, 203, 206, 287–288, 303, 305–306, 317, 343, 361, 369–370, 374, 382
WLOK Radio, 16, 139, 168, 250, 337, 367
World War I, 112, 152, 213, 240, 381
World War II, 64, 72, 84, 88, 97, 189, 195, 220, 256, 297, 308, 321, 325, 379
WREG-TV, 16, 104, 168, 204, 322

Xaviar University, 30, 75, 158, 325

yellow fever epidemics, 7, 80, 227
Young Men's Christian Association (YMCA), Abe Scharff Branch, 118, 183, 220, 251, 298, 319, 337, 377
Young Women's Christian Association (YWCA), Sarah Brown Branch, 61, 67, 95, 97, 202, 248, 278, 291, 344, 370, 377

Zion Cemetery, 90, 176, 263, 338